Homeland Security Techniques and Technologies

HOMELAND SECURITY TECHNIQUES AND TECHNOLOGIES

JESÚS MENA

FIREWALL MEDIA

(An Imprint of Laxmi Publications Pvt. Ltd.)

BANGALORE • CHENNAI • COCHIN • GUWAHATI • HYDERABAD
JALANDHAR • KOLKATA • LUCKNOW • MUMBAI • RANCHI
NEW DELHI

Jesús Mena. *Homeland Security Techniques and Technologies.*

International Standard Book Number : 81-318-0050-4

Published by **FIREWALL MEDIA**
(*An Imprint of Laxmi Publications Pvt. Ltd.*)
113, Golden House, Daryaganj,
New Delhi-110002
India
Phone : 011-43 53 25 00
Faxes : 011-23 25 25 72
011-23 26 22 79
E-mail : info@laxmipublications.com

Branches

- **Bangalore** (*Phone* : 080-26 61 15 61)
- **Chennai** (*Phone* : 044-24 34 47 26)
- **Cochin** (*Phone* : 0484-239 70 04)
- **Guwahati** (*Phones* : 0361-254 36 69, 251 38 81)
- **Hyderabad** (*Phone* : 040-24 75 02 47)
- **Jalandhar City** (*Phone* : 0181-222 12 72)
- **Kolkata** (*Phones* : 033-22 27 37 73, 22 27 52 47)
- **Lucknow** (*Phone* : 0522-220 95 78)
- **Mumbai** (*Phones* : 022-24 91 54 15, 24 92 78 69)
- **Ranchi** (*Phone* : 0651-230 77 64)

http:/www.laxmipublications.com

Edition : 2007

ISBN : 81-318-0050-4

FHO-2887-295-HOMELAND SEC. TECH & TECHNO

Economy Edition Price : Rs. 295.00

Printed at : Sanjeev Offset Press, Delhi. **C—12710/06/06**

To my father,
Clemente Mena,
Who taught me about work—and could always make me laugh.

Introduction

The genesis of this book is a white paper, "Data Mining for Homeland Security," which I wrote for a federal agency and somehow was read by the chief information officer of a federal homeland security organization. He e-mailed, complimenting me on its content and requesting much more information on the technologies discussed in the paper. This book is the result of that request.

Another source of this book is briefings I have conducted for the United States Air Force, the Department of Justice, the General Accounting Office, the Sandia National Laboratories, the Terrorist Threat Integration Center, and others. Due to changes in the industry, upgrades in software, and the evolution of these technologies, a companion course has been developed that will incorporate the latest developments, case studies, product versions, innovative services, and software demos. The course may be found at *prominer.com*.

Best,

Jesús Mena
mail@jesusmena.com.

Contents

1 Overview: The Homeland Security (HS) Tasks, Technologies, and Processes

In This Chapter

- Preamble: The HS Requirements
- The HS Processes and Objectives
- The HS Missions
- Task 1: Aggregation: The Data Components
- Task 2: Integration: Virtual Databases
- Task 3: Collaboration in Real Time
- Task 4: Categorization: Clustering Concepts
- Task 5: Intelligence Systems for Detecting Terrorist Crimes
- Task 6: Data Mining: Embedded and Distributed
- Conclusion: The Information Technology Terrain

The National Strategy for Homeland Security Report of July 2002 noted that information systems contribute to every aspect of national defense. It also found that although American information technology is the most advanced in the world, the country's information systems have not adequately supported the homeland security missions. The report noted that databases used for federal law enforcement, immigration, intelligence, public health surveillance, and emergency management have not been connected in ways that allow users to comprehend where information gaps or redundancies exist.

The report concluded that to secure the homeland better, the country would need to link the vast amounts of knowledge residing within each government agency while ensuring adequate privacy. This book will discuss how various types of software can be used to improve information sharing and systems. In addition, combating terrorism in the twenty-first century will require multiple ongoing processes, such as:

- Identity validation via data aggregation and name recognition.
- Anticipating attacks and profiling potential future perpetrators.
- Organizing, disseminating, and collaborating experts and content in real time.
- The creation of virtual databases of images, documents, HTML, files, e-mail, and so on.
- Visually mapping "who knows who and when and where have they been in contact."
- Aggregating, preparing, and mining data remotely over networks anywhere in the world.
- Detecting crimes associated with terrorism, such as identity theft, fraud, and money laundering.
- Categorizing documents, chat, e-mail, instant messages, audio, video, and so on in any language.

A major portion of these tasks can be accomplished by the use of existing data sources, services, and software for data aggregation, integration, collaboration, categorization, intelligence, and mining via an assortment of processes for the creation of a centralized self-adaptive national defense system.

PREAMBLE: THE HS REQUIREMENTS

Accomplishing these tasks will no doubt involve the use of existing technologies, as well as the development of new techniques, many of which will be developed over the coming years. One objective is clear: All these processes will require innovative types of network—centric self-evolving analyses, which must adhere to existing privacy laws that protect the rights of citizens. These information technologies are mature and sophisticated enough to enable the design of homeland security systems that can ensure these privacy rights are protected. The following are some of the key requirements of homeland security organizations:

- To have the tools to quickly interpret large data holdings.
- To have the software for information fusion in immense data environments.
- To have tools with innovative, interactive computer interfaces.
- To have systems for integrated visualization of time and space features.
- To be able to perform predictive data mining analysis and modeling simulation.

- To be able to handle all types of multimedia, including text, audio, video, geographic information system mapping, imagery, graphics, and analytical data.

Homeland security personnel will need to share information within their organizations and across multiple agencies at varying levels of clearance in multiple locations at different government levels. These organizations may include intelligence, defense, and civil organizations at the local, state, and federal levels. These organizations will need to communicate in distributed and mobile environments, requiring users to exchange information at anytime and at any place via instant messaging, e-mail, chat, and so on. Organization collaboration will require the ability to quickly find experts within a community of interest via secure networks and wireless communications with point-to-point encryption. They will require the capabilities of tracking reports, comments, and coordinating chains of analyses. Organizations will need software for sharing information and ideas online with access controlled automatically based on clearance and need-to-know basis, with capabilities such as classified messaging for managing user groups and the ability to easily initiate secure conference calls on the fly.

Homeland security organizations will require that personnel be able to sift through diverse data sources of both structured and unstructured content to find vital information and quickly identify trends and anomalies. This includes the capability for automated information maintenance, monitoring, querying and browsing, automated identity extraction, automated meta tagging, and the ability for users to easily access metadata information. This automatic metadata tagging will include all content formats, such as audio, visual, text, and imagery, and the capability to enable personnel to access it at any classification level from various homeland security organizations such as defense, intelligence, and civil, as well as local, state and federal levels.

A central requirement of the homeland security organization is the ability to manage large volumes of data across the intelligence, law enforcement, and military communities. This will no doubt require the use of software tools for trend, relationship, and predictive data analysis, which can quickly, autonomously, and automatically identify trends and anomalies in massive data sets. That software will need the capability to provide results in actionable formats as well as providing users the ability to drill down into the tool's logic, to associate entities, people and events, and specialized tools to assist with scenario planning and outcome analysis.

Homeland security organizations will require search and retrieval capabilities for ingesting and storing large amounts of data. Massive repositories will contain gigabytes of e-mail, text documents, relational database records, images, multimedia clips, geo-spatial data, and more. Organization personnel will need to immediately derive knowledge and insight from these vast data depositories, requiring tools for federated searching, content meta-tagging, directed search and retrieval, intelligent search results, dynamic hyperlinks, and software agent and blackboard-based discovery. Organization personnel will need to see query results relevant to their particular missions and clearance levels.

At the core of all applications and processes of these homeland security organizations is an army of software intelligent agents (autonomous programs running over networks). Personnel will require tools that learn from corrections of human analysts, software that monitors and adapts from observations of users' behavior, and programs that learn from users' corrections or selections. This requires software that is dynamic in behavior and that has the ability to operate autonomously and accomplish various tasks set out by users without direct human intervention or supervision.

Agent technology requires that software be embedded with the intelligence to be aware of its environment and to act on behalf of users. Seeking content and expertise it has learned that its owners require to accomplish their tasks and missions, this self-learning software acts for the users and is able to improve its behavior over time. Intelligent agent software monitors and reports to human analysts and devices over distributed networks anywhere, anytime.

THE HS PROCESSES AND OBJECTIVES

One of the key objectives is that of data aggregation. Homeland security organizations need to have access to multiple demographic and public and private data sources for identity validation of individuals at borders, ports, airports, and other transportation locations. Demographics data providers such as Acxiom monthly normalize the names, addresses, and vehicles of every individual in the United States for marketing purposes, and this data can also be used for security purposes.

Another objective is that of data integration for multiple agencies at the federal, state, and local levels. Integration requires homeland security organizations to function as a central interchange, through which a host of applications can communicate with each other, and where events trigger a series of preprogrammed actions using a combination of middleware adapter tools. The glue for doing this will likely be eXtensible Markup Language (XML), Simple Object Access Protocol (SOAP), and Web services for connecting disparate data sources for use at the various government levels.

Another urgent requirement for homeland security organizations is the ability to quickly communicate and collaborate the results of analyses, alerts, and expertise. There is the need for locating, capturing, extracting, organizing, classifying, and routing tacit knowledge often from unstructured content, as well as locating experts in specific areas, first responders, weapons of mass destruction, or counterintelligence, for collaboration and communicating in real time.

Categorization will also play a vital role in homeland security organizations in the form of the classification of semistructured and unstructured content as found in documents, news articles, press releases, forms, travel records, e-mail, chat, instant message, and so on for homeland security purposes. Categorization software can automatically tag forms of communication using various combinations of predefined semantic, syntactic, statistical, and artificial intelligence techniques to classify this unstructured content, converting it into structured formats for subsequent visual, link, clustering, and inductive pattern recognition data analyses.

Intelligence for homeland security organizations will come in the form of targeting crimes often associated to terrorism. This has to do with focusing on criminal activity such as identity theft, fraud and money laundering; for example, the USA PATRIOT Act imposes strict rules requiring verification of the identity of individuals. There exists various types of software, services, and systems that can be used by homeland security organizations to enhance their ability to detect these types of terrorist related crimes.

Lastly, data mining for homeland security organizations involves the use of standalone, embedded, and distributed advanced pattern recognition algorithms, such as neural networks, decision trees, self-organizing maps, Bayesian networks, and machine learning algorithms, for discovering hidden signatures of potential terrorists scattered across distributed databases around the world and for anticipating and thwarting future attacks. This is probably the most challenging of all the tasks in the area of homeland security, involving the development of new techniques and algorithms in the field of entity detection and scenario modeling. This area will see the development of very powerful, original, and subtle methods of discerning patterns involving seemingly unrelated data from databases scattered across networks in many locations.

The homeland security organizations' environment will be an evolving one, perpetually adjusting to the threat of terrorism in the twenty-first century. Its design must be open but secure, with 168-bit 3DES encryption and with multiple access levels to homeland security personnel from multiple agencies at various levels of government. Such systems must provide and support detailed user audit trails of every transaction and session. The applications must be incorporated into a single seamless interface for homeland security personnel, and they must be network centric and accessible via browsers over desktops or laptops, adhering to rigid accepted industry standards, such as Java 2 Enterprise Edition (J2EE). The applications must be able to be integrated into a homeland security organization's information technology framework via a single common format and syntax.

THE HS MISSIONS

In July 2002, the Office of Homeland Security published its *National Strategy for Homeland Security Report,* laying out its vision for a future "system of systems" that would meet the United States' national defense challenges. It defined six core missions as required by the United States government, discussed in the following sections.

Intelligence and Warning

This core mission deals with the major initiatives to enhance the analytic capabilities of the FBI and to build new capabilities through the Information Analysis and Infrastructure Protection Division of the Department of Homeland Security (DHS). It also set out a plan to utilize dual-use analysis to prevent attacks (dual-use refers to items used by terrorist that can be easily obtained in the free market). Key strategies involve the use of technology to improve the linkages between key intelligence databases and the ability to "connect the dots" before attacks take place: to use technology to more effectively capture and process raw intelligence. Lastly, the plan calls for the creation of a new system that facilitates intelligence sharing with state and local officials who lack high-level clearances but have a compelling need to know about key threats. Clearly, the message here is for the use of technologies to boost data aggregation, integration, collaboration, categorization, intelligence, and mining, which are the subjects of this book.

Border and Transportation Security

Major initiatives in this area include the ensured accountability of transportation security by the creation of "smart borders." Key strategies involve the use of technology to track cargo containers, verify their contents, and ensure that they have not been tampered with. The objective is to prevent the entry of hostile individuals or weapons and screen hand-carried and checked luggage for explosives; to screen cargo non-intrusively at ports of entry to prevent the importation of nuclear materials and other weapons of mass destruction, all without slowing down commerce; to use technology to verify the identity of individuals entering the United States at its land borders, both in cars and on foot, without bringing border crossings to a standstill. Lastly, this initiative calls for assisting foreign countries and international shippers with efforts to comply with a range of new U.S. and international rules for aviation, maritime, and ground transportation security. This mission focuses on the use of technologies to improve the security of our borders and in identity validation. These subjects are covered extensively in Chapter 2, "Aggregation: How to Leverage the Web, Robots, and Commercial Demographics for Entity Validation," and Chapter 6, "Intelligence: Systems for Detecting Terrorist Crimes."

Domestic Counterterrorism

Major initiatives in this area included improving intergovernmental law enforcement coordination to facilitate the apprehension of potential terrorists and the prevention of future attacks by targeting terrorists' financing. Key strategies involve assisting law enforcement agencies such as the FBI and state police with their new responsibilities for domestic intelligence gathering. In Chapter 6, special intelligence software systems are discussed for targeting money laundering schemes often used by terrorists groups.

Protecting Critical Infrastructures and Key Assets

Major initiatives in this area included using the best analytic and modeling tools to develop effective protective solutions to secure major infrastructures such as cyberspace. Key strategies involve hardening buildings, increasing stand-off, and strengthening access control at facilities that are likely terrorist targets due to their symbolic value or potential for widespread damage. It calls for improving the security of commercial and military seaports and the security of airports. This will be the subject of Chapter 7, "Mining: Pattern Recognition and Agent Technologies for Analyzing Text and Data Remotely," which involves various types of data mining techniques, technologies, and systems.

Defending Against Catastrophic Threats

Major initiatives in this area include improving the detection of attacks by developing new vaccines and antidotes to reduce the impact of biological threats. Key strategies involve establishing a system to get vaccines or other countermeasures to a large affected population before the impact of an attack reaches catastrophic proportions. It also calls for quickly detecting an airborne biological or chemical agent in public places such as a subway system or shopping mall, before the impact is widespread. A major initiative in this area will involve the collaboration of analysis and expertise, most likely involving some of the tools and techniques discussed in

Chapter 3, "Integration: The Components, Adapters, Middleware, and Web Services for Information Sharing," and Chapter 4, "Collaboration: The Technologies for Communicating Content, Experts, and Analyses in Real Time."

Emergency Preparedness and Response

Major initiatives in this area include integrating separate response plans by improving the capability of different first responder groups at an incident to communicate with each other and coordinate their efforts. Key strategies involve outfitting first responders with the necessary equipment to respond to chemical or biological attacks. At the core of this mission is allowing agencies at multiple levels and locations to communicate and share data with one another, starting with the integration of their systems, the subject of Chapter 3.

In November 2002, Congress passed legislation to create the DHS, setting the stage for the largest reorganization of the federal government since the creation of the Department of Defense in 1947. The new DHS is faced with developing responses to three major national responsibilities:

- Detection
- Integration
- Protection

Thus, federal, state, and local homeland security authorities are mobilizing to conduct threat analysis and assessment of known and suspected terrorists. What techniques and technologies would these agencies use?

In the chapters to follow, we'll describe a possible list of software components with the ability to be accessed via closed or open networks for self-synchronizing operations, populate communities of interests, and share diverse information, data sources, experts and analyses that will require the use of a wide array of clustering, calibration, organization, and classification algorithms for collecting, monitoring, routing, modeling, and disseminating their findings to decision makers in real time for proactive action against attackers and potential attacks before they occur. These software solutions will address the specifications set out by the six main missions of the National Strategy for Homeland Security and the three major responsibilities of the new DHS, specifically, detection and integration.

TASK 1: AGGREGATION: THE DATA COMPONENTS

Data aggregations systems can be used to collect data from diverse sources of government, Internet, demographic, financial, and other data depositories. A tactical infrastructure is required to enable a homeland security organization to monitor the overall state of processes for the validation of an individual's identification at point of entry border crossings and airports, as called for in the homeland security mission statements. For example, systems similar to the Computer Assisted Passenger Prescreening System (CAPPS II), which use a passenger name, date of birth, home address, and home phone number, could cross reference several commercial data sources to validate a person's identity.

The potential data matching could be performed against such sources as Acxiom's Abilitec® Unique Identification Number Database, which has been in use for years by marketers and retailers to perfect their customer mailing lists, or TransUnion HAWK®, which focuses on the use of Social Security numbers and has developed several identification validation data products for fraud detection and security checks for financial service providers, or DataQuick PropertyFinder data product, which is the world's largest real estate data depository, in use for years for by private industry and government agencies for performing real estate checks.

One year after 9/11, in testimony before Congress, FBI Director Robert Mueller indicated that a sweeping overhaul was planned for the bureau, including the construction of a data warehouse to house information from multiple FBI databases. One of the major obstacles to the aggregation of data by the government is that agencies traditionally do not communicate with each other via their respective proprietary information technology systems. They traditionally do not do this at the federal-to-federal level, much less at the federal to state and local levels. Cultural changes will need to be made, and standards will need to be established for the sharing and aggregation of this internal agency government data, and no doubt this will be an ongoing process. Eventually, the FBI warehouse might receive data from other law enforcement and intelligence agencies, including demographics from commercial data aggregators with such data attributes as the following:

- Date of birth
- AKAs for subject
- Other Social Security number
- Other names associated with SSN
- Addresses associated with subject
- Real property ownership
- Deed transfers
- Vehicles registered at subject's addresses
- Possible watercraft
- FAA aircraft registration
- UCC filings
- Bankruptcies, liens, and judgments

- Professional licenses
- FAA pilot licenses
- DEA controlled substance licenses
- Business affiliations
- Possible relatives
- Other people who have the same address as the subject
- Possible licensed drivers at subject's addresses
- Neighbor phone listings for subject's addresses

The purpose for using these types of demographics will not be for marketing to individuals, but instead will be for validating their identities at points of entry. One of these data demographic providers has already converted all 270,000 million consumer names into a unique 16-digit identification number, effectively normalizing the location of every individual in the United States and associating them with a specific physical address and vehicle number.

> *"There is far more information outside the federal government about us, as individuals, than anybody has a clue about."*
>
> ***—Steve Cooper, DHS CIO***

Already several homeland security-related products have been introduced by these demographic and data providers. For example, Acxiom has developed an identity validation product it calls Sentricx® with an identification validation fraud score, drawing and matching data from multiple personal identity databases.

Polk has introduced the Complete Vehicle Identification Number Analysis (CVINA) from its vast vehicle information depositories, while ChoicePoint is offering a new biometric service along with demographic data reports geared specifically at law enforcement and homeland security government organizations. While in the past demographics were primarily used in marketing, in the future they will increasingly be used for security applications. News reports indicate the FBI is looking to develop investigative data warehousing technology in the war against terrorism.

There are a number of data warehousing techniques for behavioral profiling and identity validation, as well as various sources of information from demographic providers, credit, criminal, government, real estate, automotive, and Web-based data created from multiple Internet mechanisms such as log servers files, CGI cookies, invisible graphic bugs, online forms, and so on.

The concept of a data warehouse is to have a multidimensional picture of individuals by merging data from disparate databases in order to gain a comprehensive view of their identities, values, and behavior. The creation of a data warehouse also commonly involves the merging of internal organization transactional data with external commercially purchased lifestyle demographics.

Many analytic technologies have their origins in data warehousing, such as query and reporting, visualization, online analytical processing (OLAP), and data mining. Query and reporting tools are used to extract data from warehouses to summarize it and present it in a report format. Data visualization is used to enable users to see large amounts of data via multiple dimensions to compare and contrast key findings to make better, informed decisions. OLAP enables users to analyze data across multiple dimensions, usually reserved to key business metrics such as products, departments, regions, and time segments. Data mining pertains to the analytical techniques drawn from artificial intelligence, statistics, mathematics, and modeling to uncover hidden patterns and trends commonly used to group individuals with similar features and behavioral tendencies.

During his congressional testimony, the FBI director indicated that new technologies are required to support new and different operational practices, including warehousing of more and new data. Investigative data warehousing is part of a much larger FBI plan to acquire and employ modern information technology to thwart future terrorist attacks. However, the design of this investigative data warehouse for homeland security applications will be radically different from those in the commercial sector. The traditional concept of the static data warehouse does not lend itself to homeland security organizations purposes, which require real-time response in which personnel must make informed decisions without an information lag.

Also as a general rule, approximately 95 percent of the data used for analytic applications in data warehouses has been historical data, which has been extracted from operational systems, transformed, and loaded into a static depository on a periodic or batch-processing basis. Again, this data warehouse model does not make much sense in the context of homeland security applications, which require networking capabilities and collaboration and analyses in real time as the data is created.

VISUALIZATION: LINK ANALYSIS

One type of software already in use by several law enforcement agencies, including the FBI, is link analysis for identifying terrorist networks and hierarchies. This investigative software is used to understand the nature of communication, the means of funding, and the sequence of events and occurrences. Link analysis can be employed by law enforcement investigators

(continued)

and intelligence analysts to examine anomalies and inconsistencies graphically, as well as the networks of relationships and contacts of humans, systems, communications, and other interactions hidden in databases. This kind of software can be used to assemble networks of associations, events, and entities with the following type of data attributes:

- Locations, such as a physical or IP address, or geo code coordinate
- Facilities, such as factories, airports, hotels, schools, or warehouses
- Organizations, such as cells, gangs, commercial or military units
- Individuals, such as names, titles, or identification numbers
- Components, such as chemicals, fertilizers, masks, acids
- Documents, such as passports, driver licenses, e-mails
- Money, such as cash, wire transfers, money orders
- Weapons, such as guns, knives, rifles, bombs
- Vehicles, such as planes, trucks, boats, cars
- Drugs, such as type, weight, source

Link analysis is the first level by which networks of people, places, organizations, vehicles, bank accounts, e-mail addresses, telephone numbers (see Figure 1.1), and other tangible entities and events can be discovered, linked, assembled, examined, detected, and analyzed. Analysts and investigators often use link analysis software to answer such questions as "who knows who and when and where have they been in contact?" The leading providers of this type of investigative software are Automated Tactical Analysis of Crime (ATAC), i2, CrimeLink, Crime Workbench, NetMap, Orion, and VisuaLink.

Link analysis, however, has its limitation in homeland security situations; the technology works best in situations where there is a limited number of observations, such as events (meetings) and entities (suspects). Its functionality rapidly deteriorates once a large number of observations or transactions begins to populate a case file or a database used for this type of visual analysis. Link analysis is also a very manual-intensive process. This kind of software is primarily a visualization tool for organizing events and associations for an ongoing investigation, not for the type of network-wide scrutiny of hundreds of thousands of records.

As the complexity and number of occurrences increase, the functionality of link analysis diminishes. In the context of homeland security, the functionality of link analysis becomes useful as a complementary tool in the analysis of relationships during the categorization of unstructured content of terms and in the clustering of concepts in large portions of text.

(continued)

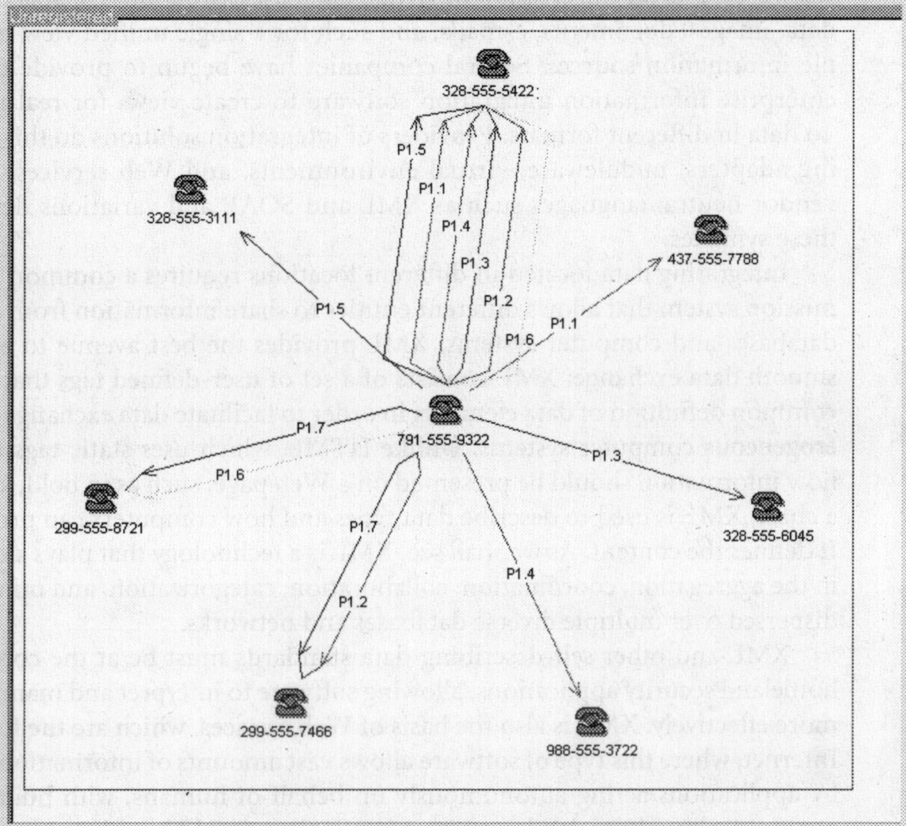

FIGURE 1.1 A link analysis graph tracking a network of phone contacts.

TASK 2: INTEGRATION: VIRTUAL DATABASES

Integration is a big part of the effort of homeland security. As Steve Cooper, the CIO of DHS, states, "There are over 16,700 municipalities in the U.S. Each one buys its own systems and equipment, and all the federal and state organizations do their own purchasing; there's very little homogeneity in this process." Integration software can be used to link some of these disparate data sources. Integration software exists for the creation of virtual databases, programs capable of accessing data, images, documents, e-mails, and such for a single unified view from multiple information sources. Several companies have begun to provide this type of enterprise information integration software to create views for real-time access to data in different formats. Providers of integration solutions do this by supplying adapters, middleware, virtual environments, and Web services, relying on vendor-neutral languages such as XML and SOAP and variations derived from these syntaxes.

Integrating data located in different locations requires a common data transmission system that allows different entities to share information from a variety of databases and computer systems. XML provides the best avenue to achieve this smooth data exchange; XML consists of a set of user-defined tags that provides a common definition of data elements in order to facilitate data exchange across heterogeneous computer systems. Unlike HTML, which uses static tags to describe how information should be presented on a Web page, such as in bold, a table or in a chart, XML is used to describe data types and how computers can process them: It defines the content. As we shall see, XML is a technology that plays a critical part in the aggregation, coordination, collaboration, categorization, and mining of data dispersed over multiple diverse databases and networks.

XML and other self-describing data standards must be at the core of future homeland security applications, allowing software to interpret and manipulate data more effectively. XML is also the basis of Web services, which are the future of the Internet, where this type of software allows vast amounts of information to be used by applications acting autonomously on behalf of humans, with built-in intelligence. Ideally, a homeland security organization should be able to create context-aware applications that are capable of understanding what the user is attempting to accomplish. Homeland security systems need to understand the user's context and be able to assemble the appropriate information and format it in accordance with the user's requirements, locations, and devices. Lastly, XML can be used to construct systems with real-time analytical capabilities and can issue alerts and perform event notification with portable digital dashboard interfaces, which are generic, hiding all of the complexity away from the users.

Using integration software tools, homeland security Web portals can be created for hosting collaboration centers, which can be used by thousands of users to view and post content culled from multiple-agency systems while communicating in real time via instant messaging with persistence capabilities. Integration software can be used to link collaboration software that allows homeland security organization personnel to seamlessly link multiple local, state, and federal subject-area experts when and where potential threats are identified.

Integration software systems are being used not only for traditional querying and reporting of massive data stores, but also to provide "dashboard" views of other systems that monitor potential security threats. For example, the New York City Department of Health and Hygiene is using iWay integration software to allow hospitals, 911 call centers, pharmacies, and first responders to collaborate on potential outbreaks of bioterrorism-related disease. The city of Norfolk, VA, is using eWork, a business process management tool from Metastorm to connect various databases and standardize processes for the emergency response activities for homeland security applications.

Web-based integration software can be used to provide real-time access to content from multiple agencies and to connect homeland security analysts, especially those charged with first responder duties as well as those monitoring border or other transportation traffic. The Bureau of Customs and Border Protection, for example, is using its Automated Commercial Environment secure data portal to distribute information about ocean, land, and air traffic that needs to be monitored in transit, before it crosses the U.S. border. The Federal Motor Carrier Safety Administration monitors the licensing of cargo truck drivers to notify Customs via the portal when a truck attempting to enter the United States from Canada may require an escalated inspection.

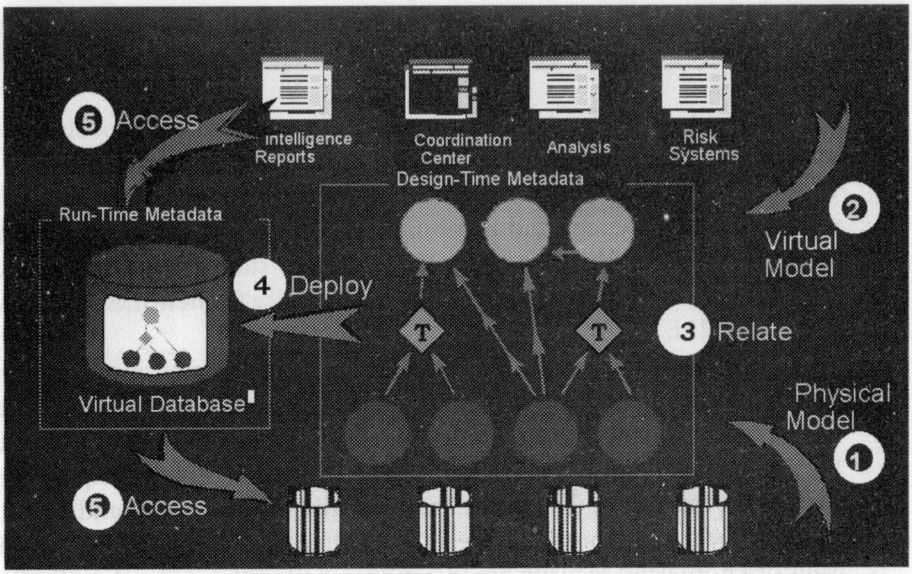

FIGURE 1.2 The virtual integration of data sources.

One of the most unique integration applications comes from Systems Research and Development (SRD), a Las Vegas firm providing software for the casino industry via its name matching Anonymous Entity Resolution technology, which allows investigators to determine whether a terrorist suspect appears in two separate databases, such as a government watch list and a car reservation system. Originally developed for background checks of casino employment applicants, SRD software not only sifts through entity identification information such as names, phone numbers, and addresses in separate databases, but most importantly it scrambles and encrypts the information using a one-way hash function, which converts the name into a character string that serves as a unique identifier, much like a fingerprint. SRD's Non-Obvious Relationship Awareness™ (NORA™) software can dynamically identify correlations across two separate databases.

Web Services and XML

Integration is also possible via a Web service, which is a software component that resides on the Internet as a URL-addressable resource. This portable architecture provides a standards-based path to application integration and superior on-demand data access, analysis, and collaboration. This is because a Web service is built on XML, which conceals the differences among disparate applications and operating systems. Web services provide a viable solution to data sharing for homeland security. Web services are especially important in the context of homeland security because they enable program-to-program communications, allowing for multiple types of silent monitoring mechanisms independent of human interaction or oversight.

Critical to homeland security infrastructures are the protocols on which Web services are based: SOAP, Web Services Description Language (WSDL), and Universal Description, Discovery, and Integration (UDDI). A Web service can be written in any language and run on any platform as long as it can communicate in conformance with these basic Web services standards. All three multivendor specifications have been integrated into Web service frameworks such as Microsoft's .NET and J2EE.

SOAP is an XML-based protocol for document-based messaging and remote procedure calls across distributed computing environments. SOAP-based messages are transport independent and are specifically designed to communicate over the Web or intranets via HTTP. SOAP can be used with other transport mechanisms, such as the Simple Mail Transfer Protocol (SMTP) for e-mail and, as we will see in Chapter 4, for collaboration in real time with other team members within the firewalls of a homeland security organization, whether they are police, firefighters, first responders, law enforcement, military, or counterintelligence. WSDL is an XML schema used to describe a Web service's abilities, grammar, and communication interfacing requirements. It provides a general description of the characteristics and capabilities of a given Web service, such as the data type, ports, and Internet addresses used for accessing and receiving messages.

UDDI is a directory services protocol for classifying, cataloging, managing, and querying Web services. UDDI consists of three types of directories: White, Yellow, and Green Pages, primarily for developing business registries that can be expanded to include homeland security organizations. For example, IBM has proposed a UDDI-compliant homeland security registry, modeled within its UDDI Registry developed for the Department of Defense (DoD), so IBM could publish and locate Web services DoD applications. Through Web services technologies, homeland security organizations could link legacy systems from intelligence agencies, military command centers, and state and local governments with new applications to facilitate information sharing. These same Web services could be used to tap into other infrastructures, such as those of utilities, hospitals, and other emergency organizations.

There is a standard known as the Web Services Interoperability Organization (WS-I), developed by BEA Systems, IBM, Microsoft, and other vendors, to promote interoperability among Web services applications. WS-I promotes profiles designed to help developers use Web services protocols in a consistent way. WS-I also crafts "usage scenarios" that address interoperability requirements within specific private industry markets and governments. The organization's government members include the Defense Information Systems Agency (DISA), which is the Department of Defense's lead organization for information technology standards. DISA is participating in WS-I to ensure that the group's implementation profiles address homeland security needs.

DISA has taken a Web services approach with the Advanced Concept Technology Demonstration, an emergency response application and hopes to benefit from Web services, such as improved data access, deployment speed, and application integration. Indeed, integration is a key theme with Web services. The approach makes application integration easier and less expensive, especially important for homeland security organizations, and the technology also simplifies training because users have to deal with only a single interface.

Most importantly for homeland security applications, Web services enable the aggregation, integration, monitoring, and communication of real-time alerts to personnel and devices via wide area networks. Web services enable the deployment of machine-to-machine monitoring for potential attacks based on predetermined rules and conditions developed by human analysts and machine learning data mining scenarios, which we will discuss in more detail at the end of this book.

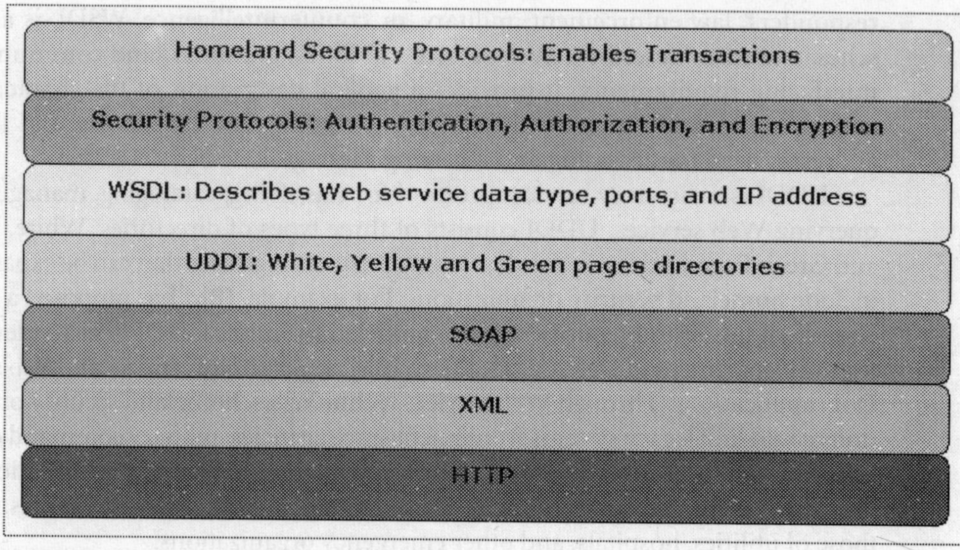

FIGURE 1.3 Web services protocol stack.

Homeland security organizations require that these tasks be organized, managed, and deployed around a set of self-evolving processes, which will use technologies to monitor transactions and generate alerts or event notifications in real time. They must be built with open industry standards to ensure portability across diverse platforms, hardware, operating systems, and information technology environments. In order to ensure such tight integration, XML and self-describing data standards must be at the core of these applications, allowing software to interpret and manipulate data more effectively. Standards can be used to create context-aware applications that are capable of understanding what the user is attempting to accomplish, assembling the appropriate information, and formatting it in accordance with the user's requirements, location, and devices.

An intelligent real-time homeland security organization reflects the need to make informed decisions and respond instantly. The pace of security in today's world eliminates information lag and requires man and machines to make timely and effective decisions. To accomplish these goals, a homeland security organization must today be organized, managed, and assembled around a set of automated applications and technologies. Increasingly, these processes must be automated along two dimensions: time and data.

Homeland security requires the use of technologies applied to individual transactions taking place in a time frame of no more than a few seconds, similar in design to that of personalization applications in e-commerce or fraud detection systems currently in use by credit card processing firms. To be useful, homeland security applications must monitor processes and generate alerts or event notifications when there are departures from expected behavior or mismatches of data occurrences, such as the use of an invalid Social Security number. These alerts must be generated and delivered via agent software quickly enough for personnel to take protective action before potential attacks take place, in a matter of seconds or minutes.

Providers of this type of information-sharing technology include Ascential, BEA, IBM, Informatica, Information Builders (iWay), IONA, MetaMatrix, Microsoft, SeeBeyond, SRD, TIBCO, Vitria, and WebMethods. IBM, through its DB2 Information Integration Data Joiner, and Oracle, via its Materialized Views, are also providing the ability to integrate their enterprise-wide databases with those of others. New firms such as Juice Software and Nimble Technology are providing the ability for the aggregated views of dozens of databases simultaneously.

TASK 3: COLLABORATION IN REAL TIME

Collaboration systems can be used by homeland security organizations to store, classify, search, retrieve, and analyze information from documents, Web sites, e-mail, and other unstructured sources, as well as databases and networks. Collaborative applications are capable of real-time interactions via instant messaging, e-mail, chat, online meetings, and application sharing. Active collaboration network software can be used for organizing and disseminating distributed structured and unstructured personalized content, as well as expertise and analyses. These programs can be used for organizing and disseminating distributed content to a community of users, with some of these tools supporting online real-time collaboration, such as chat and instant messaging. Most of these programs support four main functions:

- Automatically search for relevant text content
- Index or categorize the content
- Manage the content by routing it to a designated group of users
- Enable collaboration between recipients of the content

Some of this collaboration software uses text analysis based on natural language processing, statistical analysis, and multiple taxonomy techniques to search, index, manage, and route content to users. Most of these programs use multiple methods in parallel to identify the principal content of documents. Some use such techniques as Bayesian statistical classifiers to identify broad topic themes, while keyword and Boolean classifiers then assemble the documents into more refined

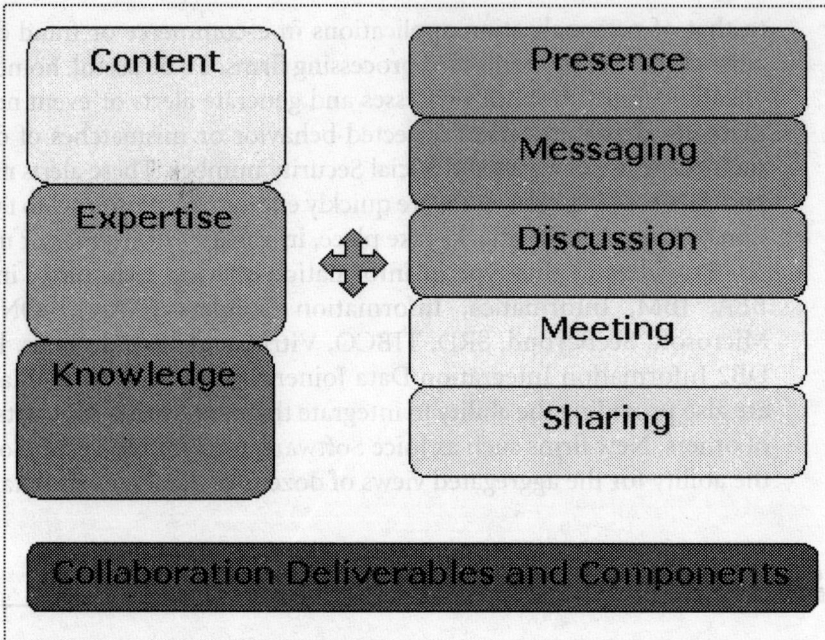

FIGURE 1.4 The collaboration map.

sub-groups of categories for sharing within groups of users in organizations. Most of these types of software products construct dynamic profiles of users by analyzing keywords in their e-mails and other documents they generate as part of their daily communication. These profiles are used to identify experts, so for a homeland security organization this might identify individuals with expertise in weapons, certain types of emergencies, water supply, languages, cultures, legal issues, and so forth.

There are collaboration products available from such firms as Autonomy, Centra, Documentum, Groove Networks, Hummingbird, Hyperwave, IBM, iManage, Intraspect, Linqware, Microsoft, Novell, Open Text, Oracle, Plumtree, Raindance, SiteScape, Traction Software, Verity, and WebEx, each of which offers unique features.

There is collaborative software for locating expertise within organizations to find out "who knows what" from AskMe, Kamoon, Sopheon, and Tacit Knowledge. There are also instant messaging systems for real-time collaboration from

AOL, Bantu, Communicator, FaceTime, Jabber, Microsoft, Omnipod, and Yahoo!. Jabber is being used for collaboration among several law enforcement agencies in the Capital Wireless Integrated Network (CapWIN). In-Q-Tel, the venture capitalist firm founded by the CIA, has invested in several collaboration software start-ups, such as the following:

Tacit Knowledge: Analyzes e-mails to identify and connect users working on similar problems. The software attempts to use internal communications within organizations to match employees working on similar problems for the creation of an Active Collaboration Network (ACN).

Tractions Software: TeamPage™ provides a writable web for a unified view of team content and communication from all sources in context. The software can be deployed quickly and easily on an existing intranet network and delivers a distribution system via a Web browser for publishing, collaboration, and content management.

Zaplet: Provides instant messaging software that turns e-mail into active collaboration documents that can be updated remotely. This Web-based instant messaging software has graphical and interactive capabilities. Its Zaplet App-mails can be one or more pages that are either predetermined at the time of creation or modified on the fly.

The Homeland Security Department's Federal Emergency Management Agency (FEMA) is using collaboration software to provide personalized content to more than four million first responders to communicate instantly so that they can plan disaster-response activities. FEMA has also incorporated a department-wide instant messaging platform from Bantu into the portal to provide real-time text communication and collaboration. The system allows users to see who is online at any given time and delivers proactive notification about time-sensitive events to enable first responders to better coordinate local, state, and federal emergency services. The instant messaging system also supports real-time alerts to thousands of people responsible for key events or response to attacks.

Additionally, collaboration software such as that from Tacit Knowledge Systems can monitor e-mail, documents, and discussion groups in order to identify experts within multiple agencies so that special alerts can be flagged directly to them. This software has the ability to create connections on the fly and can autonomously locate and link domain experts. Tacit's ActiveNet system works inside an agency intranet to continuously discover and catalog the focus and expertise of its personnel. A security feature of Tacit's ActiveNet software enables anonymous requests and information to be routed to the best-matched expert without initially revealing why the match was made.

TASK 4: CATEGORIZATION: CLUSTERING CONCEPTS

Another key technology for homeland security is that of text analysis, which allows investigators and analysts to sort, organize, and categorize gigabytes of unstructured content. Text mining for homeland security can be applied to the problem of searching and locating names or key terms such as "anthrax" used in e-mails, wireless, phone calls, faxes, instant messages, chat, and so on. Categorization software can also be used for the automatic classification of unstructured content to extract key hidden concepts from free-form documents, files, e-mails, records, and such in any language that can be "tokened," that is, tagged using XML.

Categorization software can be used to automatically generate hierarchies of categories (taxonomies) of unstructured content so that homeland security personnel can make sense of massive flows of new feeds, reports, documents, Web pages, e-mails, chat, and instant messages, enabling them to begin the task of connecting the dots. Some of the categorization software is language independent; it relies on the mathematic sequencing of words in the text, making them ideal for intelligence community agencies such as the CIA, FBI, TTIC, and DHS. This type of software can be used to tag, categorize, and route unstructured content to specific users based on monitored profiles observed over time or described by the user within a homeland security organization. Some of the classification schemes for the categorization of text include the following:

- Rule-based, manually constructed taxonomies
- Statistical, naïve Bayesian, or K-nearest neighbor (clustering)
- Support Vector (yes/no) binary classes
- Probabilistic Latent Semantic Analysis (PLSA)

Categorization software uses a variety of search methods that combine lexical parsing and clustering techniques to extract key phrases from large amounts of unstructured text. Some programs enable users to make new associations and relationships, and some generate their output via three-dimensional charts, paths, and links for further analysis. One of the largest and most extensive text mining applications is that of the Raytheon Knowledge Discovery Kit, which allows intelligence personnel to link to a centralized system using dozens of commercial off-the-shelf visualization and categorization software products. The user can search, retrieve,

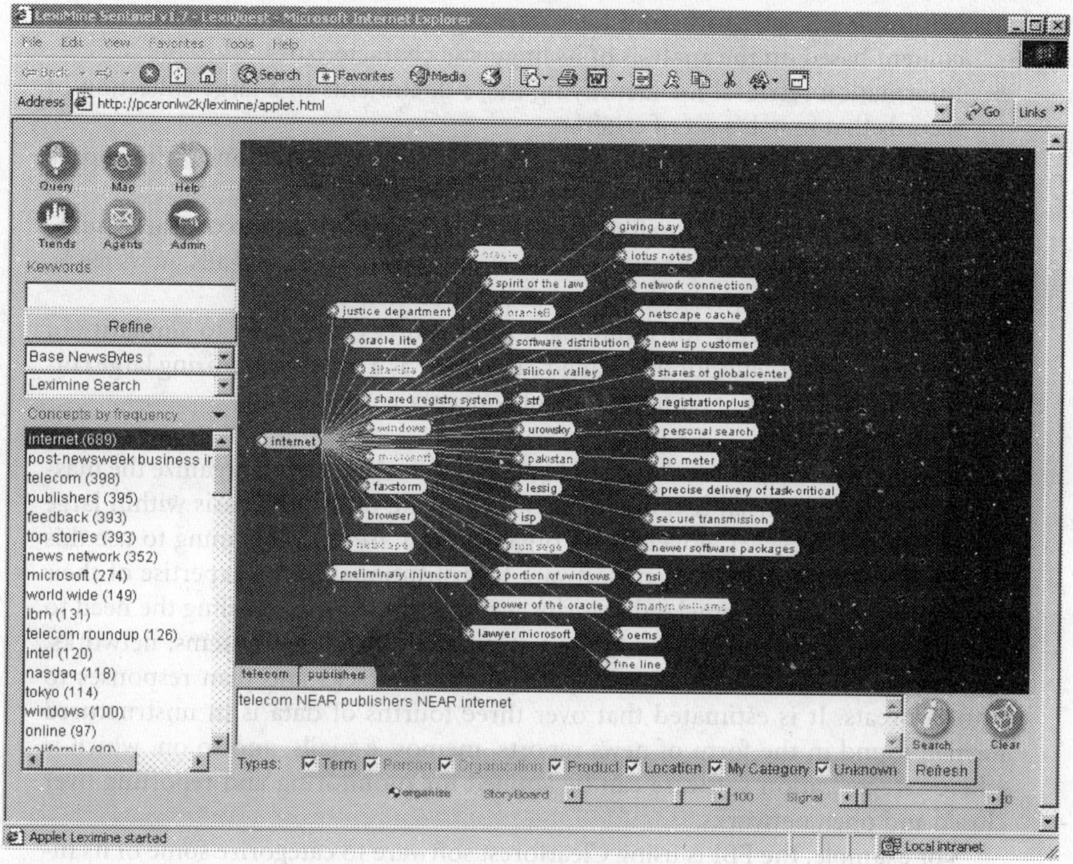

FIGURE 1.5 The visual mapping of text using LexiMine from SPSS. © 2003. Reprinted with permission from SPSS, Inc.

view, and analyze news feeds from around the world in any language with the ability to link relationships, translate on the fly, and even incorporate video and audio broadcasts.

There is a definite distinction between how categorization software works with unstructured textual information and how data mining software works with structured databases; however, both types of technologies attempt to extract some insight that can be used by the homeland security organizations. Both text and data mining will be covered extensively in Chapter 7. Most categorization software components use all or some of the following techniques:

- Natural language processing for capturing critical features of a document's content based on the analysis of its linguistic characteristics.
- Information retrieval for identifying those documents in a large collection of records that match a set of criteria.
- Routing and filtering for automatically delivering information to the appropriate destination according to subject or content.
- Document summarization for producing a compressed version of a large number of documents or collection of text, such as Web pages, e-mails, news feeds, chat, and instant messages, with an abstract of their content.
- Document clustering for grouping textual sources according to similarity of content, with or without predefined categories, as a way of organizing large collections of documents into clusters of concepts.

Private industry has been using categorization technology to organize the massive amounts of internal text documents they create on a daily basis within large organizations. However, government organizations are also beginning to use this type of knowledge management software to institutionalize the expertise of their content and experts. Homeland security agencies are likewise tackling the need to filter massive data that is often housed at different locations, systems, networks, agencies, and departments to anticipate potential attacks and plan responses to future threats. It is estimated that over three fourths of data is in unstructured format, found in the form of news reports, memos, e-mails, and so on, which is where categorization software can be applied for monitoring and reporting over closed and open networks.

For example, the FBI is using Clearforest software to categorize some of its internal documents. This software uses natural language and "rulebooks" (taxonomies) to classify facts and entities in unstructured content. The software is able to work with documents, news articles, and Web sites. Clearforest can output its correlations in the form of maps, tables, or graphs. The company's ClearResearch application is used by all FBI analysts to quickly analyze the bureau's entire document management repository—more than one billion existing documents, with up to 1,000 new ones arriving each day—to improve the way FBI terrorism-related information is used and shared. ClearResearch, as with almost all the other categorization software packages, extracts pertinent information from documents and tags it using XML.

Some of the most powerful software of this genre is that from Recommind, with its entity extraction capability, which is completely language independent and uses a Probabilistic Latent Semantic Indexing (PLSI) algorithm to automatically identify concepts in large numbers of records. Its MindServer software supports industry-specific taxonomies, including one for government. The software uses machine learning to classify and index documents based on relevancy and frequency of words, in virtually any language.

Some of the other providers of this type of categorization software technology include Applied Semantics, Ask Jeeves, Atomica, Attensity, Clearforest, Convera, DolphinSearch, Endeca, Entopia, Entrieva, FAST Search and Transfer, Google, Insightful, Intelliseek, Inxight, Mohomine, NextPage, Recommind, Stratify, TripleHop, and Vivisimo. The CIA-backed In-Q-Tel has also invested in several categorization startups in an effort to develop the type of technology required by the intelligence community it serves. These include the following:

Attensity: Transforms unstructured text into a structured, relational format for parsing into link analysis to show the relationship between key words; the software uses trending for the clustering of concepts.

Convera: Unique among these categorization tools in that its RetrievalWare product supports video content and can convert graphic images into digital format for storage and transmission. RetrievalWare also enables users to index and search a wide range of distributed information resources, including HTML, XML, text, relational database tables, and groupware repositories. Search capabilities include concept and keyword searching, pattern searching, and query-by-example.

Intelliseek: Their software can search and retrieve structured and unstructured content for internal communications, collaboration, and categorization. The Web-based software combines federated guided intelligent search, analysis, and management of Internet and database information with automated tracking and alerts for changes. Enterprise Search Server™ (ESS) is scalable and can be customized. It combines a set of classification methods: brokering, indexing, bridging, and catalog building.

MetaCarta: Its Geographic Text Search (GTS) appliance allows the user to interact with text-based information to view documents and geographic information in one logical view.

Mohomine: The MohoClassifier for National Security Organizations™ reviews text information in cables, e-mails, filesystems, intranets and extranets, including the Internet, and provides automated document classification and routing based upon learn-by-example or pattern recognition technology. The software reports on multiple defined properties such as topic, country source, subject, tone, urgency, and author, among other variables and settings.

TASK 5: INTELLIGENCE SYSTEMS FOR DETECTING TERRORIST CRIMES

Ultimately, terrorist organizations will not be able to function if they cannot have access to money and if they cannot protect their true identities from authorities. Homeland security organizations need to focus on mounting an offensive on those crimes often associated with terrorism, such as money laundering, fraud, and identity theft. Cutting off the money channels will eventually disrupt the terrorist networks. Tracking these financial channels is a major challenge because of the intricacies of international financial transactions, webs of shell offshore companies, and schemes intentionally devised to evade detection by authorities. It is imperative to provide homeland security personnel with the proper investigative tools to combat the complex and ever-changing money laundering schemes of perpetrators to investigate sophisticated money laundering schemes.

This requires an ongoing effort to uncover the sophisticated schemes devised by terrorism groups and to disrupt their financial operation of these illicit organizations. Because of the complexity of these schemes, reliance on software may not be adequate to combat these types of complicated crimes, which is where some of the following intelligence services come into play. These intelligence systems are specifically designed to detect identity theft, fraud, and money laundering, crimes often associated with terrorist activities and groups. There is also specialized software focusing on name recognition, which falls into this specialized intelligence service category.

Identity theft service providers include ID Analytics and Fair Isaac, and some of the data aggregation providers such as Acxiom, ChoicePoint, Experian, and TransUnion have new identification validation products. Identity theft will result in losses in excess of $8 billion by 2006 alone. Hoping to cash in on this growing market, the startup from San Diego ID Analytics is using models created from 200 million credit applications, 10 million of which were fraudulent. ID Analytics uses its proprietary Graph Theoretic Anomaly Detection (GRAD) algorithms to look for fraudulent signatures in credit applications to generate an ID Score. The ID Analytics scores can be used to screen and validate new credit application accounts and monitor existing accounts for potential take-over thefts.

Somewhat related to this process of identity theft is name entity recognition (NER) technology for perfecting "watch lists" and matching suspected terrorist names against an assortment of records, such as those of airline reservations. Providers of this technology include AeroText (Lockheed Martin), IdentiFinder™ (BBN/Verizon), Intelligent Miner for Text (IBM), NetOwl® (SRA), Thing Finder (Inxight), Search Software America (SSA), and Language Analysis Systems (LAS).

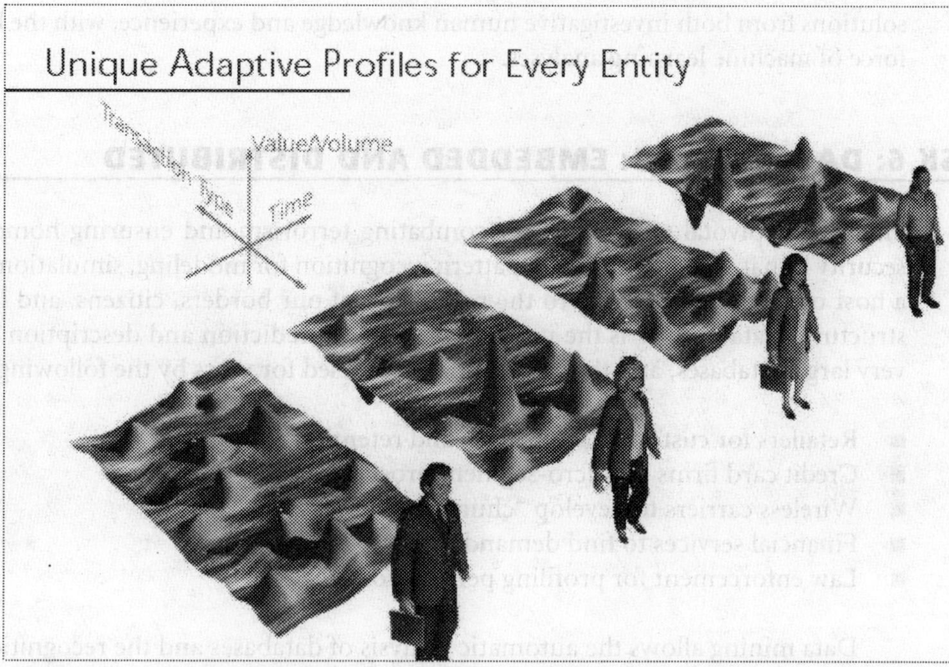

FIGURE 1.6 Searchspace's adaptive profiles.

Fraud and money laundering providers include GIFTS Software, Mantas, NetEconomy, and Searchspace. A major solution provider in the area of financial crimes is Searchspace, which has been providing its Anti-Money Laundering (AML) services and software to financial institutions since 1993. Searchspace currently monitors over 40 million transactions daily for Barclays, Bank of New York, Wells Fargo, and other banks; it also monitors stock exchanges in the United States and Europe, looking for potential insider trading activities. Its Sentinel software components look for unusual transactions or known laundering scenarios, such as unusually large or uncharacteristically frequent transactions. The Searchspace system combines both human and data mining rules to generate risks alerts at the individual, country, relationship, and organizational levels.

The core technologies of Searchspace are rooted in several artificial intelligence technologies, including fuzzy logic, neural networks, and genetic algorithms. The Searchspace software system uses both a top-down and a bottom-up approach to detecting criminal patterns, an ideal paradigm that uses the best pattern recognition solutions from both investigative human knowledge and experience, with the brute force of machine learning analyses.

TASK 6: DATA MINING: EMBEDDED AND DISTRIBUTED

Finally, the pivotal technology for combating terrorism and ensuring homeland security is that of data mining, or pattern recognition for modeling, simulation, and a host of other tasks critical to the protection of our borders, citizens, and infrastructure. Data mining is the iterative process of prediction and description from very large databases, and this process has been used for years by the following:

- Retailers for customer acquisition and retention
- Credit card firms to micro-segment prospects
- Wireless carriers to develop "churn" models
- Financial services to find demand trends
- Law enforcement for profiling perpetrators

Data mining allows the automatic analysis of databases and the recognition of important trends and behavioral patterns. Probably the most important and central technology for homeland security is data mining and related artificial intelligence technologies that make up the core of much of the software discussed so far, including aggregation, integration, collaboration, categorization, and the intelligence systems related to detecting identity theft, money laundering, name recognition, and so on. Through the use of neural networks, decision trees, and genetic and machine learning algorithms, data mining automates the manual process of searching and discovering key features and intervals in text, video, audio, and databases.

Data mining software and the systems it drives can be used to answer such questions as "when is money laundering most likely to take place?" or "what are the characteristics of a smuggler?" Data mining can be used to detect signatures of potential attacks in large, distributed diverse databases to search and find the attributes and ranges for the signatures to identify these possible threats.

> *"Data mining is an integral component of the White House's national strategy."*
>
> ***—Steve Cooper, DHS CIO***

Machine learning software can segment a database into statistically significant clusters in the search for the digital footprints of potential terrorists. These pattern recognition programs can be used to find the needles in the moving haystacks. Data mining analyses can generate graphical decision trees or IF/THEN rules that users can use to gain important insight about the attributes of perpetrators:

IF Attribute A
AND Interval 1–4
AND Attribute B
THEN Perpetrator Probability 77%

Data mining has been used over the years to discover hidden patterns, profiles, and signatures in large databases through such processes as classification, clustering, segmentation, and prediction. Data mining is also descriptive—it is about discovering signatures in databases through the following types of data mining processes:

- Classification, with neural networks
- Clustering, with self-organizing maps
- Profiling, with machine learning algorithms

Providers of data mining software components include ANGOSS, CART, IBM, Magnify, Megaputer, Quadstone, SAS, and SPSS, as well as RDBMS vendors Oracle and Teradata, who have embedded pattern recognition operations within their database software. Data mining technology has gone through an evolution since it was first developed in the mid 1980s, prior to the explosion of the Internet and distributed communications and computing. At the first level of this evolution, data had to be imported into the data mining software or linked to tables, such as those of products from SAS and SPSS.

Next, the database vendors began to embed the data mining operations within their relational databases, such as regression, factor analysis, rule induction, decision tree, clustering, and association algorithms. This eliminated the need to move the data to a centralized location and allows for the use of parallel processing. Teradata's Miner, for example, performs its data pre-processing, modeling, and deployment inside its database.

Both Teradata and Oracle deal with the problem of scalability by embedding multiple pattern recognition operations directly within their products through a set of SQL functions. The Teradata Warehouse Miner supports all the major analytical algorithms. Oracle has also embedded its data mining operations, offering it as an additional software component to its main database in order to reduce data latency, maintenance, and integration costs. SAS and IBM closely integrate their pattern

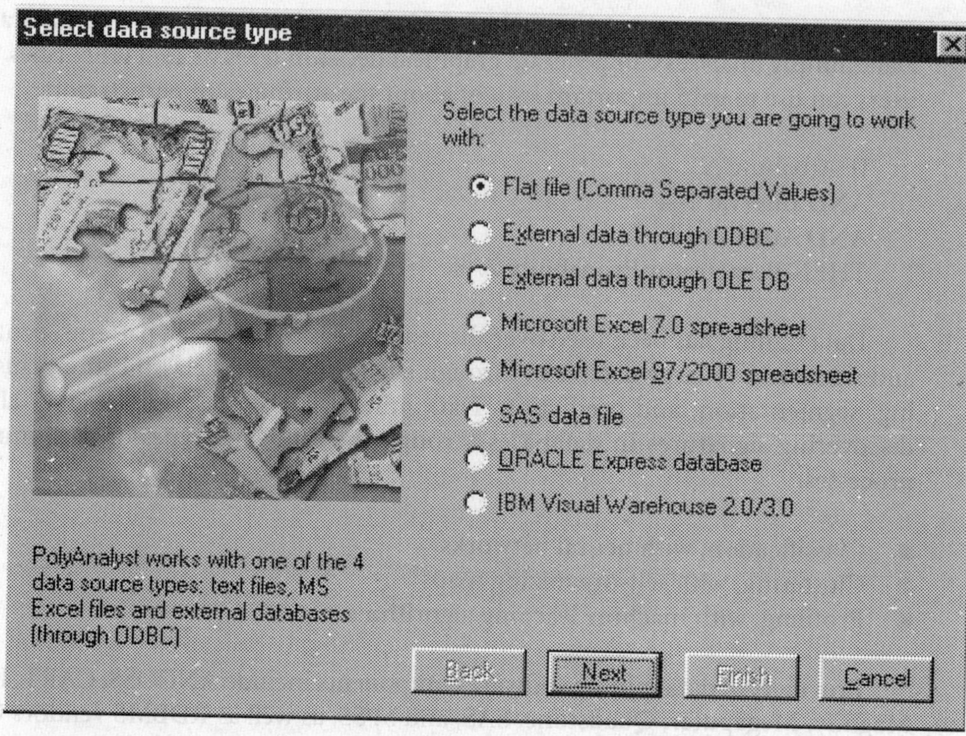

FIGURE 1.7 Data was imported or linked through ODBC to the software.

recognition components within their mainstream database software as well. However, embedding data mining functions within a database works only if the data is in a single homogenous data location from the same vendor, an unrealistic expectation in today's IT environment, especially in the area of homeland security.

The third and final progression in data mining is that in which autonomous machine learning agents are sent to prepare and mine databases in different remote locations over closed and open networks. This is an intriguing approach in light of the obstacles of homeland security, where it is difficult to move databases due to different owners and privacy concerns. As with the other types of analyses, the ability to aggregate, analyze, and distribute the results to a group of users in different locations is particularly useful in homeland security applications.

As with the other software used for categorization and collaboration, distributed data mining relies on agent-based technology. Agents are software programs that

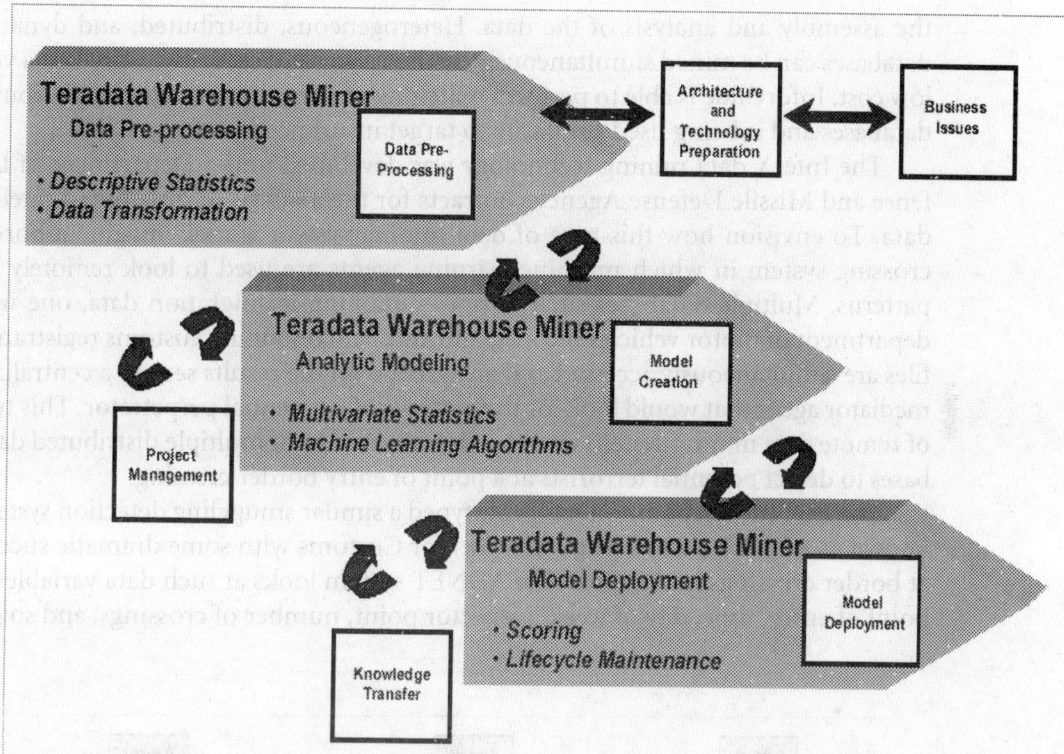

FIGURE 1.8 Embedded data mining inside Teradata database.

perform user-delegated tasks autonomously, such as retrieving, matching, or analyzing structured or unstructured data over networks. Intelligent agents are increasingly used in the area of intrusion detection for monitoring systems and networks to deter hacker attacks.

Agents can be used for distributed search and match and pattern recognition, and providers of this type of distributed data analysis include Agnik, InfoGlide, and InferX.

These networked-centric data mining software providers use agents to look for unique names or patterns in the data remotely over networks. Only the solutions move; the data stays where it is. Data ownership is maintained; scalability is achieved without the need to build expensive monolithic data warehouses, as with some of the data integrator solution providers. A virtual environment is created for the assembly and analysis of the data. Heterogeneous, distributed, and dynamic databases can be mined simultaneously, with privacy and security assured, at a very low cost. InforGlide is able to perform matching of names over multiple distributed databases and is being used primarily to target insurance fraud.

The InferX data mining technology was developed under Department of Defense and Missile Defense Agency contracts for the analysis of distributed satellite data. To envision how this type of data mining system works, imagine a border crossing system in which machine learning agents are used to look remotely for patterns. Multiple databases such as one containing immigration data, one with department of motor vehicles records, and another containing customs registration files are simultaneously accessed and analyzed, with the results sent to a centralized mediator agent that would look for the patterns of a potential perpetrator. This type of remote data mining system would collate the results of multiple distributed databases to detect potential terrorists at a point of entry border crossing.

The MITRE Corporation has prototyped a similar smuggling detection system, known as ADNET (Anti-Drug Network) for Customs with some dramatic success at border crossings in Arizona. The ADNET system looks at such data variables as point of entry, time, day of week, inspector point, number of crossings, and so on,

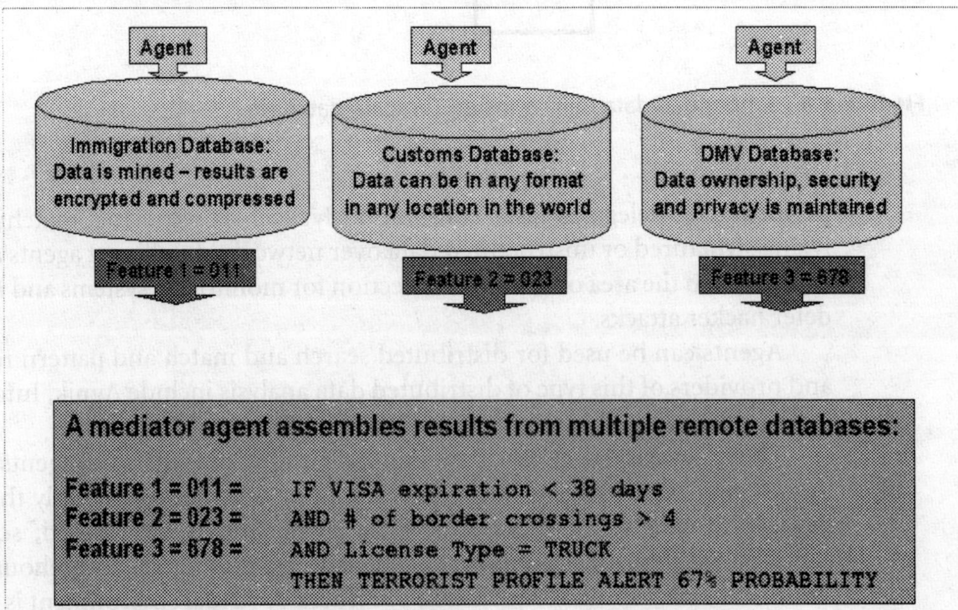

FIGURE 1.9 A pattern recognition sentry for homeland security.

based on the input of a vehicle license plate number. Conditional IF/THEN rules have been created using a very small sample data set, representing less than .01 percent, to try to target potential smugglers. ADNET is limited to a single database, with a very limited number of observations and data attributes, yet it has led to successful detection of smugglers. If a limited system such as ADNET had the capability of mining multiple distributed databases, its results would greatly improve. Similar homeland security systems could be deployed to monitor our borders, docks, airports, and other points of entry into the United States.

CONCLUSION: THE INFORMATION TECHNOLOGY TERRAIN

Ever since 9/11, data mining has been identified as a key technology in the battle against terrorism because the ultimate objective of most of these kind of analyses is the prediction of human behavior, such as fraud and identity theft, crimes often associated with terrorists. However, any kind of data collaboration and analysis, whether it is categorization of unstructured content or pattern recognition of databases for homeland security, will require the use of a network-centric, agent-based infrastructure, due to the distributed nature of our information technology environment, where:

- There are different database owners and locations.
- The scaling is of extremely large databases.
- There are heterogeneous data schemas and database platforms.
- These dynamic real-time databases are constantly changing.
- There are privacy and security issues that prohibit the movement of the data.

All these obstacles make the massive movement of databases to centralized data warehouses for data mining for homeland security impractical. However, a network-centric data sharing, collaborative, mining environment overcomes these obstacles. These types of networked solutions are a direct by-product of the dot-com revolution of the 1990s that saw the development of the Internet, intranets, wireless networks and, most importantly, autonomous agent-based technology.

In a networked environment such as ours, it doesn't matter where the databases are located because everything is designed to connect to networks and share the data—where the sum of the information is much greater than its parts. In this type of environment, intelligence can be distributed via an army of software agents to human investigators and analysts in the field in real time to an assortment of devices, PDAs, laptops, phones, wireless, and so on. In a network-centric system, all homeland security organizations are plugged in and can exchange information with each other, and intelligence such as the profiles of perpetrators can be created on the fly and distributed instantly to multiple locations. Because everyone on the network can share data with everyone else, homeland security organizations can aggregate, integrate, collaborate, categorize, and mine in real time, not only content, but also their expertise and analyses.

The Perpetual Evolutionary Tasks

Increasingly, IT systems will be organized in terms of homeland security processes to ensure that they support national defense goals and provide the infrastructure required to link all management and operational processes into a network that gives agencies and departments real-time response and intelligence. Homeland security organizations must be designed to reconfigure processes rapidly for real-time responsiveness; such agility will be possible only if they understand their objectives and how they fit under a common architecture. The concept is one of building an organization much like an organism that reacts to changes in real time, in response to a rapidly changing environment. The homeland security organization is a system of processes that responds to external stimuli and is self adaptive, made up of intelligent software components that are interchangeable and working in tandem.

As with the Internet, which was created by DARPA decades ago for the survival of the United States' information infrastructure in the event of a nuclear attack, a network-centric approach for homeland security will ultimately benefit not only national defense and law enforcement but also the corporate world, with a new wave of efficiency, speed of deployment, and lower cost for such applications as fraud deterrence, intrusion detection, CRM, e-commerce, personalization, and business intelligence. In the long run, an effective homeland security infrastructure will incorporate agent-based components for data aggregation, integration, collaboration, categorization, intelligence, and mining, resulting in a safer country. In the chapters to follow, we will focus on each of these processes in greater detail in order to see how they can function as components of homeland security techniques and technologies.

The ability to collect, analyze, and act on an ever-increasing amount of information is a daunting and constantly evolving task for homeland security organizations. Many of the existing repositories within defense intelligence agencies have grown to many hundreds of terabytes, with the need for information sharing between these organizations increasing. Current intelligence solutions require standardized access to several of these huge repositories to effectively perform their missions. The scalability, flexibility, precision, and performance required to address these demands can be achieved only by a combination of a powerful metadata repository foundation with a set of components that access and process the content represented in the repository. This model is referred to as the Information Supply Chain (ISC), also known as an enterprise knowledge infrastructure.

The creation of the Department of Homeland Security, bringing together 22 federal agencies, is the most visible manifestation of the sea change in intelligence. As stated in the beginning of this chapter from the *National Strategy for Homeland Security*, this integration of multiple agencies will be an extremely complex effort by all those involved. Interoperability of content, systems, analyses, and expertise is at a premium and must be based on the use of flexible components in an intelligently designed infrastructure.

In the past, individual agencies built self-contained solutions that needed only to meet the internal standards necessary to solve a problem specific to that agency. These standalone silos of data had the luxury of being independent, and defining their content, format, metadata, and architectural system design depended only on the specific agency's standards. With the creation of the DHS and a surge in the drive to enable interoperability, information solutions must be able to deploy today to be flexible, scalable, and standardized.

Aggregating, integrating, collaborating, categorizing, and mining this information is an ongoing process that is the foundation to intelligence gathering. It requires a comprehensive procedure, facilitated by technologies such as client-server and Web services-based techniques, which smoothly extract and allow the sharing of knowledge. With minimal interruption to workflow, it creates a semantic representation of the information that contains the collective tacit and explicit expertise of homeland security organizations. It's a strategy that includes secure advanced collection and classification capabilities, dynamic collaboration, and powerful search and information retrieval to enable analysts and decision makers to do their jobs efficiently and accurately. The intelligence process is illustrated in Figure 1.10.

Just as the private sector has created manufacturing supply chains that can share and use information across corporate boundaries, so will homeland security organizations develop an ISC to facilitate the creation and sharing of content, expertise, and analyses. Keith Herrington, Directorate Information Officer, Department of Homeland Security, defined this new ISC as an integrated suite of software components and processes, including the following technologies:

- Search/Profiling/Agents
- Collaboration
- Identity Extraction

- Categorization
- Data Translation
- Natural Language Recognition
- Link/Temporal Analysis
- Entity Relationship
- Summarization
- Geo-Spatial Analysis
- Reporting

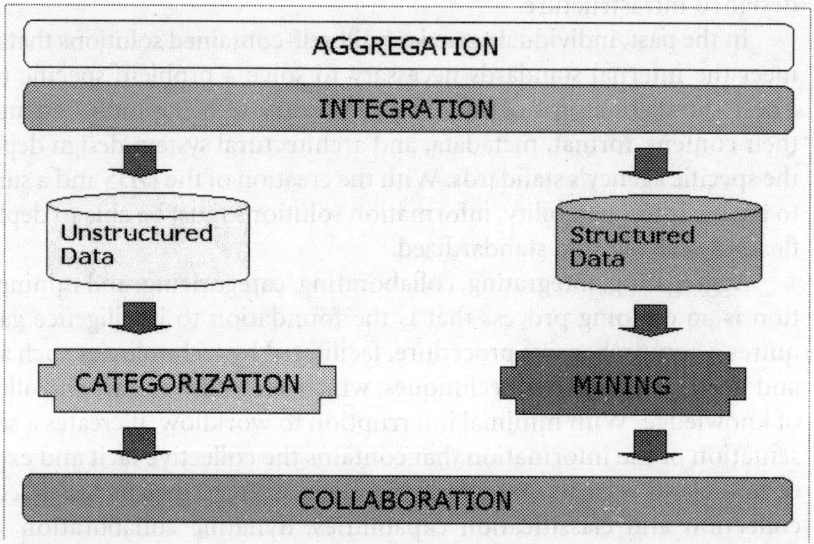

FIGURE 1.10 Homeland security information technology infrastructure.

Having an arsenal of data mining capabilities is critical to the success of homeland security, but it must done with an information infrastructure that is flexible enough to accommodate the content, metadata, and repository access necessary to support these analyses. The challenge of enabling all these intelligence analysis solutions, which may be the largest information retrieval and analysis project ever, is frightening, but the need and importance are equally unprecedented, as we are reminded every 9/11.

2 Aggregation: How to Leverage the Web, Robots, and Commercial Demographics for Entity Validation

In This Chapter

- Zero Latency
- Dynamic Data Warehouse (DDM)
- The Web: Internet Mechanisms
- Robots: Data Collection Software
- Commercial Demographics: Entity Validation
- Conclusion: From Aggregation to Integration

Terrorists are almost always ideologically, politically, religiously, or issue oriented, commonly working in small independent cells. They are sophisticated, smart, and skilled with tools and weapons and possess an efficient planning capability, with the patience and money to wait for the opportunity to strike at their time and place of convenience and advantage. Aggregating data about them is an especially challenging task. Innovative strategies are called for, as well as the use of techniques and technologies from the corporate world, such as dynamic data warehousing, the use of Internet mechanisms, and use of real-time data aggregation software coupled with the strategic use of commercial demographics for entity validation. The point is not to be ignorant about the entity of the enemy; the goal is to know who they are and how to spot them before they strike. No template exists for aggregating data about potential perpetrators, but some guidelines can be followed about what strategies to follow in the collection and organization of this data.

At the start of this book, several missions about homeland security were listed, including those involving border and transportation security, which calls for the creation of smart borders and the use of technology to verify the identity of individuals entering the country, and domestic counterterrorism, with major initiatives for improving intergovernmental law enforcement coordination and domestic intelligence gathering. Both of these missions are particularly central and relevant to data aggregation: They call for the gathering of information about individuals and the validation of their identities via the use of various techniques and technologies that will be discussed in this chapter.

ZERO LATENCY

In private industry, zero latency is the ability to react immediately to a business event, such as making a cross-selling offer for a product or service to a customer the instant he buys something. A zero latency company, for example, is one that has removed delays from its operations so that business events that occur anywhere in the organization can immediately trigger appropriate actions across all other parts of its operation. This translates to the removal of all operational inconsistencies, where users gain real-time access to real-time aggregated information. Driven by the need for profits, private industry has become more responsive, competitive, and attentive to customers; firms are extremely sensitive to their demographics, behavior, and values. Likewise, government and homeland security organizations can become more responsive and effective in meeting their mission by using some of the same techniques of private industry and by using some of the same data sources.

The challenge for organizations lies in becoming a zero latency enterprise. For a business this means it must somehow aggregate the customer and transactional data, synchronize it, and route that information across its operational units all in real time. A similar challenge exists for homeland security organizations, where instant action is required to thwart intrusions at the country's points of entry borders, as well as recognizing potential internal attacks via domestic counterterrorism. The tasks for achieving zero latency for both private industry and the government include the following:

1. Capturing the event, such as a suspected individual attempting to enter the country at a border crossing in El Paso, TX.

2. Collecting the data in proprietary formats into a single standard message format.
3. Routing the message to a hub.
4. Transforming the data into a native format on the receiving end.

This no doubt will involve some of the tools, syntax and technologies of data integration to be covered in the next chapter, but at this juncture it is important to recognize why there is a need to capture all this information and how it can be of value in the context of homeland security.

While the most common model for data aggregation in private industry has been the data warehouse for generating business intelligence, multiple organization reports, and insightful views of customers. This data warehouse model does not fully address the challenge of real-time data aggregation, which homeland security organizations must cope with. The problem with the data warehouse construct is that it is typically designed to help companies understand their customers over time and analyze their internal marketing, sales, and financial operations. A traditional data warehouse provides long-term, integrated views, but not real-time zero latency alerts.

A data warehouse is a repository for information extracted from other systems, but it is not appropriate for propagating change to other operational systems, especially those involving counterterrorism and homeland security. A data warehouse is an information depository for temporal and spatial analyses and is not designed for aggregating data from which real-time alerts can be generated to field personnel about possible intrusions at the country's borders and airports. Only in recent years has the concept of dynamic data warehouses come into vogue, with some progressive private industry companies that want to have the competitive advantage of being more responsive to their customers via the Web or wireless media.

DYNAMIC DATA WAREHOUSE (DDM)

Homeland security calls for instant data aggregation, integration, and access with the ability to issue alerts and create profiles as events take place. A DDM model can respond and deliver distributed solutions, such as entity validation to border, airport, and other homeland security personnel. A DDM can provide risk assessments, surveillance, monitoring, and profiling over networks to homeland security personnel for both real-time alerts and detailed data analyses.

Such a DDM would require that it be flexible and capable of accommodating disparate, distributed, diverse data sources. It would also require the ability to support high volume and performance, with a flexible ability to aggregate data from transactional points in support of dynamic creation of multiple data marts for specific homeland security applications. The DDM would be designed to handle the flow of the information specific to the needs of different homeland security agencies and personnel. The system should also provide full access to all current and historical data available from internal government databases as well as key external data sources as determined by homeland security personnel.

A DDM model aggregates data based on homeland security requirements and may consist of a group of interrelated logical and physical databases that contain the aggregated information for meeting specific homeland security missions and tasks. Lastly, the DDM would aggregate data as acquired from internal processes such as border crossings or external data providers such as demographics data resellers like ChoicePoint. It may also require the search for specific Internet-related information aggregated by spiders or robots scanning for suspected IP addresses and e-mail addresses captured via the various Internet mechanisms in use by e-businesses. It would also aggregate data resulting from analytical processes that determine the need to acquire and use specific information such as personal identifiers' activity or inactivity, for instance Social Security numbers or financial related account information indicative of possible money laundering activity. The actual physical location of the DDM can be any RDBMS server, centralized or distributed.

THE WEB: INTERNET MECHANISMS

Terrorist cells around the world use the Internet for scheduling, meeting, and organizing. The Web has become a terrorism-assistance tool that allows them to do things in secrecy. Encrypted messages can originate from anywhere in the world because the Internet is so ubiquitous. Reportedly, steganography and watermarking techniques for data hiding are being used by these groups. Using the Web, terrorists are sending encrypted messages in electronic files—hiding pictures and maps of targets in sports chat rooms, on pornographic bulletin boards, and on Web sites. The Web offers entry to any user from any country; with so many points linked together that tracking terrorist activity is often impossible. Bin Laden's Al-Qaeda and other terrorist groups have reportedly used encryption programs available free on the Web. There are deciphering techniques for tracking and monitoring some of this activity, but that is outside the scope of this book. There is, however, some basic data created by Internet users that is universal and common every time a browser visits a Web site.

With the advent of the Internet and the networking of databases across the globe, new mechanisms have been created for aggregating browsing information and user behavior for analysis and real-time action. There is a multitude of these mechanisms, programs, and technologies, including some innocuous-sounding techniques known as *cookies*, *bugs*, and *forms*, that are used to silently aggregate clickstream data about users and their behavior for such purposes as personalization of content and optimization of online e-commerce.

These Internet mechanism can have a dual purpose in monitoring for homeland security purposes, especially in light of the fact that the Web is being used by terrorist groups to communicate and organize their attacks worldwide. Internet mechanisms commonly used by marketers for personalization can be converted and applied to homeland security purposes, to track and discover the identity and location of potential terrorists, as well as to monitor the content of their communications. Terror organizations are known to use chat rooms to keep in touch by e-mail and to coordinate attacks via the use of cybercafes. The following section discusses several of these Web-based data components.

IP Addresses

IP stands for Internet Protocol. An IP address consists of 32-bit numbers, normally expressed in four octets as a dotted decimal number. Here is what a typical IP address looks like:

203.217.36.138

Every machine on the Internet has a unique IP address, with a server having a static IP address that does not change very often. A home machine that dials up through a modem often has an IP address that is assigned by the ISP when the user dials in. That IP address is unique only for that session, and it may be different the next time he dials in. This way, an ISP needs only one IP address for each modem it supports, rather than for each customer.

Each computer on the Internet has an IP address that uniquely identifies it from all other computers on the Internet. When a user sends or receives data, the message gets divided into small chunks called *packets*. Each of these packets contains both the sender's Internet address and the receiver's address. Each packet is sent first to a gateway computer, which is normally a networking device called a *router* that understands a small part of the Internet. The gateway computer reads the destination address and forwards the packet to an adjacent gateway that in turn reads the destination address and forwards the packet further until one gateway recognizes the address as belonging to a computer within its immediate neighborhood or domain. That gateway then forwards the packet directly to the computer whose address is specified. What is important about IP addresses is that they are written to log files, recording all sessions and capturing additional information such as Web page requested, time, keywords used, and cookies.

Log Files: Clickstream Data

When a person looks at a Web page and clicks on a link, it instantly creates a transaction, which gets aggregated and recorded at a server log file, generally in the following format:

```
207.237.176.5- -[17/Jan/2003:14:00:15 -0400] "GET /cgi
bin/ncommerce3/CategoryDisplay?
cgrfnbr=12178&cgmenbr=1&homecategory=118&View.x=23&View. y=9 HTTP/1.1"
200 - COMPANY=SELF:1:929630485:929630485:11929628000822906249
:929630485; SESSION-ID=10878083,w293AYY5nzEQhy6LIRt25Ip1fkq6gXZ7VodE
52AK/5Z1bDp 19yASQfdRQ4plBOfR" "https://www.company.com/cgi-bin/
ncommerce3/CategoryDisplay? 4.1 Loganalyzers
cgrfnbr=118&cgmenbr=1&homecategory=118""Mozilla/4.0 (compatible; MSIE
4.01; Windows 95)"
```

One of the most basic Web data components is the log file, which originally consisted of seven fields known as the Common Log Format as created by the National Center for Supercomputing Applications. The seven fields consist of the following information:

1. The remote host field identifies the browser host IP number or DNS hostname:

   ```
   prominer.com or 204.58.155.58
   ```

2. The RFC931 remote log name identification field, 99.9 percent of the time a dash:

   ```
   -
   ```

3. The AuthUser field is an authenticated ID or password for accessing a protected area:

   ```
   jmena iujsd23
   ```

4. The date and time field in Greenwich Mean Time:

```
Thu July 1712:38:091999
```

5. The request or transaction field as it comes from the client, such as:

```
"GET" index.html/products.htm
```

6. The HTTP status code returned to the client usually (Success) transaction:

```
200
```

7. The byte size field of the document transferred or the transaction:

```
3234
```

As you can see, log files were designed primarily to track server traffic; they were never intended to record individual's interactions or their demographics. The Extended Common Log Format, which is used by most of today's commercial Web sites, adds the Referrer, Agent, and Cookie fields to the original seven fields of the Common Log Format:

1. The Referrer field identifies the search engine and keyword used to navigate to the site; it can also identify a routing banner ad:

```
http://search.yahoo.com/bin/search?p=data+mining~ /index.html
```

2. The Agent field identifies the browser used by the visitor, a totally useless bit of information:

```
Mozilla/2.0 @Win2002; I)
```

3. The Cookie field is a header tag, which can be used to identify new or returning visitors:

```
.snap.com TRUE/FALSE 946684799 u-vid-0-0 00ed7085
```

The Extended Common Log Format can reveal what a Web user was looking for and when he came to a site. The same field can also identify what search engine he used or if he was routed from a banner ad placed at another site. The Referrer field can tell which site is generating the most visits to a site and the most critical cookie file, which can contain personal identification numbers and other browsing behavior information.

Log analyzer software exists for decomposing server files into reports that can be used to find out where visitors to a Web site came from, what search engine and keywords they used to find the site, how many of them are returning visitors, and how long they stayed. Almost all servers generate detailed log files of every transaction. They all aggregate tremendous amounts of data about browsers continuously and can provide the following type of aggregated information:

- What times of the day and days of the week a server is busiest
- What browsers and operating systems visitors are using
- What pages of a site were viewed and how often
- What sections of a site are visited and at what times
- The average view time for a given Web page
- What search engine people use to find a site
- What keywords people use to find a site
- From which pages people enter a site
- Who the most frequent visitors are
- How many visits a site received
- What errors people encounter
- Where people come from

One of the most effective log analyzer tools is WebTrends; the following are some of the types of basic reports it is able to generate:

- Average Time to Serve Pages, for determining performance of a Web site
- Visits by Hour of the Day, for identifying peak hours of traffic to a Web site
- Server Cluster Load Balance, for maximizing the server's effectiveness

There are commercial and academic log analyzers that decode log files and provide some basic analysis and reporting. An alternate way of monitoring data from a site is via the use of packet sniffer software or network monitors, which observe the movement of packets from servers to browsers in order to report on how visitors arrived at a site. These tools monitor the flow of communication between servers and browsers. One of the advantages of packet sniffers is that, because they look at the meta tags of Web pages being passed, they can be configured to monitor the activity of large farms of distributed servers. Both log analyzers and packet sniffers are able to report on a very critical component of clickstream data: cookies.

Cookies

Cookies are programs than enable a Web server to send pieces of information to a browser, where it is stored in the user's computer, ready for future access, usually for recognition and tracking. Cookies are embedded in the HTML data that flows back and forth between a user's computer and the Web servers he visits. Cookies were originally implemented to allow user-side customization of Web content. For example, cookies are used by Amazon to track what a user purchases, in order to make targeted recommendations in future visits. This is done through the writing of certain data attributes by a Web server to a browser's machine and then using that data as tracking tokens and unique identifier values.

FIGURE 2.1 A view of a cookie file.

Cookies commonly have six parts that a Web server can modify directly on the browser machine. These data attributes usually are the variable name, the variable value, the expiration date/time, the domain name, the domain path, and the security flag. In addition, the cookie may also contain a field that shows when the cookie was last modified, but this is not under the direct control of the Web server. The purposes of these cookie attributes are as follows:

The Variable Name: This is simply the name selected by the server to describe the variable that's being stored in the cookie on the browser. Depending on the server's purpose or objective, this name may or may not describe what the cookie's purpose is. It can be a unique identification number such as this one, which is also recording the time and referring search engine used along with the keyword:

```
timestamp_id_0051-6789JM-07/06/2003_8:90am_google_homeland_security
```

The Variable Value: This is the data that the cookie is actually storing, where the Web server stores information about a Web browser. Internet standards limit the information a server can store in a browser to 4 kilobytes of data. This can contain any kind of information a user has entered or that the server has observed. For example, in the following, a book shopper profile is being generated:

```
Name:Jaime_Bustamante/Products:Books/Sections:Accounting/IPAddress:
855.987.987.001/Number_of_Visits:5/AmountofPurchases:3/Demographics:
GrayPower
```

The Expiration Date/Time: This is the date and time at which the cookie expires or is no longer valid. After a cookie expires, the browser is free to discard it if it so chooses. The expiration date and time are set by the server in Greenwich Mean Time (GMT) format: WDY (weekday-optional) DD (date) YYYY (year) HH (hour) MM (minute) SS (second):

```
720587163128823809105616643110561664311056166431
```

The Domain Name: This is the name of the Web server that created the cookie and has exclusive rights to use, view, and write to that cookie. If a server does not belong to the same domain as the Web server that created the cookie, the server is denied access. For example, *www.foxnews.com* is not allowed to access cookies that have been created by *www.abcnews.com* and vice versa:

```
washingtonpost.com
```

The Domain Path: This is the path on a Web server for which the cookie will be valid, a tracking mechanism that allows some cookies to be valid for certain parts of a Web site and other cookies to be valid for other parts of a Web site:

```
mortgageWebcenter.com/CheckRates/Search
```

The Security Flag: This is set to either TRUE or FALSE. If it is TRUE, it means that this cookie should be considered to be secure using HTTPS, SSL and should not be passed over the Internet in unencrypted form. If it is FALSE (as most cookies are), it means that the server and the browser can pass the cookie back and forth without encrypting it:

```
FALSE
```

The Creation Date/Time: Some browsers also keep track of the date and time that a given cookie was created or last modified. This field is not controlled by the Web server, it changes only when the server modifies a cookie:

```
1577836800
```

Cookies aggregate user-specific information transmitted by the Web server onto the user's computer so that the information might be available for later access by that server. In most cases, not only does this cookie information go unnoticed, so does access to it. A Web server automatically gains access to relevant cookies whenever the user establishes a connection to it, usually in the form of Web visit. When a cookie is stored in the user's computer, it is essentially a tagged string of text containing their preferences, personal information, or actions at a Web site and can be read by that Web server. The cookie is automatically transferred from the user's machine to a Web server with stored personal information, preferences, or historical actions.

Bugs

A Web bug is a graphic on a Web page or in an e-mail that is designed to aggregate information on who is reading the page or message. Web bugs are invisible because they are typically only 1-by-1 pixels in size. They are represented as HTML IMG tags, with some containing cookies for monitoring purposes. Bugs represent another Web mechanism for aggregating data and any graphic on a Web page can serve the function of aggregating information from a browser to a centralized server. The term "bug" is used to denote a small, monitoring data-aggregating mechanism; other terms to describe the programs include clear GIF, 1-by-1 GIFs, invisible GIFs, and beacons. Bugs can aggregate and broadcast an assortment of information to a server without a browser's knowledge, including the following data attributes:

- The IP address of the browser that fetched the Web bug from the server
- The time an e-mail was opened and viewed by a recipient

- The URL of the page that the Web bug is located on
- The time the Web bug was viewed
- The URL of the Web bug image
- A previously set cookie value

Ad networks such as Doubleclick use Web bugs to add information to a person's browsing profile. The profile is created by a browser cookie set and managed by the ad network and is stored in a centralized server belonging to the ad network, basically to track what Web site a user visits. It is an attempt to provide targeted advertising and personalization. Web bugs are also used in e-mail to find out if a particular message has been read by the recipient and to timestamp when the message was read. The e-mail bug can aggregate and broadcast the IP address of the recipient, and it also can report how often a message is being forwarded and read. Web bugs can also be used in newsgroup messages to track and monitor the individuals who log on and read messages in a particular newsgroup. Such data aggregation mechanisms can be used to monitor people in specific news-related, religious, regional, and political newsgroups, for example. The following is a sample of the code of a bug:

```
img width='1' height='1' src="http://www.m0.net/m/logopen02.asp?
vid=3&catid=370153037&email=SMITHS
%40tiac.net" alt=" ":@IMG SRC=
"http://email.bn.com/cgi-bin/listening?
x=ABYoAEhouX":
```

Forms

Another mechanism for aggregating data about individuals is via registration and purchase forms. Through the use of forms, Web sites are able to aggregate information using programs or scripts that collect data from visitors and write their content to a database. Server processing of form submission data can take several directions, the most common of which is the launching of an action that executes a lookup or an event such as a registration or a purchase. The most common is the input of a search keyword to a search engine. The important aspect of this activity is the aggregation of data by the server from the browser and its documentation to a database.

The techniques for aggregating this information via forms can involve the common gateway interface (CGI), a popular protocol by which browsers interact with servers. It is a robust and versatile method by which browsers communicate with data providers on the Internet. CGI is a method by which Web servers are able to aggregate information from browsers and communicate that input with information from other sources, such as offline demographics or internal organization databases. Java can also be used with forms, as well as JavaScript at the server side with Active Server Pages and LiveWire. Forms enable the aggregation of information from browsers that can be written to databases, which can be merged, matched, and monitored.

ROBOTS: DATA COLLECTION SOFTWARE

There is a tremendous amount of information available on the Web, but aggregating it is problematic for several reasons, including client and session cookies, dynamically generated URLs, client-side scripts, page redirects, site navigation, interaction with forms, and secure protocols. However, data aggregation software exists that allows homeland security agencies to tap into information that is available on the Internet and its databases. These data aggregation systems can extract data from Web sites, automatically transforming it into structured data formats, such as XML, which can be used immediately in new applications and be made available for subsequent analyses and deployment into new applications, eliminating the need to deal with data in its unstructured format. The explosion of the Internet worldwide has created a ubiquitous environment in which information is being created on a daily basis in many languages, some of which is being used by terrorists to communicate and coordinate their efforts. Having the ability to collect this Web-based data requires automated tools. The following sections provide descriptions of these types of data aggregation agent-based robots.

AIS

Automated Info Solution (AIS) offers an information extraction tool it calls the Kapow Web Collector, which is a multiplatform, multi-OS, multi-database, multiprotocol data collection tool written in Java. The software is composed of several sub-components it calls *robots*. RoboMaker is a component for the creation of data-aggregation robots, RoboRunner executes data collection robots in batch mode, and RoboManager monitors and manages the robot's lifecycle and performance. The robots can consolidate multiple Web sites into one central location in a repeatable, automated method. A free evaluation copy of the software is available at the company's Web site at *http://www.automated-info-solutions.com*.

Fetch

This software platform, as with AIS, consists of three major sub-components. The first is AgentBuilder, an interactive visual environment for constructing data aggregation agents. AgentRunner is an execution system that automatically performs the tasks specified by the agent and produces the structured data ready for use in any subsequent application. AgentAdministrator provides the continued maintenance of the data aggregation agents. The core technology embedded in the Fetch agent platform was developed by Fetch company founders at the University of Southern California. The basic idea is that the user provides examples of the data to extract, which the agent then automatically learns. In this manner, extraction rules are created, rules that monitor the quality of the data being extracted.

According to Fetch, this approach enables them to regenerate agents automatically even when the format of a Web site changes. A Fetch agent is a software program that enables online sources to be queried as if they were databases. The Fetch agents aggregate semi-structured data sources. These are sources where there is no explicit structure or schema, but where there exists an implicit underlying structure. Many Web sources, such as e-mail messages, have some underlying structure in which data can be aggregated from specific fields such as the date, sender, addressee, title, and body of the messages.

Fetch's AgentBuilder allows users to mark up sample pages from a Web site. The system then uses the template to generate a set of extraction rules that extract other pages. Fetch uses a greedy-covering inductive learning algorithm to search, which incrementally builds the extraction rules from the examples used to train it. According to Fetch, it enables them to generate extraction rules efficiently from a small number of training samples. This is made possible by exploiting the hierarchical structure of the source to constrain the learning problem. This approach also has the advantage of being able to extract data from pages that contain lists, nested structures, and other complicated formatting layouts. Fetch also automatically performs statistical verifications and repairs agents in response to changes in Web site layouts or content formats.

Mobular

Mobular offers truly unique software in the area of data aggregation and distribution with potential value in the area of homeland security. Its technology offers a high degree of portability and speed. In the late 1990s, NASA scientists David Noever, Ph.D., and John M. Horack, Ph.D., developed Mobular Engines™ to aggregate, compress, and mobilize both structured and unstructured data with self-contained search and navigation capabilities. Their data aggregation breakthroughs allow entire databases to be delivered via e-mail or Web browsers, where they can be searched and navigated in lightning-fast speed. With Mobular Engines, a user in effect can "clone" an entire online database (or subset thereof) or large group of documents and deliver them in e-mail, with full search and navigation capabilities to be run locally on the recipient's computing device, whether it is a PC, PDA, or cell phone.

Mobular takes an entire online database, converts it into its special format, adds its built-in search engine and navigation, and puts it into its compressed and self-expanding package that travels very easily via e-mail. Since the database and search engine are running locally on the recipient's machine, performance is lightning fast. Searches run anywhere from ten to hundreds of times faster than what's possible even via a broadband Web connection. The Mobular Engine works with no special plug-ins, attachments, PDF, or other special software. The Mobular system can aggregate text and images, indexing the content and adding powerful search and retrieve features along with navigation capabilities and delivering it in a compact file.

The secret to the fast performance of the Mobular Engine technology lies in its proprietary portable database and built-in search engine design, both of which are delivered to and installed at the client computing device. Unlike traditional Web architectures, with the Mobular Engine, the entire database and search engine are delivered to the end user's computing device, so that searches and navigation happen instantaneously. There's virtually no perceptible lag because the end user's computer doesn't have to communicate back and forth with a server. The database and interactivity software programs remain resident in an e-mail program, browser's cache file, or a self-contained "save to desktop" Windows executable, all of which will still function when the system is offline.

Mobular's spidering and iterative data aggregation technologies are able to distill and index information from all manner of source formats or any combination of formats. Mobular uses a streaming data mechanism in the format of a tiny 3K e-mail footprint that, when opened, presents the user with a complete easily navigable document or database. Most importantly for homeland security agencies, Mobular Engines can not only be deployed via e-mail and Web browsers, they can also be used be viewed via wired mobile devices, like PDAs and Web-enabled cell phones, which is especially critical for first responders, border, and counterintelligence personnel. Next we move on to another important source of information that a homeland security organization may want to use as part of its tasks, missions, and analyses: commercial demographics, lifestyle and neighborhood information, real estate and vehicle data, and so on.

COMMERCIAL DEMOGRAPHICS: ENTITY VALIDATION

One of the key objectives of data aggregation for homeland security is to assemble composites of potential perpetrators. This involves a strategy of aggregating data sources for data mining analyses to uncover specific patterns or conditions of abnormal consumer behaviors and lifestyles, coupled with the mismatching of certain government and financial activity records. In the following section, some of the largest commercial demographic providers are discussed. Marketers for years have use these demographics to micro-segment and target their sales at the geo code (households) level, based on the physical location of a person's residence. Rather than using this data exclusively for marketing, it can also be used for security and the validation of the identity of individuals; in fact, the Computer Assisted Passenger Prescreening System II (CAPPS II) has tested this in the validation of airline passengers using Acxiom data. The following sections discuss some of the largest demographic and data aggregators.

Acxiom

Acxiom is one of the world's leading data and demographics provider. Their InfoBase® List National Consumer File is a comprehensive, national consumer list covering over 111 million households and more than 176 million individuals. The InfoBase is one of the largest collections of U.S. consumer and telephone information, and marketers have used InfoBase for years for database or file appending, analytical services, mailing lists, and e-mail data enhancement. It is a very accurate, comprehensive, and multisourced data source. Acxiom starts with over 500 million names and addresses compiled from multiple sources, including county recorder, county tax assessor files, other list compilers, and telephone directories. The file is totally rebuilt every quarter, with interim refreshes.

One of the most powerful data aggregation technologies from Acxiom is AbiliTec®, which links their demographics to data records to effectively reduce the number of duplicate matches. It then uses a component it calls BestAddress to identify the most recent address for that data record. Finally, demographic and real property data is applied to each record in order to get the most accurate, comprehensive data match possible. Acxiom then converts the names of 270 million individuals, which may have multiple or truncated last, middle, and first names, and converts them to unique 16-digit identification numbers, effectively normalizing and improving the accuracy by which individuals can be matched to physical mailing addresses. AbiliTec aggregates and updates its database monthly, processing 80 percent of all directory phone listings and 50 percent of all National Change of Address changes. Acxiom processes over 42 billion data records, performing address changes and cleansing processes, while assigning its unique AbiliTec identification numbers. Originally developed to improve the accuracy of mailing lists for marketers and retailers, this file can be used by homeland security organizations to validate the identification of individuals at key checkpoints such as borders and airports or security locations warranting an extra level of protection.

Another of Acxiom's data products is Personicx®, a household-level segmentation system built with InfoBase data, which places all U.S. households into one of 70 distinctive segments based on specific consumer behavior and demographic characteristics. For more than 30 years, marketers have been using segmentation systems to tailor their marketing programs and gain quick, accurate analysis of their most profitable customers. Using the same core data from InfoBase, Acxiom has developed Sentricx®, a data reference product designed to combat fraud by enabling data-driven identity verification of customers and prospects at the point of sale, in call center and Internet environments, and on applications for credit accounts, demand deposit accounts, or insurance polices. Businesses have always had a need to validate an individual's identity, a need now shared by the government in the aftermath of 9/11.

Clearly, products like Sentricx can also be used for homeland security purposes by enabling data-driven validation of individual identities. By accessing multiple reference databases in real time or batch mode, data products such as Sentricx can be used to validate the identify of individuals at point-of-registration transportation desks, such as those at airports, and point-of-entry borders. Sentricx offers rapid access to a wide array of data from multiple and diverse database sources, with flexible design for incorporating their data into multiple applications. One of the key strategies that Acxiom claims for this data product is its breadth of data accuracy and its rapid capability for integration into applications for personal identity verification.

Flexibility to incorporate Sentricx into existing systems means that powerful identity verification can be implemented where and how it is needed to minimize fraud exposure and improve homeland security. Acxiom claims very robust data integrity for Sentricx, which combines data from multiple sources. It provides what Acxiom calls "in-wallet" data, information that is commonly found in a person's wallet or purse such as a credit card or driver license, in combination with "out-of-wallet" data for verification and entity validation purposes, making an ideal product for homeland security. The following data components can be packaged into the Sentricx data product for entity verification and validation:

- Name and address information
- Phone numbers

- Date of birth
- Social Security number
- Additional household members
- Own/rent
- Previous addresses
- Likelihood-of-fraud scores based on matches/mismatches of the data noted above

Acxiom is providing the Sentricx data product to leading financial institutions and insurance companies, who have experienced significant savings associated with fraud reduction as a result of their use of the product. Sentricx's combination of breadth of data categories, depth of data on any given record, and flexibility in implementation make it a robust data-driven identity verification and entity validation product for homeland security applications.

The firm also markets Acxiom Information Security Services (AISS) for background screening via various type of record searches. AISS provides multilayer, 100 percent in-person real-time Federal Credit Reporting Act-compliant reports including but not limited to criminal, credit, driving, employment, and education verifications for security applications for businesses, which again lends itself to homeland security purposes. There is an assortment of AISS products available from Acxiom, typically used by businesses to perform background checks, but which are very relevant to identity validation for homeland security applications. The following sections discuss some of these products.

TRUST

TRUST (Tracking Residences Using Social Security Trace) uses a person's Social Security number to trace back prior addresses associated to it. This is in situations where an individual may not want this information revealed or disclosed in job, insurance, or credit applications. Using these prior addresses, for example along with data association software from Systems Research and Development (SRD) or COPLINK, which will be discussed in subsequent chapters, links may be uncovered of relationships between terrorist cell members.

Criminal Record Search

Acxiom's Criminal Record Search provides in-person, real-time searches of criminal background records. AISS researchers obtain criminal records from counties, municipal courts, and statewide repositories.

Driving Record Search

Acxiom's Driving Record Search looks at department of motor vehicle records at the state level.

Employment Credit Report

Acxiom's Employment Credit Report can provide insight into an individual's financial responsibility as well as verify previous employment and past address information.

Social Security Number Trace

Acxiom's Social Security Number Trace is one of the most effective methods of validating an individual identity. A person's Social Security number (SSN) is considered to be one of the most abused pieces of personal information and is a key component of identity theft, a crime often associated with terrorism. Using a product such as this, a homeland security organization can detect suspected misuse of an SSN by an individual in opening a bank account or obtaining another type of identification document such as a driver license or visa.

Other Types of AISS Verifications and Checks

- Education
- Certificate and Licenses
- Employment
- Civil Record Search
- Workers' Compensation Search
- Drug Screening
- Sexual Offender Registry Check
- AISS COMPLETE SAMPLE REPORT (Includes)
    - Employment Credit Report
    - (Including Hawk Alert: Use of an SSN not issued by Social Security Administration)
    - Statewide Criminal Record Check
    - Civil Suits (Federal Region)
    - Misdemeanor Criminal Record Check
    - County Criminal Record Check
    - Federal Criminal Record Check
    - Education Verification
    - Employment Reference
    - State Driving Record

- Worker's Compensation Records
- County Civil Record Check
- Tag and VIN Search

Products such as Sentricx, TRUST, and the various AISS record searches can be used with data integrating name or address matching software components, such as those from SRD's Non-Obvious Relationship Awareness™ (NORA™) program to dynamically identify correlations across disparate databases and identify associations of suspected terrorist residing in the United States using erroneous Social Security numbers or other illegal methods of identification.

ChoicePoint

ChoicePoint is another source of data specifically concentrated on reducing fraud and mitigating risk by providing its information to the insurance industry. It has branched out to also provide decision-making intelligence to businesses and government. Through the identification, retrieval, storage, analysis, and delivery of data in multiple formats, ChoicePoint today feeds cross-referencing information to businesses, as well as federal, state, and local government agencies. For example, its AutoTrackXP and ChoicePoint Online provide Internet access to more than 17 billion current and historical records on individuals and businesses and allow users to browse through those records instantly. With as little information as a name or Social Security number, data products can cross-reference public and proprietary records, including identity verification information, an individual's relatives and associates, corporate information, real property records, and deed transfers. These easy-to-read online reports are used to locate people and assets and detect and prevent fraud, and they lend themselves to homeland security applications requiring the validation of a person's identification.

Another type of report available from ChoicePoint is Discovery PLUS!™, which is also available online. This report compiles a comprehensive report on an individual, including current and previous addresses, relatives, assets, corporate involvement, and derogatory information. The report lists where no matches were found. Discovery PLUS! can also match and return with a vehicle identification number. The Info:PROBE™ report, also available via ChoicePoint Online, can check millions of records simultaneously and provides a "shopping list" of databases that contains records that match the search criteria. An agency client can select which databases it wishes to view. No matter how many records are viewed, fees will not exceed $100 per search. It also returns lists where no matches are found.

ChoicePoint also offers a National Comprehensive Report through its AutoTrackXP system that enables searches of national and state databases for a summary of assets, driver licenses, professional licenses, real property, vehicles, and more. This report supports the ability to add associates, including relatives or others linked to the same addresses, as the subject of an investigation. This type of report of entity association clearly has applications in the area of homeland security and law enforcement.

ChoicePoint Public Records is partnering with Voyager Systems, Inc., to provide law enforcement and public safety organizations with a fully integrated wireless data access application. Subscribers can check criminal records, immediately accessing outstanding warrants through local, state, and federal criminal justice databases, to verify the identity of subjects encountered in the field and display mug shots for positive identification. The integration of the Voyager Query™ wireless application and ChoicePoint's public record data runs on virtually any handheld device and wireless network to provide secure, portable delivery to mobile devices for field personnel. The system provides end-to-end application encryption with a 4 to 10 second average response time and is available 24/7 through the ChoicePoint network operations center.

Another data product with potential homeland security applications is that of ChoicePoint's CORE™ report. CORE is designed for users who need to draw from a vast number of information resources, including ChoicePoint's 17 billion public records and proprietary data, notes, interviews, photos, financial records, and police reports. With CORE, homeland security users can quickly and convincingly present investigative findings through compelling diagrams, reports, and images. This report enables AutoTrackXP® subscribers who have purchased CORE to download AutoTrackXP basic and national comprehensive reports for link analysis. In addition, CORE offers simultaneous downloading of multiple AutoTrackXP reports for batch processing. CORE pulls public record data directly into databases or spreadsheets for analysis; it can merge data automatically with other internal databases.

ChoicePoint also offers a high level of authentication services using a combination of personal data and biometric elements to provide a higher method of identification. ChoicePoint's identification services organization can perform on-site, online, or off-line identity validation and confirmation. ChoicePoint makes the service so that an organization can integrate it via an API into any integrated credentialing application, such as credential monitoring, traditional digital certificate issuance, rights and privilege monitoring, and certificate revocation. The process involves the following sequential steps:

1. Identity Verification (establishes unique identities)
   a. Verifies name, SSN, date of birth, and drivers license number and ensures they are all valid and unique.
   b. Matches this information against a separate credit source.
   c. Verifies that the person is who he claims to be.
2. Identity Validation (establishes valid identities)
   a. Knowledge engine validates whether an enrollee is who he claims to be by posing unique questions only the applicant can answer.
   b. Questions are developed using ChoicePoint's extensive public record databases.
3. Identity Confirmation (confirms a level of trust with the identity)
   a. Builds on identity verification in step 2.
   b. Uses formula to determine normal transactional history for the individual.
   c. Compares individual's actual history with formula to confirm valid identity.

After these steps are completed, a credential can be issued to the individual for use in trusted transactions or for storage in any secure device, such as a smart card. Clearly, this type of validation system can be used as part of a homeland security organization's effort to improve the protection of vital infrastructure locations.

Claritas

Claritas invented the U.S. geo-demographic industry when it launched the first PRIZM segmentation system in 1974. PRIZM is the original and most widely used neighborhood target marketing system in the United States. It segments neighborhoods into distinct consumer cluster types with unique behavioral traits. Claritas traditionally has worked on target-marketing projects for businesses and marketers to identify who their customers and best prospects are. The demographics describe what they are like, where they are located, and the areas where they live and determine how to reach them most cost-effectively. PRIZM's neighborhood clustering system, however, also can be used for homeland security applications to assign a lifestyle label to an individual that can enhance an analyst's knowledge about the individual through segmentation analysis in combination with other databases to create decision rules in the form of behavioral profiling. For example, the Beltway Snipers that terrorized the nation's capital had demographics that clearly did not match those of the suburbs of Virginia or Maryland. Although by itself this did not warrant their detention, it could have elevated concerns about their presence at the multiple sites of the shootings.

Fifteen unique clustering algorithms are used to segment PRIZM grouping by Claritas. The firm focuses on the key factors in each density-affluence domain that account for the most statistical difference among neighborhoods within that group. PRIZM neighborhood assignments are updated each year to reflect the demographic changes occurring in neighborhoods. Accurate and reliable demographic estimates and projections are critical to this process. Claritas taps into over 1,600 local government and private sources to develop current-year estimates and five-year projections of hundreds of demographic variables at all levels of geography across the United States. The accuracy and reliability of Claritas demographic estimates have been used in courts where they have been submitted as admissible evidence in cases involving site location disputes between a parent company and its franchisees.

Claritas pioneered the concept of PRIZM links and interlocks in the 1970s by putting PRIZM on major syndicated survey databases, including Simmons Market Research Bureau and Mediamark Research, Inc. In the 1980s, audience measurement interlocks with Arbitron, Nielsen, and Scarborough were added, along with most compiled lists used for direct marketing. Today, PRIZM is available on virtually all industry-standard databases, direct marketing service bureaus, and primary research vendors. Marketers have used PRIZM for market research, analysis, targeting, and media planning.

The starting point in the creation of PRIZM is the U.S. Census, where PRIZM models are re-created upon completion of the census every 10 years. The assignment of PRIZM clusters to neighborhood geography is performed annually, using the latest geographic rosters, updated demographics, and behavioral data. The primary geographic unit for demographic-factor analysis and system development is the census block group, the smallest neighborhood geography consistent with statistical reliability and data availability (block groups average 250–550 households).

Factor analysis of census data reveals several dozen demographic and lifestyle variables in six categories that explain most of the statistical variance between neighborhood types: social rank, household composition, mobility, ethnicity, urbanization, and housing. Cluster analysis of these factors produces the basic neighborhood types. These basic clusters are tested, refined, and calibrated with actual consumer-purchase data. Behavioral tests and enhancements to PRIZM tap millions of consumer-purchase records from multiple sources covering auto buyers, magazine subscribers, real estate transactions, consumer credit, direct marketing response, and consumer-expenditure data. The resulting system provides a flexible framework for decision-making that is consistent from one level of geography to another. For instance, the PRIZM assignments for the 5-digit ZIP

Code can be instantly and accurately translated into assignments for block groups, tracts, or ZIP+4s. Marketers use systems like PRIZM to identify, locate, and reach their best marketing opportunities.

PRIZM divides the U.S. consumer into 15 different groups and 62 different segments. The following is a sampling of the information provided for each group and segment:

Group S1: Elite Suburbs
Group U1: Urban Uptown
Group C1: 2nd City Society
Group T1: Landed Gentry
Group S2: The Affluentials
Group S3: Inner Suburbs
Group U2: Urban Midscale
Group C2: 2nd City Centers
Group T2: Exurban Blues
Group R1: Country Families
Group U3: Urban Cores
Group C3: 2nd City Blues
Group T3: Working Towns
Group R2: Heartlanders
Group R3: Rustic Living

Group S1: Elite Suburbs

The five clusters of social group S1 rank in the first and second deciles of Claritas' education and affluence scale, making this one of the nation's most affluent social groups. S1 clusters share high income, education, investment, and spending levels. High concentrations of wealthy Asian immigrants populate these clusters. Beyond these shared patterns, there are marked differences. The Elite Suburbs group consists of the following segments:

01. Blue Blood Estates: Established executives, professionals, and "old money" heirs who live in America's wealthiest suburbs. They are accustomed to privilege and live luxuriously; one-tenth of this group's members are multimillionaires. The next affluence level is a sharp drop from this pinnacle.

02. Winner's Circle: These "new money" families live in expensive "minimansions" in major metropolitan suburbs. They are well-educated executives and professionals who are married and have teenagers. Big producers and big spenders, Winner's Circle families enjoy globe trotting.

03. Executive Suites: These households are single and married couples that have bought their first houses and condos. They have more children than the other clusters in the S1 social group. Although they are less affluent then Cluster 02, they are equally ambitious, well-educated, and competent—they are just 10 years younger.

04. Pools and Patios: Empty-nester executive and professional couples are living the good life in their "post-child" years. Their dual incomes support rich, active lives filled with travel, leisure activities, and entertainment. Many live in the highly populated northeast corridor of the United States.

05. Kids and Cul-de-Sacs: Similar to Executive Suites and Pools and Patios, Cluster 05 ranks high on all affluence measures. Although married couples and children still dominate this cluster, some married couples without children are moving into Kids and Cul-de-Sacs. These suburban folks lead busy lives centered on family activities.

Group U1: Urban Uptown

Group U1 ranks as the nation's second-most affluent social group. Major market concentrations are dense, with over 94 percent of total households in the top 10 TV markets. For over two decades, these clusters have had high concentrations of executives and professionals in business, finance, entertainment, and education. More recently, U1 clusters have absorbed a wave of upscale immigrants from Eastern Europe, Asia, and the Middle East. The Urban Uptown group consists of the following segments:

06. Urban Gold Coast: The highly educated, professional singles and married couples of Cluster 06 live in large urban apartment and condo complexes. Most are found in such densely populated areas as New York City and Washington, D.C. Very few of these busy, affluent Urban Gold Coasters have children or own cars.

07. Money and Brains: Cluster 07 is a mix of family types: singles, married couples with children, and married couples without children. These families own their own homes in upscale neighborhoods. Dual incomes provide luxuries, travel, and entertainment.

08. Young Literati: Although less affluent than Money and Brains, Cluster 08 is more educated. Young Literati executives, professionals, and students live in apartments, condos, and townhouses near private urban universities. They have few children, leaving them free to pursue active lives filled with travel, art, and fitness.

09. American Dreams: These immigrants and descendants of multicultural backgrounds in multiracial, multilingual neighborhoods typify the American Dream. Married couples, with and without children, as well as single parents are affluent from working hard at multiple trades and public service jobs. They have big families, which is unusual for social group U1.

10. Bohemian Mix: Dominated by mobile, highly educated singles, Bohemian Mix is an eclectic group of executives, students, artists, and writers who prefer to live in rented high-rises. Very few children are found in this multiracial cluster.

Group C1: 2nd City Society

The three clusters of social group C1 top the economic scale in hundreds of America's "second" and "satellite" cities. They are highly educated with big incomes. Most own their homes and are executives and professionals in local business, finance, health, law, communications, and wholesale. They are far more conservative than their upscale S1 peers who live in the suburbs of major metropolitan areas. The 2nd City Society group consists of the following segments:

11. Second City Elite: The movers and shakers of America's smaller cities are the prototypes for Second City Elite. Most are married without children; some have teenagers. They hold professional and white-collar management positions. Most have attended college or are college graduates.

12. Upward Bound: Upward Bound members are computer literate, earn dual incomes, and fly frequently. Most are married and have kids and live in new, single-family homes. These college graduates work in management or professional occupations.

13. Gray Power: As the population ages, this cluster's numbers are increasing. Found in retirement communities across the United States, these affluent retirees are playing golf, monitoring their health, and tending their hefty investment portfolios. They are married couples or singles with high school and college education levels.

Group T1: Landed Gentry

The four clusters of social group T1 cover a vast amount of American geography. T1 is the fourth-most affluent group. Large, multi-income families with school-age kids, headed by well-educated executives, professionals, and "techies" dominate this group. Above all, the clusters share serenity because T1 neighborhoods lie far outside the metropolitan beltways in America's most spectacular coastal areas and uplands. The Landed Gentry group consists of the following segments:

14. Country Squires: Yearning to escape urban stress, Country Squires have moved away from our major cities to the outer suburbs to find tranquility in the country. They are well-educated professionals and white-collar managers who are married with children. Fourth in affluence, this cluster has "big bucks in the boondocks."

15. God's Country: Like Country Squires, the large families of Cluster 15 prefer to live away from the city. They are well-educated professionals or white-collar managers. Dual incomes support an active lifestyle that is centered on family and outdoor activities.

16. Big Fish, Small Pond: Married couples with and without children dominate this conservative, family-oriented cluster. They are very similar to God's Country, just slightly less affluent. Most are high school graduates and have taken some college classes. These captains of local industry enjoy investing in their homes and vacationing by car in the United States.

17. Greenbelt Families: Cluster 17 families are younger and less affluent than some of the other clusters living in America's smaller cities. These heavily mortgaged, married couples have lots of children. Because of their heavy debt, they depend on family entertainment and outdoor sports for recreation.

Group S2: The Affluentials

The five clusters of social group S2 represent the upper-middle income suburbs of major metropolitan areas. S2 is the fifth-most affluent group. These clusters share above-average incomes and rentals; an eclectic mix of homes, condos, and apartments; a broad spectrum of business, technical, and public service jobs; and daily commuting—but very little else. The Affluentials group consists of the following segments:

18. Young Influentials: The high-tech, educated folks of Cluster 18 have managerial and professional jobs and live in rented urban high-rises. Although many of their contemporaries have married and settled down, these childless, live-together couples prefer their sophisticated urban lifestyle, supported by dual incomes. They are the last of the Yuppies.

19. New Empty Nests: Their hard work in professions and industries has rewarded Cluster 19 with the affluence that comes from double incomes. Most of these married couples are in their "post-child" years, are more conservative than Young Influentials, and can be found mostly in the Northeastern and Northwestern corners of the U.S.

20. Boomers & Babies: Cluster 20 ranks second out of all PRIZM clusters for married couples with children and ranks first in total households with children, many of whom are pre-schoolers. Cluster 20 folks are found mostly in the Western United States, where they are executives and "techies" in various fields.

21. Suburban Sprawl: The native and foreign-born people in Cluster 21 have educated themselves and are now working as executives, administrators, and technicians. Their diligence has enabled them to leave their multilingual neighborhoods in America's major metropolitan areas and move to the suburbs.

22. Blue-Chip Blues: Topping the blue-collar ladder, the dual income, high school-educated Blue-Chip Blues parents head large suburban families. During the past two decades, their kids grew up and left, and blue-collar employment opportunities declined sharply. A small core of Blue-Chip Blues remains, concentrated in the Great Lakes area.

Group S3: Inner Suburbs

The four clusters of social group S3 comprise the middle-income suburbs of major metropolitan areas, straddling the United States' average. Otherwise, the clusters are markedly different. Two clusters have more college-educated white-collar workers; two have more high school-educated blue-collar workers; two are young; one is old; one is mixed. All show distinct, variant patterns of employment, lifestyle, and regional concentration. The Inner Suburbs group consists of the following segments:

23. Upstarts and Seniors: Cluster 23 shows that young people and seniors are very similar if they are employable, single, and childless. Upstarts and Seniors share average educations and incomes in business, finance, retail, health, and public service. Preferring condos and apartments, they live in the Sunbelt and the West.

24. New Beginnings: Concentrated in the boomtowns of the Southeast, the Southwest, and the Pacific Coast, New Beginnings is a magnet for many young, well-educated minorities who are making fresh starts. Some are divorced, and many are single parents. They live in multi-unit rentals and work in a variety of low-level, white-collar jobs.

25. Mobility Blues: These blue-collar counterparts of New Beginnings are young, ethnically mixed, and very mobile. Many are Hispanic and have large families with children. These breadwinners work in transportation, industry, public service, and the military.

26. Gray Collars: The highly skilled blue-collar workers of Cluster 26 weathered the economic downturn of America's industrial areas and now enjoy a resurgence of employment. Their kids grew up and left, but the Gray Collars stayed in the Great Lakes "Rust Belt."

Group U2: Urban Midscale

The five clusters of social group U2 are the backbone of the middle-income, urban-fringe neighborhoods in America's major metropolitan areas. Group U2 is also highly concentrated, with 75 percent of the total households in the top 5 TV markets and 96 percent in the Top 25. Group U2 averages below the affluence mean. The U2 clusters have high population densities and ethnic diversity, use public transportation, and enjoy all the perks and survive all of the risks of urban life. The Urban Midscale group consists of the following segments:

27. Urban Achievers: Cluster 27 is the most affluent of the U2 clusters. Often found near urban public universities, these neighborhoods are ethnically diverse with a blend of youth and age. Single students mix easily with older professionals who work in business, finance, and public service.

28. Big City Blend: The most ethnically mixed of the U2 clusters, Big City Blend has many Hispanics, Asians, and other foreign-born immigrants. Less affluent than Urban Achievers, Cluster 28 folks have large families and work in white- and blue-collar jobs. They live in older, stable, high-density urban row-house neighborhoods.

29. Old Yankee Rows: More languages are spoken in Cluster 29 than in the other U2 clusters. Recent Asian and Latin American immigrants live in these "magnet" neighborhoods concentrated in the Northeast. Although they have the same mix of white- and blue-collar jobs as Big City Blend, they are less affluent. They tend to be single and live in rental multi-unit apartment complexes.

30. Mid-City Mix: Like the other clusters in U2, Mid-City Mix is above average in ethnic diversity with a similar mix of service, white-collar, and blue-collar employment. Living in urban row-house neighborhoods, they are found in the Northeast and around the Great Lakes. Cluster 30 is three-quarters Black and has a high incidence of college enrollment.

31. Latino America: With the nation's highest index for foreign-born immigrants, Cluster 31 represents a giant step in achievement for the young families of Latino America. They have many children and are concentrated in New York, Miami, Chicago, and the Southwest. Although they live in rented houses and have blue-collar jobs, they are moving up and are college bound.

Group C2: 2nd City Centers

The five clusters of social group C2 describe the midscale, middle-density, satellite cities surrounding major metropolitan areas, as well as many smaller, second-tier cities. The C2 clusters have a lower cost of living and are generally better off than their peers in group U2. With some exceptions, these clusters are predominantly white. Otherwise, they differ in age, marital status, education level, occupation, and lifestyle. The 2nd City Centers group consists of the following segments:

32. Middleburg Managers: These business executives, professionals, city officials, bankers, and retailers are the solid citizens of America's smaller cities. Half of Middleburg Managers are older and married with grown children. The other half is young and single with no children. Thanks to their above-average incomes, they can pursue leisure activities in clubs and sports.

33. Boomtown Singles: Young people in the fast-growing smaller cities in the South, Midwest, and West fall into Cluster 33. They are young professionals and "techies" in public service and private industries who live in multi-unit rentals. They like music and outdoor activities such as boating and skiing.

34. Starter Families: Unlike most of their contemporaries, Starter Families opted for early marriage and parenthood. Cluster 34 folks have large families and work in blue-collar jobs. The solo parents in this cluster have young children. They prefer living in the natural beauty of the Pacific coast areas, the Rockies, and the states bordering northwestern Canada.

35. Sunset City Blues: Cluster 35 is just as affluent as Starter Families, they are just older. At the end of their careers in police work, fire fighting, and other blue-collar occupations, Sunset City Blues are ready to retire. A few relocate to the mountains or to Florida, but most stick close to home near the Great Lakes and the Mohawk Valley.

36. Towns and Gowns: Many college towns and university campus neighborhoods are divided into half locals (Towns) and half students (Gowns). Cluster 36 is primarily composed of 18- to 24-year-olds on limited budgets and highly educated, but perhaps underpaid, professionals. Both of these groups have a taste for prestige products that are beyond their means.

Group T2: Exurban Blues

The four clusters of social group T2 cover the midscale, low-density towns on the outskirts of all major metropolitan areas and second cities. Group T2 is comparable to groups S3, U2, and C2. Three of these clusters are predominantly white, show an even age distribution, own their homes, and are married and raising kids. The Exurban Blues group consists of the following segments:

37. New Homesteaders: More highly educated than the other clusters in T2, the New Homesteaders professionals and executives work in local service fields of administration, communications, health, and retail. The younger married couples have children. Life is homespun with a focus on crafts, camping, and sports.

38. Middle America: Sitting just above the U.S. median household income, Cluster 38 is aptly named. These are family neighborhoods with many married couples. Busy with kids and dogs, they enjoy fast food, sports, fishing, camping, and watching TV. Middle America families are found coast to coast.

39. Red, White, & Blue: Cluster 39 is more blue-collar and industrial and less affluent than Middle America. They are skilled workers in mining, milling, manufacturing, and construction jobs. Concentrated in the Great Lakes industrial area, the Appalachians, and the Western highlands, these folks love the outdoors.

40. Military Quarters: Located on or near military bases, Cluster 40 appears around our principal harbors and other defense installations. Composed of military personnel living in group quarters, the demographics of Cluster 40 are atypical. Fully integrated with the highest index for adults under 35, Military Quarters members like fast cars, action sports, and bars.

Group R1: Country Families

Social group R1 now rivals groups S3, U2, C2, and T2 in midscale affluence and, thanks to lower living costs, suffers less poverty. Found in hundreds of small towns and remote exurbs, the group covers all but a few television markets. Composed of white, married couples, many with children, these country families work in industrial and agrarian occupations. They own their houses and mobile homes. The Country Families group consists of the following segments:

41. Big Sky Families: Cluster 41 households are well-paid craftsmen, machinists, and builders who live in scenic locales in New England, the Tidewater, the Great Lakes region, and the Rockies. Their family-centered lifestyles focus on hobbies, hunting, and boating. Most are high school graduates or have attended some college.

42. New Eco-topia: Found in the rural areas of the Northern Pacific, the Rockies, and northern New England, Cluster 42 is the only R1 cluster with an above-average education level. New Eco-topia has an even mix of white- and blue-collar jobs. A high index of personal computers reflects the high-tech industries in those pristine areas.

43. River City, USA: These solid, blue-collar folks in New England and the Mohawk Valley through the corn, grain, and dairy belts to the Pacific orchards are raising their children in single-family homes. Fourth of July parades and front porches are important to River City, USA. Most Cluster 43 members are high school graduates or have attended some college.

44. Shotguns & Pickups: Found in the Northeast, the Southeast, the Great Lakes, and the Piedmont industrial regions of the United States, Cluster 44 is the least affluent of the R1 clusters. They lead the group in blue-collar jobs. Most are married with school-age children. They attend church and also enjoy hunting, bowling, sewing, and attending auto races.

Group U3: Urban Cores

With the nation's lowest incomes and highest poverty ratios, U3 is the least affluent social group. These clusters live in multiracial, multilingual communities of dense, rented row houses and high-rise apartments. They have high indices for singles, solo parents with pre-school children, and unemployment. The Urban Cores group consists of the following segments:

45. Single City Blues: Cluster 45 is found mostly in Eastern mega-cities and in the West and includes many singles. Often found near urban universities, this cluster hosts a fair number of students. With few children, it is a mixture of races, transients, and night trades and is best described as a "poor man's Bohemia."

46. Hispanic Mix: The bilingual barrios concentrated in Chicago, Miami, Texas, Los Angeles, the Southwest, and the Atlantic metro corridor describe Cluster 46. Large families with lots of small children live in these neighborhoods. They rank second in the percentage of foreign-born and first in transient immigration.

47. Inner Cities: Concentrated in America's poorest neighborhoods in large eastern United States cities, these young, African American single parents live in multi-unit rental complexes. High unemployment and public assistance are prevalent here. When work is available, they have service and blue-collar jobs. They have grade school and high school education levels.

Group C3: 2nd City Blues

The four clusters of social group C3 cover the downtown neighborhoods of hundreds of second cities on the fringe of major metropolitan areas. With lower living costs, these clusters are better off than their big-city cousins (social group U3). Coupled with pockets of unemployment, broken homes, and solo parents, this group also includes a wide range of occupations, including agrarian, clerical, retail, labor, transportation, and public and private sector services. The 2nd City Blues group consists of the following segments:

48. Smalltown Downtown: Cluster 48 is made up of students and those looking for fresh starts and first employment. Smalltown Downtown neighborhoods are found mostly west of the Mississippi. These young and single folks often live near city colleges and work in low-level, white-collar sales and technical jobs.

49. Hometown Retired: At opposite ends of America and the age scale, Cluster 49 is mostly in the Appalachians and central Florida. A few pockets are found in the West. Hometown Retired is third in singles, second in ages 65+, and first in retirement. They take bus tours, collect stamps, and enjoy playing cards and chess.

50. Family Scramble: Although Cluster 50 is found in many markets, it is centered across the Southwest and Pacific areas. It ranks third in Hispanic population and has an above-average number of Native American members. Ranked 62nd in higher education, Cluster 50 shows all the scars of poverty, but they are managing by working in transport, labor, and service.

51. Southside City: The neighborhoods of Cluster 51 are scattered throughout the Southeast, the smaller Mississippi delta cities, the Gulf Coast, and the Atlantic states. Over 80 percent of its households are African American. Ranked 61st in median household income, their low cost of living and jobs in labor and service keep these families afloat.

Group T3: Working Towns

The four clusters of social group T3, with thousands of remote exurbs and satellite towns, are found outside major metropolitan areas and second cities. T3 is considerably better off than groups U3 and C3. The T3 clusters have lower education levels and incomes and work in blue-collar occupations. They own or rent single-family homes amid awesome scenery. They enjoy crafts and going to church. Otherwise, they are distinctly different. The Working Towns group consists of the following segments:

52. Golden Ponds: The scenic rustic towns and villages near coastal, mountain, valley, and lake areas coast to coast are where Cluster 52 neighborhoods can be found. Golden Ponds seniors have retired here to live in cottages among their country neighbors. They are not as urban or as affluent as other retirees.

53. Rural Industria: Low-cost, non-union labor proliferates in Cluster 53, the most industrial cluster of the T3 group. Hundreds of blue-collar mill towns on America's back roads are home to Rural Industria folks. This predominantly white cluster has an above-average index of Hispanic ancestry.

54. Norma Rae-Ville: Centered in the South, the Mississippi delta, and the Gulf Coast and Atlantic states, Cluster 54 is the blue-collar labor pool for the nation's clothing and home furnishings industries. With grade school and high school education levels, many families in this biracial cluster live below the poverty level.

55. Mines & Mills: As its name implies, Cluster 55 folks live in scenic splendor and work in America's mines and mills across the United States. Mines & Mills neighborhoods are in the Appalachians, across the Ozarks to Arizona, and up the Missouri River to the Montana coal fields. The population is older, mostly single with few children.

Group R2: Heartlanders

The two clusters of social group R2 describe the nation's agrarian heartland, centered in the Great Plains, South Central, Mountains, and Pacific, with a few pockets in the East. They are comparatively self-sufficient with a low cost of living. They are large, multigenerational families living in low-density houses and mobile homes. A mix of Hispanics and Native Americans, they are fiercely independent. The Heartlanders group consists of the following segments:

56. Agri-Business: Famous for very large families with lots of kids, countless animals, apple pie, and going fishing, Cluster 56 is in the greater Northwest from Lake Michigan to the Pacific. Occupations include farming, forestry, fishing, ranching, mining, and other blue-collar employment. Most cluster members are high school graduates or have attended some college.

57. Grain Belt: Feeding the United States, and sometimes the world, Cluster 57 is our bread basket. Centered in the Great Plains and South Central regions, life is tied to the land and ruled by the weather. Mostly self-sufficient, family- and home-centered, these families are poor only in money.

Group R3: Rustic Living

The five clusters of social group R3 describe thousands of remote country towns, villages, hamlets, and reservations scattered across the United States. Because the five R3 clusters have lower-middle incomes and a low cost of living, they are a promising market. These married couples and elders share mobile homes, kids, and carpools. They work as craftsmen and laborers in agriculture, mining, transportation, and construction. The Rustic Living group consists of the following segments:

58. Blue Highways: On most maps, the interstates are colored red and the older highways are blue. Cluster 58 follows these remote roads through our mountains and along our coasts, deserts, and lake shores. Blue Highways families are young with lots of children. They hunt and fish, attend tractor pulls, and love country music and camping.

59. Rustic Elders: Cluster 59 ranks as the third-oldest cluster in the United States with the lowest incidence of children in social group R3. It covers the nation but is concentrated in the Great Plains and along the West Coast. Although the life here is pure country, there is a surprisingly high index for health walks, golf, boating, and volleyball.

60. Back Country Folks: Cluster 60 is located in the Eastern Uplands along a wide path from the Pennsylvania Poconos to the Arkansas Ozarks. These are the most blue-collar neighborhoods in the United States Centered in the Bible belt, many members enjoy Christian and country music.

61. Scrub Pine Flats: Cluster 61 is located mainly in the coastal flatlands of the Atlantic and Gulf states from the James to the Mississippi rivers. These humid, sleepy rural communities with their mix of African Americans and whites exist in a timeless agrarian rhythm.

62. Hard Scrabble: Scratching a living from hard soil describes those who live in our poorest rural areas. Reaching from Appalachia to the Colorado Rockies and from the Texas border to the Dakota Badlands, life is hard for Cluster 62 folks. Mining occupations and chewing tobacco show the highest indices in Hard Scrabble.

For marketing purposes, mid-June can almost be considered the beginning of the year. That's when Claritas' Annual Demographic Update is released. The update is our set of current-year estimates and five-year projections developed by Claritas' demographers for hundreds of census variables. These estimates and projections include populations and household totals, age, race, sex, and income variables. Claritas also includes wealth and income-producing assets and consumer expenditure data in the update. Geographic rosters are also updated at this time, including Metropolitan Statistical Areas (MSA), Designated Market Area (DMA), Congressional District, 3- and 5-digit ZIP Code, and Yellow Page Directories (YPD).

Claritas spends months each year analyzing fresh demographic data from many sources, including local governments, consumer databases, and postal delivery counts. Its goal is to locate and use the best sources of local level data available in order to build the most accurate picture possible of demographic growth or decline from year to year about individuals in the country, information once the main domain of marketers, but that can also be applied to homeland security for enhanced entity validation, verification, and behavioral profiling. Claritas' local level data is also referred to as small-area or local market data because it reflects demographic characteristics at the smallest geographic levels—the neighborhood, block group, and census tract. Since the U.S. Census Bureau does not develop nationwide sets of data estimates for the tract and block group level, data suppliers must acquire and incorporate local level data into their own small-area demographic estimates and projections.

In developing its annual demographic updates, Claritas applies both a *top-down* and a *bottom-up* process. In the bottom-up process, Claritas uses local level data to assess demographic growth and decline at the local level. While in the top-down process, Claritas uses U.S. Census Bureau estimates and other federal data to develop totals for demographic variables for larger areas such as cities, counties, and states. These independently produced estimates serve the important function of methodological control, a checks and balance measure to ensure that any indications of demographic change are consistent across all data sources.

These types of residential neighborhood demographics coupled with other identification validation sources can reduce the false positives that often lead to the detention of individuals because of similarities of their names to those in homeland security watch lists. Although originally developed and used by marketers and retailers, these demographics can also be used by homeland security organizations to enhance their ability to validate the identification of individuals. The perception of the public is important, and a homeland security organization should be viewed as being highly efficient as it goes about its missions.

DataQuick

DataQuick is the premier provider of real estate-related information in the United States. Its PropertyFinder can be accessed via the Web to instantly connect to DataQuick's robust nationwide real estate database by entering as little as a partial address, an owner's name or a parcel number. PropertyFinder can verify real estate ownership, identify absentee owners, locate other residences owned by individuals in other locations, and more. It can append real property information to individual records. With as little as a name or an address, a user can conduct a nationwide search and receive results in about 10 seconds. Data File Enhancement appends property-related information to large volumes of data containing thousands of records or targets. Situations may exist in which knowing about real estate ownership and the transfer of titles of property among known or suspected terrorists and their supporters may be of value to investigators and analysts in the area of homeland security. In situations where this kind of real property information is warranted, DataQuick is a key data aggregator in this area.

Experian

One of the three major credit bureaus in the country offers lifestyle demographics via its INSOURCE™ database. The INSOURCE database contains information on over 215 million consumers in 110 million households across the United States. Experian combines data for INSOURCE from hundreds of public and proprietary sources; it claims that it updates it more frequently than any other data aggregator to provide the most accurate picture of U.S. consumers. Experian, as with all the other major demographics and data aggregators, provides data enhancement services. The INSOURCE family of data that is available for both enhancement and list services includes:

- Individual/household demographics
- Property
- Telephone numbers
- Direct response/consumer response
- Summarized data statistics
- Segmentation tools
- Area level data

As with Acxiom, Experian provides a wide range of identification validation products that can be used by homeland security organizations to improve their information processing tasks.

Polk

Polk is the leading source of automotive-related information. Polk has served the automotive industry for 80 years and is the longest-standing provider of automobile records in the United States. Founded in Detroit in 1870, Polk launched its motor vehicle statistical operations in 1922 when the first car registration reports were published. It now provides automotive solutions to nearly every segment of the motor vehicle industry as an analytical consultant and statistician, as a provider of database-marketing services, and as a supplier of vehicle histories to private industry and government.

Polk collects, compiles, and interprets state vehicle registrations and title information, enhancing this information by supplying demographics and lifestyle information associated with automobiles and trucks. Polk has the most accurate and complete vehicle-related data. Typically manufacturers, dealers, aftermarket firms, and auto finance and insurance companies have used this data to understand what vehicles are being purchased and what their customers look like. Polk focuses on knowing what automotive consumers buy, where and when they buy them, and what they are likely to buy next. However, this type of vehicle-related information also has a potential application and benefit in the area of homeland security, especially in the area of border protection, where this type of "automotive intelligence" can be used to enhance data aggregation and analysis. This is especially true in light of the annual information it aggregates and makes available on nearly 200 million cars and trucks in operation in the United States and Canada. The databases available from Polk are extensive; the following is a partial listing:

- Active Auto Buyer
- Analytic Services
- Antique File
- Auto Tracker New Vehicle Statistical Report
- Automotive Financial System (AFS)
- Automotive Loyalty Excelerators
- Automotive Profiling System (APS)
- Automotive Purchase Predictor (APP)
- Bankruptcy Data
- Business Lists
- Commercial Account File
- Commercial Bus File
- Commercial Trailer File
- Commercial Vehicle Registration System (COVERS®)
- Commercial Vehicle Registration System for Fuel Tax (COVERSft)

- Complete Vehicle Identification Number Analysis (CVINA®)
- Covers®.net
- Custom Market Analysis
- Custom Target Marketing
- Dealer Direct Team
- Decision Point
- Demographics
- Do-It-Yourself/Do-It-For-Me Lists
- Driver License Booklet
- Electronic Market Area Reports (eMAR)
- Fare
- Fleet Find
- Fleet Reports
- Focal Points®
- Garage Predictors
- Lifestyle Data
- Mapping Services
- Marketing Program Evaluations
- National Vehicle Population Profile (NVPP®)
- New Vehicle Data
- Niches
- Parts & Service CRM Solutions
- Planning Potential Reports
- Polk Cross Sell
- Polk eSolutions
- PolkOne
- PSYTE®
- Polk Recall
- Polk Total Market Predictor™
- Recover Service
- REGIS®.Net
- Registration Manuals
- Research Sampling
- Self-Reported Auto Data
- Service Marketing and Retail Targeting (SMaRT)
- Surrender Title
- Tele-Plan®
- TeleStat®
- TIP® Access
- TIP®Net

- Unified Files
- Used Vehicle Data
- Vehicle History
- Vehicles in Operation (VIO)
- Vehicle Identification Number Analysis (VINA®)
- Vehicle Insurance Symbol (VIS®)

Some of this vehicle-related information can be used to track the purchases of vehicles, such as large trucks by targeted suspects; the movement of these suspicious vehicles can be monitored and associated to other legal entities. Legal titles of these vehicles can also be tracked and associated to financial institutions and the accounts of individuals or companies for the source of purchase funds. For example, one of the Polk products is CVINA®, which is provided with special software via networks for fast, efficient validation of ID numbers in commercial trucks, trailers, and passenger vehicles. With Polk CVINA®, homeland security agencies can verify VIN accuracy, validate the entire 17-digit VIN including the check digit, correct VIN errors, generate standard vehicle descriptions, return full spellings of vehicle make and series names, and obtain more than 20 other elements of vehicle data, including exact gross vehicle weight (GVW) and gross combined weight (GCW) dating back to 1992. Insurance records can be cross checked, associated demographics of the owners of trucks and automobiles at border crossings or strategic bridges can be aggregated and again, using other type of software components such as those from SRD, InforGlide, and InferX, data matching and data mining analyses can be performed in real time to search for potential attacks or perpetrator profiles, especially those involving large trucks licensed to carry dangerous chemical materials.

SRC

SRC provides a very inexpensive desktop system it calls DemographicsNow with demographics 2003 estimates and 2008 projections for just $995 per year or a low monthly rate. The package includes access to maps and reports for all U.S. geographies and addresses. Geographies include custom drive times, counties, census tracts, block groups, U.S. places, DMAs, MSAs, ZIPs, and more. The product includes easy-to-use preformatted summary, comparison, and rank reports using over 1,100 variables with any U.S. geographic location. Fully interactive maps are available with adjustable ranges and custom color schemes. As with the other demographers, this firm is focused on the typical users of this type of consumer information. The software contains modules for chain supermarkets, chain drug stores, and discount stores. The system can easily be adapted to homeland security applications, especially for those first responder situations where graphical maps of areas and distributions of populations are important data components to aggregate for situation analyses and scenarios. This type of desktop demographic software is very inexpensive and easy to use, making an ideal tool for police, fire, and other small local level homeland security organizations.

TransUnion

TransUnion (TU) is another of the major credit bureaus providing data and demographics. TU excels in the areas of monitoring accounts and setting risk thresholds, security screening of individuals, and predicting and averting fraud. TransUnion supplies data as well as analytic services, models, and segmentation tools. According to the firm, new technologies and new distribution channels have created new ways to perpetrate fraud, and TransUnion offers a suite of identity and fraud detection solutions that are among the most innovative in the industry. TransUnion offers both standalone solutions and complementary capabilities to maximize effectiveness. TransUnion ID verification and fraud detection solutions include the following:

Fraud Detect and Fraud ID-Tect: Fraud Detect is an information validation system designed to prevent application fraud. Fraud ID-Tect is an enhanced version that lets the client customize and deepen the validation analysis.

HAWK®: This is a very effective data product with high value for homeland security applications. HAWK identifies high-risk or potentially fraudulent addresses, Social Security numbers, or telephone numbers.

Year of Issuance (YOI): Used in conjunction with HAWK, YOI allows the client to detect Social Security number misuse and identify conflict in the Year of Issuance. Another homeland security tool.

HAWKeye®: This product offers fraud protection, but it does not access credit information because it uses only public records and individual identification data component fields from the complete credit report.

ID Search®: Provides fast, prioritized verification of identifying information in order to create more efficient application processes and better customer service, reduce fraud, and minimize return mail. This product can also be used for entity validation.

ID Searchplus®: Helps verify application information by matching a consumer's name, address, and/or Social Security number against TransUnion's credit reporting database. ID Searchplus delivers current/previous addresses, SSN, phone number, DOB, aliases, consumer statements, and number of inquiries on file.

Office of Foreign Assets and Control (OFAC) Advisor: Helps credit grantors comply with new federal regulations, including the USA PATRIOT Act, as well as minimize risk and avoid significant financial penalties. With OFAC Advisor, every time a credit report is pulled or uses other selected products, the customer's information is checked automatically against an expanded OFAC list.

Reverse Phone Append: This product helps verify an individual's information and identity by providing access to a multisource database of residential and business telephone listings.

Fraud Detect Model®: This product enhances the effectiveness of Fraud Detect or Fraud ID-Tect to further streamline the entity validation process.

TRANSALERT®: offers a complete application-fraud prevention system that issues alerts about a significant number of recent inquiries on a credit file and differences between information on an inquiry and the contents of existing credit file databases.

TOTAL IDSM: This is a quick and easy identity verification and application analysis service.

The TransUnion suite of identity verification and fraud detection solutions is among the most innovative and comprehensive in the industry. In addition, the company will develop custom identification and fraud detection solutions that fit any business or government agency requirements. Homeland security applications can benefit from the type of reports that TransUnion is able to create from its vast depository and experience in identification verification and validation.

CONCLUSION: FROM AGGREGATION TO INTEGRATION

As we move from the task of data aggregation to that of data integration, we shift to a discussion on the methodology to organize and link these internal and external data sources. Specifically, we will discuss the use and creation of application servers and organizational portals. An application server is a software layer above the operating system that provides shared services and functionality for a network of users, in this case those of multiple homeland security organizations. There are two types of application servers: Microsoft Windows, which uses its Component Object Model, and those that adhere to the Java 2 Enterprise Edition (J2EE) specification. These platforms are used both for creating interactive public Web sites and for building thin client applications. Microsoft and vendors of J2EE application servers, such as BEA, IBM, Oracle, and Sun, sell suites of servers, collections of software components that run on application servers. These components include an integration server that enables applications to connect with programs and databases running in other platforms and the portal server.

A portal server is a collection of server-based software components that run on the application server and produce, in a browser environment, programs running on the application server. In this chapter we discussed some of the types of data a homeland security organization may want to aggregate for analysis and in meeting its missions. In the following chapter will we discuss some of the more technical aspects of information sharing and data integration, such as how to make this information available to homeland security personnel via portal servers, which provide a consistent, user-customized platform in which to aggregate and interact with applications.

Portal servers enable rapid application development, so thin client user interfaces can be quickly created to provide access to business logic running on the application server. Homeland security administrators can use portals as an agency-wide gateway, so that when a user signs on to a portal, that user's identity and access permission grant him access to specific levels of information and programs based on predefined clearance levels. For example, Versant offers application server software that it claims is faster in coming up with information integration solutions involving accessing disparate data sources than a typical relational database. In this context, the use of special integration software can be used to enhance data aggregation for homeland security applications.

3 Integration: The Components, Adapters, Middleware, and Web Services for Information Sharing

In This Chapter

- The Integrators: Framework Providers
- The Future: From 22 to 1 in 2002

Interoperability among government information systems is critical to winning the war on terrorism. However, the Homeland Security Report of July 2002 found that databases used for federal law enforcement, immigration, intelligence, public health surveillance, and emergency management have not been connected in ways that allow users to comprehend where information gaps or redundancies exist. The report concluded that to secure the homeland, the country would need to link the vast amounts of knowledge residing within each government agency.

The demands of homeland security dictate that federal, state, and local government agencies remove the barriers that block exchange of vital data and services, and they must do so quickly, efficiently, and effectively to ensure no future attacks take place. The current situation is that government systems can't communicate, but with the advent of the Terrorist Threat Integration Center (TTIC) and the new Department of Homeland Security, there is a new vision for integrated data, experts, systems, and analyses. The question is how to best bridge the cultural, legal, political, and technical obstacles to make interagency data integration happen.

THE INTEGRATORS: FRAMEWORK PROVIDERS

Most of the integrator providers discussed in this chapter offer complete integration software frameworks with messaging, middleware, adapters, workflow, monitoring, and modeling component programs and capabilities. Many software vendors in this market offer single integration technologies, such as messaging middleware, adapters, workflow, and activity monitoring. The software firms included in this section offer complete integration solution frameworks, which homeland security organizations require in dealing with multidepartmental environments. The obstacles to information sharing for homeland security go further than mere technological solutions and integration software; there are agency, legal, and most importantly cultural barriers that will take time to overcome. However, a start is a discussion on the integration solution providers, discussed in the following sections.

Integrator: Ascential

Ascential offers an integration product called DataStage, the core component of its Enterprise Integration suite, enabling a homeland security organization to integrate multiple data sources for the construction of real-time data warehouses. DataStage supports a multitude of heterogeneous data sources, including text files and almost any database, including partitioned ones and Web services. DataStage supports real-time integration and can capture messages from Message Oriented Middleware (MOM) queues using adapters to seamlessly combine data into conforming operational and historical analysis perspectives.

Ascential Services is a service-oriented architecture (SOA) enabling middleware that provides enterprise-wide benefits of the Ascential Enterprise Integration Suite across a continuum of time constraints, application suites, interface protocols, and integration technologies. DataStage also consolidates, collects, and centralizes information from various systems and mainframes using native COBOL generation and a single design environment. It generates COBOL applications and the corresponding custom JCL scripts for processing all mainframe flat files, IBM DB2, IBM

IMS, and Teradata. Ascential Connectivity for Enterprise Applications comprises a set of data integration PACKs (Packaged Application Connectivity Kits) that provide seamless connectivity within private industry's most widely used enterprise applications, such as SAP, Siebel, Oracle, PeopleSoft and may also be applicable to homeland security systems.

Integrator: BEA

BEA Systems is a leading supplier and integrator of open Java 2 Enterprise Edition (J2EE) application servers. Its WebLogic Integration product is a set of extended J2EE services and tools with an integration hub, a process engine, adapters, and data transformation functions. WebLogic Integration is one of the few total integration platforms providing a single modeling and execution environment. BEA also is a major supplier of transactional processing middleware via its Tuxedo product line.

WebLogic Integration (WLI) is the business integration component of the WebLogic Server platform. It uses all the major middleware services built into the J2EE platform and uses adapters to integrate with non-J2EE applications and components. The WLI integration software supports human interaction through a graphical interface for custom workflow client activities. BEA offers an extensive list of application and technology adapters, as well as event adapters to listen for application events. For example, a homeland security organization might want to use such integration software to link disparate systems using this "listening" feature for issuing alerts or sending information from one application to another. Layered over the adapters and event adapters, the integration tool translates application data and events to a common XML-based integration framework, making this system ideal for homeland security systems. As with most of these top-of-the-line integrators, WLI Studio has a fully graphical interface that enables the user to define transactional processes, flows, and interactions for a "click and integrate" functionality. Application integration and data integration plug-ins to the Studio component can connect data transformation and translation operations.

BEA Tuxedo handles transaction coordination among multiple systems and supports thousands of concurrent users with massive data volumes and high throughput. Tuxedo's core components include the transaction manager for naming, message routing, load balancing, configuration management, transaction coordination, and security, queue services, and domains that provide a framework for configuring servers into autonomous groups. Tuxedo supports most major operating systems, including Microsoft, UNIX, and Linux. A Tuxedo Control component integrated with BEA WebLogic Workshop enables Simple Object Access

Protocol (SOAP) access for Web services. BEA is a very mature and complete data integrator software provider, and because it supports so many platforms, including Web services, it will be a critical component for collaboration among homeland security organizations at multiple government levels and locations.

The Cultural, Legal, and Technical Obstacles

First, government agencies must break down the cultural barriers that for years have resisted interoperability. The cultural mindset of agencies toward sharing data is the major obstacle to data integration. Organizations have to be able to share the information inside their firewalls. People have to understand and see very clearly why the new way is better than the old way, and that sharing information will lead to a more effective government and a secure national defense. Data aggregation is pointless without interagency data integration, which will lead to collaboration, intelligence, and analysis.

Secondly, legal obstacles must be dealt with using post-9/11 legislation, which actually facilitates the exchange of this information. There are legal processes and existing government policies that can impede these data integration efforts. There are laws that prevent the sharing of information, and there are privacy rights and civil liberties that need to be dealt with using new homeland security legislation enacted after 9/11 that can be used to make data integration possible for the common good without the violation of citizen rights. There is also a need to consider integration of external data sources such as utilities, financial, and commercial demographics for homeland security objectives. The software is mature enough to ensure that privacy and security are maintained, and there is agent technology that enables the data to not be moved. There are features that enable only those with clearance to view certain sections of records or files and only with legal instruments and authorizations.

Thirdly, there is the challenge of the technology, which is actually the easiest one to overcome. Integration standards, tools, and techniques can be applied to solve the challenge of data aggregation, collaboration, categorization, intelligence, and mining.

Agencies can use integration architecture standards such as the Government Interoperability Framework. Based on a Web services model, the Government Interoperability Framework combines Internet-based standards, such as XML and SOAP, with robust security, a centralized service registry, and agreements among agencies on data schemas. The result is a seamless, secure fabric of services that promotes data sharing among agencies and provides government with a crucial resource for combating terrorism and improving homeland security.

Integrator: IBM

IBM is a leading proponent of data integration and offers its software solution via its WebSphere brand, even though many components are not J2EE based. The key components of its integration software suite include WebSphere MQ, providing core message-oriented middleware; WebSphere MQ Integration Broker, a high-performance, rule-based message broker; and associated application adapters. IBM also offers WebSphere InterChange Server, a process-oriented integration server and associated adapters: WebSphere MQ Workflow, a process engine for long-running flows, including human interaction; and WebSphere Business Integration Modeler and Monitor, components for process modeling and activity monitoring. Homeland security organizations can also obtain the WebSphere Business Integration Server, a packaged suite combining all these software components: WebSphere MQ Workflow, WebSphere InterChange Server, WebSphere Business Integration Adapters, WebSphere MQ Integrator Broker, and WebSphere Business Integration Modeler. The WebSphere Business Integration Server achieves end-to-end process integration by using multiple process engines, each with its own implementation-modeling tool, all linked by adapters.

IBM also offers an Enterprise Edition of WebSphere Application Server itself, which in addition to standard J2EE services includes a transactional process engine for both long- and short-running flows; a feature called container-managed messaging that separates business logic from messaging logic; and special business rule beans that integrate business rules with J2EE applications. IBM WebSphere MQ is messaging middleware that facilitates application communication across heterogeneous networks, a key feature for homeland security systems. WebSphere MQ runs on more than 35 different platforms, including J2EE, where it serves as a Java Messaging System (JMS) provider. The MQ middleware includes a Queue Manager application that ensures messages are either delegated to their proper queues or routed to another queue manager. The Queue Manager supports persistent and non-persistent messages and can recover persistent messages in the event of a system crash. To guard against the loss of important information, the Queue Manager does not remove sent messages from the queue until they have been received by the correct destination application. This security feature can enhance the use of this software component for integrating 24/7 homeland security systems.

WebSphere MQ Integration Broker (WMQI) is a message broker that runs on Windows, UNIX, and Linux, in addition to IBM OS/390, OS/400, and z/OS. WMQI routes received MQ messages through a series of processing nodes on the WMQI server, which uses rules to filter, route, and format messages as well as generate and send new outgoing messages. WMQI is offered in three versions: WMQI

Event Broker is a basic message broker, bundled with WebSphere Business Integration; WMQI Integration Broker adds message transformation, routing, and InterChange Server integration; and the full WMQI product adds business rules and formatting. WebSphere InterChange Server is the core integration server, executing transactional business processes called *collaborations*. Collaborations are typically short running but include conditional branching, error handling, and transaction recovery.

WebSphere Application Server (WAS) V5 Enterprise Edition turns IBM's J2EE application server into a build-to-integrate platform for processes based on Java components and Web services. WAS V5 supports several integration innovations: a flow container-managed messaging and business rule beans. The flow contains business processes composed using WebSphere Studio Application Developer Integration Edition, which can generate XML. IBM has added support for TCP/IP, Java, EJB, HTTP, and Web services. In all, IBM offers a wide array of options, methods, and configurations for data integration of diverse heterogeneous data sources and applications. IBM is a big supporter of open systems and industry standards, which are critical components for homeland security organizations.

Integrator: Informatica

The Informatica Data Integration Platform uses active metadata to speed the data integration processes. Metadata means data about data. Its Active Metadata uses a repository server in combination with a metadata repository to optimize data use, maintain lineage, and ensure end-to-end data integrity. This active environment extends to incorporate other metadata sources and retains the memory of the data and its use to deliver notification of environment changes and up-to-date documentation. The platform separates the runtime environment from the designer, thus the integration engine can determine how to execute processes without generating system-specific fixed code or requiring hand coding. The design can capture transactional data from an organization's application integration message queues as well as deliver information from a data warehouse or other applications and systems. A key feature of the Informatica Data Integration Platform is broad interoperability through an open and extensible metadata-centric framework for seamless interaction with native connectivity to disparate systems; this design optimizes integration flexibility.

The Informatica Data Integration Platform uses an object-oriented development environment. From project design, operation, and evolution, the platform promotes reusability. This differs from code-based or code-generating solutions that rely heavily on developer expertise, which take more time to develop and are error-prone and hard to modify and reuse. This object-oriented approach is fundamentally codeless, separating the logical design of data integration from the physical operational environment-allowing designers to focus on the "what" and not the "how." For a homeland security organization, it would allow non-IT personnel to provide guidance for integrating systems and applications at a very high level. Its SuperGlue system integrates metadata from disparate systems and offers visualization and analysis capabilities for enhanced understanding of a homeland security organization's IT environment. SuperGlue also provides analysis and reporting capabilities via a Web-based dashboard for monitoring and analyzing data quality, content, use, and performance in a network-centric architecture.

The Benefits: Speed and Accuracy

There are many obstacles and technical concerns that make data integration difficult, but the benefits by far outweigh these obstacles. The benefits of homeland security integration are the ability to access information quickly and accurately and the ability to connect independent database silos and integrate data, experts, analyses, processes, and applications across multiple agencies at the federal, state, and local levels. If data integration is to succeed, it must be through mutually agreed multiple-agency requirements. A robust data integration architecture should allow agencies to participate in whatever manner they are capable given their resources, instead of mandating forced compliance. This "opt-in" data integration design is vital to implementing a trustworthy privacy and data ownership policy. By integrating their data or applications, agencies should not be affected negatively in their operations or in their existing information resources, databases, or networks. This type of data integration solution should ensure that agencies are able to share their internal data in a secure manner relatively easily without negatively affecting their missions.

Sharing information between agency IT systems and among public jurisdictions historically has presented a tough challenge for the government. The situation persists for a number of reasons. Different government databases often represent the same data in different ways. Where one system stores a person's first and last names in separate data fields, another may store both names in a single field. Similarly, databases may use different codes to represent the same information. Agencies also must ensure the security of exchanged messages and data, a requirement that typically dictates the use of some form of encryption, which also involves connectivity issues such as deciding which network and communications protocol to use. These obstacles can be solved via the use of technologies and solution providers featured in this chapter.

Integrator: Information Builders (iWay)

iWay is a leading provider of adapters to the industry. Its XML Transformation Engine (iXTE) product supports and serves as a universal translator for integrating XML with over 140 different applications, all major relational databases, transactions systems such as IBM CICS, IMS/TM, BEA Tuxedo, Bull, packaged applications (SAP, PeopleSoft, Siebel), and all major file formats. Using a drag-and-drop user interface called the XML Transformation Workbench, non-technical personnel can create transformation templates for linking application servers, integration brokers, and custom applications. iWay requires no programming knowledge and honors existing encryption and security while allowing user-defined extensions. The Transformation Engine uses programmable agents, queuing, scheduling, and recovery.

iWay Software supports the full spectrum of bulk data and direct data integration to application integration and broker-based solutions. The software is based on open, flexible standards, offering over 250 codeless adapters, one of the largest in the industry. The XML Transformation Engine provides a visual environment to transform and map disparate information systems with each other. The XML Transformation Engine uses iWay Intelligent Adapters to connect to over 200 e-business formats, packaged applications, legacy systems, and data. Using just XML and SQL, developers can connect public processes that use EDI, HTML pages, XML, and other documents to private processes using iWay Intelligent Adapters that communicate with almost any information system. The XML Transformation Engine is a 100 percent Java-based transformation and integration engine that accepts documents from MQSeries, TCP/IP, HTTP, SOAP, e-mail, and file systems. The engine applies a series of transformation steps that can read from or update back-office systems through iWay Intelligent Adapters.

The iWay Adapter Classes include the following:

- e-Business adapters for transforming e-business exchange formats such as EDI, SWIFT, FIX, HIPPA, HL7, and dialect-specific XML documents into formats compatible with XML and non-XML-based resources.
- Transaction systems adapters support automatic transaction invocation, message transformation, and error recovery for transaction systems such as IMS/TM and CICS.
- Application systems adapters provide object-level support for packaged application systems such as SAP, Siebel, PeopleSoft, Ariba, Oracle, and Lawson.
- Data adapters support proprietary databases and filesystems such as VSAM, Adabas, IMS, IDMS, MUMPS, and Model 204.

- Emulation adapters use screen-scraping technology to integrate 3270 and 5250 applications through terminal emulation.
- Technology adapters support application frameworks, message queues, networking protocols, and so on.

iWay's Universal Adapter Framework is open and works with .NET, J2EE, Web services, or a combination of all three application frameworks. iWay's Universal Adapter Framework can be reached using the following application programming interfaces (APIs):

- J2EE™ application servers that support the JCA standard
- Data-level APIs such as JDBC, ODBC, OLE DB, and ADO
- Integration brokers and message queuing systems
- BizTalk Server and the .NET framework
- SOAP-based Web services

iWay also provides native support for these platforms and environments:

- BEA WebLogic
- SOAP-Based Web Services
- IBM WebSphere Application Server
- Microsoft BizTalk Server
- IBM WebSphere MQ, MQI
- Visual Studio.NET
- XML Transformation Engine
- Oracle 9iAS
- SUN ONE
- SoftwareAG EntireX
- Fujitsu Interstage
- SAP eXchange Infrastructure (XI)
- JMS
- PeopleSoft Application Integration Broker
- TIBCO
- SonicMQ/XQ
- Q-Link BPM

Information Builders (iWay) and Homeland Security

iWay Software and Information Builders have also recently packaged the technologies that make up their core competencies, such as integration and business intelligence, into five integrated government suites. These suites are targeted toward helping federal, state, and local agencies implement solutions that are driven by today's homeland security initiatives.

Each package consists of two major components: an Integration Component (iWay) and an Information Delivery Component (WebFOCUS). The Information Delivery Component is a limited-use license of the WebFOCUS Pro Server. The integrated government suites consist of one generic bundle, the Information Exchange Suite, and five related bundles that coincide with ongoing budgeted homeland security initiatives.

iWay Integrated Justice Suite: This is targeted toward projects that will help automate the criminal justice supply chain.

iWay Critical Infrastructure Protection Suite: This suite is targeted toward projects that involve critical infrastructure protection, such as utilities, water supply, bridges, and tunnels.

iWay Bioterrorism Response Suite: This is targeted for use with the data gathering and syndromic surveillance projects associated with bioterrorism initiatives.

iWay Health Alert Network Suite: Targeted for use with first responder and health alert network projects.

iWay Transportation, Port, and Border Security Suite: This is targeted toward projects that will secure ports and borders.

iWay Information Exchange Suite: This is a general-purpose Business Activity Monitoring (BAM) solution that can be used when a solution requires both iWay and WebFOCUS. This is one of the most flexible and powerful integrators in the industry.

The Middleware: The Intermediary Layer

Integration requires application connectivity across heterogeneous platforms, databases, and networks. This may also require a central interchange through which a host of applications can communicate with each other. Message brokers respond to incoming requests and application events with a series of preprogrammed actions, some of which are driven by models created by analysts, while others may be the result of categorization or data mining analyses.

Middleware has served the function of integrating existing applications; this is the layer of software that sits between applications, such as networks and databases. The function of this middleware is to act as an intermediary that handles all the tasks required to enable applications to communicate with each other, eliminating the need to modify the networks or databases. There are several layers of middleware operations, the first of which is connectivity and data integration, a key requirement for homeland security applications. This functional layer sets the foundation infrastructure for moving data and invoking procedures or methods distributed across heterogeneous systems between agency networks and the Internet.

The connectivity and data integration layer of middleware deals with the core communications issues of data translation and transformation. Translation involves the conversion of data from the existing application to a common representation used for integration. Transformation deals with the mapping of the data elements translated between the formats and data structures used by the applications being integrated, such as from one state agency to a homeland security organization. There is also another middleware layer dealing with a common broker facility through which users or applications can access data or invoke procedures or methods on any integrated application. Several software vendors provide this type of integration solution, but there is a new technology wave developing toward the use of XML to provide a context in which applications can send and receive messages and documents that describe their content machine-to-machine. It is through Web services that these standardized mechanisms can communicate with other applications, initiate discussions, and exchange XML-defined data. These are the technologies that will speed up the integration process for homeland security organizations.

Integrator: IONA

IONA is a middleware vendor known primarily for its CORBA object request broker (ORB) named Orbix. However, recently IONA has shifted its focus from CORBA orientation to Web services. The Orbix E2A Web Services Integration Platform is aimed at essential organization integration via Web services. The Web service integration technology is included in IONA's Orbix E2A e-business platform. Orbix E2A is comprised of the Orbix E2A Web Services Integration Platform for the Internet standards-based integration of existing applications and processes, whereas the Orbix E2A Application Server Platform is aimed at the creation and deployment of new distributed applications and processes using CORBA, J2EE, and Web services. Each platform contains the deployment tools needed to collaborate and integrate applications at the appropriate level.

Orbix E2A Collaborate Enterprise Integrator is a distributed, Java-based integration platform that includes adapters, transformers, routing nodes called hubs, and a messaging backbone. Its Enterprise Messaging Service is a JMS provider supporting secure, reliable asynchronous messaging for integration flows. The Transformation Service translates, formats, splits, and merges application-specific messages. The Hub Service provides content-based message routing, while the Adapter Service connects the broker to IONA's application and technology adapters. The Web Services invocation adapter links Collaborate Enterprise Integrator with Web services activities. The Collaborate Edition also supports multiple protocols such as RosettaNet, Electronic Business XML (ebXML), and EDI. IONA also offers Orbix E2A XMLBus Edition, a J2EE-based Web services container that can run standalone or on an application server.

Integrator: MetaMatrix

MetaMatrix offers a product, MetaBase, that helps an organization discover and map the disparate data sources in its computer systems and describes the way the organization's users can access that information. Organizations can use MetaBase to create the physical metadata models that describe how the databases, data feeds, flat files, XML documents, and other data sources store information, as well as the virtual metadata models that describe how the organization's users and applications integrate, organize, and use that information.

Users can not only model the existing data sources, they can also capture some of the transformational logic performed when combining and using more than one data source. This separate, virtual layer of information can represent a virtual database that presents the way the organization's users would like to transform, integrate, and view the information. The MetaBase Repository offers a single storage location for metadata information about all the data sources an organization has access to. The organization can safely maintain the information with version control and check-out/check-in model management capabilities. Within this repository, the organization's users can search throughout the multiple and diverse information sources for particular columns, tables, tags, or other information structures based on descriptions, names, and keywords.

An organization can use discrete meta objects to build a complete picture of the organization's data sources. When assembled into a complete description of a data source, the meta objects form a metadata model that contains the full name spacing for each element within the data source. This metadata model offers many easy-to-navigate ways to browse metadata, including Unified Modeling Language diagrams, hierarchical tree views, tables, and searches. A piece of metadata, called a meta object, contains information about a specific information structure. For example, an address book, in a very basic database, would probably include a field or column for the ZIP Code. This column or field in a database would have the following properties:

- It would be named ZIP Code.
- It would be five numeric characters long.
- It would be located in the Street Address Table.
- It would represent an identifier used by the United States Postal Service to speed delivery.

This definition represents metadata about the ZIP Code data in the address book database. It abstracts information from the database itself and is useful to describe the content of the organization's enterprise information systems and to determine how a column in one enterprise information source relates to information in another database. MetaMatrix MetaBase supports a number of metamodels out of the box and also enables each organization to extend the metamodels so that it can model its own custom data sources in such a way as to relate to its or other sources. MetaMatrix supports industry standards such as OMG's Meta-Object Facility (MOF™), Common Warehouse Meta-Model (CWM™), XML Metadata Interchange (XMI®), and Uniform Modeling Language (UML™). MetaBase provides an open environment for metadata management.

The MetaMatrix Server works with MetaBase to provide a single integrated virtual database for all the organization's applications. The MetaMatrix Server can use the physical and virtual metadata models as a map to the data stored in the organization's disparate data sources. The applications can place queries based on the virtual metadata models, which can collect and combine result sets from the various physical data sources. The application receives a single result set, defined by whatever transformational logic and functions the data modelers have created.

MetaMatrix Server provides a standardized platform for data integration. Using virtual databases, the MetaMatrix Server provides real-time access to information in its native store without moving data, a definite advantage for homeland security systems because it addresses some security and privacy concerns. Serving as a core infrastructure element, the MetaMatrix Server provides a single access point to an organization's physical information resources. Deployed on J2EE-compliant application servers such as IBM WebSphere or BEA WebLogic, the MetaMatrix system integrates multiple information sources. Homeland security organizations can easily access and integrate diverse databases and information systems.

First, an organization develops metadata models with MetaBase to describe these systems. These metadata models then act as virtual databases that allow users and applications to query for real-time results from the modeled systems.

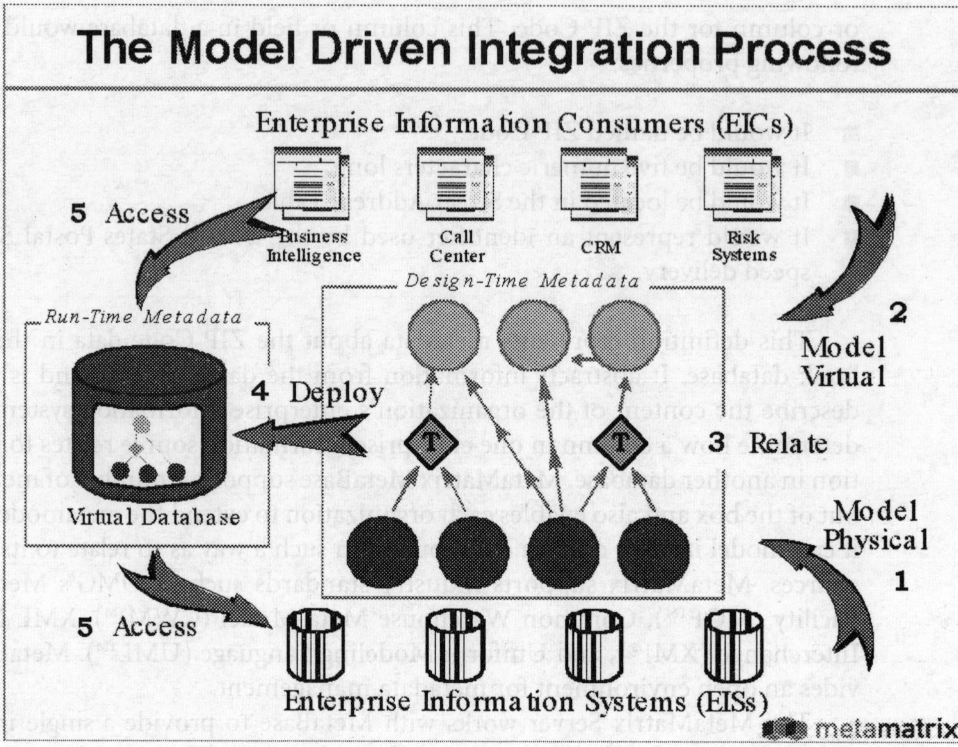

FIGURE 3.1 MetaMatrix's virtual modeling data integration architecture. © 2004. Reprinted with permission from MetaMatrix, Inc.

The Architecture: The XML Glue

Homeland security integration design will likely be dependent on networked communications, enhanced security, and real-time selection of process participants. It will depend on reliable, secure, and transactional messaging over HTTP integration framework using public-process models based on a government-agreed XML document and data exchange standard vocabularies, multi-agency profiles, and cross-agency agreements. XML allows applications to send and receive messages and documents that describe the nature of their content in machine-readable format. XML is a broad specification for creating descriptions of data for the purpose of exchanging information between applications. A set of XML-based protocols defines the processing parameters for XML documents and creates vocabularies that enable the exchange of data by industries and the government, including homeland security organizations.

The integration middleware will use messaging over HTTP or Simple Mail Transfer Protocol (SMTP) as specified by standards such as ebXML or the federal government's own developed framework. Homeland security integration will require the use of standards-based middleware and/or Web services whose underlying protocols have become part of the J2EE development environment. Integration typically is based on messaging middleware over HTTP or SMTP as specified by such standards as ebXML. Connectors provide application connectivity, event detection, and translation of application objects and methods into a common integration framework.

Laying down this type of framework will allow agencies and their users to integrate data, applications, and analyses via shared dashboards, common interfaces, and Web services. This will not only allow the integration of disparate databases and applications, but it will also hide the complexity of each by providing a generic interface, reducing the training of homeland security personnel.

Web services are made up of a set of standards that allow programs to invoke a predetermined set of processes across Internet Protocol (IP) networks through the exchange of XML self-describing messages riding on top of HTTP. Unlike humans who receive a Web page via the Internet, the recipients of Web service messages are machine applications or programs. The ubiquity of the Internet, intranets, extranets, and wireless networks gives Web services the ability to reach almost any device or user anytime and anywhere. Web services are always invoked by an XML message; their most intriguing capability, especially in the area of homeland security, is that they allow programs, rather than humans, to exchange information and actions. For example, Web services can be created to aggregate, integrate, and disseminate data to human analysts in an organized manner at predetermined times for just-in-time analyses. Web services can also feed pre-processed data to devices for machine-learning data mining analyses that can discover important trends or patterns for human attention and pre-emptive action.

Microsoft has proposed a Government Interoperability Framework (e-GIF) using a Web services concept and open Internet standards such as XML and SOAP to meet the interoperability demands of public jurisdictions. The framework builds a solid IT infrastructure, institutes reliable security processes, and promotes collaboration and data sharing. The framework's XML-based Web services architecture allows programs to communicate in a standards-based way, even if they are written in different programming languages and are operating on different computing platforms. The XML standard focuses on content and business context instead of how the content is displayed or printed, enabling systems to exchange and interpret documents without human intervention. In addition, recently developed XML schemas reconcile the disparate tag structures, content, and data types that are commonly encountered when agencies attempt to link together multiple information systems.

The proposed framework also includes security services designed to ensure that only authorized users gain access to sensitive data. These security services use a modular design and isolate agency applications from underlying user-identity technologies. Therefore, participating homeland security agencies can easily adopt new identification technologies without altering their applications. Homeland security agencies participating in the framework would control access to their data by granting access to groups of individual users. Additionally, local, state, and federal government agencies can choose the specific data they want to share or not share rather than the "all or none" approach most systems use today. This allows them to maintain full control over their data, which law may restrict them from disclosing, even when shared with other outside agencies.

This type of Web service design ensures data ownership and privacy, disclosing only predetermined sections of records or documents. For example, a person's Social Security number may not be accessed by an outside agency, but an individual's address could be shared. A DMV record from California may be shared with a homeland security organization outside the state but without moving the data itself, which is prohibited by statute. The flexibility is to allow data integration without sacrificing an agency's responsibility for nondisclosure and an individual's right to privacy and civil liberties.

This type of open framework includes request manager servers that manage the flow of information among participating agencies and document interchange capabilities that give users additional flexibility for publishing information and notifying information recipients. Homeland security organizations also may add data-mining capabilities, analytical applications, and other business intelligence tools designed to create knowledge from raw information. By creating and using standards-based middleware such as J2EE specification, which encompasses messaging, and adapters, this type of framework makes it possible to switch applications or integration servers.

Integration of applications and databases by multiple homeland security agencies means they can be accessed remotely in spite of different platform architectures. There are different methods by which this communication, access, and integration can take place. For example, there are different methods of communications, principally

1. Remote procedure call (RPC)
2. Messaging-oriented middleware (MOM)
3. Transaction processing (TP)

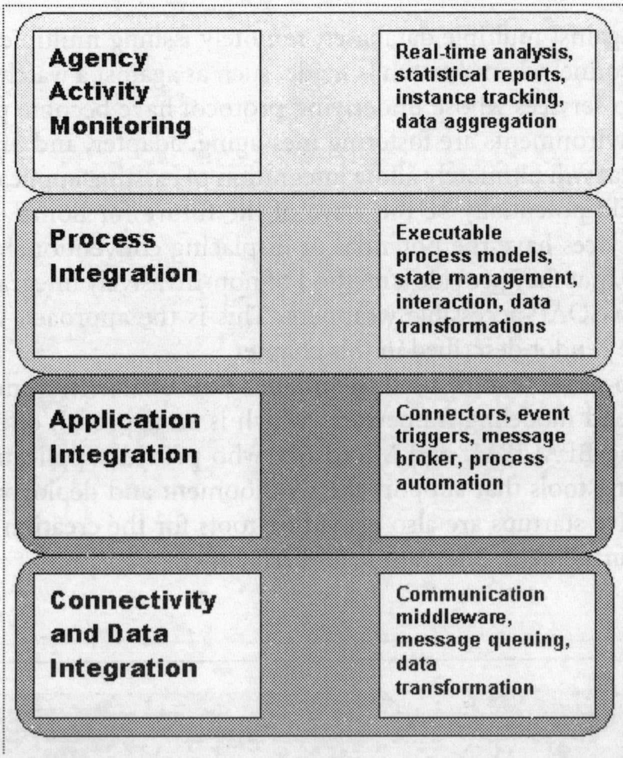

FIGURE 3.2 Homeland security integration functional map.

Specifically, RPC allows an application to call a function or object method on a remote application system as if it were local. MOM allows applications to communicate using messages via a store-and-forward design. This eliminates the need for participating applications to be immediately available, enabling them to work via different networks and alternate messaging gateways. Lastly, TP provides transactional integrity when applications update multiple databases. When these databases are distributed over networks, a common scenario for homeland security applications, TP monitors and coordinates so that updates take place on all systems.

Web services provide a standardized mechanism through which applications can discover other data and applications; they can initiate independent intelligent remote procedures and exchange XML-defined information for homeland security purposes. This is an especially compelling technology for homeland security applications, as it enables the ability to create systems that can monitor events, such as border crossings data entries or airline registrations, and independently validate a match against multiple databases, remotely issuing multiple alerts to devices and key personnel when a match is made, such as against a watch list.

Web services whose underlying protocol have become part of J2EE development environments are fostering messaging, adapter, and process modeling standards that will ultimately allow integration of existing applications without coding and could potentially be the wave of the future for homeland security agencies. Web services have the potential of displacing conventional integration architectures, in that they provide a method of non-invasively integrating existing applications via SOAP-accessible wrappers. This is the approach with WebMethods, a software vendor described in this chapter.

Web servers can be used to initiate a flow of activities and sub-processes in an end-to-end modeling framework, which is an approach offered by several firms, including BEA, IBM, and Microsoft, who provide application servers and programming tools that support the development and deployment of Web services. Innovative startups are also providing tools for the creation of Web services and their management, integration, and reliability.

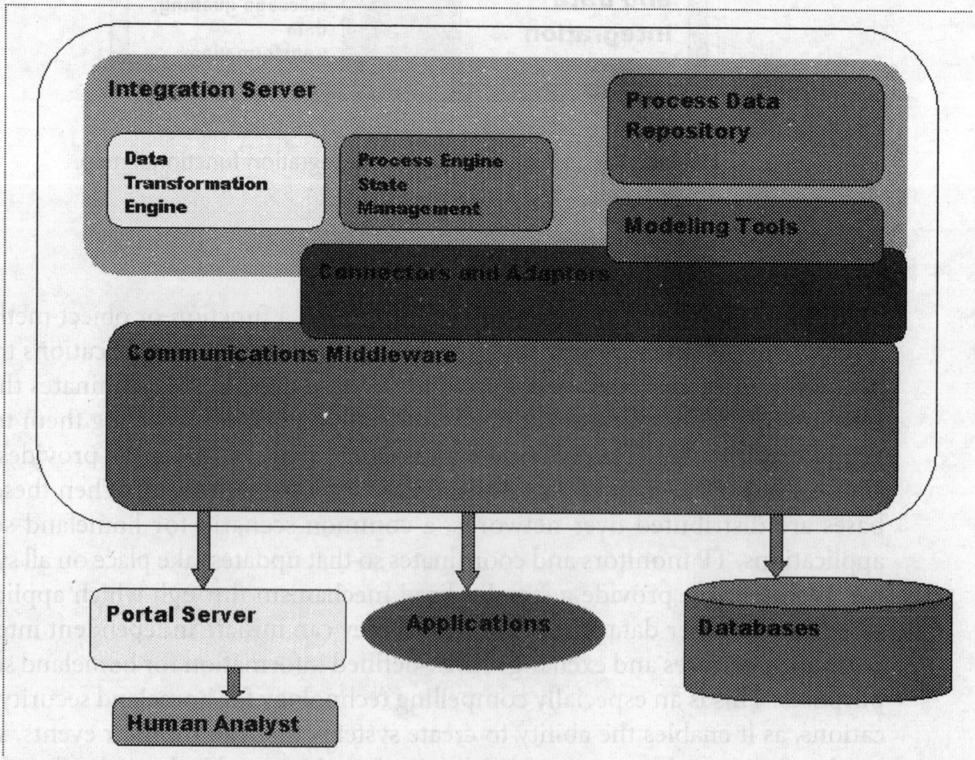

FIGURE 3.3 Homeland security integration architecture.

Integrator: Microsoft

Microsoft's primary business integration components are Windows core services, Host Integration Server, and the BizTalk framework. Windows' core services for integration include Microsoft XML Services (MSXML), Microsoft Data Access Components (MDAC) connectivity services, and Component Object Model (COM+) application services. MSXML is a core service of Windows 2000 and successor operating systems that allows Windows components to create, send, receive, and understand XML messages. Microsoft provides tools for delivering XML Web services through the .NET Framework and Visual Studio .NET.

Windows MDAC services include ActiveX Data Objects (ADO), a high-level programming interface supporting creation of front-end database clients and middle-tier business objects in both client/server and Web-centric architectures. Windows COM+ services provide transaction and security boundaries around business logic components that can be used to manipulate data as it flows through an organization's data resources. COM+ includes Microsoft Transaction Server (MTS), a transactional application server, and supports Microsoft Distributed Transaction Coordinator. Microsoft Host Integration Server is a set of transactional gateways, services, and adapters that facilitates integration between the Windows platform and host environments. BizTalk is Microsoft's XML-based business integration framework. BizTalk Server includes a core messaging engine, a process engine, and a set of design tools.

Integrator: SeeBeyond

SeeBeyond offers a complete integration platform, including long-running process management, workflow, business-to-business integration, and Web services. SeeBeyond's process-oriented Business Integration Suite includes the eGate Integrator, eInsight Business Process Manager, eIndex Global Identifier, eXchange Partner Manager, and eXpressway Integrator partner on-ramps. eGate Integrator is a distributed integration platform that can separate tasks into small, lightweight processes and run them on as many servers as needed, balancing the traffic and transaction load over the servers to maintain acceptable response times. eGate Integrator is composed of Intelligent Queues, Business Object Brokers, and eWays. eWays brokers events between applications and Intelligent Queues, with each one reading incoming data streams to which it has subscribed, routing the data to its intended destination, and executing the business logic associated with a particular action. eWay Adapters includes a large set of prebuilt application and technology adapters. The eWay Extension Kit allows developers to build custom adapters. eGate Integrator offers packaged processes called Intelligent Bridges that simplify deployment of common integration flows.

SeeBeyond also has an XML converter for use with eGate for graphical translation of application data to and from XML. eIndex Global Identifier provides an integrated view of customer information, linking and cross-referencing data from disparate application systems and databases. The eXchange Partner Manager is built on the eGate Integrator foundation and is used for business-to-business integration. The eXpressway Integrator is a rapid-implementation framework for trading partners to register their profiles and configure external connectivity using partner on-ramps. It could easily be configured to link government agencies for homeland security applications and processes.

INTEGRATOR: SRD

A unique content integration solution comes from Systems Research & Development (SRD), a Las Vegas firm that has developed a search and match technology for discovering entity resolution via its Non-Obvious Relationship Awareness (NORA™) software. The software performs cross-reference matching of databases to identify potentially alarming non-obvious relationships between entities. For example, companies have been using the software to generate NORA Intelligence Reports™ representing alerts focusing investigations and audit resources on areas of possible concern, such as a casino job application containing a phone number associated with an organized crime member. SRD defines real-time entity resolution to be a data quality problem, which it solves by identifying the most accurate data available. According to SRD, organizations often have multiple records in their systems, many with slight variations in name, address, phone number, or other differentiating items, even though these various records in fact pertain to the same person or organization. Entity resolution determines whether multiple records that appear to describe different people or organizations are actually records for a single person or organization. Once it is determined that two or more people or organizations are actually the same, the entity resolution software provides a comprehensive, unified view of all available information about that person or organization.

The software standardizes names and addresses on individuals so that information on residence, banking, phone number, and affiliations can be identified, enabling those records to be cross-referenced for potential terrorist activity or relationships. NORA uses "fuzzy logic" algorithms to perform link analysis and uncover associations that are normally difficult for humans to detect. While link analysis has and is being used by law enforcement to discover relationships via visual maps, the technology is limited, and once records or observations such as bank accounts or cell numbers get large, link analysis breaks down. NORA's link analysis, however, works on discovering

(continued)

hidden relationships in digital data using brute computing power and fuzzy (continuous) logic algorithms.

Not confined to a single language, NORA operates across a variety of platforms. The data structure lends itself to acquiring and analyzing information from an unlimited number of sources. NORA technology can quickly search through vast sources of data to identify relationships both human and digital, such as visa addresses and credit card numbers. The basic concept behind NORA was created in the early 1980s to detect credit fraud. NORA searches for similarities across people and company records by evaluating names, addresses, phone numbers, credit card numbers, and so on. NORA uses special processes to detect inappropriate relationships that may be ignored or missed by existing technology and loss prevention methods.

Obviously the digital technology can now be applied to the area of homeland security, so that, for example, NORA can be used for matching watch lists such as the FBI's Most Wanted Terrorist list of individuals who are wanted in connection with terrorist acts committed against the U.S. NORA technology was designed to concentrate on people and relationships and to identify suspected relationships that would otherwise go unnoticed. NORA's analytical capabilities could prove useful to government intelligence agencies trying to ferret out terrorist cells entrenched in communities. NORA creates a data warehouse for storing information where users can quickly add new information and cross-check it with other entries. So, for example, the Terrorist Threat Integration Center (TTIC) could cross-check lists of Al-Qaeda and Taliban prisoners at the Guantanamo Bay naval base or trace relationships among suspected terrorists being held in the United States. Likewise, the FBI could quickly check airline passenger lists to determine whether a suspect at an El Paso airport is the nephew of a known Egyptian terrorist, once shared an address with another terrorist suspect in Germany, or uses the same credit card or bank account number as a suspect in New Jersey. NORA analyzes data in near real time, returning query results in seconds. Similar technology is available from other companies and will be covered in the last chapter of the book: Infoglide and COPLINK™.

Integrator: TIBCO

TIBCO introduced the concept of The Information Bus (TIB), a distributed publish-subscribe integration platform that enables organizations to transmit, receive, filter, and personalize digital information in real time automatically. TIBCO is primarily used for real-time information delivery in financial services. TIB also facilitates real-time, two-way communication between distributed computer networks and mobile information devices such as handheld computers, pagers, and digital cellular telephones, making it an ideal provider for homeland security organizations, such as first responders, fire, and police.

TIBCO provides integration software through two product lines: ActiveEnterprise for application integration inside the firewall and ActiveExchange for organization-to-organization integration. ActiveEnterprise is a family of over a dozen software components based on a variety of technical architectures, many with overlapping functionality. ActiveEnterprise components can be grouped in the categories of messaging middleware, adapters, integration servers, system management tools, and business activity monitoring. TIBCO Rendezvous, the core middleware for ActiveEnterprise, is a distributed platform for both publish-subscribe and request-reply messaging with real-time information delivery.

TIBCO IntegrationManager is a process-oriented integration server, including a transactional process engine and modeling tool supporting both short- and long-running processes. TIBCO BPM is another process-oriented integration server combining workflow, application integration, and Web services. It uses a distributed server architecture that uses TIBCO Rendezvous for client/server communications. A graphical user interface allows users to design and model processes without coding. Processes can be saved as XML templates or Web services for reuse. TIBCO BusinessWorks is yet another alternative integration framework, positioned as a rapid design and deployment solution for smaller organizations.

MULTISTATE ANTI-TERRORISM INFORMATION EXCHANGE: AN INTEGRATION CASE STUDY

The Office of Justice Programs, U.S. Department of Justice, initiated funding for a pilot proof-of-concept project titled the Multistate Anti-Terrorism Information Exchange (MATRIX). The MATRIX pilot project was initiated in response to the increased need for timely information sharing and exchange of terrorism-related information among members of the law enforcement community. The MATRIX pilot project is an effort to increase and enhance the exchange of sensitive terrorism and other criminal activity information between local, state, and federal agencies. MATRIX applies and integrates existing and proven technology to provide a new capability to assist law enforcement in identifying and analyzing terrorist and other criminal activity and appropriately disseminating it to law enforcement agencies nationwide in a secure, efficient, and timely manner.

The organizational structure for implementation and operation of the MATRIX pilot project ensures each participant a voice in the project's administration. The MATRIX pilot project has been awarded a $4 million budget by the Office of Justice Programs,

(continued)

Bureau of Justice Assistance, U.S. Department of Justice, for database, hardware, and software integration and network support to a multistate coalition of law enforcement agencies, which currently is comprised of the following states: Connecticut, Florida, Georgia, Michigan, New York, Pennsylvania, Ohio, and Utah.

One of the prime objectives of the project is to use factual data analysis and data integration technology to improve the usefulness of information contained in multiple types of document storage systems. The MATRIX project is implementing factual data analysis from existing data sources to integrate disparate data from many types of Web-enabled storage systems to identify, develop, and analyze terrorist activity and other crimes for investigative leads. This capability will facilitate integration and exchange of information within the participating states, including criminal history, driver license data, vehicle registration records, and incarceration/corrections records including digitized photographs, with significant amounts of public data record entries.

Provision has been made for the inclusion of data sources from additional states, should expansion be authorized. One of the project objectives is to use data analysis from existing data sources to save investigative hours and significantly improve the opportunity for successful conclusion of investigations. Information submitted by a state may be disseminated only in accordance with restrictions and conditions placed on it by the submitting state, pursuant to the submitting state's laws and regulations. Data will be made available only to law enforcement agencies and on a need-to-know and right-to-know basis. Data access permissions will be conditioned on the privileges of the user making the inquiry.

A second major objective is to provide a mechanism for states to become nodes on the Regional Information Sharing Systems (RISS) network, a secure intranet (riss.net) for electronic information exchange among participating agencies. The communications backbone for the MATRIX project is RISS, an existing secure network with a proven track record of transmitting sensitive information among law enforcement agencies. In addition to linking the six regional RISS center resources, this network currently provides connectivity for the High Intensity Drug Trafficking Areas, United States Attorneys' Offices, other federal agencies, and several state law enforcement systems. This network is based on standards that will allow other state and federal systems to interoperate. The riss.net system represents a cost-effective solution and a way to rapidly implement the project. Each of the participating MATRIX state agencies is establishing electronic connection as a node on riss.net. End-user accounts will be enabled for authorized participating state and local law enforcement agency users in each state. This connectivity will allow secure communications with other participating agencies, as well as the RISS centers, and allow secure access to the Web-enabled document storage systems.

The MATRIX system is designed to encourage the exchange of information via secure state Web sites. For networking and information sharing to be effective, data

(continued)

must be made available over the network to authorized users. Utilizing the access controls employed by the RISS system, secure Web sites are being created and deployed for each state to enable information to be disseminated to the appropriate audience. These Web sites provide a familiar vehicle for MATRIX participants to post and review anti-terrorism and alert information. This system will ensure that state and local law enforcement officers—the individuals most likely to come into direct contact with terrorists or other criminals—have the best information (accurate and complete) available to them in a timely manner. It will also provide a mechanism for local officers to share important information they collect on the street with other local, state, and federal authorities. Implementation of this pilot capability represents an important component of an overall prevention strategy, critical to United States homeland security.

Integrator: Vitria

Vitria's BusinessWare platform provides an integrated modeling and execution environment for data workflow, integration, and support of an increasing number of packaged vertical solutions called Vitria Collaborative Applications. In the latest version of BusinessWare, all process elements, including flows, data transformations, queries, and workflow activities, are encapsulated as reusable service-oriented components, which can be nested and chained to construct complex business properties and can be invoked as a Web service, EJB, CORBA object, or Web client.

BusinessWare abstracts the transport layer from the process model using ports, allowing transports to be mixed and matched as needed. Vitria offers a library of packaged application and technology adapters that can be configured using a graphical connection modeler, as well as the Connector SDK for building custom adapters. BusinessWare allows any activity or sub-process to be exposed as a Web service that can be invoked by other BusinessWare components or called externally. Vitria Business Cockpit and Real-Time Analysis components provide business activity monitoring by funneling process events into an analytical engine, configured by a graphical reporting tool. Users can configure their own key performance indicators and reports as well as set real-time alerts. Vitria Collaborative Applications (VCA) are fully tested, documented, and maintained vertical industry solutions layered on application-specific process models, data objects, transformations, and Cockpit reports. Vitria and its system integrator partners have developed VCA solutions for banking risk management, USA PATRIOT Act compliance, financial, and insurance industry applications, with the potential of doing the same vertical development in the area of homeland security.

Homeland Security (HS) Requirements

HS integration will need to build communication middleware to allow applications to access data and invoke procedures and objects within other databases and applications distributed throughout government networks and databases at the federal, state, and local levels. This integration framework will feature several software components, including adapters and connectors to provide an interface for translating between disparate native APIs and events of specific applications and database management systems (DBMS) into a common syntax and format. The framework will also require message brokers to validate, filter, route, and transform incoming messages into outgoing messages based on message content and rules. Lastly, these incoming messages and events will be used to trigger instances of predefined processes or actions based on models or rules developed by HS personnel or data mining analyses.

HS models can be detailed templates for invoking an agency process, and they can be machine processes such as identifying data components and their sequence. They may be human rule-based, triggering the conditional branching, splitting, and joining of data from a series of sequential databases. HS integration models can be developed to activate nested sub-processes and search and append routines. Integration tools increasingly support the ability of these models to be written in a process description language, increasingly XML-based, representing the output of a graphical process modeling tool component. Once loaded on a process engine, the model becomes executable. These types of integration models can be triggered by events, such as an incoming message, a firing rule, or an API call, creating a flow of activities as prescribed by the model. Models may also be data mining based, constructed via machine learning rules, so that agents can be invoked to issue alerts or retrieve nested data retrieval routines.

HS integration will require the capability to collect and monitor data in real time 24/7 from disparate systems, networks, and databases and aggregate it for event reporting or modeling. Integration middleware must be able to provide a common architecture for controlling activities across distributed heterogeneous agency systems, and they also must be able to transform their content for calculation and analysis. Analytical views typically involve real-time monitoring and instance tracking, using events generated by processes. These views may trigger the need for drill down or create an event, and issue an alert. In some instances monitored events may trigger alerts requiring notification to HS personnel or the routing of data components to processing or visualization systems or data mining models for scoring or for further analysis and correlation. In time the sophistication of HS integration monitoring models will evolve to new levels of real-time data collection and analysis.

Integrator: WebMethods

WebMethods introduced the technology of Web-based business-to-business integration. Its current WebMethods Enterprise is an event-driven, hub-based message broker using their Sockets core publish-subscribe messaging middleware. Adapters provide the connection between an application and the WebMethods Enterprise integration system. More than 50 of these adapters are available for various databases, middleware systems, and packaged applications. The broker manages event queuing, delivery, filtering, and security; to achieve scalability, additional brokers can be added to the system.

WebMethods Enterprise is extensible through components called agents, standalone programs that can respond to numerous event types. WebMethods offers packaged, customizable agents to provide a framework for handling integration logic, executing business rules, and facilitating complex data transformations. For example, a data transformation agent can be used to translate between old EDI formats and current XML. Software agents are used for creating a unified view of heterogeneous applications, such as when two organizations have different data reporting systems with a need to integrate, a very likely scenario for a homeland security organization.

WebMethods Business Integration provides a graphical modeling and monitoring tool for long-running business processes. WebMethods Manager is a system and network management framework based on the Open Management Interface (OMI) standard. WebMethods Integration Server relies on synchronous (request-reply) point-to-point communication of XML documents over Web transports such as HTTP. WebMethods represents a new services-oriented platform based mainly on the Integration Server and Flow architecture. It uses Enterprise Broker as a central hub to which multiple integration servers are connected. While enterprise adapters are still supported for backward compatibility, the new development environment focuses on connection through integration server adapters. WebMethods provides a secure, reliable, transactional process framework for Web services.

THE FUTURE: FROM 22 TO 1 IN 2002

Integration is one of the highest priorities for homeland security and anti-terrorist deterrence. The integration of both existing systems and new application projects is a major driver of today's federal and state government agencies. Achieving a fully integrated homeland security infrastructure is a significant challenge for IT organizations. In private industry, standardized examples exist for assisting government.

RosettaNet is a supply chain initiative that has standardized dozens of Partner Interface Processes (PIPs) for the electronic components industry, such as PIP3A4 for purchase order processing, in which an XML PO is sent and returned via a Accepted, Rejection, or Pending status. Similarly, homeland security organizations can begin to develop preset and pre-agreed protocol frameworks for coordinating, communicating, and integrating their communications, data, analyses, and expertise.

As we have seen, the emerging technology of Web services can transform and simplify the way organizations integrate applications, information, analyses, and communication processes. Web services represent a new way to link systems together and automate agency and departmental processes, eliminating much of the complexity and expense associated with traditional organization integration technologies. More importantly, Web services will be a catalyst for service-oriented architectures, enabling real-time analysis by accelerating the flow of information and decisions across homeland security organizations.

The Homeland Security Act of 2002 brought 22 agencies into the new Department of Homeland Security with the hope that the consolidation will enable more effective coordination. This can occur only through more effective data integration, the lifeblood of both human and machine mining analyses. The Act requires that the agencies continue pursuing related but diverse goals to oversee and ensure the safety of our country's infrastructures and citizens. It assigns primary responsibility for investigating and detecting terrorist acts to federal, state, and local agencies, many of which have never integrated their data systems. The war on terror will require an intergovernmental effort to coordinate and integrate intelligence as the agencies monitor millions of communication, transportation, trade, and financial transactions.

Data aggregation and integration are the foundations to enable data mining algorithms to assist analysts in their monitoring for potential patterns of attacks. Data mining algorithms overcome human abilities to objectively find the digital needles in the moving haystacks. The algorithms offer immense number crunching speed capacity and infallibility. In the near future, data aggregation, integration, and analysis will be the key processes for meeting the missions of homeland security organizations and solving the problems of identifying and assessing threats.

For years private industry has been constructing predictive models of consumer behavior, fraud detection, and financial risk. Homeland security organizations must also develop capabilities for detecting anomalous activities. Both sectors face similar challenges in integrating personal and demographic information from disparate database sources. The challenge for homeland security organizations, however, is that new algorithms and techniques for data mining must be developed, because quantifying the risk of terrorist attacks is anecdotal, and there is little or no data for constructing models for predicting potential threats.

4 Collaboration: The Technologies for Communicating Content, Expertise, and Analyses in Real Time

In This Chapter

- Collaboration Components: Presence, Messaging, Discussion, Meeting, Sharing, and Virtual
- Collective Knowledge: Locating, Extracting, Organizing, and Routing Tacit Knowledge
- Threat Matrix Collaboration: Multi-Agency and Multimedia

One of the urgent requirements of homeland security organizations is the capability to quickly communicate and collaborate on content, expertise, and analyses. There is a multitude of network-centric collaboration software systems from the business world that can be applied to the needs of homeland security personnel in communicating and working more effectively in pursuit of their missions. Collaboration focuses on locating, capturing, extracting, organizing, classifying, and routing tacit knowledge, often from unstructured content found in internal documents, reports, e-mail, chat, and instant messages. This collaborated intelligence can be sent to users based on predefined profiles or specified requests. Collaboration software applications facilitate human and devices interaction, and they enable for the creation of virtual workspaces and virtual meeting rooms. These virtual work planning, analysis, investigative, and response environments eliminate the physical constrains of time and location.

Collaboration tools eliminate the need to have group meetings, conference calls, or in-person contacts; homeland security personnel can instead use the ubiquitous Web and other networks to collaborate either at times that are convenient for them or in real time via various devices: wireless, PDA, laptops, and so on. Almost all collaborative software products support standard communication facilities such as chat and text/audio/video conferencing in addition to document and application sharing, whiteboard, browsing, annotation of documents, tracking workflow, and calendar sharing. Collaborative systems exist with the explicit purpose of identifying experts within a large organization; these systems are designed to create *expertise profiles* and disseminate them across internal networks. These systems enable less-experienced personnel to identify individuals they can ask for assistance and team with for future collaboration. For a homeland security organization, this could span the range from emergency response teams to terrorist intelligence specialists; in either case there are always experts in specific areas.

Co-workers can view and edit documents stored in a common area, a shared workspace. Documents and reports can be updated as edits are made by team members. Document sharing goes further than uploading and storing documents on a common server; most collaborative systems offer more sophisticated management of files, including group members' access privileges, control of user access to those documents, versioning, and annotating. Users can access the collaborative system through a browser via a password, where the changes or updates to documents are recorded via a tracking control system. These collaborative features are especially compelling for a homeland security organization, in which users need to share information within their agency and across multiple external departments at varying levels of clearance, including intelligence, defense, and civil personnel.

Application sharing involves not the document directly but the application, which is used to create or modify the document. For example, sharing a word processor between two people enables them to access both the menus and the functions of the same program to create a single document. This may require each participant to have the application with which the document was produced, such as a word processor or spreadsheet application, or it may be literally sharing one person's application. In this case, only the originator needs to be running the application, and the collaborator merely sees an image of that application sent across the network but can interact with it as if it were on his desktop. A whiteboard facility enables a group of collaborators to collectively create a document such as a watch list, a plan of action, a map of a section of a city, or a diagram of a building. Locally, the whiteboard program looks like a simple drawing package, but in a live session, changes made to it by any participant appear on every participant's machine.

It may be used to support brainstorming, annotation of a diagram, editing and modifying a draft document, and so on, and this can enable a team of analysts, for example from various agencies specializing in different aspects of homeland security such as border safety, transportation, intelligence, defense, and so on, to coordinate a plan of action from their own desktops or laptops.

Although e-mail is the most widely used collaboration medium, instant messaging is gaining ground. The capability to find other members of a team in an instant message network is becoming a basic requirement for current collaboration systems. Some of the Web-based instant messaging services from AOL, Microsoft, and Yahoo! have been upgraded for organizational use with improved identity management, archiving, administration, maintenance, and security features for use by large organizations. Even mobile users can now be alerted and connected and exchange instant messages using *presence* features with file sharing, combined calendaring, and other collaborative functions linking them to other groupware applications. For homeland security personnel such as first responders, medical, emergency, police, and fire, this instant messaging feature may be most applicable because it enables the coordination and communication of vital information with headquarters and other experts on toxics, bombs, buildings, chemicals, and so on.

COLLABORATION COMPONENTS: PRESENCE, MESSAGING, DISCUSSION, MEETING, SHARING, AND VIRTUAL

Collaboration software enables users of geographically dispersed homeland security organizations to share information and expertise via distributed networks. The tools enable knowledge to be networked, briefings, intelligence, and analyses can be shared, joint decisions can be made instantly, documents and presentations can be authored by teams of analysts, with their findings being communicated in real time to multiple locations. For example, intelligence gathered in the Middle East can be viewed and shared by analysts in Asia, Europe, and the United States simultaneously, with analyses collaborated in real time.

The key components of collaborative software systems lie in how and when data is shared. The functions of these collaborative programs include many generic features, as seen in Figure 4.1.

Presence: Instant-messaging features, such as buddy lists that track and find participants or services for availability and possible collaboration.

Messaging: Instant messaging, e-mail, short message service (SMS), as well as store-and-forward messaging features.

FIGURE 4.1 Collaborative system components.

Discussion: Chat, threaded discussion, voice and video conferencing, and Weblogging features. (A Weblog is a personalized journal page in HTML.)

Meeting: Scheduling, calendaring, task tracking, and agenda management features.

Sharing: Shared document creation, work products, audit trails, logs, versions, and archiving features.

Virtual: Real-time application sharing, shared virtual whiteboards, shared browsers, shared use of a desktop application, and help desk support features.

One of the distinguishing abilities of collaborative software is that it enables users to interact with various forms of unstructured communication content such as e-mail, chat, instant messages, files, records, and documents in support of ongoing processes. For homeland security applications this may expand to include field intelligence, news feeds, and other types of strategic real-time communication such as video and audio streams, or it may pertain to the scene of a terrorist attack in which the coordination of various agencies and personnel needs to take place. The key property of collaborative tools is how and when data and experts are shared, because of the nature of our networked world; space and time is irrelevant, enabling knowledge and intelligence to be anyplace a Web browser can be accessed.

Collaboration can be either synchronous, where each participant waits for a response from other participants before continuing, or asynchronous, where a participant goes on to another task without waiting for a response. Real-time collaboration systems support interaction in the same time frame as if the participant were physically present. Real-time application sharing superimposes collaborative capabilities on a desktop or Web-based location, so that more than one user can interact in a shared presentation, whiteboard, master document, intelligence report, news story, mug shot photograph, and so on.

Another dimension of collaborative systems is whether they operate on a persistent or non-persistent manner. In most modern tools, persistent features will be the dominant mode, such as instant messaging communications. Depending on how they are configured, collaborative systems can handle a mixture of public and private data. Private data takes the form of a user's preferences, skills, expertise, profiles, identity, a personal address list, and level of access to security information. Public data includes documents, logs, work products, sessions, directories, archives, news stories, recordings, and Web sites.

Today's collaboration software is designed to interface with other applications. Vendors often provide a set of APIs and Web service interfaces in an effort to provide tight integration with other software components. Collaborative software vendors recognize the importance of being able to communicate with a variety of other software applications. Because of this integration capability, when selecting a collaborative tool it is important that it support key industry standards. These standards encompass such functions as presence, instant messaging, e-mail, chat, discussion tools, meeting support, shared persistence, and application sharing. The following is a more detailed description of these standards, which are critical to a homeland security information technology environment, as seen in Figure 4.2.

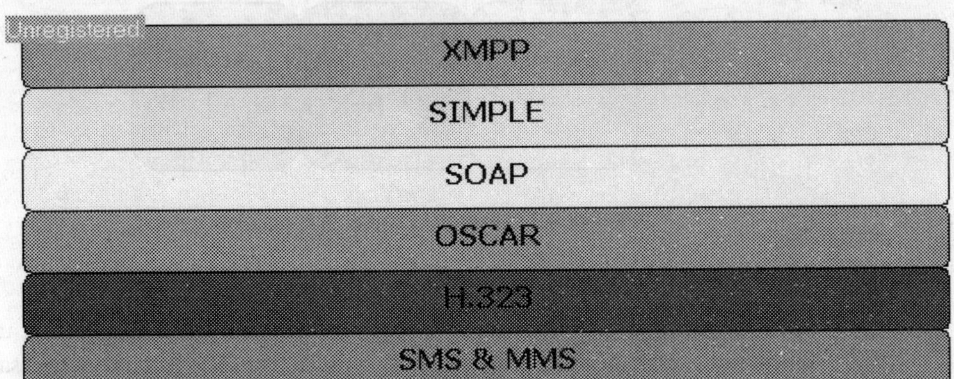

FIGURE 4.2 Instant messaging standards for collaboration.

Instant Messaging Standards: These are current and developing standards for discovery and presence.

XMPP: Extensible Messaging and Presence Protocol is an Internet Engineering Task Force (IETF) proposed protocol for open, XML-based messaging and presence interactions.

SIMPLE: Session Initiation Protocol for Instant Messaging and Presence Leveraging Extensions is an application of Session Initiation Protocol (SIP) to the area of instant messaging.

SOAP: Simplified Objects Access Protocol with features for presence description as part of its access facilities.

OSCAR: This is the AOL proprietary protocol.

H.323: The International Telecommunication Union (ITU) standard applying to audio and video conferencing, handling session issues such as call-signaling and call-control, and framing protocols.

SMS and MMS: These are mobile messaging service standards. The European Telecommunications Standards Institute (ETSI) developed SMS as part of the Global System for Mobile Communications; it is a text-only messaging service. The MMS standard allows graphics, animation, video and sound; the standard was established by the Open Mobile Alliance.

E-mail Standards: Almost all the collaborative tools discussed in this chapter support the following Internet e-mail standards, as seen in Figure 4.3.

FIGURE 4.3 E-mail standards for collaboration.

SMTP: Simple Mail Transfer Protocol defines how the Internet uses mail servers to exchange mail with each other. It defines the format of message headers, including the location of fields such as From, To, Reply-To, and Date.

POP and IMAP: These are the Post Office Protocol and Internet Mail Access Protocol standards, which define how interactions between clients read and create e-mail and how the server deals with and stores the messages. POP downloads e-mail from the server to the client, while IMAP enables the client to access messages stored in the server without deleting them.

MIME: The Multipurpose Internet Mail Extension standard defines how non-text content such as images, audio, video, and HTML can be included in e-mail by allowing multiple parts in a message containing different content.

A Discussion Standard: Network News Transport Protocol (NNTP) defines how treaded discussion schemas are handled.

A Meeting Standard: iCalendar or xCal is the standard for storing schedule or calendar information.

A Shared Persistent Standard: The SyncML standard defines data synchronization.

Application Sharing Standards: The ITU T.120 standard defines how data conferencing deals with the interchange of data. The T.126 standard defines whiteboards, T.127 defines file transfer, and T.128 defines program sharing.

All of these standards, as seen in Figure 4.4, are important in ensuring that team members can collaborate and communicate in multiple modes of media. The standards ensure intelligence and expertise can flow to members of homeland security organizations from multiple levels of government in distributed locations around

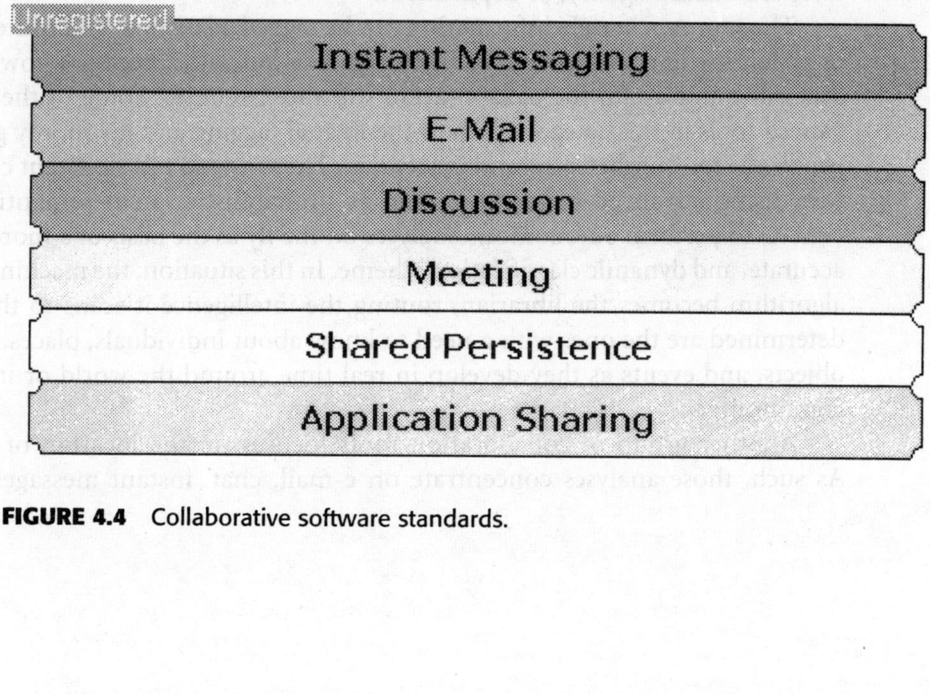

FIGURE 4.4 Collaborative software standards.

the country and the world. Ensuring that collaborative software supports these standards will ensure point-to-point, broadcast, global awareness, and computer supported collaborative work (CSCW) can stream seamlessly.

COLLECTIVE KNOWLEDGE: LOCATING, EXTRACTING, ORGANIZING, AND ROUTING TACIT KNOWLEDGE

Every organization, including those devoted to homeland security, possesses explicit and implicit knowledge in its data and people; collaborative tools are designed to apply this information and expertise. Some of these collaboration tools are very dependent on the technology of text mining, or categorization, which is the topic of the following chapter. In fact, there is some overlapping in the functionality between the software discussed in this chapter with that discussed in the next, because to an extent both deal with knowledge management.

Advances in linguistics analysis have enabled producers of collaboration software components to design automatic tagging functions via XML to extract information and categorize it in a hierarchy of relevant categories. These categories are created using a combination of predefined semantics, syntactic, statistical, and document format rules that users can modify with their own classification schemas. In other words, the taxonomy generation process can be autonomous, semi-manual, or controlled by the user. For example, for a homeland security organization these categories can be set by geographical regions, weapon types, terrorist groupings, biological or chemical classes, or other predefined categories relevant to the tasks and missions of each agency, or department.

The more accurately information can be tagged, classified, and routed to users or systems within a homeland security organization with a need to know, the more accessible and useful the collaboration software becomes. Some of the more advanced tools in this category eschew the formal tagging and taxonomy generation process as too cumbersome and inaccurate. They instead rely on latent clues in the text, using advanced algorithms such as probabilistic latent semantic analysis (PLSA) to perform autonomous analyses on the fly as the basis of a more relevant, accurate, and dynamic classification scheme. In this situation, the machine-learning algorithm becomes the librarian, routing the intelligence it scans to those it has determined are the ones with a need to know about individuals, places, locations, objects, and events as they develop in real time around the world or in the local community.

Another group of collaboration tools focuses on the location of expertise. As such, those analyses concentrate on e-mail, chat, instant messages, reports, directories, and other types of communicated content as it flows between individuals in an organization for building dynamic expertise profiles. These software systems rank concepts in the text according to relevancy and frequency, creating expertise profiles based on these rankings. These profiles can also be created from structured sources such as an organization's Lightweight Directory Access Protocol (LDAP), a common directory service standard. The components are flexible enough to allow users to access their profiles and alter them and to change and control the information about their areas of expertise, which is being made available to others with access to the collaborative organization information system.

Collaboration is the process of collecting, tagging, classifying, organizing, and applying an organization's internal content and expertise. It's about the strategic management of its knowledge assets. For homeland security organizations, this means using these types of software to apply the information that is being collected by the law enforcement personnel at the street level, researchers, academia, and the intelligence communities, as well as other monitoring agencies, government entities, news feeds, and sources of real-time information. It also applies to identifying and profiling experts in various key technologies, such as counterintelligence, intrusion detection, or bio-terrorism, for quick collaboration in the event of such an attack. These types of knowledge assets can be used by homeland security organizations to harness intelligence and expertise assets. The collaborative tools can collect, distribute, and route to those with a need to know at the instant events occur, or better yet, before events or attacks happen.

Benefits of Collaboration: One Mission, Different Cultures

Homeland security collaboration is a complex system of agency-specific processes and technologies coupled with diverse departmental cultures, all working for a common mission and made possible by the use of these types of communication programs. Collaborative tools enable users to share what they know or what information or intelligence they have gathered and discovered. The benefits are clear; it makes for a smarter, more effective, and responsive homeland security organization at the local, state, and federal levels. Homeland security agencies are able to capture, organize, and disseminate both explicit and tacit knowledge. The explicit information may be in structured formats, located in agency databases, employee directories, or watch lists, as well as unstructured content such as e-mail, reports, memos, chat, and instant messages. Agencies can also benefit from tacit knowledge; this is the experience or special training that certain homeland security employees have in such areas as counterterrorism, espionage, law enforcement, smuggling, weaponry, money laundering, border security, transportation, first response, and fire fighting.

Homeland security collaboration tools enable agencies to reuse the experience and knowledge they have gained over time. It institutionalizes and applies departmental and agency best practices, in-house expertise, and lessons learned so that prior mistakes are not repeated and so that weaknesses and flaws in security systems and processes are avoided in the future, and incremental improvements are made in homeland security investigations, analyses, and alerts. Collaboration enables analysts and investigators to find the right information and experts at the right time when needed. It enables users to sort through reports, publications, e-mail, and other forms of internal and external communications more effectively and with better results. These collaboration software components are a way to build and maintain the cache of valuable content and the experience a homeland security organization accumulates. Collaboration software transforms a homeland security organization into an organic engine, learning and evolving as it goes about the tasks of protecting its citizens and country.

Collaboration tools support the extraction of information from unstructured sources scattered inside a firewall's organization, as well as those found outside in open sources such as the Web. Some tools convert that unstructured content into a structured format, storing it in a repository for easy search and retrieval, as well as link analyses. One of the side benefits of a homeland security organization using collaboration software is that it shifts the cultural tendencies of data hoarding from the past to data sharing for the common good of national defense. This subtle shift encourages data sharing through organization-wide policies, championing the collaboration of information, analyses, and experts. It emphasizes a strategy of identifying, capturing, sharing, and reusing knowledge to improve response, intelligence, and the overall efficiency of the homeland security organization.

In the end, collaborative software programs enable a homeland security organization to use its staff more efficiently. Projects become virtual through the elimination of geographical constraints. Teams also become virtual and, in doing so, more effective because the best possible combinations of talent and experience can be assembled since not everyone is required to reside in the same location, such as inside the Beltway or at a state capital. Another side benefit is that these virtual team members are empowered to be more creative and innovative. Teams can collaborate on what they do best; members can research, investigate, write, and perform their tasks while gaining significant time and at a cost saving to a homeland security organization. Some of the newer versions of these collaborative tools are able to support instant messaging with file sharing, and mistakes are reduced significantly because no e-mails are being exchanged. Analyses and investigations can be conducted and communicated in real time, shared with all team members simultaneously and globally.

The Collaborators: Acquire, Learn, and Discover

Vendors offering collaboration software components covered in this chapter are organized in the following sections according to their core functionality:

1. Collaboration suites commonly using search and discovery techniques
2. Expertise identification collaborative systems
3. Instant collaboration systems using real-time technologies

As the next chapter will demonstrate, often these collaborative applications will overlap in functionality with categorization programs because they both focus on the clustering of concepts from unstructured data. The collaboration software discussed here integrates a set of applications and technologies, which can be used to support homeland security organizations and their personnel via intelligence management; expertise communication, shared analyses, and personalized content delivery.

Autonomy

Founded in 1996, Autonomy is one of the first collaborative engines on the market; it uses Bayesian networks and Information Theory to categorize content and users. Autonomy software identifies the patterns that naturally occur in text, based on the use and frequency of words or terms that correspond to specific ideas or concepts. At its software core is Autonomy's Intelligent Data Operating Layer (IDOL) server, which integrates unstructured, semistructured, and structured information, including text, voice, and video, from multiple repositories, clustering the concepts it identifies.

At the heart of IDOL is the Dynamic Reasoning Engine™ (DRE™), a scalable, multithreaded process that analyzes and delivers targeted content to users. The DRE is based on probabilistic modeling techniques, which perform the following core operations:

Concept Matching: Accepts a piece of content as input and returns references to conceptually related documents ranked by relevance or associated contextual distance.

Automatic Summarization: Accepts a piece of content and returns a summary of the information containing the most salient concepts in the content.

Active Matching: Accepts textual information describing the current user task and returns a list of documents ordered by contextual relevance to the active task.

Contextual Retrieval: Accepts a Boolean term or natural language query and returns a list of documents containing the concepts sought, ordered by contextual relevance to the query.

Autonomy manages user profiles based on the documents they access, create, and retrieve. This profiling mechanism also enables interfaces such as ActiveKnowledge and ActiveWindows Extension to provide users with relevant documents in the context of their current work processes. Autonomy supports community development and collaboration through its Collaboration and Expertise Networks. Autonomy can identify networks of experts within an organization, map the relationships among people and documents, personalize automatic content delivery, and generate alerts to people on the basis of their community and expertise profiles.

The Autonomy infrastructure is based on a set of connectors that enable it to process content from a variety of databases and content management systems. The IDOL server provides the key functional operations of classification, indexing, and searching, which can be accessed via the Portal-in-a-Box interface for information retrieval, visualization, and expertise location. The Department of Homeland Security purchased Autonomy software, as have other government agencies around the world.

Centra

The Centra platform provides the capability to perform real-time business meeting and collaborative events. The Centra collaboration interfaces include capabilities for audio conferencing, application sharing, real-time data exchange, shared workspaces, and session recording and playback, all accessed via a browser interface. The Web-based software enables real-time communication and collaboration via integration with the users' desktops. Centra supports three main processes: Web Seminars, Self-Service Meetings, and Virtual Classes. All are standardized on one application with one point of access from any Web browser or IBM/Lotus or Microsoft application, such as Outlook. The software integrates with Oracle and Microsoft databases, LDAP, and Microsoft Active Directory.

Documentum

Originally developers of a document content management platform, the firm has expanded into the collaborative suite market via several acquisitions. The current version of the software includes the Enterprise Document Management (EDM) component for scanning, capturing, and storing paper documents. The EDM component integrates with other desktop software, such as Microsoft Office, and offers workflow automation, life cycle management, search, and retrieval. The Digital Asset Management component collects, stores, searches, browses, and manages multimedia data, including images, audio, and video. Users can incorporate the content in storyboards or PowerPoint presentations and other desktop applications. The Record Manager component enables the administration of multiple media, including e-mail, documents, images, video, and audio.

The eRoom component supports the collaboration of work teams via shared folders and calendars, portal views, and In boxes. eRoom combines content management, a workspace, and a repository in a Web-based collaboration workspace environment. Users can save content, create workflow engines, and create links to content for publishing on Web pages, on an intranet, or within an organization portal. Content can be shared across multiple workspaces, with search capabilities, group calendaring, offline access, and the tracking of document versions. Real-time meetings and presentations can take place via a Real Time Services (RTS) component.

Documentum's Content Intelligence Services (CIS) architecture supports the automatic classification and discovery of unstructured content. The software runs on Windows-based servers and can be accessed either through a browser or through Windows clients. It integrates with Microsoft Office, Outlook, and LDAP servers. The Department of State, Department of Energy, Food and Drug Administration, Federal Aviation Administration, and the U.S. Navy and Army have purchased Documentum software.

Groove Networks

Groove Network's Workspace is a desktop collaboration peer-to-peer system that enables participants to collaborate on documents and projects. Groove Workspace uses XML messages for communication and XML objects for storing messages. The software real-time capabilities include collaborative editing and viewing of files and presence: the capability to see who else is connected to the system. Workspace enables threaded discussions, chat and instant messaging, voice communications, shared calendars, location of users, and automatic notification of updates of content. Groove Workspace integrates with Microsoft SharePoint, Office, and Project, as well as IBM Lotus products. The National Institute of Standards and Technology (NIST) has approved the cryptographic module used by Groove software, Crypto++, to Federal Information Processing Standard 140-2 level. The FIPS 140-2 is a U.S. government standard that provides a benchmark for implementing cryptographic software. NIST specifies best practices for implementing crypto algorithms, handling key material and data buffers, and working with the operating system.

The current version of Groove Workspace obtained the first Department of Defense (DoD) certification for collaboration interoperability. Groove Workspace has been certified for interoperable with the DoD Defense Collaboration Tool Suite (DCTS), a standards-based means for collaboration within the U.S. defense and intelligence communities. DCTS evolved from a 1999 congressional mandate to the U.S. defense and intelligence communities to address the lack of interoperability in their collaboration tools. The mandate: Develop a strategy for implementing collaboration tools throughout the DoD, and validate a prioritized list of functional requirements for DoD collaboration tools. DCTS provides voice and video conferencing, document and application sharing, instant messaging, and whiteboard functionality to support defense planning. DCTS, which takes advantage of commercial off-the-shelf (COTS) software, gives U.S. military and intelligence personnel the capability to link various command, control, communications, computers, and intelligence systems for sharing data, conducting collaborative planning, and consulting on information from worldwide locations. The following is a case study on the use of collaborative software in the Iraq conflict. The author thanks Groove Networks for its contribution.

LESSONS FROM IRAQ: A GROOVE NETWORKS CASE STUDY

Information Technology for Crisis Management Conference

Presented by Robert Kirkpatrick, Groove Humanitarian Systems Group
Helsinki, Finland: 13 September 2003

Introduction

To combat hierarchical bureaucracies, terrorist groups long ago mastered the cellular form.

Terrorist cells, as we now know all too well, are agile, resilient, and highly adaptive. Today I am going to describe how a team of Groove volunteers and a group of humanitarian actors in the field used similar, cellular principles of organization in their work in Iraq. So please let me begin by adding another title to my official topic. I shall indeed describe *Collaborative Tools and Spaces in Humanitarian Intervention: Lessons from Iraq*, but I shall subtitle it: *A New Self-Organizing Architecture for Virtual Space.*

During Operation Iraqi Freedom, I worked with members of the Humanitarian Operations Center in Kuwait to develop Groove-based software tools for needs

(continued)

assessment and coordination of relief. In response to unanticipated information sharing needs, our team of volunteers in Massachusetts, together with a physician in Kuwait already familiar with our technology, built these tools over the course of several days. The tools, organized into virtual "shared spaces," were loaded in the field onto laptops of both civilian and military personnel in March, during the few days before and after the onset of conflict. Membership in these spaces spanned several continents and soon came to include military medical and civil affairs, UN-OCHA, CENTCOM, DFID, USAID, State-HIU, ICT vendors, public health experts, and NGOs such as IMC, PHR, IRC, and others. These groups were able to use the shared spaces as a kind of neutral ground for coordinating operations and sharing information both between headquarters and the field, as well as between themselves.

Admittedly, not everything went as we might have hoped. One critical organization had difficulties exporting data into a database, and another was unable to use the software because it had not been approved. I extend both of these organizations an apology. These problems might have been avoided by training and preparation in advance, but as is often the case in emergencies, there was simply no time, and their participation was sorely missed. We were newcomers unaware of the terrain—a group of nighttime volunteers at a commercial software company, trying to help. Yet, in spite of all that did not occur, what did occur was still remarkable and, I believe, instructive. These solutions were not planned by anyone. They emerged from the field, at the intersecting edges of organizations. They were designed directly by those who knew what was needed. The tools and membership of the virtual spaces evolved over time as the needs changed. My team and I had both opportunity to observe and the honor to participate. I would like to share with you some of what we learned. First, allow me to provide a bit of context.

Architecture Matters

Many solutions intended for use by field personnel in Iraq were client/server systems configured, deployed, and maintained at central headquarters. Although servers are ideal for use as data repositories, where people are interacting primarily with information, they can present problems during emergencies, when people most need to interact with one other. Organizations that had deployed a combination of e-mail and web server-based tools for data collection, collaboration, and sharing of select information encountered a range of technical and social challenges related directly to client/server architectures. Five of these are described here.

Servers may be difficult to reach. Users in the field frequently work offline, and when they are connected, it is often over slow and intermittent satellite links. Requests to Web servers time out. When users cannot connect to the server, they cannot reach either their data or one another.

(continued)

Headquarters may be slow to react. Solutions designed at the center are often unable to adapt to rapidly changing needs in the field. Personnel in the field have a perspective that is sometimes difficult to articulate to headquarters. They frequently cannot wait for IT to understand their needs and formulate appropriate solutions.

Agility is more valuable than planning. The situation in Iraq was, and remains, volatile, unpredictable, and fluid. Users must be able to develop solutions in the field quickly, without concern for supporting network infrastructure.

Teams form spontaneously. Field personnel need to "swarm" around problems, creating ad hoc teams with members of other organizations securely, without outside assistance.

Servers make poor "neutral ground." When successful coordination requires negotiation, ownership becomes an obstacle. If military and civilian actors wish to share a server, who owns it? Make changes, and at whose request? Who pays the bills? Client/server architectures foster territorial behavior. Whoever owns the server will be perceived as owning the solution, and the resulting tension over control of turf works against any spirit of cooperation, consensus, and sharing of information.

Peer-to-peer systems such as Groove, however, in which there is no central server, and in which data is replicated on each user's computer, are intrinsically neutral ground. The spatial neutrality provided by this architecture may help to build trust during the process of negotiation. Let me tell you a bit about this technology.

Ray Ozzie, the inventor of Lotus Notes, founded Groove Networks in 1997 after leaving Lotus. During his time at Lotus, Ray had come to recognize that the client/server architecture upon which systems such as Notes are based presents a number of infrastructure-related obstacles to cross-organizational collaboration. He designed Groove to overcome these obstacles. Groove is a secure, distributed, asynchronous collaboration platform well suited for use in austere environments. By this I mean that it has six distinct features, which have proved useful for humanitarian work in Iraq:

Collaboration. Users create virtual shared spaces, add software tools and content to use within the spaces, invite others to be members of the spaces, and then interact to solve problems. When all users are online, each member of a shared space sees the actions of the others. The system has built-in instant messaging and contact management, and notification of new content. Presence and awareness features indicate what other team members are online, and what spaces they are currently working in. Out-of-the-box tools include chat, voice-chat, shared files, threaded discussions, calendars, whiteboards, document review, meetings, customizable forms, and project management.

Secure. All data on disk and over wire is password-protected and encrypted at 192 bits with unique keys. Because encryption occurs at the application layer, Groove may

(continued)

be used for secure communications over insecure physical and wireless networks. Users only enter spaces via explicit invitation from current members; without an invitation, there is no way even to discover that a space exists. Space members authenticate each other's identities. All data transmitted is digitally signed for tamper-detection. The software makes extensive use of roles and permissions.

Distributed. Groove is serverless, in the sense that tools and data are synchronized onto each user's computer. If there are 10 members of a shared space, there are 10 copies of the data, each of which automatically synchronizes directly with other users' copies. If a laptop is lost, 9 other copies of the data still exist, and the user may easily be reinvited into the shared space. User identities, password policies, and account backup, on the other hand, may be administrated centrally by each organization using a Groove Management console.

Asynchronous. Groove works by capturing users' actions and queuing them for dissemination to other peers. Since all data is stored locally on each device, users may continue to collect data and work even while offline; any changes they make are queued and then synchronized with others at the next opportunity. Interrupted communications resume where they left off, and data is sent intermittently until synchronization is achieved. Groove peers discover one another and synchronize automatically on local networks without any access to the Internet and on wireless networks even without a Wireless Access Point. If a connection is lost, work may continue uninterrupted.

Austere Environments. For efficiency, Groove peers do not synchronize by sending one another new versions of modified data; rather, they send only XML metadata commands describing how to produce the changes. That is, if I add a line to a 200 kilobyte diagram in a Groove whiteboard, my device only sends other members' devices a description of the attributes of that line—a mere 1 kilobyte of data. In a sense, Groove transmits verbs rather than nouns. For changes to files, Groove calculates the binary differential between the two versions and transmits only the change. Although initial transport of a new file is no different that it would be via e-mail or download, changes are very efficient and, because data is already stored on each computer, reads incur no bandwidth cost at all.

Platform. Groove's collaboration and synchronization services support thousands of APIs in multiple programming languages and rich web services interfaces for use in developing custom tools. Groove supports a large number of data exchange standards, programming languages, and protocols. Groove interoperates natively with Outlook, Lotus Notes, Internet Explorer, and MS Office. Groove shared spaces may

(continued)

integrate directly with relational databases, GIS systems, RSS news feeds, web portals, wikis, document repositories, and other center-based resources. The Humanitarian Systems Group has built a variety of free tools for relief, reconstruction, development, human rights, and peace.

The Solution

On March 15th, 2003, UNOCHA released the final version of the Interagency Rapid Assessment Form for Iraq (RAF). Everyone sensed that conflict would break out in a few days, and it was feared that a massive humanitarian crisis might ensue. Coalition Civil Affairs personnel, who would be doing the first round of assessments, were beginning to deploy north with photocopies of the form and a few hours of assessment training. A number of organizations needed assessment data for coordination purposes, and several databases had already been prepared. There was, however, no mechanism for distributing and submitting the forms. Paper is easily damaged. Handwriting may be difficult to read. Coalition Civil Affairs were planning to radio their assessments back from Iraq by reading out one field-value pair at a time. (The RAF is a large form, containing in excess of 300 fields.) Others were planning a combination of courier, fax, and manual data entry. A tablet-and-sat phone-based system had been developed, but it was a pilot project and only six tablets were available.

Recognizing the need for a solution, Dr. Eric Rasmussen, a civil-military medical coordinator in Kuwait familiar with Groove's capabilities, contacted us and asked for our help. Over the weekend, three volunteers at Groove Networks built a Groove-based version of the RAF form and deployed it into several shared spaces. The RAF form, essentially, is an HTML form loaded inside of Groove. The membership of these spaces included Coalition forces, UNOCHA, DFID, and a number of NGOs among others. Users in the field completed these forms while offline and synchronized with others later—instantly sharing the assessments with space members everywhere. The use of chat and sharing of maps and photos was common among assessment teams. Phones were unreliable, and many users switched to Groove's VOIP tool. Assessment data was exported to relational databases at the HIU and the HIC for Iraq and published to the Web. Assessments continued to flow into this space until early June.

As areas of Iraq fell to Coalition forces, medical supplies intended for Iraqi hospitals began to arrive from governments all over the world. Cargo planes landed in Kuwait and Jordan, and ships converged on the port of Umm Qasr. This tide of assistance caught the HOC staff unprepared. No communications system was in place to inform them either of available assistance or of current needs. Many of them learned about the donations from news reports. No one knew that these shipments were

(continued)

coming, nor what they contained, nor which Iraqi facilities needed them, nor who could provide overland delivery, nor what military escort was required. In less than 24 hours, our team helped Dr. Rasmussen assemble a set of three shared spaces that were used for medical relief logistics. Membership was both civilian and military, spanning a number of organizations. Information streamed in from assessments and news reports. Hospitals in need of drugs, and patients in need of specialized treatment, were matched up with offers of evacuation and supplies finally moving into the recently de-mined port. Transport was found, and escort was arranged. Users shared maps, satellite images, handbooks, policy manuals, treatment protocols, news articles, pharmaceutical inventory lists, PowerPoint presentations, and other content.

Conclusion

During the war, we learned many lessons about how this technology works in austere communications environments. Although the technology was not designed explicitly for such circumstances, it worked well over sat phones. Users in the field confronted the unanticipated, defined their own requirements, designed their own solutions, formed new teams, and did what needed to be done. Data flowed back and forth between center and edge, military and civilian. Some users spent weeks disconnected from the Internet but coordinated with others in the field using ad hoc wireless networks. Many of those organizations are still working in Iraq, with new spaces being created as relief has given way to reconstruction. Groove is even being used in the Baghdad palace.

Yet the most valuable lesson we learned belongs more to the domain of social science than to that of technology. The psychosocial significance of distributed architecture was unanticipated. In retrospect, however, it makes sense. Homo Sapiens is by nature a territorial creature. In the real world, if trust is high, we may willingly congregate in any physical "shared space" to solve our mutual problems. If trust is low, power is at stake, and negotiation is required, geography suddenly matters. Neutral ground is essential. In the virtual world afforded by networks, the social issues persist. Servers are bound by location and, as such, are a poor locus of neutrality. Ownership, no matter how well meaning, undermines efforts to establish a sense of symmetrical power, thereby increasing the likelihood of competitive behavior. When the server is removed, and everyone owns a copy of the data, the medium becomes transparent, and users focus on the problems at hand. Barriers to cooperation are lowered, and shared spaces may be created for the pursuit of specific, limited, common goals.

In conclusion, what we have seen in Iraq is that humanitarian actors benefited from a new technological enabler of cellular structure—not to subvert the hierarchy, but to advance its aims by endowing it with an elastic adaptability, speed, and

(continued)

resilience. Enabling field personnel to self-organize on virtual neutral ground, even while disconnected from central authority in time and space—swarming, acting, and disbanding in response to events—created new conduits of power that both overlaid and cross-linked existing hierarchies and facilitated greater responsiveness during humanitarian action. Certainly, many barriers to interoperability cannot be overcome by technology. But architecture matters. That we now know.

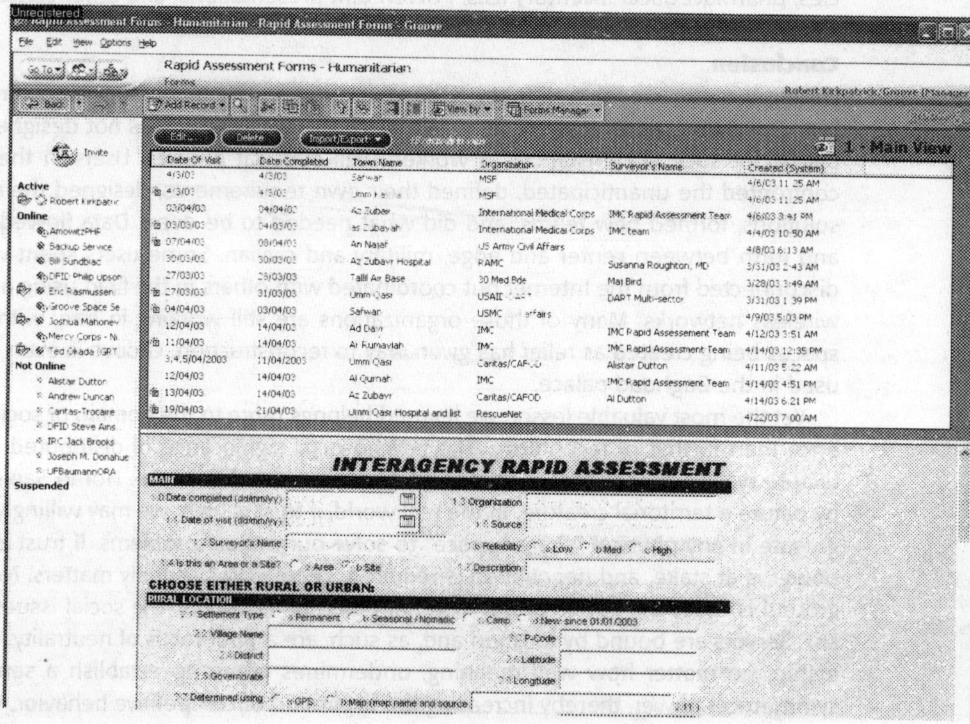

FIGURE 4.5 A view of the Groove software interface. © 2004. Reprinted with permission from Groove Networks.

Hummingbird

Hummingbird's approach to providing a complete collaboration suite is to package individual products that can be integrated and customized by users. An organization can add the products as it evolves through its collaborative efforts, strategy, and needs. Hummingbird KM, Search Server, and Collaboration modules provide natural language processing for searching unstructured content: documents, filesystems, Web pages, e-mail, and so on. The system uses a neural network for browsing and discovery. The Hummingbird Collaboration module contains a meetings feature that provides the capability to schedule single or multiple meetings around any object in a collaboration project. The secure collaboration environment ensures that only project participants who have access to the item in question will be able to see the related meetings. The calendaring feature enables users to create events and invite users to participate in projects and can be synchronized with Microsoft's Outlook. Hummingbird supports personalized content delivery and expertise location. KM enables users to conduct single, unified searches across multiple unstructured information sources, including Lotus Notes, Microsoft Exchange Server, Web sites, file repositories, document management systems, multimedia libraries, and more. Additionally, structured data sources such as databases and enterprise operational systems are also indexed via the Hummingbird SearchServer.

Hyperwave

Hyperwave is a leading supplier of Collaborative Knowledge Management and eLearning solutions, which empower private industry and government agencies to gather, manage, share, and reuse knowledge and experience securely. Hyperwave's eKnowledge Suite supports content classification, indexing, and searching and includes content and document management for structured and unstructured documents. The eKnowledge Suite can also be expanded to include Hyperwave's Team Workspace for personalized content delivery, expertise location, and collaboration for project members working in different locations. Created in five easy steps using a wizard, various tools such as group calendars, task lists, notes, and e-mail integration are also available. The eKnowledge Suite's discovery capabilities include probabilistic concept search, matching and retrieval of related terms, and automatic classification using the Autonomy or Verity engine. The Hyperwave eKnowledge Portal component provides integration with other applications via messaging, including the eKnowledge Suite, enabling users to consolidate all content and activities for a given project in a single location. Hyperwave has been adopted by several intel and Department of Defense agencies, including the U.S. Air Force, U.S. Army National Ground Intelligence Center, the Joint Warfare Analysis Center, and the Space and Naval Warfare Systems Center.

IBM

The IBM WebSphere Portal Extended Solution collaborative components include Lotus Sametime and Quickplace modules and the Lotus Discovery Server (LDS) for automatic classification and taxonomy construction. LDS uses advanced vector mapping, clustering, and metrics in the classification process, and an editor is included for modifying the taxonomy. The collaborative tool can generate a map grouping documents to individuals and locations. Profiles are created based on users' interaction with documents whose contents reflect a categorical topic. Clicking on a person's name in the map brings up that person's expertise profile, with an option to automatically address an e-mail to the person identified, initiate an instant message, or add the individual's name to a community or shared place.

IBM Lotus Sametime uses an Enterprise Meeting server for managing multiple online meetings; it integrates with Notes and MS Outlook for the coordination of users' calendars. Sametime is also capable of integrating with other instant messaging systems using the SIMPLE protocol, such as MSN Messenger Content. Sametime has the capability to share and send files while chat sessions are underway. Sametime Everyplace is a mobile version with a programmable API for real-time alerts. A counterpart component to Sametime, Quickplace lets users create team workspaces to collaborate on documents, meetings, and coordinate plans, tasks, and resources. It enables content creation, searching, and indexing. When Quickplace is integrated with Sametime, users can communicate via instant messages and attend Web-based conferences. The software integrates with Lotus Notes, Microsoft Outlook, and Office.

iManage

iManage WorkSite is an integrated suite of components focused on document management, collaboration, knowledge management, portal, and content workflow. The iManage sub-components WorkKnowledge, WorkTeam, and WorkPortal unite document management, collaboration, knowledge management, and workflow tools within a Web portal, running on Windows NT or a Java open platform. WorkTeam provides customizable virtual workspaces in which geographically disperse teams can be organized into projects with threaded discussions, calendars, and shared URL link lists. iManage offers a number of products that significantly extend the collaborative capabilities of the WorkSite applications suite. The Immigration and Naturalization Service Office of the General Counsel and Department of Justice have purchased iManage software.

Intraspect

Intraspect's Core Services support collaboration via e-mail, desktop applications, and Web-based workplaces, which collectively can create a group memory or repository. Its c-spaces are secure collaborative workspaces, and its c-mail services use e-mail as the access point for collaboration. Users can perform real-time search and retrieval, access, update, and check documents in and out, all via e-mail. Using graphical, template-based tools, users of the framework can create or modify workspace "teamplates" to build custom functionality, augment the base data model, and customize, integrate, or replace the user interface.

Linqware

Linqware is a server-based peer-to-peer e-meeting application, providing presence detection, instant messaging, application sharing, dynamic archiving, and retrieval. Its Collabrix software provides collaboration with 40 to 128 bit industry standard SSL encryption security, with administrative controls to establish user rights and privileges, limiting access to non-secure environments and managing all system activity.

Microsoft

Microsoft NetMeeting enables real-time collaboration among participants; it supports video and audio conferencing, a whiteboard, text messaging, lists of participants, file transfer capabilities, and remote desktop sharing. Security features include user authentication, data encryption, and password protection. Microsoft Placeware is a real-time interactive communications tool; its Auditorium supports hosted conferencing. It runs on Java-enabled browsers. Microsoft SharePoint Team Services is a content server that enables users to share drafts of documents in a common Web-based workspace; it supports document searching, indexing, and automatic updating. SharePoint can be set up with as many as five levels of permission and membership. SharePoint Team Services provides collaboration capabilities, including team and Web site creation, team lists, document discussions, membership managed surveys, and document libraries. When combined with SharePoint Portal Server, it can provide a platform for collaboration within an organization. Microsoft's .NET platform can expand its capability to integrate Exchange and Outlook, Content Management Server, and NetMeeting into a complete collaborative suite. Microsoft's Exchange communication features include instant messaging, buddy lists, chat, audio, and video conferencing.

Novell

GroupWise incorporates e-mail, calendaring, scheduling, document management, indexing, searching, workflow, collaboration, secure instant messaging, and mobile access capabilities. GroupWise's licensing model is user based rather than device centric. GroupWise is a cross-platform collaboration product that enables users to work with others over any type of network, wired or wireless, including the Internet. It integrates e-mail and scheduling services with tasks, instant messaging, contact and document management services, and extensive mobile-access capabilities.

GroupWise includes support for Palm and Pocket PC and two-way access to Blackberry RIM and Synch ML devices.

Open Text

Livelink is Open Text's collaborative portal. It supports document management, information retrieval, and workflow automation. Collaboration features include shared discussion, links, calendars, and task lists. It also includes support notification of changes and federated searching of multiple instances. Open Text also has developed modules containing features and applications for specific industries, such as telecommunications, high technology, manufacturing, pharmaceuticals, finance, and may develop similar modules for homeland security. Livelink provides natural language capabilities that enable searching by natural language queries and a Recommender module for the location of human experts. Open Text also offers workflow capabilities through enhanced forms management. Livelink MeetingZone provides an online meeting environment with follow-up task lists, meetings, and automatic capture of minutes to a repository. Virtual teams can combine tools, utilities, and content via a browser interface. Both of Open Text's records management software packages, Livelink and iRIMS, received the Classified Records certification, along with the mandatory DoD 5015.2 certification. Open Text met the security requirements as part of its DoD 5015.2 certification, which is required for all records management solutions used by the Department of Defense and other U.S. federal agencies. The new Management of Classified Records certification has become important to ensure the highest level of security of records as the demand to share information among federal agencies grows.

Oracle

Oracle's Collaboration Suite uses an integrated inbox where users access their voice mail, e-mail, and shared files. Oracle's iMeeting provides Web conferencing, co-browsing, voice streaming, instant messaging, and meeting playback. Other components are Oracle Email, Oracle Voice Mail, Oracle Calendar, Oracle Files, and Oracle Ultra-search, all of which use the Oracle database and application server as their foundation. Collaboration Suite uses its relational Oracle database and its Oracle Application Server infrastructure to offer customers messaging and collaboration applications that enable them to simplify business communications and consolidate information, while reducing hardware, software, and administration costs.

Plumtree

The Java-based Collaboration Server combines views of active projects with e-mail, documents, and directories. Its projects are made up of "portlets" that encapsulate task and document management, threaded conversations, project calendars, templates, and group announcements. The Collaboration Server builds its own relational database for storing and hosting all documents and data related to each collaborated project. The Collaboration Server lets people across an organization work together on projects—setting schedules, assigning tasks, sharing documents, and exchanging ideas. Designed to integrate with Plumtree's Enterprise Web Suite, the Collaboration Server transforms applications delivered by the Plumtree Corporate Portal into interactive workspaces where project teams can drive initiatives and interact with other resources such as e-mail and documents.

Raindance

Raindance Communications provides hosted telephone and conferencing services comprised of both Web and phone communications for visual sharing and interaction. The service enables meeting leaders to initiate a phone conference at any time by using a dedicated toll-free number and an assigned PIN. The moderator can call and add participants, lock the conference for security, mute individuals or groups, and track responses. The Raindance system can e-mail the meeting after the conference with a report outlining the discussion. The conferencing servers are hosted on redundant UNIX systems with multiple levels of security and layered firewall protection.

SiteScape

Enterprise Forum includes workflow, wireless support, online discussions, share and revise files, chat, meetings, shared calendars, and organize tasks. WebWorkZone is a hosted version of Enterprise Forum, and SiteScape also offers eMeetings for voice and video Web meetings, virtual presentations, whiteboards, and application sharing. With Forum, users can host online discussions, share and revise documents and files, chat; schedule meetings using shared calendars, organize tasks, and quick message teammates. SiteScape Forum is flexible and designed to run in multiple environments. It is Web based and can be accessed by PCs or PDAs.

Traction Software

Traction's Enterprise software expands the concept of Weblogs, personal Web-based journals, to support working communication, collaboration, and information sharing for groups of users working within or across organizations. Traction supports a mix of public and private online discussion between users. The streams of thoughts and opinion can be interleaved with collected source information to provide context and to support analysis over time. Project importance, topic, author, and time organize the Enterprise Weblog, with each project having a permission access list. Individuals can see and search the union of all activity their

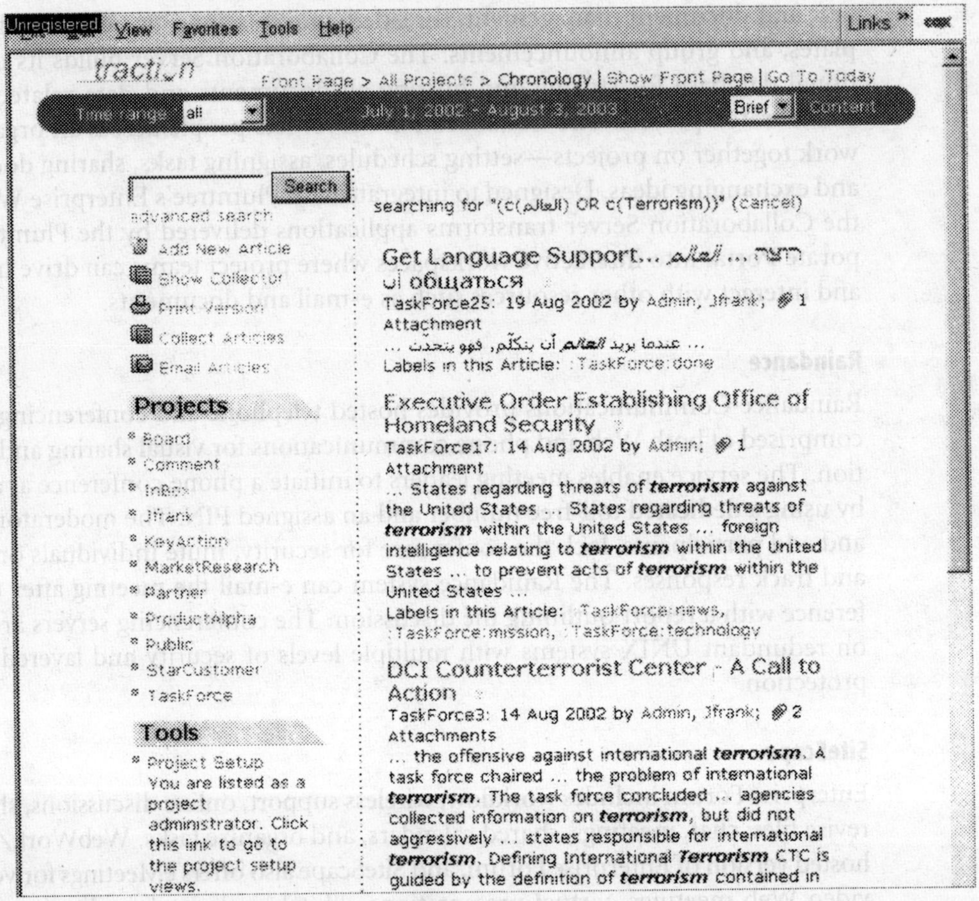

FIGURE 4.6 A view of the Traction software interface. © Traction Software, Inc., 2003. Reprinted with permission.

permission level allows them to read. Comments and discussion about a particular article can be posted to more restricted projects, such as an individual analyst's notebook or investigation, so that people with appropriate permission can hold a private conversation with the complete discussion in context. The software is designed for collaboration for groups with a common goal, such as Watch Center, Analyst, or Operations teams. For example, homeland security units can create project workspaces to facilitate case-related communication as well as capture and track events, evidence, or other investigation-related materials.

Verity

Verity is one of the original full-text search engine providers and now supports enterprise-wide collaboration via knowledge management and a portal. Verity provides a three functional tier infrastructure for discovering, organizing, and connecting content and experts. In the first tier of discovering, Verity's search engine enables users to perform natural language queries; it supports multiple languages and both parametric and wild card searches. The search engine component is available as a standalone product called UltraSeek. The Organize tier is the content classification and indexing component; it uses a combination of automatic classification, business rules, and concept extraction for automatic taxonomy creation and the clustering of concepts. Verity uses Logistic Regression Classification for the categorization of content. The third tier, Connect, is a profiling system for the location of expertise, community identification, and recommendation component. It performs a profiling function that returns the names and contact information of people who are possible experts in a specific area or who may be candidates for an emerging community of practice.

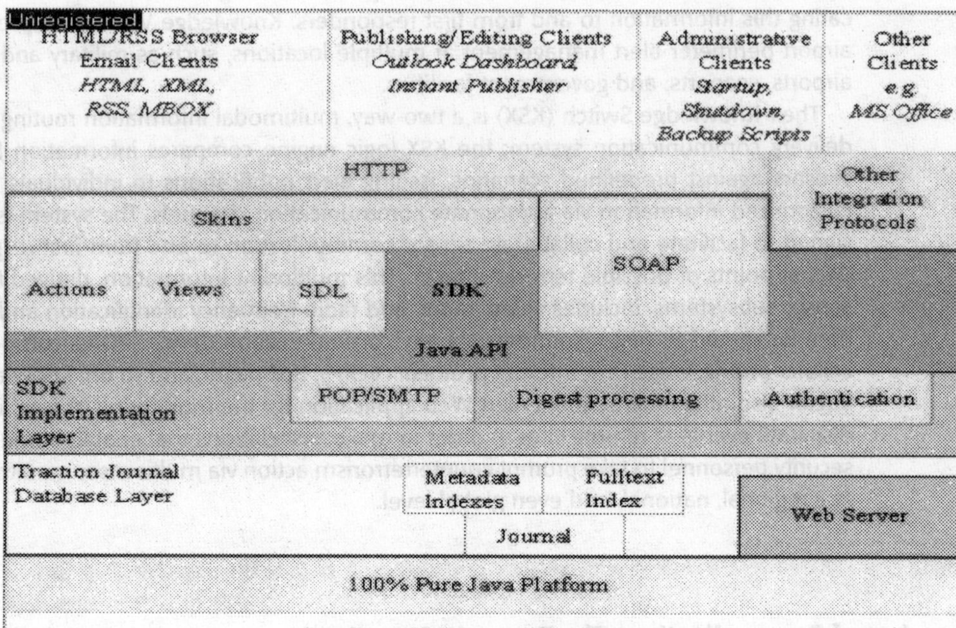

FIGURE 4.7 A view of the Traction software architecture. © Traction Software, Inc. 2003. Reprinted with permission.

WebEx

WebEx is a hosted online meeting and conferencing service provider. Its MediaTone meeting and conferencing services incorporate rich media, application and data sharing, and real-time videoconferencing. Sharing capabilities include zooming and annotation tools for documents and applications. Participants can save annotated documents for offline viewing without the need to have the original application installed on their computers. WebEx Exchange enables users from different venues to schedule and start meetings, maintain a common calendar, receive or leave messages, chat, and use instant messaging.

THE COLLABORATION OF SENSORS: A KNOWLEDGE VECTOR CASE STUDY

Knowledge Vector provides a system for collaborating sensor data to homeland security applications and its personnel, such as those found at airports. They offer an integrated threat alert and management system that aggregates data from existing security and surveillance systems, converting it into a single format and communicating this information to and from first responders. Knowledge Vector can provide airport perimeter alert management at multiple locations, such as military and civil airports, seaports, and government facilities.

Their Knowledge Switch (KSX) is a two-way, multimodal information routing and delivery communication system; the KSX logic engine compares information from sensors against predefined scenarios, issuing alert notifications to individuals with customized information via appropriate communication channels. The system is designed to facilitate and collaborate sensor communication to and from first responders at points of possible terrorist attacks. This multipoint information, derived from sensor subsystems, includes video, radar, and radio frequency identification and can then be routed to first responders via any communication device: PDAs, computer, cellular phone, voice over Internet protocol (VOIP), text pager, and so on. Knowledge Vector also offers the Sentinel Alert Web application for the monitoring of seemingly disparate events at remote sites in order to make associations that enable homeland security personnel to take prompt counterterrorism action via multisensor monitoring at a regional, national, and even global level.

Experts and Personalization: The Dynamic Organization

Collaborative software exists for locating experts within an organization by scanning their e-mail, chat, instant messages, and other documents they generate in their jobs over time. The software continuously captures and stores data about every interaction that occurs to develop expertise profiles. The programs then monitor the questions that get routed to these experts and what answers were provided; in the background it rates them and their response times, capturing it all dynamically. The software typically analyzes this expertise data to produce reports for administrators on both inquiries and responses by these experts.

These expertise locator and profiling systems apply the tacit and commonly undocumented knowledge that human experts acquire over time via specialized training and work experience. Employees in homeland security organizations can gradually learn how to use these types of collaboration systems to assist them in future tasks or as events occur. For homeland security organizations, these types of systems can provide key and tactical intelligence in both locating and collaborating with experts in dirty weapons, pattern recognition technologies, foreign policy, emergency procedures, and a host of other special fields.

There also are collaborative systems that create static and dynamic profiles for delivering personalized content to users in an organization that is relevant to their tasks, responsibilities, missions, and positions. These types of software systems provide both targeted and relevant content and the technology to manage its delivery to profiled users. As users interact with information systems, networks, and data depositories, profiles of what content they deal with on a daily basis are recorded in a knowledge base so that domain and specific topics or events are associated with those users. For a homeland security organization, profiles of experts can be developed dynamically as new events occur, either via threats or as investigations or attacks occur.

The collaborative program then automatically routes new content that matches its user profiles of interest. These personalization content delivery systems also issue alerts to profiled users when new events occur, such as when a databases is updated or when changes in documents take place. They also can identify new experts as they enter an organization, alerting others of new-found expertise. In all, it makes for a highly dynamic work environment in which content and expertise is aligned and directed to those with a need to know as events and analyses occur. Again, for a homeland security organization, this type of software can be used to alert those first responders, investigators, or analysts the system recognizes as having the clearance levels and "need to know" as events, explosions, contaminations, sightings, arrests, attacks, and so on take place.

Expertise Collaborators: Who Knows What

The following systems are designed specifically for the location of experts within an organization. As with private industry, homeland security organizations will recognize that expert knowledge that is often tacit and undocumented exists with a person, and that individuals often learn most effectively and quickly by a process of collaboration and direct communication with resident experts.

AskMe

AskMe uses the concept of employee knowledge networks to describe what its software does. As with other tools in this market space, the software creates employee profiles from existing data sources and uses this information to direct individuals within an organization looking for answers for resolving current problems. The software delivers knowledge from experts to individuals seeking solutions and captures that expertise for future searches by other knowledge seekers. This collaborative software model assumes there are groups within any given organization where there is a need to recycle and manage the knowledge, content, and expertise acquired for a particular and specific domain. AskMe uses natural language processing techniques coupled with user-provided expertise ratings in associating seekers of solutions to experts. The software also performs dynamic profiling of experts, collection of best practices, profile-based content delivery services, rules development, and the automation of workflow within an organization.

Kamoon

Connect is an expertise locator tool that takes a systematic approach to the process of identifying and managing expertise. It supports end-users by enabling them to locate experts on particular topics, and then it monitors the interaction between the requestors and expert providers. Kamoon uses a workflow engine based on policy rules for matching requests and experts. These rules are based on a person's role in an organization, the availability of a previously asked question, and the accessibility of the available experts. Kamoon tracks all interactions, including any real-time chat between questioners and experts, and is continually adding to its knowledge base and dynamically updating its user profiles. Kamoon's Expertise Engine enables organizations to customize the routing of questions to support specific practices; the engine uses a series of IF/THEN rules in routing seekers to experts.

Sopheon

Sopheon's Accolade product works primarily through e-mail in locating and collaborating with experts. Its rating system allows users to rate both the content of the response and the expert. As with some of the other expertise location and management products, Accolade also provides community forums. Sopheon's software focuses on corporate research and development.

Tacit

KnowledgeMail is Tacit's collaborative product and expertise location tool. It works by continuously analyzing company e-mail to determine the areas of expertise for each employee in an organization. Once an individual has been identified as an expert in a particular area, the system will automatically route queries on that topic to them from other employees. These same profiles can route e-mail messages or news stories from the Web to the appropriate individual in an organization. Although the profiles are created via an automated process, the expert has the final approval on its accuracy and is given the option on what is disclosed to others in the organization about his expertise. Tacit ESP is a taxonomy-independent search and analysis engine that monitors activities in e-mail, content repositories, and input streams, enabling the location of experts via analysis of a range of document and databases. Users can search using keywords, Boolean expressions, or natural language queries. The system returns a ranked list of people and resources, along with relevancy ranking. The reporting and analysis capabilities enable an organization to identify and measure collaboration activity, expertise gaps, and internal flow of relevant knowledge. In-Q-Tel, the CIA VC firm, was one of the seed investors of Tacit, which it saw had the potential to provide a collaborative solution to the intelligence community it serves.

Mapping Collaboration: Search, Retrieval and Categorization

There are various goals and methods in collaboration, and one of the principal ones is to *acquire, learn,* and *discover.* This involves methods for seeking specific information, data, content, or knowledge. The technologies involve search and retrieval and the categorization of unstructured text and data mining systems for classification. The techniques provide a search and classification of unstructured content housed in networks or databases of an organization. Search capabilities give users access to the breadth of content gathered from internal and external sources. Collaboration in this context often involves the use of autonomous learning agents, that is, programs that search for content across multiple databases inside and outside an organization, using natural language processing and advanced search and retrieval techniques. Summaries of these content searches are returned on the basis of relevancy and frequency, based on either keyword matching or the clustering of concepts.

Another method to acquire, learn, and discover for collaboration in an organization is to locate experts, investigators, and analysts working on related subject areas, such as specific terrorist cells or methods of attacks, weapon types, cargo shipping, modes of transportation, or task forces. This involves expertise location and the creation and maintenance of dynamic profiles of experts based on workflow of their documents, e-mails, instant messages, chat sessions, and other unstructured content, where the system must be self-learning and adaptive, modifying these profiles as workflow evolves.

Yet another method to acquire, learn, and discover for collaboration is to monitor events, news, developments, alliances, trends, and changes, and use profiling techniques to route new content via targeted delivery services. In these cases technology is used to sniff, filter, and retrieve relevant content from internal and external sources, routing it to users based on self-adaptive profiles of recipients' interests. These profiles are developed by the detection of a user's current information related to his specialty or content interests, including the dynamic notification of previously accessed databases or documents.

Lastly, another method to acquire, learn, and discover for collaboration involves the data mining of database sources of structured content. This involves technology for mining a collection of distributed databases and directories to extract rules and patterns and populate the data structures for humans to view for knowledge discovery.

Another goal of collaboration is to *create*, *combine,* and *refine* content, to provide a centrally managed workspace for users to locate experts and documents and engage in threaded discussions, send e-mail, chat, or instant message. Collaboration also involves the *cataloging* of content, storing and indexing information via various types, and performing autonomous automatic classification via personal and Web knowledge content management systems. To index and categorize content in multiple routines that are relevant and meaningful in a personalized manner makes the results available for browsing, visual display, reuse, or recombination.

A final goal of collaboration is to *apply* and *deploy* the results of collaborative efforts via organizational portals, providing access to group, branch, department, agency, or department knowledge bases and applications via a single user interface. This involves using collaboration software to access and share investigations, inquiries, and queries in progress, and to disseminate personalized content to specific profiled need-to-know users in a shared collaboration space. It includes providing in-context access to specific intelligence on a step-by-step basis during the performance of a task, capturing new information, conditions, and events, and capturing ancillary data during these ongoing task accomplishments.

Instant Collaborators: Presence Messaging

The collaboration vendors discussed in the following sections provide enterprise-level instant messaging (IM), presence, and chat products.

AOL IM

AOL offers its enterprise version of its instant messenger service (EAIM) via an AIM Enterprise Gateway and a desktop client AIM. EAIM includes access control, auditing and archiving, and reporting, along with group screen names, presence functions, and chat rooms to encourage team collaboration. The AIM Enterprise Gateway (AIM EG) is an enterprise server software product developed for AOL by FaceTime. It is provided with a software developer kit for integration into an organization's infrastructure.

Bantu

The Bantu instant messenger and presence platform are available as a hosted service or as licensed software installed at onsite servers. Bantu IM is a Web-based application written in Java and requires no client software. Bantu servers run on a wide array of platforms, including UNIX, Linux, Solaris, and Windows. The Bantu IM enables users to see others online for instant real-time collaboration. Bantu also offers Mobile Messenger software, which is a Wireless Application Protocol (WAP) client that runs on PDAs and cell phones. Lastly, Bantu also provides subscription-based hosted IM services via its service center in Virginia.

Communicator

Communicator is a secure instant messenger offered as a hosted service or self-maintained application. It features identity management, access control, content aggregation, and instant messaging. The Communicator Hub IM is an HTTP-based application with Secure Sockets Layer (SSL) encryption security features. There are application and browser versions of Communicator Hub IM. The application version works on Windows, Mac, and UNIX platforms, while the browser version works on all current versions of major browsers. The application version is a Java-based application designed for desktops, and the browser version is non-Java based. Users access Communicator Hub IM with assigned usernames and passwords, with the server doing the authentication; the Hub includes address books, contact lists, presence, and other customizable alerting options.

FaceTime

FaceTime provides server-based real-time computing (RTC) to detect, control, and administer the use of instant messaging and chat. The FaceTime IM Guardian is an enterprise security gateway designed and optimized for managing complex, real-time communication technologies such as IM and peer-to-peer (P2P) communications, Web teleconferencing, and voice over IP (VOIP). IM Guardian works hand-in-hand with FaceTime's suite of enterprise IM management and control solutions, such as IM Director for management and control. Specialized versions of FaceTime IM Director applications are available. For example, there is a Risk and Security Management module, enabling organizations to safely deploy IM applications on public network infrastructures such as AOL, Communicator, Lotus, Microsoft, and Yahoo!.

Jabber

Jabber is an open XML protocol for the real-time exchange of messages and presence between any two points on the Internet. The Jabber protocol is free, open, decentralized, and secure, with multiple open-source implementations for servers, clients, and development libraries. Common extensions of the software are managed by the Jabber Foundation. The RTC Jabber communication platform supports instant messaging and embedded streaming of XML data into other vendors' applications, devices, and services. Jabber software is built on an XML-based protocol; they also offer Extensive Instant Messaging (XIM) Jabber, a full-feature IM client Jabber Messenger (JIM), the Jabber Communications Platform for developing real-time applications and services, and tools to enable instant messaging on mobile devices. The Jabber Communications Platform is made up of the Jabber server, the Jabber Messenger desktop client, and the Jabber Webclient for integration with LDAP directories.

THE CAPITAL WIRELESS INTEGRATED NETWORK (CAPWIN): A JABBER CASE STUDY

Jabber's commercial platform, XCP, is a core component of the Capital Wireless Integrated Network (CapWIN) system. CapWIN is a wireless integrated mobile data communications network being implemented to support federal, state, and local law enforcement, transportation, and public safety agencies in the Washington, D.C., metropolitan area. The purpose of CapWIN is to greatly enable and enhance communications for first responders during critical incidents by integrating data and messaging systems, effectively creating the first multistate, interjurisdictional transportation and public safety integrated wireless network in the United States. CapWIN provides a "communication bridge," allowing mobile access to multiple criminal, justice, transportation, and hazardous material data sources, as shown in Figure 4.8.

A consortium of law enforcement, fire, transportation, and emergency medical agencies in the Washington, D.C., region created CapWIN. The system will be the first multijurisdiction, multidiscipline network of its kind in the nation and will eliminate many of the communication bottlenecks that now hamper emergency response coordination. Law enforcement agencies will be able to communicate instantly using Jabber's secure, real-time instant messaging platform, allowing better coordination between users in multiple agencies responding to an emergency. Individuals can instant message each other or create secure online "incident rooms" to communicate with multiple individuals in real time. For example, a police officer arriving at an emergency can create an incident room and request assistance from other available

(continued)

agencies or officers, regardless of where they are located. Some of the objectives of CapWIN are as follows:

- Make extensive use of commercial-off-the-shelf (COTS) products.
- Be an open, scalable, and reliable Web-based architecture.
- Make extensive use of technology standards.
- Provide minimal impact to existing systems.
- Provide low total cost of ownership (TCO).
- Make efficient use of limited bandwidth.
- Provide better use of limited resources.
- Provide enhanced data security.

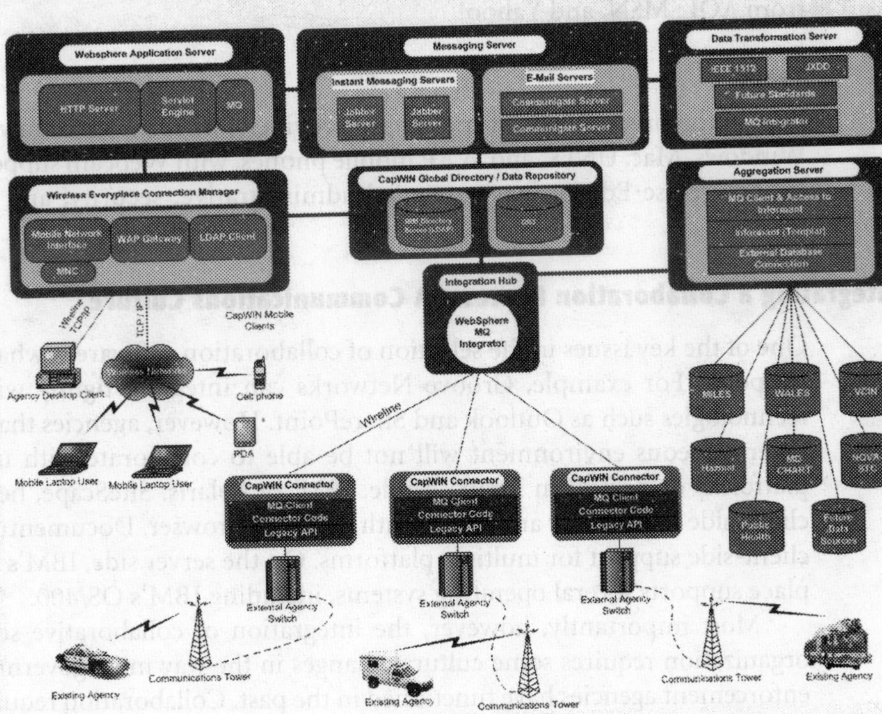

FIGURE 4.8 This is a schematic of the CapWIN communication bridge system.

Microsoft

Microsoft offers its MSN Messenger Connect for instant messaging for organizations; it supports PC-to-phone connections, PC-to-PC voice and video connections, data conferencing, whiteboarding, directory integration, and authentication. The instant messaging client for Exchange uses Microsoft's Active Directory to add a layer of security and identity control. Microsoft also is embedding its messaging tools in Exchange and its XP operating system with video conferencing features.

Omnipod

Omnipod provides a secure, client/server RTC platform with instant messaging and integrated file sharing applications. Omnipod puts emphasis on security via the use of a 168-bit Triple Encryption Standard (3DES) SSL in its instant messaging and file transfer applications 3DES features the capability to import buddy lists from AOL, MSN, and Yahoo!.

Yahoo!

One of the original instant messenger providers, its software is downloadable for Windows, Mac, UNIX, and WAP mobile phones, with Webcam support and video. Its Enterprise Edition has expanded administrative, security, and maintenance features.

Integrating a Collaboration Process: A Communications Culture

One of the key issues in the selection of collaboration software is what platforms it supports. For example, Groove Networks can integrate tightly with Microsoft technologies such as Outlook and SharePoint. However, agencies that operate in a heterogeneous environment will not be able to collaborate with users running platforms or devices in Linux, Apple, IBM, or Solaris. SiteScape, however, offers client-side support for any device with any Web browser. Documentum also offers client-side support for multiple platforms. On the server side, IBM's Lotus Quickplace supports several operating systems, including IBM's OS/400.

Most importantly, however, the integration of collaborative software in an organization requires some cultural changes in the way most government and law enforcement agencies have functioned in the past. Collaboration requires establishing new communication channels; it requires that some analysts and investigators share their intelligence and knowledge in implementing these new technologies. Because of these fundamental changes, successful collaboration initiatives will require leadership from executives with very clear directives.

Once organizations have begun to share their content, expertise, and analyses, they may discover unique abilities and intelligence that can be used to champion collaboration as a process of high value to the mission of homeland security. The goal is to encourage workers to communicate freely with one another for the better good of the organization and national defense. One of the first steps in fostering a collaborative environment and infrastructure is to define explicitly what knowledge sharing is and what value it can bring.

Existing employees need to be trained in information sharing and how to work in a team-oriented environment; a collaborative work style should be emphasized. In all, collaboration should be designed and planned as an ongoing process, not as an end in itself. This requires a well-defined methodology, not just procuring and installing a software product. With time, a framework for replicating best practices of collaboration can be expanded and developed, gradually evolving as a method of emphasizing internal communications for the improvement of intelligence and the overall mission of homeland security.

Key Issues in Collaboration: Five Factors

There are several issues and concerns any homeland security organization must face as it incorporates some of these collaboration software solutions. They include privacy, language, security, scalability, and storage.

First, as evidenced by a description of the functionality of some of these software products, an organization must look at user documents, e-mail, chat, and instant messages in determining users' expertise and in routing relevant content to them. As such, the issue of a person's privacy must be addressed, and a policy must be communicated and agreed upon within the organization.

Secondly, because of the very nature of homeland security, the software used for collaboration must support machine-assisted search and translation of multiple languages in all types of content. With regard to the issue of security of information and knowledge bases, a model must be forged for the classification of documents and users' right of access to certain intelligence. The software used needs to incorporate search and indexing algorithms to ensure security and a proper level of access to indexes.

Next is the concern over scalability and the need to manage multiple knowledge bases, content, and taxonomies in a way that enables them to flow easily and securely over multiple heterogeneous platforms and networks. The final issue is that of increasingly expanding volumes of data and how to manage the deluge of information in an intelligent and strategic manner by filtering, extracting, abstracting, and routing only the intelligence that is relevant to a particular analyst or investigator.

THREAT MATRIX COLLABORATION: MULTI-AGENCY AND MULTIMEDIA

The essence of effective homeland security collaboration revolves around sound multi-agency information sharing and a real-time communications infrastructure. Working homeland security teams must communicate information related to potential threats, including news feeds, translations, scenario creation, hypotheses, memos, pictures, reports, events, sitings, papers, recordings, videos, and other forms of data and media. One of the toughest challenges of homeland security projects will be information sharing, collaboration of expertise, and getting executives, managers, and analysts to work in interagency environments with cross-functional initiatives.

There are many ways to collaborate and share information, as evidenced by the descriptions of some of the software systems discussed in this chapter, and homeland security information technology specialists must be careful not to let the abundance of choices obscure desired policy or operational objectives. Often, government officials rely too heavily on supposed experts in private industry, such as outside consultants and large system integrators. At times they fail to fully understand the core missions of a collaborative project and can divert limited resources and waste precious time, such as in creating new databases or systems when it would suffice simply to use existing sources that have been in use for years by private industry, such as that of demographics data sources. These newly created systems may ultimately miss the mark and simply serve the purpose of creating new revenue for professional outsourcing specialists and firms.

The point of some integration and collaboration projects will be to draw information from a structured database at a given moment, such as querying a terrorist watch list while processing a visa application. Often this type of task comes down to finding the simplest and most secure way to connect one system to another, and it can involve using existing commercial software components such as those covered in the previous chapter. Other initiatives will try to give homeland security analysts access to unstructured data such as memos, e-mail messages, or news feeds. This involves some of the technologies covered in this chapter as well as the next. These programs can absorb an enormous amount of data and provide a way to categorize it; they can extract relevant facts and identify possible patterns or links among them for analysts to use. Some of these programs aim to provide virtual workspaces for collaboration, enabling employees from one agency to find and work in real time with employees from another agency, whether they are across the street or across an ocean. As seen in this chapter, some of these programs can provide collaboration and location of both content and expertise. There are many variations on these types of collaborative models and programs; no single software does it all, so the challenges for homeland security executives will be to select, design, and deploy systems using the right components with the proper level of security, data lifecycle management, and user training. Systems must be portable and flexible, with generic interfaces built with interchangeable platforms.

Such homeland security systems will require a conscientious effort toward improving government information technology practices, such as the use of enterprise architectures and the use of industry standards. In the end this will result in more effective government agencies and a more secure country. The new priorities of homeland security are transforming traditional approaches to government collaboration and information sharing. Before, budgets and project funding drove those who built these software systems, failures were typical, and delays common. Today that is no longer acceptable; if a vendor fails to deliver on a project or a program doesn't work, no longer can a homeland security organization afford the luxury of not meeting its deadlines or objectives. Too much is at stake after 9/11.

No longer is failure to communicate or collaborate between agencies self-imposed, and no longer can goals be matched to resources and budgets. Such luxuries cannot be counted on anymore. Today, commercial software exists with which multiple agencies can be linked to enable them to connect the dots. Programs exist that can be called upon to support seamless agency collaboration; only existing data hoarding cultures stand in the way. The collaborative tools are as varied as the expertise of agencies and the information they aggregate and store. Software is available for the construction of portals for housing sophisticated collaboration centers, which can be used by thousands of users to view and post content culled from multiple agency systems while communicating in real time via instant messaging. There also are online collaboration tools that enable agencies to seamlessly link multiple local, state, and federal subject-area experts when a potential threat is identified. Collaborative systems can be used to provide dashboard views to monitor potential security threats at borders and transportation hubs. Indeed, many of the most valuable new functions will be built by linking resources that already exist. Agencies in the past saw no need to link disparate data sources, but today that is no longer the case. The intelligence is in the networking of content and expertise.

Current collaborative commercial systems can provide secure, scalable, Web-based access to content and expertise from multiple agencies. Homeland security portals can provide real-time data and experts to connect analysts and investigators, including those charged with first responder duties or other first-line defense missions such as monitoring border traffic. These portals will enable multiple agencies to share information about ocean, land, and air traffic that needs to be monitored in transit, before crossing the U.S. border. Collaborative software could be used by the Federal Motor Carrier Safety Administration, which monitors the licensing of cargo-truck drivers, to notify homeland security personnel via a portal that a truck attempting to enter the United States from Canada may need to have an elevated level of inspection. Similar types of systems can be used to feed information to the portal from wireless transponders and Global Positioning System units, which are attached to cargo containers to monitor if they are tampered with en route.

Such portals can provide real-time access to the supply chain of data required by homeland security agencies and can incorporate an understanding of the use of such information along with rules for data access and sharing. Users can be assigned an administrative ID account so that the tracking of their use is monitored. Real-time collaborative software can be deployed to provide an organization wide instant messaging for real-time text communication. It can enable users to see who is online at any given time and deliver proactive notification about time-sensitive events to better coordinate local, state, and federal emergency services. These portals can be divided into "swarming teams" of groups, with administrators from individual agencies controlling their own content. Each administrator also dictates who can access specific documents and who can join knowledge centers that are developed to enable users to collaborate via threaded discussions.

Homeland security collaborative portals can be packaged with advanced capabilities, such as secure audio and videoconferencing, enabling users to enter a team workspace and establish virtual meetings. Software can go to the user's desktop and go away once he stops using it. Because portals and instant messaging can link known specialists in emergency response, homeland security organizations can set up in advance the mechanisms to identify ahead of time experts who may be needed to quickly collaborate for a wide variety of threat scenarios. Homeland security organizations can also create connections on the fly for locating and linking experts during and after an attack. Homeland security organizations and their executives need to continuously discover and catalog the focus and expertise of agency personnel by examining data collected in e-mail messages, from discussion groups, or from published work. Task forces need to study and identify experts within and outside government for collaboration in the event of attacks via several terrorist scenarios using an assortment of weapon types.

Linking people to address potential homeland security requests is a clear need for first responders, but law enforcement and intelligence agencies also are tackling the need to filter massive reams of data that may be housed at several different organizations. For example, federal agencies can check information found on visa applications against the counterterrorism data in the State Department's Tipoff system to help prevent suspected terrorists from gaining entry to the United States. Originally designed for use only by State employees, the system can feed information to other agencies, with a common database they can use to share information relating to possible terrorist threats, activities, and identities. In this case, as with many in the homeland security context, much of the value comes not from building a brand new system, but from capitalizing on resources and skills already in place.

Historically, federal intelligence agencies thought that keeping investigative information and systems hidden from one another was the most effective way to keep an eye on potential terrorists. Various legal and technical barriers contributed to the long-standing divide, not to mention the occasional turf battle. Now, however, with new security threats, these government organizations are working with one another, as well as with state and local agencies, to improve the flow of security-related data. Initiatives are under way to open up government internal networks so data can move more freely from employee to employee. This involves linking such networks as CIA's Intelink, the FBI's Law Enforcement Online (LEO), the State Department's OpenNet, and the Justice Department's Regional Information Sharing Systems (RISS).

The FBI's LEO network is an online service for domestic law enforcement officers and criminal justice officials. In service since 1995, the network has approximately 32,500 members. LEO has become the home to the Joint Terrorism Task Force Information Sharing Initiative pilot program, designed to integrate federal, state, and local databases in specific regions and then expand nationwide.

The Justice Department's RISS network has been in use for more than two decades and helps state and local law enforcement agencies exchange information. Consisting of six regional centers that share intelligence and coordinate efforts against criminal networks that operate across jurisdictions, RISS serves more than 6,200 law enforcement agencies in 50 states.

The CIA has been focusing on Intelink, the network emerging as the top rung on the information-sharing ladder. All of these agencies are moving to integrate and collaborate their data via these existing networks and databases.

While these networks currently enable thousands of homeland security users to access classified and unclassified information, a great deal of work remains to be done before all the data needed during an investigation is available via a few keystrokes. Collaborating on all this data has less to do with the technical aspects and more to do with getting greater interagency coordination, amendments to current laws, new agency procedures, and cultural changes in agencies and their analysts and investigators. The ultimate goal is to connect different intelligence networks with the type of collaborative software covered in this chapter with portable, generic, Web-based interfaces so that they can easily find and examine pertinent information.

The easy flow of information should cut the time local, state, and national investigators, officers, and analysts need to piece together snippets of data. Ideally, a

Virginia state trooper should have access to data that would enable him to know that a person detained at a highway stop had his visa revoked by the State Department. The desire for better integration among law agencies' systems is not new, and these networks have been in place for years. However, not until 9/11 was the need to integrate and collaborate all this data a national priority. The evolution of technology and the acceptance of standard protocols such as IP and virtual private networks have made it simpler for agencies to exchange information securely using widely available networks. But more importantly, there has been a growing recognition that different government groups need to share information. Historically, investigators in one jurisdiction often did not know that data that could assist them in an investigation was available in another department's system. The Beltway shootings dramatically demonstrated this, with the suspected snipers having been stopped repeatedly near the shooting. The investigators, not having access to the data to see this, could not connect the dots.

At the federal level, there are issues of security. For example, intelligence groups have classified information with very specific limits on access levels: Top Secret is accessed by select officials in agencies such as the CIA and FBI; Sensitive is information of a military nature and is primarily accessed by the Defense Department; Policy data is accessed by individuals who develop the policies that outline who should have access to what; and then there is unclassified data. However, these levels of data access and classification can be set for integration and collaborative software agency systems via some of the programs described in this and prior chapters to control cleared users to restricted access to parts of or all the data.

Homeland security organizations will determine the network and system interfaces to move data from place to place and who will have access at what level. This can be done by focusing and using existing industry standards such as Secure Sockets Layer (SSL), X.509 digital certificates, public-key infrastructures, Standard Generalized Markup Language, eXtensible Markup Language, Web services, and browsers. The idea is to provide pointers to data locations rather than extracts of the data itself. As discussed in Chapter 2, "Aggregation: How to Leverage the Web, Robots, and Commercial Demographics for Entity Validation," the idea is not to move the data, but instead to move users and analysts to where the data is stored. That means that individual agencies would be responsible for providing authorized users with access to specific data on their systems, rather than supplying their data, or exporting it, to a system maintained elsewhere. The data stays where it is, but aggregation, integration, and collaboration by homeland security organizations and their personnel take place using agent technology. No doubt a big challenge to these processes will revolve around access to personal information.

The U.S. Constitution provides citizens with basic protections, such as a right to privacy, so agencies have to be extremely careful about safeguarding this information. Who should be granted access to this sensitive data? For example, the State Department is now struggling with how much information can be shared about immigrants in the United States. Corporations were concerned that if they made their vulnerabilities known, someone could use the Freedom of Information Act (FOIA) to gain that data and damage their public image. However, Congress included a provision in the USA PATRIOT Act that exempts critical infrastructure information from FOIA requests.

The CIA, the FBI, and the Justice and State departments all have been examining ways to open their networks with some of the features such as secure e-mail, online chat rooms, bulletin boards, and access to selected applications and databases. Now the goal is to collaborate these information sources between agencies, to make information available to whoever has the need and authorization to see it, whether they are FBI agents, CIA analysts, border customs inspectors, state police officers, or first responders. Homeland security organizations face an enormous challenge in addressing a multitude of threats to national security.

In order to counteract potential future threats, these government organizations need to create the necessary infrastructure to manage critical data and share it efficiently with appropriate state, local, and federal agencies. Some of these collaborative software suites provide a framework to access information from disparate sources and securely share that information across various agencies, empowering homeland security organizations to efficiently coordinate, plan, and prevent terrorist activities and coordinate emergency responses better. In the next chapter we will see how text mining technologies and software can serve homeland security organizations in coping with a sea of documents, e-mails, news feeds, and other unstructured content.

5 Categorization: The Techniques for the Clustering of Concepts from Unstructured Content

In This Chapter

- Categorization Techniques
- The Evolution of Categorization of Unstructured Content
- Categorization for Homeland Security

Categorization is the organization and classification of semistructured and unstructured content, which for homeland security organizations may involve the analysis of a massive flowing amount of documents, spreadsheets, news articles, press releases, tables from relational databases, online forms, query results, directories, travel records, financial files, e-mail messages, chat sessions, instant message archives, Web server logs, and so on. It may even involve multimedia objects such as digital images, graphics, audio and video files, animation, and engineering drawings. However, for the most part categorization for homeland security purposes will probably focus on capturing, extracting, organizing, and routing unstructured text as it is found in documents, reports, Web pages, news feeds, and e-mail.

Categorization software uses a combination of advanced multiple linguistic analyses as well as neural networks, machine learning, and proprietary algorithms to automatically tag text and classify it. These categorical tools can analyze huge amounts of text, generating a hierarchy of relevant classes of topics using a variety of predefined semantic, syntactic, statistical, and artificial intelligence techniques to classify them. They do this in an effort to sort and classify unstructured content into a semblance of categories of key concepts.

These categorization software tools vary in their accuracy and in the method by which they go about tagging and classifying unstructured content. Some are more autonomous than others; for example, in spite of the benefits of autonomous tagging and taxonomy generation, some software such as Recommind eschews the classification process as too cumbersome and inaccurate. More advanced products rely on latent clues in the text, which can be analyzed on the fly in a more accurate and dynamic classification scheme. Due to the classification scheme for tagging content, some of these text-mining tools are language independent, making them ideal for homeland security applications because they rely on the structure and positioning of words rather than linguistics for the classification of documents.

Because some of these tools can classify documents flowing to and from individuals by examining their e-mail, chat, instant messages, and documents, they can also be used to identify experts in organizations, similar to collaboration tools covered in the previous chapter. Many of these categorization products create dynamic expertise profiles based on the text that flows to and from individuals. They rank concepts in the text according to relevancy and frequency, building up profiles based on the results of their schematic ranking. These profiles can also be created by using information from an organization's internal Lightweight Directory Access Protocol (LDAP) to personalize content delivery.

Unstructured content, whether text or rich media such as images, audio, and video, must first be indexed, classified, and tagged with metadata in order for categorical tools to be able to retrieve and route its output to those profiled as requiring the information. As we found out in Chapter 2, "Aggregation: How to Leverage the Web, Robots, and Commercial Demographics for Entity Validation," metadata is data about data. It identifies what a document is about. Unlike structured databases where metadata clearly defines each data field in a table, unstructured documents such as text and rich media have no clear definition, which is where categorical tools come in: They automate the tagging and organization process.

For homeland security applications, this type of software can be grouped into those that perform clustering of concepts or keywords and those that perform text extraction, along with search and retrieval functions, and lastly those that do link and relationship analysis of text. However, all must first go through some sort of conversion and tagging of unstructured content, converting it into a structured format for visual display. There is categorization software that performs multiple language translations, while some generates link analysis. Ideally, a combination of tools and functions is probably the best solution for homeland security and threat integration analyses, where one tool would capture the unstructured content, categorizing it into key concepts and parsing over to another for converting it into a structure format for visual display by yet another specialized instrument for clustering or decision tree analysis via a data mining tool.

CATEGORIZATION TECHNIQUES

Two key goals in the autonomous organization of unstructured text are precision and recall. Precision is measured according to the correct classification of documents into relevant categories, and recall is measured in terms of all of the relevant documents that were correctly classified out of all that existed. To boost performance categorization, software vendors use various search and retrieve functions, such as content identification, which lists the locations where content can be found, such as an intranet, databases, and servers. Crawling is another function, also known as *spidering,* in which the indexing engine follows all the hyperlinks in the unstructured content. Most modern index and search engines no longer work in batch mode but continuously update the index to ensure the metadata is always current. The techniques are constantly evolving with each new update and software version, and with continuing consolidations and mergers of key players in the marketplace.

Another function of categorization is classification, or indexing, which is the key differentiating factor between categorization engines. Indexing techniques range from organizing full text by words of a Web site or document to complete semantic analysis of their content. Full-text search engines will index all the words in a document or Web page as well as any metadata associated with that document. In an HTML file, keywords can be designated using a <META> tag. The search engine will use this metadata during its indexing and classification of key words. The effective ranking of retrieved documents is a critical component of categorization engines and is measured as a value of its relevance.

Statistical and artificial intelligence algorithms may also be used for weighting relevance to calibrate the frequency of terms in documents, their position in a document, their proximity to other words, and other types of associations and hidden relationships. The algorithms may include clustering ones, such as k-nearest neighbor from statistics, the AI-based Self-Organizing Maps (SOM), or other types of pattern recognition technologies such as Bayesian inference, Support Vector Machines, and neural networks.

Bayesian Networks: Categorizing Uncertainty

Bayesian networks attempt via inference to assess the probability that a document actually contains content that is relevant to a term, given that the term occurs in a number of documents. Mathematically, this technique compares the number of occurrences of the search term in a single document with the number of occurrences of that term in a group of documents. If a term occurs more frequently in one document than in others, the categorizing engine infers a higher relevancy and generates a higher score for that document. Bayesian networks are models for representing uncertainty in knowledge; they use probability theory to manage uncertainty by explicitly representing the conditional dependencies between the differences of data components. Bayesian networks compute conditional probabilities between independent conditions. For example, let's consider the following scenario: A person walks outside and finds that the street and lawn are wet. He concludes that it has rained recently. Furthermore, the person decides that he does not need to water his roses. Assume the following set of rules:

rain or sprinklers → street = wet
rain or sprinklers → lawn = wet
lawn = wet → soil = moist
soil = moist → roses = okay

We can directly transform this into a graph. By considering each variable as r.v. with possible states of true and false, we can construct conditional probability tables for r.v. that reflect our knowledge of the world (see Figure 5.1).

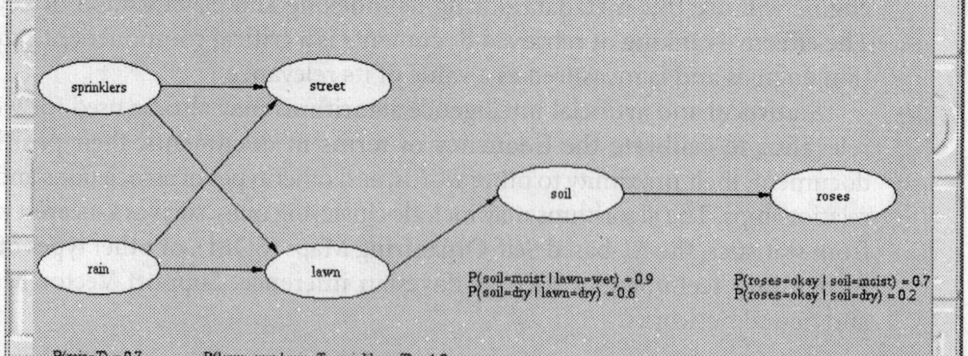

FIGURE 5.1 Sample Bayesian network.

Let's compute the joint probability of the world where the roses are okay, the soil is dry, the lawn is wet, the street is wet, the sprinklers are off, and it is raining:

P(sprinklers = F, rain = T, street = wet, lawn = wet, soil = dry, roses = okay) = P(roses = okay | soil = dry) × P(soil = dry | lawn = wet) × P(lawn = wet | rain = T, sprinklers = F) × & & P(street = wet | rain = T, sprinklers = F) × P(sprinklers = F) × P(rain = T)

Substituting the appropriate numbers from the tables, we get $0.2 \times 0.1 \times 1.0 \times 1.0 \times 0.6 \times 0.7 = 0.0084$ as the probability of this scenario.

Conditional tables at each node must contain all possible combinations of assignments. For space purposes, we give a reduced collection.

Support Vector Machines: Categorization via Vectors

As previously mentioned, support vector machines (SVMs) is yet another technique for categorizing unstructured content. SVMs analyze patterns of text and their relationships, treating a document as a collection of words and phrases that have meaning and can be represented mathematically as a vector. The vector's dimension represents the terms it contains, and its magnitude represents the number of occurrences of the words. SVMs calculate the similarity or dissimilarity of documents by comparing these vectors. Like other classification algorithms such as CART, SVM can work only with number values, so terms are converted prior to modeling and categorizing them. Also like neural networks, SVMs require training sessions with data sets of terms in order for modeling and categorization to take place.

Neural Networks: Mapping Meaning

Neural networks are a very important pattern recognition technology developed during the late twentieth century and applied to a variety of data and text mining problems. In describing how neural networks work in the classification of unstructured content, it is important to take a short historical review over their development. In the 1930s, Alan Turing discovered a way to represent logical propositions in algebraic form. He went on to develop a so-called universal machine and a conceptualization of the mind as a computational function. His work is the foundation of modern computer science. It is also the foundation for a great deal of modern cognitive science—the idea that the mind operates as a physical symbol-processing device, and that thinking is very much like working through a logical proof.

In 1943, Warren S. McCulloch and Walter Pitts invented a way to conceive of the operation of neurons, the nerve cells that make up the brain, as abstract computational devices. Small networks of neurons could be organized to perform each of the basic logical functions (AND, OR, and NOT) that were the building blocks of all the logical relationships of humans. This work gave the first hint of how the brain might actually produce thinking. The main problem, however, was that there was no obvious way to build complex interlaced, dynamic networks out of these simple elements.

At about the same time, Donald Hebb proposed that the brain learned by strengthening these connections between neurons, as they became activated at the same time. He proposed that memories were the result of cell assemblies learning to activate one another. In other words, the process of learning was based on the strength of the associations of the links between neurons. Each input neuron codes for the presence of a particular feature or the value of a specific feature. The neuron could be turned on when the feature is present and turned off when it is absent, or the degree to which it is turned on could depend on the strength or value of the input feature. In the case of categorization of text, each input neuron would be designed to respond to the presence of a specific word in the input text. A learning process would cause the network to learn the mapping from the input samples by changing the connection strengths (weights) among the various neurons in response to examples used to train its models.

Eventually Frank Rosenblatt came up with a way to allow the networks of McCulloch and Pitts to program themselves on the basis of their experience. He called these networks "perceptrons" because he used them as automatic perceiving devices. His method employed feedback (the perceptron learning rule) to change the strength of the connections among the neurons. For example, he could set up his perceptrons to learn a specified classification task in which some input patterns were to be classified into one group and other input patterns were to be classified into a different group. One output neuron, for example, would be intended to be active when the patterns from group 1 were presented to its inputs and be inactive otherwise. Another output neuron would be intended to be active when patterns from group 2 were presented and inactive otherwise. He provided the network with examples of each of these types of patterns and their appropriate classifications. If an output was supposed to be active in response to a particular pattern and it was not, then the connections leading to that output neuron were strengthened. If it was supposed to be inactive and it was not, then connections leading to that neuron were weakened. This discovery led to a way to let a "synthetic artificial brain" organize itself on the basis of a training experience; it was one of the first attempts at pattern recognition via software.

A few years later, Marvin Minsky and Seymour Papert wrote a highly critical critique of Rosenblatt's perceptron in which they pointed out that it could not solve some very basic problems that humans could solve. Therefore, perceptrons could not be the basis for computational intelligence, the emulation of human intelligence, or pattern recognition. The problem they used to make their argument was that of the XOR, or exclusive OR problem. The XOR starts with a set of marbles, some of which are green, some red, some are large, and some are small. The marbles that are large or green but not both, or those that are small or red but not both, belong in group 1, the keeper group; others belong to group 2, the loser group.

The experiment starts by reaching into the marble bag and pulling out a marble. It is large and red—is it a keeper or a loser? It is large, so maybe it's a keeper, and it's not green, so therefore it is a keeper. The next one is small and red, so it is definitely a loser.

	Large	***Small***
Red	Keeper	Loser
Green	Loser	Keeper

A perceptron could readily learn to classify the red and the green or to classify the large and the small, but it could not learn the unique combination rule that is shown in the table. The XOR problem is one that is not linearly separable, meaning that there is no line that one could draw on the table that would put all of the members of group 1 on one side of the line and the members of the other group on the other side. Rosenblatt's perceptron learning rule could only learn problems that were linearly separable. With their paper, Minsky and Papert froze all interest and funding from the government in the area of neural networks for several years.

In 1986 David Rumelhart and James McClelland published a paper that described how to build multilayer perceptrons that could solve problems that were not linearly separable. Their work led to a sudden rebirth of interest in neural networks as a computational basis both for pattern recognition and for artificial intelligence. Their work led to an explosion of research into using neural networks to solve a number of problems that had resisted solution under the traditional logical approaches, such as linear regression and other statistical processes.

Neural networks are particularly well suited to solving problems that are difficult to describe verbally. They can seemingly without effort solve problems that are difficult to solve using traditional methods. Neural networks are pattern recognition systems designed to replicate the way humans learn, by training, testing, and subtle adjustment to errors over time. However, by harnessing the computing power of today's CPUs, they can quickly converge on pattern recognition solutions, such as those facing private industry and the government.

Neural network models are brain-style software computational models; they mimic biological structures. They consist of webs of highly interconnected computational neurons, each interacting with the other neurons in the network through connection paths analogous to the axons and dendrites of real human neurons. These network models have been found to be very successful at problems such as pattern recognition and others that have resisted solution by more conventional computational approaches. In their most general form, neural networks consist of a set of input neurons that receive activation by environmental stimuli and events, a set of output neurons that return information, and one or more groups of neurons between the input and output neurons.

Neural network-based categorization systems do not use rules, but instead can automatically "train" on their own by being exposed to training document examples, which occurs when they are exposed to samples by users. Systems that use neural network technology sometimes require very large training sets, which are split into two parts: a training set and a testing set. In the training set, samples of documents with terms such as "biological pathogens" are fed in order for the neural network to iteratively adjust the weight of its internal nodes until it learns to recognize and correctly classify this category of documents. Once trained, the system can be exposed to an unseen test set in which a number of documents with "biological pathogens" are contained, and the neural network-based categorization system should be able to correctly identify a high percentage of them and classify them into a predetermined category.

The brain solves the problem of understanding the meaning of sentences by forming vast interconnected networks among the words and their meanings. These vast networks allow people to make inferences, understand analogies, and do the myriad other things that people use words to do. Similarly, neural networks can be used to form learning associations to organize large groups of classes from unstructured repositories. Neural network-based categorical systems have been used in the area of litigation support.

Clustering Concepts

Clustering is yet another method of categorization of unstructured content. It can be done by using either a k-nearest neighbors statistical algorithm or SOM neural network. Clustering is the process of grouping documents based on the co-occurrence of words or concepts in a large group of documents. The clustering algorithms look at the placement of words with respect to each other, their placement in the document, their frequency, and how close the terms appear to each other. A search for a word or a term will return documents in a cluster that are the most relevant based on distance proximity as measured by the algorithms. Clustering classifies documents by measuring associations among documents that have the most topics in common, forming categories of clusters into taxonomies.

One of the advantages of categorization by clustering is that no training is required, and for homeland security applications this is critical because in most instances agencies will be dealing with highly dynamic content, such as news feeds. Clustering assembles documents that share keywords or phrases that are statistically similar, and each cluster is representative of text associated with related topics. Once primary clusters are identified, categorization software creates a larger taxonomy. For example, a cluster may be created where the words "research project," "biological pathogens," and "Jihad" are found, but another cluster may also be created where only "research project" and "biological pathogens" are associated, in which case the potential of an alert is lessened.

A rather unique and innovative approach to the categorization of textual documents and Web sites has been developed by Vivísimo, a search engine that licenses its technology and its proprietary clustering engine algorithm. Vivísimo performs the automatic organization of documents into groups or clusters, which differs from other techniques such as classification, taxonomy building, tagging, and so on. Instead of producing a flat list of groups, the engine organizes groups into a hierarchy or tree, so that users can zoom in on items of interest while keeping visible an overview of all the topics. Vivísimo's clustering methods interleave the process of forming groups with the step of describing them, much like people might do by hand. Vivísimo forms a group of clusters and judges to ensure it is concise, accurate, and distinctive, and otherwise it is rejected. Vivísimo's clustering technology has achieved a very high rate of accuracy both in the categorization of internal documents within organizations and in the ranking of Web sites, where sometimes less is more, especially when searching through large volumes of records.

On the Web, Vivísimo works more or less like any other search engine: The user types in a query, hits the Search button, and gets back *x* number of searches, but the handy difference is that in a frame to the left of the search results, Vivisimo presents a short, clickable list of the popular topics in the search results. For example, using the GuruNet interface, which uses four popular search engines—All The Web, Google, Teoma, and Vivísimo—a search was generated using the keywords "terrorist cells." The results were as follows:

All The Web: 391,550 hits

Google: 509,000 Category: Society → Issues → Terrorism → Counterterrorism

Teoma: 119,200 Refine Suggestions to narrow search: Terrorist Network, Sleeper Cell, and so on

Resources Links: Terrorist Organizations Intelligence Analysis

Vivísimo: 169, and to the left a screen broke the results into these subcategories:

- Terrorist cells (169)
- Al-Qaeda (29)
- Activities (19)
- Terrorist Network (17)
- Terrorist attacks (19)
- Sleeper (14)
- Europe (8)
- World Trade Center (6)
- Government (7)
- FBI, Cities (9)
- Buffalo, Alleged Terrorists (5)

As this example demonstrates, the clustering technology of Vivísimo dramatically squashes the matched records and provides additional, concise lists of related topics for further analysis.

Linguistic Analysis Techniques

Another group of techniques for organizing unstructured text comes from linguistic categorization using morphological analysis, syntactic analysis, semantic analysis, and entity extraction. Morphological analysis, or stemming, concentrates on recognizing the roots of words, so that it knows that "bomber," "bombing," and "bombed" are the stem of "bomb" and classifies and indexes them accordingly. Syntactic analysis looks at the position of a word in a sentence and uses grammatical rules to identify its components. For example, the sentence "Wolfowitz says U.S. must act against terrorist threats even if intelligence is 'murky'." identifies the subject (Wolfowitz) the verb (act), the object (threats), and so on. Semantic analysis, on the other hand, relies on language- and domain-specific taxonomies or ontologies in its classification scheme, so that it recognizes the difference between "*The Matrix* was shot in Alameda, CA" and "The Al-Qaeda shot down a plane." Finally, entity extraction is the process of identifying known words in a document and inferring meaning on the basis of position of the words in a phrase or a sentence. For example, in "The Al-Qaeda shot down a plane," it would understand that the Al-Qaeda is a terrorist group.

Together these techniques are used to emulate natural language processing (NLP), which is the way humans speak, read, and write. Natural language text and retrieval systems attempt to understand the patterns and idioms of spoken and written text in processing user queries. Since NLP processing is language specific, the patterns vary between, for example, English and Arabic. In this instance, lexicons are used to assist the categorization process by using regional lists of entities, such as cities, countries, phrases, and names of organizations. Some NLP software providers license their engine, rules, and lexicon in order for users to integrate their software components into their applications. Some categorical software providers claim that by combining both NLP and statistical or machine learning techniques, or by the use of proprietary patented algorithms, their software can "understand" human questions and answer them directly. NLP software providers have also developed industry- and government-specific ontologies to improve the categorization process. For example, an NLP engine using an information system domain ontology would know that the text string "java" refers to that of a computer language and not coffee or an island.

Mapping Content

Taxonomy is a hierarchy of topics grouped along the lines of their natural relationship. For example, the Yellow Pages and Yahoo! are two common examples of taxonomies. Taxonomies are used to complement full-text classification and retrieval, and most products have the capability for users to add, delete, or change topics. Most products come with prebuilt starter taxonomies that users can refine, but the process of refining them can be time consuming, requiring skilled intervention and guidance. This equates to human intervention and time, two requirements that a homeland security organization often does not have. The process of developing the taxonomy starts with the selection of the training data sets to be categorized. Domain experts select these representative sets of documents with a sampling for each section of the taxonomy. The data is then "spidered" in order to extract key concepts, from which clusters are created and a taxonomy structure is developed, which must be reviewed by subject matter experts to ensure it is correct. Once the taxonomy structure is ready, a larger data target is used to populate taxonomy with links and pointers. From there, metadata is extracted, usually in XML format, with the last phase of the process being the maintenance of the taxonomy.

The objective is that once classification rules have been developed for this taxonomy, new incoming documents, e-mails, files, and so on are automatically categorized when they are introduced to the system. Ideally, the system is constantly learning and adjusting categories on the basis of new content. In a fairly static corporate, legal, or medical environment, this can realistically function quite well, but in a homeland security situation, where the unexpected is the expected scenario, this may not work. To automate the training process, some tools will read and process documents, apply linguistic and semantic rules, and create tagged versions of the documents, which domain experts can review and validate. Tagged content makes the accuracy of categorization software more precise and allows for parametric searches. For example, once a document is tagged, its <META> tags such as <AUTHOR>, <ABSTRACT>, and <LOCATION> can be extracted and its related text used to produce a catalog that lists only the matching items, such as <AUTHOR>, John Brennan; <ABSTRACT>, TeeTick; <LOCATION>, McLean, VA. Such tagging is a fundamental premise of XML.

Personalized Content

Categorization software can also be used to direct specific unstructured content to employees of an organization based on profiles it develops. Either categorization profilers can be told explicitly what content a user wants to receive or autonomous agents can observe a user's selection of content and applications. An agent can create profiles containing metadata about users of an agency or departmental portal and use those profiles to determine what to present and route to each of them. The categorization component can deliver to users specific content based on keywords housed in the users' profiles, with updates as new content is created through multiple content streams from Web sites to document repositories. Also, databases can be monitored by information delivery services to route personalized data based on user interests at the frequency they specify. Categorization software uses profiling to push content through the use of intelligent agents, similar to the methods used by collaboration software, covered in the previous chapter.

Profiles can be set up by system administrators or by the users themselves through system menus. These profiles can be static, set by the user manually, or dynamically built over time and created by software agents that monitor information flow to and from users, monitoring for keywords used in their e-mail and in their queries over the Web and intranets. Categorization by mining users' e-mail is increasingly important in view of the growth of this medium of communication in organizations. By 2005, the number of e-mail messages sent annually worldwide will reach 9.2 trillion, according to market research firm IDC. However, the use of e-mail, instant messaging, and Web browsing to customize and personalize content, as we discussed in the previous chapter, may create problems for a homeland security organization because it may infringe on a user's privacy. Policies need to be set and consent needs to be provided by users for this type of monitoring to take place.

A primary goal of categorization software is to automatically collect and route relevant information from unstructured content to users based on profiles of interests and positions. Some of the more advanced programs automate the process of extracting this unstructured text, converting it into structured information, and populating databases with a set of XML tags. This method of information extraction and automatic tagging relies on semantic learning, in which words, names, and phrases are analyzed prior to categorization. Some products combine categorization, information retrieval, and natural language processing with the goal of identifying key concepts, relationships, and events in documents. In the following section we will provide an overview of some of the best software in this category.

The Categorization Providers

The primary goal of these software systems is to collect, categorize, and make available to analysts the unstructured data from within and outside an organization, a process often referred to as either *search and discovery* or *text mining.* Because so many systems now use natural language processing, it is more and more possible for systems to infer the user's meaning and intent and to present results that enable the user to discover hidden key concepts not immediately explicit in the original query. Many of these software systems use a combination of technologies to cluster concepts and present their results to a user in a way that enables him to gain actionable insight, which for a homeland security organization could mean decisive proactive engagement.

Applied Semantics Gets Googled

Applied Semantics uses natural language processing to provide content categorization, summarization, and metadata creation. Its platform, Conceptual Information Retrieval Communication Architecture (CIRCA), includes ontologies of millions of concepts and relationships. Unlike typical search engines, which retrieve information on the basis of the exact string of text the user enters, CIRCA maps words in the document with concepts in the ontology. CIRCA technology understands, organizes, and extracts knowledge from Web sites and information repositories in a way that mimics human thought, enabling it to be more effective in its retrieval.

Applied Semantics technology is used primarily by the publishing industry. It uses its news processing software to helps newspapers, e-publishers, and content aggregators reduce their operating costs and increase productivity during newswire capture, editing, archiving, and syndication, which is very similar to the functions performed by intelligence agencies that commonly monitor foreign Web sites, news feeds, and other sources of foreign events on a daily basis. A key application of the CIRCA technology is its AdSense product that enables Web publishers to understand the key themes on Web pages and deliver highly relevant and targeted advertisements. Google acquired Applied Semantics in 2003.

Ask Jeeves: Social Networking

Ask Jeeves provides natural language question answering and advanced search technologies for organizations via the Web and networks through its Jeeves Solution software. The Ask Jeeves Web search portal and its enterprise search solution use the Teoma search engine, which employs a subject-specific popularity ranking method. Teoma, which means "expert" in Gaelic, uses the concepts of *refinement* and *relevance* in its search algorithms. Instead of ranking results based upon Web sites with the most links leading to them, Teoma performs a dynamic ranking of a Web site to find its subject-specific popularity among communities of similar pages to determine its relevancy on both the Web and an organization's intranet.

According to Ask Jeeves, the most accurate result when searching on the Web is *content relevance* because, like social networks in the real world, the Web is clustered and made up by small local communities that are grouped around Web pages closely related to the same subject. Teoma is a search technology that uses communities and associations to target Web sites; creators argue that this is how things naturally occur on the Web. This unique method allows Teoma to generate more finely tuned search results, exposing dimensions of the Web that have previously gone unseen by other search engines. This method provides preference to pages that are linked from other pages having the same subject matter; it is a method of categorization by social networking. The tool is designed for customer support and self-service and can index up to 200,000 documents; it accepts keywords and Boolean and full sentence queries, and it performs natural language processing to extract meaning from queries. Using this concept of searching on the basis of social networking, terrorist-related links could be developed in the analysis of Web sites, e-mail addresses, instant messages, chat sessions, and other types of interactive digital communications via the use of the Teoma search engine.

Atomica: GuruNet

Founded originally as GuruNet, the firm also offers Atomica Enterprise, which ships with targeted, predefined search templates. The software works with standard Lightweight Directory Access Protocol directory services so that users can access only internal data sources for which they have set permissions. GuruNet is still available for free on the Web. Its search interface provides links to four main search engines: All The Web, Google, Vivísimo, and Teoma. It also includes several search accessories, called GuruNet Library, with references to thousands of online sources. Atomica stores meta-information about internal data sources, the Metasearch Engine queries multiple locations, and the Topic Builder unifies content across multiple data sources and integrates all data with enterprise security with a Windows client application.

Attensity: From Unstructured to Structured

The core function of Attensity's software is to convert unstructured text into a more usable structured format. Their software has the capability to extract pieces of data from free form text and combine it with structured information. The software has the capability to automate the extraction of relational events from free form text so that a text string such as "John Doe bought C4 from John Smith in Cairo on Oct. 4, 2002" can be extracted into a table format in the following subsets:

Event: Bomb
Bomber: John Doe
Arms Dealer: John Smith
Location: Cairo
Date: Oct. 4, 2002

The text extraction technology is highly accurate and can work with unknown words, misspellings, and ungrammatical constructions; nearly 100 single-spaced pages can be processed per second. Attensity's text extraction technology relies on structural linguistic principles in its translation from free form text to relational tables. For purposes of analytical processing, each row in a relational table represents an event and each column an attribute of that event. Clearly this tool has features that could be used for homeland security and intelligence applications, which is probably why In-Q-Tel was one of its venture capital investors.

The government intelligence version of the software is able to deal with linguistic constructs peculiar to that environment. It comes with a series of tools that enable users in classified environments to perform knowledge engineering processes without direct involvement from Attensity's implementation staff. The government version is integrated with various third-party products, including System Research and Development's Non-Obvious Relationship Awareness (NORA), enabling data extracted from free form text to be used for link analysis, trending, and data matching and association applications. One of the possible applications of Attensity software is in the conversion of unstructured text field reports into a structured format that lends itself to visual, link, and data analysis such as clustering, decision trees, predictive modeling, and other types of techniques to be discussed in more detail in Chapter 7, "Mining: Pattern Recognition and Agent Technologies for Analyzing Text and Data Remotely."

Clearforest: Classifying for the FBI

Formerly ClearResearch and formerly Instinct Software, this categorical software can be used for the analysis and visualization of a large collection of unstructured content such as documents, e-mails, and records. Clearforest software is based on an information extraction clustering technology it refers to as Unstructured Data Management (UDM), which employs natural language processing techniques coupled with "rulebooks" that define the way its classification engine identifies entities and facts in documents. Rulebooks are available from Clearforest in industry-specific taxonomies for the classification of documents, news feeds, articles, Web sites, and other unstructured content for financial, intellectual property, law enforcement, life science, government, and publishing market sectors.

Clearforest automatically reads and interprets text from multiple sources for purposes of identifying patterns, connections, trends, and features. The software tags documents via XML and outputs visual interactive formats, enabling the identification of new entities, facts, or events previously unknown to the user. The software can assimilate textual data of any size and structure, and it can extract key terms, assigning them to meaningful categories (taxonomies) and establishing their relationships. The result can be generated in a variety of visual formats such as maps, tables, and graphs. The software can automatically identify new and relevant concepts for tagging documents, such as new and emerging groups or technologies, and can be used to track and alert for all new terms, concepts, and groups. The names of key players, graphic and textual representation of their comparative distribution, interactive recursive cross-references, time-based charts of appearance, and visual maps of links between members of any category can be mapped in an interactive manner. The FBI is using Clearforest to tag and organize its internal documents.

Convera: Multimedia Categorizer

Convera's flagship RetrievalWare software enables users to search for and collect text, images, and video from databases, intranets, and the Internet. It identifies and indexes patterns in digital data, allowing for misspelled words and other inconsistencies when it performs searches. Convera also offers its Screening Room document imaging and video capture software. Convera's RetrievalWare (formerly Excalibur) information retrieval engine uses adaptive pattern recognition processing (APRP) and semantic network searching. APRP analyzes and matches binary patterns to locate similarities and proximity relationships, such as misspelled words or closely matching bitmap images. Semantic network searching recognizes word meanings and relationships and allows users to expand or narrow a search by offering semantically related words and phrases.

Convera provides a knowledge base of more than half a million word definitions and a million and a half word relationships to distinguish different meanings of words and yield greater precision in responding to natural language queries. The search engine's semantic network can expand queries for more complete recall and can be used for research and discovery searches. It includes a thesaurus and conducts morphological analysis, beyond simply stemming, tracking idioms, recognizing multiple meanings of words, and fuzzy searching. The engine can perform cross-lingual searches based on internal semantic networks for English, French, German, Spanish, Italian and Dutch.

Convera supports over 200 document types, including Lotus/Domino, FileNET Panagon, Microsoft Exchange, and Documentum, and can perform native bridges to Oracle, Sybase, Informix, and MS SQL databases. It also includes an ODBC bridge for other databases. A security model tracks authorization status across all instances of RetrievalWare, with additional security and authentication interfaces for third-party proxies and cross-repository authentication. A Java Server Page Toolkit is provided to allow programmers to customize indexing, the interface, searching, relevance rank, and result display functions. It provides APIs in C, C++, COM, ASP, and J2EE. .NET client and servers, Web services, and XML queries are also included. Additional modules support categorization tools with multiple level taxonomies and a Video Analysis Engine for automated shot-boundary detection, clip similarity matching with pattern recognition.

An important differentiator for Convera in the categorization of unstructured content market is its ability to work with video. Its Screening Room component converts video images to digital format and creates a storyboard of viewable thumbnail images; it also extracts any closed caption text. Screening Room Capture analyzes and categorizes the images. Video Asset Server stores the resulting metadata and indexes, as well as any annotation or closed-caption text, along with the content. Screening Room is aimed at people who are creating and managing large tape libraries or large numbers of digital assets. Instead of looking up entries in a card catalog or even a computer-based file system, with Screening Room users can simply execute a natural language query on the system to automatically scan the database, locate the best matches based on the query they entered, such as "show me YXZ record of EVENT taped on MMDDYY," and receive a set of metadata about that video. A user of Screening Room could determine if that was the video he was looking for without having to watch the entire tape. The Naval Research Laboratory is using Convera software in The Optical Retrieval Project Electronic Documents Online (TORPEDO) project. This video clipping application has potential for other homeland security applications.

DolphinSearch: Neural Network Classifier

DolphinSearch deals with the concept of indexing in a very unique manner; rather than creating categories via natural language processing or categorical programs processing to classify text into taxonomies or other methodologies that capture the semantic or meaning of relationships among documents, it uses neural networks to create what it calls "semantic profiles" in documents. DolphinSearch first starts by reading through and learning a repository of documents loaded into its file server. DolphinSearch goes about reading each document, extracting the text, breaking up each document into paragraphs of text, and transforming each paragraph into a mathematical value that can be used to train the neural network.

The neural network then forms connections among words that are strongly related to other words and that occur frequently in sentences and make up the same meanings. As the network reads the documents, it learns more and more about how each word is used in the context of the documents. Spurious or accidental relationships are "washed out," leaving behind only the most important and most dominant meanings and relationships. Through this process, DolphinSearch can learn from an entire set of documents that it reads, and the user has the option of feeding specific documents as part of the training process.

DolphinSearch employs this patented neural network methodology to read documents, extract their meaning, and perform searches based on this training. The software forms semantic profiles from these analyses, and these profiles are mathematical representations of the meaning of words and their relationship to the other words in the documents. These semantic profiles capture meaning and reduce ambiguity. When the software is used for a content search, DolphinSearch compares the semantic profiles of the query to the semantic profiles for each of the documents the software has been trained on. It then ranks the resulting document list by the degree of similarity between the semantic profile for the document and the semantic profile for the query. The result is a true fuzzy semantic search. Everything DolphinSearch knows about the meanings of words it learns from the documents it reads. Acronyms and words that are used in a unique way in the documents are learned as they are used, not confused with more generic meanings.

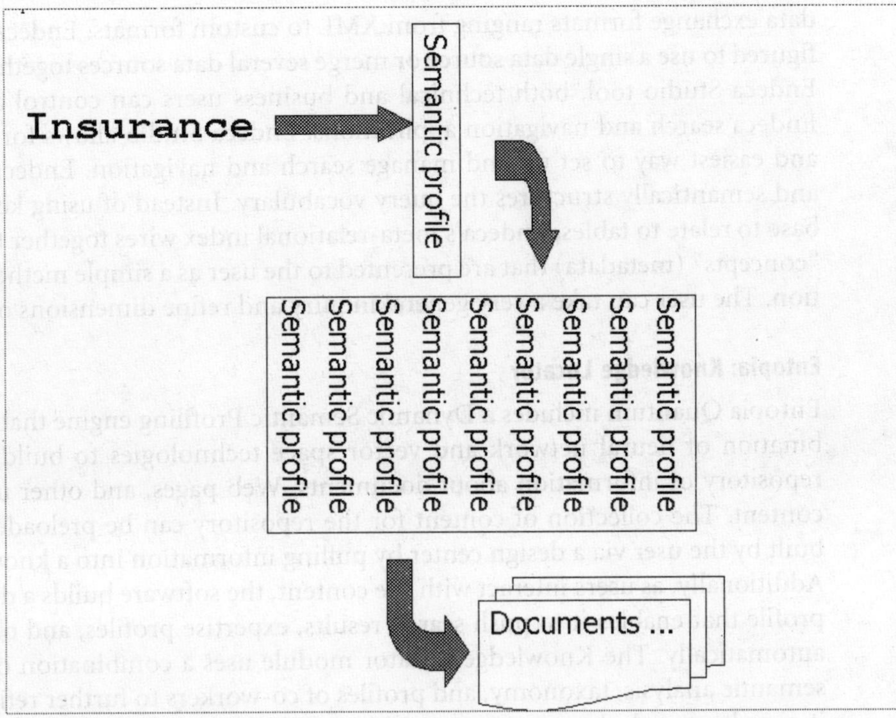

FIGURE 5.2 DolphinSearch using a semantic profile to search for a word in documents.

Endeca: Structure and Unstructured Searcher

Endeca uses a technique called Guided Navigation, which is based on its meta-relational indexing technology. Its enterprise search product, ProFind, uses Guided Navigation to present results to users in a way that lets the user see a range of categories associated with the query term and to browse the categories in a step-by-step fashion. The Endeca Navigation Engine platform supports a variety of operating systems, over 225 file formats, numerous enterprise repositories and databases, and over 20 foreign languages. It is also the only approach to searching that bridges structured and unstructured data. At each level of navigation, choices are presented to the user that reflect the current relationship between the query term and potential results.

Endeca imports data from over 225 existing formats and numerous content repositories into its own index format. The platform supports industry standard data exchange formats ranging from XML to custom formats. Endeca can be configured to use a single data source or merge several data sources together. Using the Endeca Studio tool, both technical and business users can control all aspects of Endeca search and navigation applications. Endeca Studio allows for the quickest and easiest way to set up and manage search and navigation. Endeca normalizes and semantically structures the query vocabulary. Instead of using keys in a database to relate to tables, Endeca's meta-relational index wires together thousands of "concepts" (metadata) that are presented to the user as a simple method of navigation. The user can take a very general inquiry and refine dimensions on the fly.

Entopia: Knowledge Locator

Entopia Quantum includes a Dynamic Semantic Profiling engine that uses a combination of neural network and vector space technologies to build a metadata repository of information about documents, Web pages, and other unstructured content. The collection of content for the repository can be preloaded or can be built by the user via a design center by pulling information into a knowledge base. Additionally, as users interact with the content, the software builds a dynamic user profile that enables it to push search results, expertise profiles, and other sources automatically. The Knowledge Locator module uses a combination of keywords, semantic analysis, taxonomy, and profiles of co-workers to further refine searches; it simultaneously locates content and experts across disconnected information repositories in an organization or on a network. It locates relevant documents based on their semantic content, on user activity surrounding such content, and on expertise related to the query. The K-Bus Knowledge Locator uses proprietary algorithms to ensure that the true relevancy of information is calculated just-in-time, using metadata created from the concepts contained in documents, collaboration efforts including discussions and edits, popularity and the lifecycle of information, as well as searcher's profile, social activity, and organizational context, thereby dramatically improving the quality (and not the quantity) of search results.

Entopia's Collaboration solution is based upon an enterprise server infrastructure that opens the doors of secure interactive collaboration. With Collaborate features installed and enabled, users and administrators are empowered with advanced security options, shared and private folders, threaded discussions, check in-check out, version and change control, and messaging notification. As knowledge is shared, changes are automatically sent to the database.

The Link/Temporal Analysis is exemplified in Entopia's knowledge visualization capabilities, which may be used to display a graphical, semantic network representation of the relationships between concepts contained in content when a query is selected. Entopia's Enterprise Social Networks Analysis solution is a diagnostic tool that enables managers to optimize information flow by identifying topic-based networks created by community leaders, subject matter experts, and peers. Entopia can perform multi-repository searches, expertise identification, social networks analysis, real-time collaboration, content management, free-form text classification, knowledge visualization, and storage resource management.

The K-Bus metadata repository is capable of handling extracted entities, and the Entopia Semantic analyzer includes a powerful entity extraction function. The combination of semantic concept tagging with the vector space support in K-Bus, which is done when documents are discovered, supports either dynamic or static categorization. The semantic processing offered by Entopia's K-Bus uses both linguistic and statistical processing to support any language. This suite of software components can be configured by a homeland security organization to find, collaborate, and communicate expertise and unstructured content over distributed locations.

Entrieva: Document Navigator

Entrieva's SemioMap software extracts phrases from documents to create topics and build conceptual maps and navigable diagrams of linkable constellations. Users can discover documents related to topics from these diagrams, and the software supports up to 200 document formats and databases. Entrieva provides the capability to monitor any data stream continuously, pulling in data that meets the established criteria of users and notifying them in real time of new updates. SemioTaxonomy uses the same categorizing technology to generate topics for inclusion in a hierarchical taxonomy. SemioTagger indexes the documents and builds a database of key concepts to be included in the taxonomy. The user is given the option to manually refine the topics generated by the algorithms and modify the classes or go with the automated process. A Topic Library is available with preconfigured taxonomies for a variety of industries. SemioSkyline is a 3-D viewer component for browsing documents' relevance without having to retrieve and read them.

FAST: Search and Transfer

FAST Search and Transfer combines search and real-time filtering technologies to solve the problem of searching and processing large volumes of information from continuous news feeds and large organization intranets. This feature makes this tool ideal for monitoring news developments and communications for intelligence purposes. Its core products include FAST Data Search for Internet and enterprise data; the product is scalable to hundreds of terabytes of data and users. FAST Web Search is a Web indexing solution used by Web portals and search engines. The high-speed crawler can scale millions of pages and hundreds of queries per second, and it can interface with standard databases including Oracle. It can handle XML hierarchies and multiple file formats, it supports over 50 languages, linguistic query features include stemming and spell checking, and it supports synonym lists, manual recommendation, and business rules.

Google: Search Appliance

Google offers its search technology to organizations via its Search Appliance. The software delivers Google's portal search capabilities to intranets with additional security and administrative features. Google can be configured to crawl protected areas on an intranet and return its search results only to users authorized to see the content. For example, a homeland security organization could set the search parameters to match the clearance levels of its users. Google uses a combination of text matching and ranking techniques to return results relevant to a query. The page ranking is based on the number of pages in the intranet that link to the given page; thus it is most functional in intranets supporting hyperlinks. There are more than 100 weights that determine a Google page rank; for example, a page indexed by the search engine will be listed if it is an exact match, but it will be ranked lower on the list than an exact match found on a more tightly linked page.

The engine's advanced search option allows users to filter results so that only more-recent pages are shown. Appliance uses Google's PageRank relevance sorting algorithm and provides excellent control of exactly which servers and directories are indexed. It handles over 200 file types, including HTML, PDF, PostScript, RTF, Microsoft Word, Excel, PowerPoint, WordPerfect, and Lotus. Appliance supports 28 languages and allows users to restrict searching to one of them. Its crawls are protected using Basic Authentication (passwords) and SSL, and it supports proxies. The appliance is designed for intranets and firewalls, with real-time reporting of indexing progress, including special listings for locations and problems.

Insightful: Meaning from Text

Insightful is a data analysis and research company offering a variety of search and retrieval products. InFact® is based on the company's expertise in business analytics, statistical data mining, and unstructured content retrieval. InFact uses natural language processing, including a proprietary algorithm, Latent Semantic Regression (LSR), for the reduction and classification of text, resulting in a document matrix. This technology allows InFact to extract meaning from text in a way that enables it to deliver answers to questions, rather than merely providing a list of sources in response to a query. InFact can be used to validate hypotheses, recognize patterns, understand causes, and predict outcomes from large amounts of textual information via intelligence analysts. Insightful also offers other data mining desktop and server level tools for analyzing structured data sets. Insightful products include InFact, Insightful Miner, S-PLUS®, StatServer®, and S-PLUS Analytic Server®, and the company's clients range from the National Institutes of Health, the U.S. Department of Defense, and 92 percent of the Top 25 ranked companies in the Forbes 500.

Intelliseek: Intelligent Searcher

Intelliseek's federated search product is the Enterprise Search Server (ESS). In addition to its ability to query multiple sources in parallel and collate results, ESS provides a number of features that enhance search and retrieval, particularly for intelligence applications. It has its own index and search capability for data sources that are not natively indexed, and it can produce a structured catalog from both structured and unstructured content. It adapts to results from its queries such that, over time, it routes queries to specific content sources on the basis of categories it has developed. It provides content tracking and personalized content delivery to alert users when topics have changed. Intelliseek also licenses its Content Mining Services to Independent Software Vendors (ISVs), System Integrators, and other application developers. These technologies include:

Phrase Miner: Intelliseek's phrase-mining toolkit uses a combination of methods to discover not only simple keywords in text but also longer phrases that distinguish one set of documents from another. From any document collection, it can mine discriminative phrases for a variety of tasks, including text mining and the discovery of trends.

Sentiment Miner: Intelliseek's technology scans text for statements indicating the author's opinions about a topic or any indication of subjective language. Sentiment Miner is modeled to detect correct interpretations, even in the face of complex grammar and word structure.

Classifiers: Once Intelliseek technology has identified and extracted specific features, classification tools sort the extracted data into meaningful sets or categories. Intelliseek applies one or more of numerous classification algorithms, including Rule-based, Bayesian, Decision Trees, Winnow, Maximum Entropy, and Support Vector Machines, to get the best performance for a given categorization need.

Extractors: Intelliseek's engineers and language specialists can train the software to identify specific text features or entities, customizing it to extract specific entities and features from regions of text.

ESS offers four types of searches:

Brokering: Passing a query to a source using its own search syntax and interpreting the response appropriately. Brokering is the choice where a Web-accessible search interface exists for the source and when maintaining security is the highest priority.

Bridges: This is used to search large data repositories when performance is a concern or existing search capabilities are inadequate. Bridges communicate directly with the application layer to provide secure, fast searches. Intelliseek currently offers a bridge to Lotus Domino and is developing others.

Indexing: Creates and maintains full-text indexes and search interfaces to content that is currently not accessible. This content may be stored in a number of locations, such as e-mail, shared drives, and Web content.

Catalog Building: Creates searchable, structured catalogs from semistructured content on the Internet.

ESS includes administration tools and an Agent Development Kit (ADK) that provides secure access to administrative services to allow users to add, edit, and remove search sources and terms easily. The architecture of ESS makes it easy to integrate into Enterprise Information Systems, for example, to create knowledge portals for news monitoring. Because of the attractive features it provides to intelligence gathering organizations, Intelliseek received funding from the CIA's In-Q-Tel venture capital firm. Its functionality makes this software an ideal vehicle for homeland security applications requiring the categorization of text and its dissemination to users.

Inxight: Categorization Engine

The SmartDiscovery search product focuses on unstructured data management. Aside from including a search engine, it is capable of taxonomy creation and categorization, entity extraction, document summarization, and content recommendation. The SmartDiscovery software can automatically organize unstructured data for more targeted information access. It dynamically enables the browsing of information via link analysis, speeding up document retrieval and delivery and enabling more accurate and thorough searches of document collection. The software supports multilingual documents and can perform automated meta tagging of millions of documents and thousands of categories. The Categorizer component assigns documents to categories from a group of subject taxonomy, using linguistic and statistical algorithms. Factiva, AltaVista, Oracle, SAS, and Verity use this categorization engine.

The MetaText component extracts and stores topical metadata about documents, including summaries, related documents, people, places, and things. Inxight includes a metadata repository and a search engine with concept search, full-text, and Boolean queries. Visualization is provided via its VizServer component, which displays maps of data in relational databases and unstructured data repositories for data and text mining processes. The metadata repository is based on entity extraction for identifying companies, locations, and key people. It can store in XML in the database or back in its original environment. Languages supported are Danish, Dutch, English, Finnish, French, German, Italian, Norwegian (Bokmål), Norwegian (Nynorsk), Portuguese, Spanish, and Swedish.

Mohomine: Extractor and Classifier

Mohomine develops technology that automatically classifies and extracts text from unstructured content. Its two primary products are the mohoClassifier and the mohoExtractor. The pattern-recognition techniques used by Mohomine can process huge volumes of text data, approximately 300 pages per second. The software is language independent and, according to Gartner, the marketing research firm, achieves a 60 to 90 percent classification accuracy rate. It uses a learn-by-example architecture combined with easy-to-understand and use APIs. Mohomine also received funding from In-Q-Tel and was acquired in 2003 by Kofax, the product-development subsidiary of the DICOM Group.

NextPage: Scaling for Security

NextPage is a content management vendor that has a focus on the publishing industry. Its NXT product is a complete electronic publishing suite for storing, assembling, securing, and distributing content online on CD/DVD or within corporate intranets, with federated search and navigation features. It indexes and classifies information and aggregates the index to enable users to search a range of content across widely distributed sources with a single query. NXT returns query results with links and summaries. It also provides a navigation view of the located content to enable browsing and discovery. The search engine component of NXT lends itself to the task of scaling millions of documents, which a homeland security organization may require. The software features include natural-language and content-based searching via keywords, Boolean operators, phrases, wildcards, stemming, synonyms, fields, proximity, nesting, and so on. It recognizes XML tagging for field data and is compatible with many file formats, including PDF, Microsoft Word, Excel, and PowerPoint.

Recommind: Software That Understands

Recommind's MindServer product suite uses machine-learning techniques for autonomous classification and indexing. It extracts and clusters concepts automatically, without the need for advanced training sets, taxonomies, or human intervention. It automatically creates thesauri based the frequency of words it find in documents, news feeds, or Web pages. The MindServer platform includes retrieval, categorization, and recommendation functions. The Categorizer component supports multiple repositories and multiple file formats. The Categorizer component includes taxonomy management functions. The Recommender component provides recommendations to users on the basis of usage profiles and can recommend documents, products, and people. Recommind's entity extraction capability has been recognized as being able to identify people, places, names, companies, and other entities in documents in over 300 file formats in 135 languages. The software can be used to construct industry-specific solutions in life sciences, media, publishing, legal services, and government, including homeland security applications.

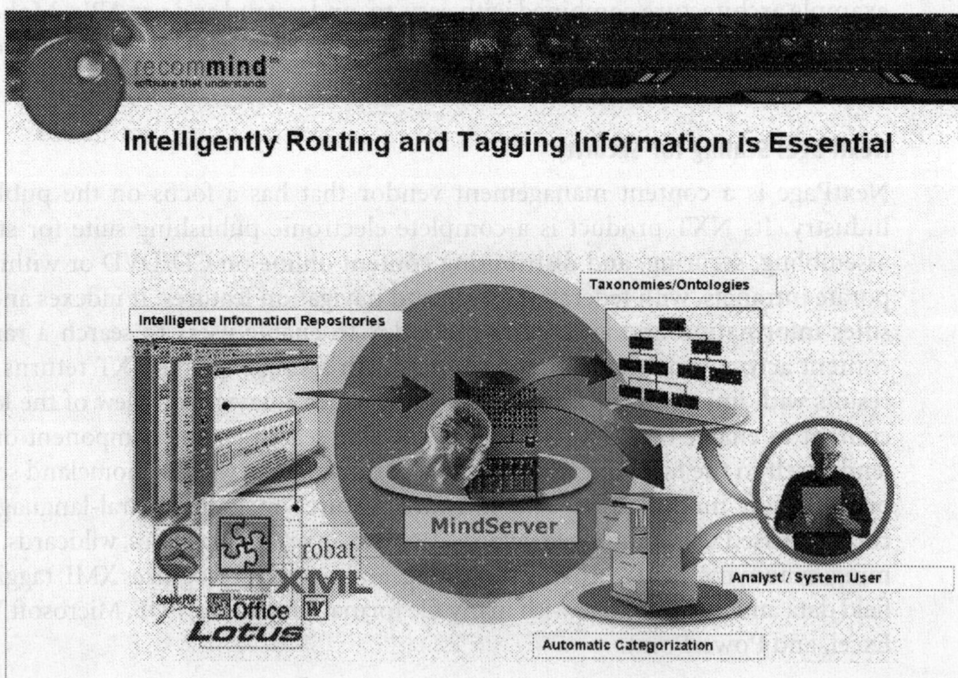

FIGURE 5.3 Recommind software interface. © 2004. Reprinted with permission from Recommind.

The MindServer engine performs semantic analysis on a body of documents and learns terminology commonly used in the field or institution. The Intelligent Retrieval (IR) module uses probabilistic relevance scores to improve rankings and can integrate personal profiles and expert recommendations. The Recommender system can alert users to new information on topics and perform social networking functions. This categorization software system was designed specifically for difficult research problems.

Stratify: Discovery and Classification

Stratify's Discovery System provides automatic classification and discovery of unstructured content through a suite of technology components. The Discovery Classification Server uses natural language processing, statistical analysis, and taxonomy-based classification techniques. A taxonomy lifecycle management application called Taxonomy Manager compares results from multiple classification technologies to produce the best classifications. Taxonomy Manager can read existing taxonomies in its categorization process and has tools for fine-tuning content after processing; it also supports development of customer-specific taxonomies. The Discovery Server user interface and other applications rely on Stratify technology to organize search results and related documents by topic area rather than as flat lists of links.

TripleHop: Targeted Relevance

TripleHop MatchPoint provides a single search point for structured and unstructured data, including databases, Lotus Notes, e-mail, filesystems, the Internet, intranets, and other repositories. Its indexing and retrieval technologies use advanced SVM algorithms for concept-based searching, and users have the option of using keyword searching as well. MatchPoint creates a profile for each user that is based on specific searches the user commonly runs and clickstream analysis; correlations are also created on related topics via collaborative filtering. MatchPoint is able to identify users in organizations who are likely to be experts on topics, based on the content they search. MatchPoint uses three layers of information processing:

Information Discovery: This layer captures both structured and unstructured data located on the Internet, an organization's intranet, e-mail servers, internal databases, Web pages, documents, PDF files, spreadsheets, and other data sources.

Classification: This layer uses SVM algorithms to organize and associate the text.

Information Retrieval: This layer routes the retrieved unstructured content by relevance to users of an organization.

Vivísimo: Human Classification

Vivísimo provides document clustering search engine technology. Its core product, the Clustering Engine, performs on-the-fly clustering of documents, automatically creating categories and arranging them in hierarchies that can be browsed using a folder-like interface. The Vivísimo Clustering Engine uses the following classifications of human-like criteria:

- Concise
- Understandable
- Accurate
- Distinctive

The Vivisimo Clustering Engine displays only the returned title and abstract for each matched result. The similarity between documents is based only on this raw material, the visible text of the search result, not the entire article. The proprietary Vivísimo algorithm clusters them based on textual similarity. This raw similarity is

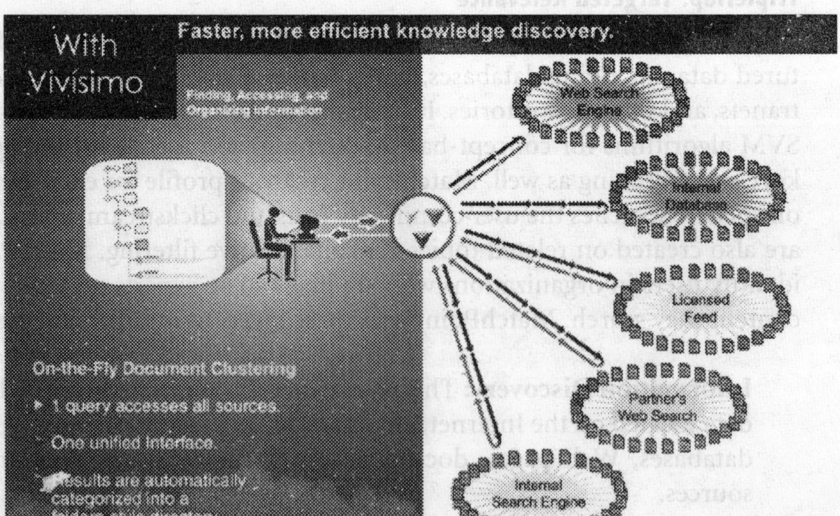

FIGURE 5.4 Vivísimo on the fly document clustering. © Vivísimo, Inc. Reprinted with permission from Vivísimo.

augmented with the four heuristics listed above, so textual similarity is only one of the two factors that determine the eventual clusters. The other factor summarizes human knowledge—coded by Vivísimo's programmers and partly invented by them—of what users wish to see when they examine clustered documents.

Vivísimo does not use a predefined taxonomy or controlled vocabulary, so every cluster description is taken from the search results within the cluster. The Vivísimo Content Integrator integrates query results from multiple search engines or databases and uses the Clustering Engine to cluster the results for display. The Enterprise Publisher creates publishable hierarchies of collections of documents from an organization. The published hierarchy provides a navigable view of a specific collection of content on an intranet or a public Web site.

THE EVOLUTION OF CATEGORIZATION OF UNSTRUCTURED CONTENT

As we see, there is a variety of techniques, technologies, and tools for the categorization of unstructured text. However, at the most basic level the process can start with the construction of a set of rules for classifying documents. Typically, these systems organize documents based on keywords in the title or in the content. The drawbacks of a rule-based approach are that they require significant manual development and testing and typically have limited coverage and, as a result, some degree of error. They require constant maintenance and supervision to achieve acceptable results and tend to work best in a highly structured environment. In a less-defined environment, rules-based systems break down completely, which for a homeland security organization simply would not be a viable option.

Then there are the keyword search and retrieval systems, which in the context of homeland security are also restricted in their capabilities because each term is treated as a separate entity; semantic relationships between words tend to be ignored. Thus, single keyword approaches in general do not account for query variability, which is why this approach as a rule lacks retrieval accuracy and often performs poorly in ranking results. Single term queries do not offer meaningful ways to refine a search. For example, in cases where the number of hits exceeds any reasonable limit, they do not offer an interactive form of retrieval. A query is either successful or unsuccessful, and in the context of homeland security this type of categorization, again, is simply not a viable option. When it's unsuccessful, the user has to figure out how to rephrase the query until the desired result is obtained.

An improvement over keyword search and retrieval is Naïve Bayes categorization, a statistical technique for analyzing the document set and automatically assigning documents to classes or categories. The strength of Naïve Bayes is that it is able to learn from examples. In an ideal situation, it will identify terms that have a high probability of occurring in documents belonging to a category. These probabilities are then used to discriminate between different categories. Unfortunately, the real world is far from ideal, and in a typical application, 50 to 100 or even more manually labeled examples are required per category to ensure that the resulting categories are of high quality, which makes this categorization technique particularly weak for homeland security applications, where samples are few.

At the next evolution phase of categorization is vector-space retrieval models, in which the software maps documents via points in a high-dimensional space, where each dimension corresponds to a particular term. Then similarities between documents as well as between documents and a query are computed by measuring the distance between points in this space. Sophisticated term weighting schemes have been developed to give more weight to terms that are assumed to be more important, that is, that are assumed to be more indicative of a given topic and categories. In this phase, vector-space software can handle partial matches, cases where no document exactly matches the query. They also make good use of the frequency information for result set ranking. However, vector-space models are conceptually similar to keyword-based approaches in that they ignore the semantic dimension of words. Vector-space systems, therefore, are not able to differentiate between different meanings of words; "cell" as in a terrorist group and "cell" as in the biological unit are not distinguished. Vector-space systems also are not able to identify words that occur in a common context. A query via the keyword of "plane" using a vector-space system would miss documents or news feeds with "aircraft," "747," "jet," and so forth. Thus, vector-based systems fail to take the semantic dimension of words into account, resulting both in the introduction of substantial noise in the retrieval of matched results and the system failing to find potentially large numbers of related documents, e-mail, news stories, and other unstructured type of content.

As we have learned, some software systems come with taxonomies specific to industries, and others come with technologies, such as neural networks, that can be trained with a set of documents to create categories of clusters. There also are concept-based retrieval systems, which index documents by using concepts instead of single words or phrases. While this is a promising route to improve retrieval accuracy, most concept-based retrieval systems rely on linguistic resources, typically thesauri or semantic networks that have to be created and maintained by human experts. These approaches have been only moderately successful in very specialized domains, such as the medical and legal fields. Concepts are typically used for indexing documents as well as for normalizing and expanding queries. Concept-based systems also tend to be brittle; that is, they are extremely expensive to maintain even if domain-specific thesauri are available, and they are still unlikely to reflect the particular terms and concepts contained within a proprietary document collection, resulting in further manual effort. A second drawback is that thesauri deal only with synonyms, but synonyms are only one type of semantic relationship between words. For example, thesauri would not come close to capturing all of the semantic relationships between the terms "credit card," "visa," and "immigration."

Because of some of the limitations of keyword, vector, thesauri, and concept-based systems, categorization for homeland security software will need to rely on machine learning algorithms such as probabilistic latent semantic analysis (PLSA) and other techniques to automatically identify and categorize relevant concepts and topics from large collections of unstructured content sources. These types of algorithms perform statistical analyses of word occurrences in documents and identify repeatable contexts, topics, or concepts in which a certain group of words occurs. They typically do not require any manual input in the form of lexicons, thesauri, or topic annotations, but operate in a completely automatic manner known in data mining as *unsupervised learning,* the outcome of which is a predictive model or a compressed, quantitative statistical description of a data set drawn from a collection of documents, files, news feeds, Web pages, e-mails, or any other type of unstructured content.

One of the major advantages of categorization of unstructured content for homeland security using machine learning algorithms is that the process is

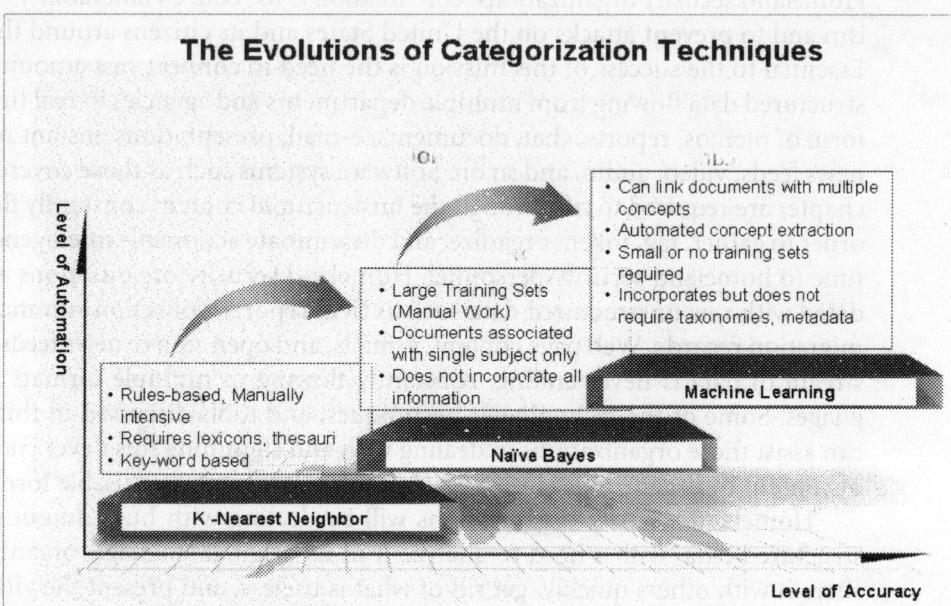

FIGURE 5.5 From rules to training to automatic learning.

language unconstrained. The algorithms can quickly identify key concepts and topics autonomously, unlike linguistic approaches, which are based on lexical semantics. These machine-based techniques are not language, industry, or domain specific; they do not require a dedicated thesaurus, but instead they learn directly from the unstructured content. The advantage for the homeland security organization is that this type of software can be used on any language, as long as the language can be tokenized and the extracted concepts are specific to the given document repository and are adapted to the language, technical terms, and specific jargon.

Obviously, rebuilding similar thesauri by hand for each domain would be prohibitively expensive and time consuming. Instead, the machine learning algorithms can categorize the content and create a numerical model, where each word has some probability to occur in a certain concept or cluster. This allows the user to quantify the relationships between words; there are no thesauri or linguistic resources that provide such quantitative information. Ideally, it is a trade-off in which machine and man combine to create the ideal system using the brute force of computers and the knowledge and experience of human intelligence and homeland security experts.

CATEGORIZATION FOR HOMELAND SECURITY

Homeland security organizations' core mission is to reduce vulnerability to terrorism and to prevent attacks on the United States and its citizens around the world. Essential to the success of this mission is the need to connect vast amounts of unstructured data flowing from multiple departments and agencies in real time in the form of memos, reports, chat, documents, e-mail, presentations, instant messages, news feeds, video, audio, and so on. Software systems such as those covered in this chapter are required to sift through the unstructured content constantly flowing in order to gather, tag, token, organize, and disseminate actionable intelligence in real time to homeland security personnel. Homeland security organizations are inundated with raw unstructured data such as field reports, collection summaries, immigration records, Web page content, e-mails, and open source news feeds, and the stream of data is never ending, constantly flowing in multiple formats and languages. Some of the technologies, techniques, and tools discussed in this chapter can assist those organizations in dealing with and stemming this never ending flow of content by organizing it into a manageable, intelligent, and usable format.

Homeland security organizations will be dealing with huge amounts of unstructured data, with a need to analyze it in its original language, organize it and share it with others quickly, get rid of what is useless, and present the vital intelligence that is of the utmost importance to the people who need it at different levels of government and at different locations. Software that can analyze this type of

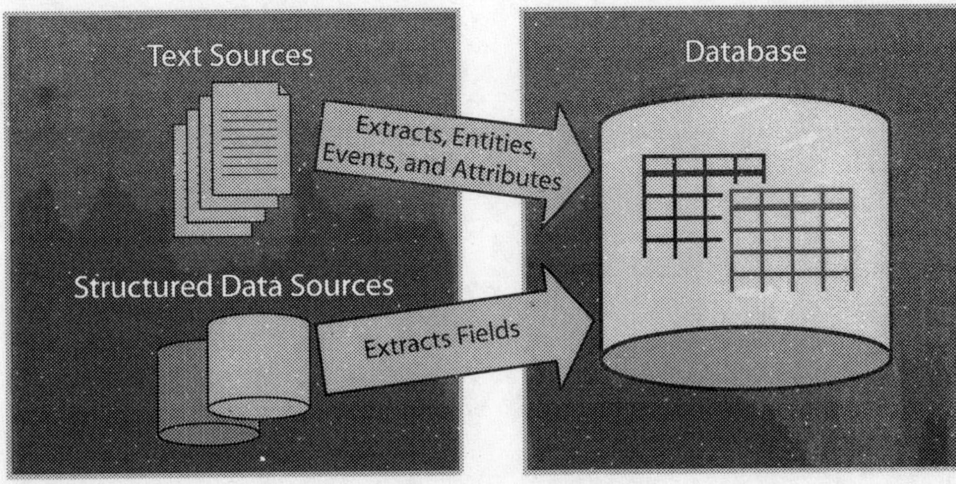

FIGURE 5.6 Extracting intelligence from unstructured text.

unstructured data will be required for interpreting it in multiple native formats and languages. The software will be needed for categorizing the text into categories and routing and delivering it to homeland security personnel when and where they need it. This kind of software, coupled with that which will be covered in subsequent chapters and that which was covered in prior ones, is required for harnessing both unstructured and structured content, in order to glean vital intelligence faster and more accurately than ever before.

Data classification, extraction, and visualization technologies are required, combined with linguistic analysis tools that can uniquely recognize the subtle differences, meanings, and relationships between disparate sources of unstructured information, in much the same way the human mind does. Software is needed that can understand the concepts in massive amounts of text with powerful metadata extraction, taxonomy management, automatic entity extraction, document summarization, concept and full-text search, tools to automatically process and understand text content from multiple languages. However, reliance solely on this type of software and technology is a mistake. Categorization relies on human interaction and decisions, which may be too slow and limited in scope. Homeland security organizations must deal with a distributed environment in which information is generated dynamically, often with the intent to deceive analysis, which is the subject of the last two chapters of this book: intelligence and mining. Keep in mind that no single technology is the answer—they all are.

6 Intelligence: Systems for Detecting Terrorist Crimes

In This Chapter

- Identity Theft
- A Crime of Our Time
- Terrorist Theft
- Visa Theft
- Technologies for Detecting ID Crimes
- National Report on Identity Fraud
- ID Score by ID Analytics
- ID Fraud Intercept by Fair Isaac
- The Fair and Accurate Credit Transactions Act of 2003
- Name Recognition
- Language Analysis Systems (LAS)
- Money Laundering

Many of the techniques that are relevant to detecting terrorist activity can be associated with related crimes, such as identity theft, fraud, and money laundering. The USA PATRIOT Act passed by the U.S. Congress in the wake of the terrorist attacks of September 11, 2001, imposed stricter anti-money laundering requirements; this included an expansion of the "know your customer" rules requiring verification of the identity of individuals to guard against the use of illicit funds in business transactions. Analytical techniques and technologies can be used to discover previously unknown relationships between individuals and organizations, and through the use of cross-database analyses, questionable entities can be uncovered. Businesses in the U.S. are required to file suspicious activity reports (SARs) with the Treasury Department, reporting transactions of a certain size and character. Private industry is increasingly turning to specialized intelligence service providers to assist in this area. This chapter discusses some of the premier intelligence software and service providers in the areas of identity theft, name recognition, and money laundering. Also discussed are some intelligence workflow programs, such as Mitopia from MitoSystems, a data fusion environment platform that offers a methodology for constructing an integrated system solution for homeland security organizations.

IDENTITY THEFT

Seven of the 9/11 hijackers, none of whom actually lived in the Commonwealth, obtained Virginia driver's licenses by submitting false proof of Virginia residency. One of the seven, Ziad Jarrah, was involved in the failed attempt to fly Flight 93 into a target in the Washington, D.C., area; two were aboard the airplanes that crashed into the World Trade Center; and four were aboard Flight 77 when it was flown into the Pentagon. Virginia has always required both proof of identity and proof of Virginia residency to obtain a Virginia driver's license. There is a long list of documents that can be used to establish identity and residency. The loophole of the law that the terrorists exploited allowed them to establish Virginia residency by submitting a notarized affidavit of another Virginia resident. For example, two of the 9/11 hijackers paid $100 to an illegal immigrant—who had himself fraudulently obtained his Virginia driver's license—to execute the residency affidavit for the hijackers before a notary public. With this notarized affidavit, the hijackers had sufficient "proof" of Virginia residency to obtain Virginia driver's licenses, which in today's environment is often sufficient evidence for establishing credit or opening a bank account.

After the connection with the 9/11 hijackers was discovered, the Virginia Department of Motor Vehicles (DMV) moved quickly to change its procedures. Within days the notarized forms were taken off the list of acceptable documents. Still, it is unnerving to discover how some of these terrorists had stolen the identities of other individuals with relative ease. Not long after the FBI announced its list of the 19 hijackers, reports discredited at least nine of the names as phony. In at least two others—Salem Alhazmi, who was on the flight that crashed into the Pentagon, and Abdulaziz Alomari, whose plane struck the World Trade Center's north tower—had passports that had been stolen in burglaries. The problem with Virginia's DMV entity validation requirements, as with those in the 49 other states, is a lack of consistency and standards. Israel, which has for decades battled the threat of terrorism, is perhaps the most experienced in this problem and has opted for individuals to voluntarily submit their biometric profiles to validate their identity. This is an option the United States is moving to implement, but in the absence of such a system, other methods must be pursued in an effort to validate an individual's true identity.

The problem of identity theft has expanded rapidly with the growth of automation and the Internet and is now entrenched as a critical issue in the war on terrorism. Nearly all of the 9/11 hijackers obtained false documentation that enabled them to base themselves in the United States while plotting their attacks. The threat posed by identity theft as well as the economic effects it has on its citizens requires the strategic attention of homeland security organizations. There are commonly three documents used to establish false identities: driver's licenses, Social Security cards, and birth certificates. Members of Al-Qaeda were able to obtain driver's licenses in three different states that enabled them to board U.S. airlines on 9/11. The problems of identity fraud are not unique to a few states such as Virginia; the problem is that each state tends to accept different documents in validating the identity of individuals prior to granting them a driver's license. Each state has different laws regarding what documents may be used to prove an individual's identity or residency to obtain a driver's license.

The problem is not only with individuals obtaining false driver's licenses. Identification procedures are full of inconsistencies that enable perpetrators to take advantage of the multiplicity of systems. Many of the 9/11 terrorists also obtained fraudulent Social Security cards or numbers through theft of legitimate Social Security numbers of others or through the use of counterfeit documents. While it has become increasingly obvious in the past few years that identity theft can cause financial damage, it is now becoming apparent that it can cause damage of a much more serious nature involving national defense.

Individuals can obtain fraudulent Social Security cards by inventing a number, stealing an existing Social Security card, buying a counterfeit card, or obtaining counterfeit documents such as passports, birth certificates, or INS papers. The Social Security Administration is responsible for preventing some of this fraud, but weaknesses in its system make it difficult to detect all cases. Much of the fraud in both the Social Security system and driver's licensing systems is related to fraudulent birth certificates. Because these records are kept in many places by local registrars and there is no national standard for these documents, it is easy to create counterfeit birth certificates or alter legitimate certificates.

There are two major forms of identity theft. True name fraud is when a perpetrator uses a consumer's personal information, often in the form of a Social Security card, to open new accounts in the consumer's name. There is also account takeover fraud, which occurs when perpetrators gain access to a consumer's existing accounts and make fraudulent charges. Other types of identity theft include Social Security fraud, the use of a false Social Security number in tandem with a false or stolen identity, and so-called bust-out schemes where perpetrators use credit card terminals obtained by a shell or front business to make charges to fraudulently obtain credit cards. This last type of crime is clearly profit motivated and is not a threat to national security. However, there are several data products for validating the legitimacy of Social Security numbers, including those of TransUnion's HAWK and ID SearchPlus.

Effective counter measures will be difficult to achieve in any event because the integrity of any verification system hinges on the security of the documents that underlie it. One of the fallacies of the system is its reliance on fabricated "breeder" documents to create authentic ones. For example, a false birth certificate can become a breeder document and be used to obtain genuine identity documents such as a U.S. passport, driver's license, or Social Security card. In addition, a Social Security number can be illegally obtained by applying for a card at a Social Security Administration office using an altered breeder passport along with a doctored INS form, making it appear that a person is lawfully in the country with a job. It is clear that the revamping of these record-keeping systems is required in which technology becomes a key to the validation of a person's unique identity. However, so far the United States has rejected the concept of a national identification card, and it would appear such a system will not be accepted until future attacks in the homeland make it clear a standardized system is required.

Terrorist financing is a subset of identity theft, financial fraud, and money laundering typologies, which can be difficult to detect, and most likely will be perceived as suspicious activity rather than immediately pinpointed for what it truly is. Financial institutions have serious concerns about how to implement identification validation processes that ensure they comply with anti-terrorist financing regulations. Terrorists often resort to identity theft, opening accounts in other people's names and then bringing in funds not in line with the account behavioral profile. The 9/11 terrorists opened 14 accounts at a Florida bank, using false Social Security numbers and other documents.

A CRIME OF OUR TIME

In what is probably the first major survey of its kind, the Federal Trade Commission (FTC) reported that nearly 10 million people in the United States were victims of identity theft on an annual basis, with the number increasing. The study also concluded that it took a total of 300 million hours to correct and cost a total of $5 billion, according to the FTC report. It was the first federal survey that tried to measure the extent of the problem. The FTC estimated that 27.3 million people have, in the past five years, had their personal information, such as credit card account numbers or Social Security numbers, misused to buy products fraudulently or establish credit for another person. More than a third of them, or 9.9 million, had such experiences in the past year, the FTC said. Such fraud, the FTC reported, cost businesses $47.6 billion, or $4,800 per victim; for individuals, losses and expenses incurred to correct problems averaged $500.

What is disturbing for homeland security organizations is that the FTC report recognized identity theft as a "crime of the times" and said its survey showed a significant increase since 9/11. Previously, government statistics on identity theft were limited, such as the 400,000 consumer complaints filed with the FTC since the fall of 1999. However, the recent findings indicate that in the past three years the number of such criminal acts has become considerably higher. The FTC's findings were based on a random telephone survey of 4,057 adults; the FTC surveyed a large group, believing they would have a difficult time finding victims. Unfortunately, that was not the case. The survey found that 4.6 percent of respondents said they were identity-theft victims in the past year, a response rate that the FTC report translates into 9.9 million victims, applied to the entire U.S. adult population.

The biggest problem in prior years, the survey found, involved misuse of existing accounts, such as unauthorized charges on credit cards or telephone bills. However, the report findings indicate that not only is identity theft on the increase, but it is being done to establish false identities, rather than simply to make purchases, which is where the concerns of homeland security come into play. According to the FTC Bureau of Consumer Protection study, 23 percent of identity theft occurred because personal information such as driver's licenses, credit cards, and mail was lost or stolen. In 13 percent of the cases, theft occurred during transactions, including the theft of information taken from a credit card receipt during or after a purchase, or through purchases made via the Internet, mail, or phone. The FTC report found that nearly half of all victims (49 percent) did not know how their identity was stolen.

In a related study, government investigators conducted a special test of security as it relates to identity theft and homeland security. Investigators were allowed to drive a truck into a Justice Department courtyard, using false ID cards they obtained from DMVs in Arizona, California, Maryland, Michigan, New York, Virginia, Washington, D.C., and South Carolina, where they were able to use forged documents to get a driver's license. The Homeland Security Department says there are aggressive efforts to beef up security and training to counter identity theft. However, this government test confirmed how easy it is to deceive homeland security organizations with bogus identification documents. The undersecretary for border security at the Homeland Security Department indicated that upward of 60,000 fraudulent documents are confiscated at borders annually, and that training is being enhanced so that agents will spot fake documents. However, the problem seems to be a lack of identification standards and a reduction in the number of documents currently being accepted for the validation of an individual's identity.

How are identities stolen? Perpetrators use a variety of ways, such as buying data on the black market, stealing mail, going through trash receptors, "skimming" the data from credit cards through illegal devices at ATMs or retailers, hacking into online transactions, and completing a change of address form to reroute mail. A new scam is to send e-mails requesting verification of financial information. Customers of Yahoo!, Citibank, AOL, Earthlink, PayPal, BestBuy.com, Discover Card, and SonyStyle.com have been targeted. The scam technique of *spoofing* or *phishing* involves sending bogus e-mails to trick customers into giving out personal information. The phisher sends out a legitimate-looking e-mail that claims to be from a company the reader does business with, informing the reader there is an account error, possible fraud, or other problem with the account, and asking for validation information.

TERRORIST THEFT

Identity theft is often associated with other criminal violations, including bank fraud, credit card fraud, wire fraud, mail fraud, money laundering, bankruptcy fraud, computer crimes, and fugitive cases. The use of a stolen identity enhances the chance of success in the commission of almost all financial crimes. The stolen identity provides a cloak of anonymity for the perpetrators while the groundwork is laid to carry out for their future attacks. This includes the rental of mail drops, post office boxes, apartments, office space, vehicles, and storage lockers, as well as the activation of pagers, cellular telephones, and various utility services, especially those associated with terrorists' infiltration, surveillance, planning, and attacks.

Identity theft is not new to law enforcement and intelligence agencies. For decades perpetrators have changed identities to avoid capture, and check forgers have assumed the identity of others to negotiate stolen or counterfeit checks. What is new today is the pervasiveness of the problem. Identity theft is not a separate and distinct criminal problem, it is a component of terrorism. Advances in computer hardware and software along with the growth of the Internet have significantly accelerated the role that identity theft plays in crime and terrorism. For example, the skill and time needed to produce high-quality counterfeit documents have been reduced to the point that nearly anyone can be an expert. Multimedia software used by professional graphic artists can now be used by terrorists.

Today's software enables novices to easily manipulate images and fonts to produce high-quality counterfeit documents. The tremendous growth of the Internet and the accessibility it provides to such an immense audience, coupled with the anonymity it allows, results in otherwise traditional fraud schemes being magnified when the Web is used as part of the ploy. Communication and collaboration of plans can take place from anywhere in the world. This is particularly true with identity theft-related crimes, such as computer intrusion into the databases of credit card companies, financial institutions, on-line businesses, and so on to obtain credit card or other identification information.

The impact of identity theft is greater than just the loss of money or property. The threat is made graver by the fact that terrorists have long used such crimes as Social Security number fraud to enable them to obtain such things as cover employment and access to secure locations. These and similar means can be used by terrorists to obtain driver's licenses and bank and credit card accounts through which terrorism financing is facilitated. Terrorists and terrorist groups require funding to perpetrate their agendas. The methods used to finance terrorism range from the highly sophisticated to the most basic. There is virtually no financing method that has not at some level been exploited by these groups, and identity theft is a key catalyst, fueling many of these methods. For example, an Al-Qaeda terrorist cell in Spain used stolen credit cards in fictitious sales scams and for numerous other purchases for the cell. They kept purchases below amounts where identification would be required. They also used stolen telephone and credit cards for communication back to Pakistan, Afghanistan, and Lebanon. False passports and travel documents were used to open bank accounts where money for the mujahadin movement was sent to and from countries such as Pakistan and Afghanistan.

Countering such fraud schemes as those that are being used by terrorists to fund their terrorist activities involves targeting ploys being committed by loosely organized groups to conduct criminal activity with a nexus to their financing. The tasks involve identifying a number of groups made up of members of varying ethnic backgrounds engaged in widespread fraud activity. Members of these groups may not themselves be terrorists, but proceeds from their criminal fraud schemes have directly or indirectly been used to fund terrorist activity and/or terrorist groups. Through the targeting of this type of identity theft activity and money laundering crimes, the links to terrorist financing will likely result in the identification and dismantling of previously unknown terrorist cells. Prior to 9/11, this type of terrorist financing often avoided law enforcement scrutiny, but since those attacks this activity can no longer be ignored, for these crimes are the financial lifeblood of terrorists.

Data mining initiatives can also be taken by homeland security organizations to identify potential terrorist-related individuals through Social Security number (SSN) misuse analysis. For example, by taking SSNs identified through past or ongoing terrorism investigations and providing them to the Social Security Administration for their validation, once the validity or non-validity of the number has been established, analysts and investigators can generate watch lists and look for misuse of those SSNs by checking immigration records, DMV records, and other military, government, and fee-based data sources, such as those of Acxiom, ChoicePoint, Experian, and TransUnion.

Incidents of suspect SSN misuse can be separated according to type, with predicated investigative packages being forwarded to the appropriate homeland security personnel for further follow-up. Given the alarming nature of the threat posed by identity theft and the potential nexus to terrorism, these types of crimes warrant the attention of homeland security organizations to aggressively investigate this type of illegal activity. Additionally, the owners and operators of the nation's infrastructures should be alert to the possible use by terrorists of official identification, uniforms, or vehicles to gain access to sensitive facilities for purposes of planning or carrying out attacks.

These official identifications refer to recognized implements of federal, state, and local governments and private sector entities. These extremist elements may use breeder documents to create identities in order to illegally obtain official identification, uniforms, or vehicles in furtherance of terrorist activities. These attempts to acquire official identification, uniforms, or vehicles would be consistent with the tactics and techniques of Al-Qaeda and other extremist groups. Al-Qaeda and other terrorist groups likely view the theft or other illegal acquisition of official identification, uniforms, or vehicles as an effective way to increase access and decrease scrutiny in furtherance of planning and operations.

Potentially, Al-Qaeda or other terrorist groups can systematically pursue the illegal acquisition of identities in order to gain access to secured locations and the use of official identification, uniforms, or vehicles in the execution of terrorist attacks. Terrorist groups have used police or military uniforms to mask their identities and achieve closer access to their targets without arousing suspicion. This was illustrated in December 2002, during the suicide bombings that targeted the Chechen government headquarters in Groznyy, Russia. Terrorists in South America, the Philippines, and Pakistan have commandeered or stolen emergency medical services vehicles and uniforms or cleverly designed imitations in order to facilitate the execution of their attacks on key facilities.

In an effort to understand the extent of official identification, uniform, and vehicle thefts, the Department of Homeland Security has conducted surveys of selected members of the law enforcement community in several states. The surveys revealed that hundreds of official identification cards, badges, decals, uniforms, and government license plates were reported stolen or lost. Additionally, a number of private companies have reported receiving suspicious inquiries about renting official delivery vehicles, and emergency services representatives have received unusual requests for detailed vehicle descriptions. There is no historical baseline to compare recent theft or suspicious inquiry data, and the intent or resolution of many of the thefts cannot be determined. Scenarios have been developed by government agencies that point to the possibility of attacks aided by the use of identification theft.

The worldwide proliferation of individuals or companies that traffic in high-quality imitations of official identification, uniforms, or vehicles is a related issue that increases the possibility such items could be used to facilitate future terrorist attacks and further complicates efforts to prevent their acquisition. For example, the New York City High Intensity Drug Trafficking Area (HIDTA) Task Force reported that it had identified a Japanese Web site selling near-exact replicas of badges from law enforcement agencies such as the U.S. Secret Service, FBI, Drug Enforcement Agency, U.S. Marshals Service, and Los Angeles Police Department. Reports have been made regarding the theft and sale over the Internet of a large number of United Parcel Service (UPS) uniforms. These reports raise the attention of homeland security organizations on the potential security concerns of missing or stolen identification, uniforms, or vehicles.

Possession of some combination of official identification cards, badges, decals, uniforms, government license plates, and vehicles tends to reduce suspicion and might allow an individual or vehicle greater access to sensitive facilities. For this reason, the Department of Homeland Security (DHS) urges departments and agencies to keep comprehensive records of all official identification cards, badges, decals, uniforms, and license plates distributed, documenting any anomalies and canceling access to items that are lost or stolen. Officials also suggest the safeguarding of uniforms, patches, badges, ID cards, and other forms of official identification to protect against unauthorized access to facilities. The DHS is developing technologies for improving identification card technology to eliminate reuse or unauthorized duplication.

VISA THEFT

In a terrorist global war, visas can be deadly weapons. One method enemies wishing to enter the United States have used in the past is the nonimmigrant visa, which can be obtained from any of the 211 American consulates around the world. The length of stay varies, depending on the type of visa. However, nonimmigrant visas represent the overwhelming majority of individuals entering the United States. For example, during the year 2000, 33.7 million visitors, students, and temporary workers entered the country. Nonimmigrant visas are ideal for supporting attacks that require brief or repeated trips to the United States. All of the 9/11 hijackers entered the United States using nonimmigrant visas; the 19 terrorists received a total of 23 visas from five different consular posts over a four-year period. Detection of individuals on a terrorist watch list can ensure that these nonimmigrant visas are not issued to a suspected terrorist, but Sheik Omar Abdel Rahman, convicted of conspiracy in the 1993 bombing of the World Trade Center, managed to obtain one under an assumed name via identification theft.

Terrorists can also enter the United States through the permanent immigration system, obtaining a green card to live in the country or become a naturalized citizen. Each year, approximately 900,000 foreigners enter the United States in this manner because they have a relative in the United States, possess a specialized job skill, are seeking asylum as a refugee, or have won a visa lottery that admits about 50,000 a year. One study of 28 known militant Islamic terrorists found that 17 of them were in the country legally, either as permanent residents or as naturalized citizens. The prevalent use of identity theft and false travel documents makes the current system particularly vulnerable to abuse. In 2001, officials at border crossing points seized over 100,000 falsified documents. Over 50 percent of those documents were border-crossing cards, alien registration cards, and fraudulent visas and passports; needless to say, terrorists have used such materials.

Homeland security organizations must organize themselves in addressing the long-term threat of terrorists with visas and continue to improve the intelligence-sharing process. The current immigration process is a hodge-podge of legacy information systems and post-9/11 policy changes and organizational tinkering. As the system operates today, providing intelligence support for visa issuance begins with TIPOFF. Established in 1987, TIPOFF is run through the Department of State's Bureau of Intelligence and Research as a clearinghouse for sensitive intelligence information provided by other agencies. It includes full biographic records on approximately 85,000 terrorist names, photos, fingerprints, and other source documentation.

TIPOFF receives highly classified intelligence data, sensitive law enforcement information, and diplomatic reports from the U.S. intelligence community through a variety of classified and unclassified communications networks. In addition, declassified information on suspected terrorists, including their name, date and place of birth, nationality, and passport number, is made available as a terrorist watch list. In addition to name records, including over 12 million related to terrorist and criminal activity provided by the intelligence community and the Drug Enforcement Agency, TIPOFF data is entered into the Consular Lookout and Support System (CLASS) system, which consular officers use to run checks before issuing a visa.

While the DHS is responsible for overall supervision of the immigration system, the CLASS database and day-to-day consular affairs are managed by the Department of State. As the system operates today, providing intelligence support for visa issuance begins with TIPOFF. However, advances are being made in improving the current visa and terrorist detection system. The first is the establishment of the Terrorism Threat Integration Center (TTIC), which is designed to be a central location where all terrorist-related intelligence, both foreign and domestic, is gathered, coordinated, and assessed. TTIC is composed of personnel from the FBI, CIA, Department of Defense, Department of Homeland Security, Department of State, and other intelligence agencies. The center will perform the following tasks:

- Optimize the use of terrorist threat-related information, expertise, and capabilities to conduct threat analysis and form collection strategies.
- Integrate terrorist-related information collected domestically and abroad in order to form the most comprehensive threat picture possible.
- Create a structure that ensures information sharing across agency lines.
- Provide terrorist threat assessments for the national leadership.

TECHNOLOGIES FOR DETECTING ID CRIMES

Data mining, identity validation, name recognition, and money laundering detection technologies could be particularly useful for the TTIC in developing and collaborating on an accurate terrorist watch list. However, funding for research and development of the Defense Advanced Research Projects Agency's Terrorism Information Awareness program was cut due to concerns about the possible abuse of data mining technology, based on unfounded speculation. Existing oversight and implementation structures could be modified to control the use of such new technology. If successfully developed and applied within the confines of the law, these techniques and technologies could offer numerous benefits to U.S. counterterrorism efforts. Data mining research and development should be encouraged and, as we will see in the following chapter, can be used to combat terrorism and better support organizations such as TTIC.

At the first level of data mining is the use of visualization tools, such as those offering link analysis from such firms as i2, NetMap, Orion, and VisuaLink. These tools can be used to search for associations of suspected accounts and to track terrorist financing schemes. This type of investigative software can be used to review transactional and reference data from many databases. For example, if a terrorist manages to slip through security systems with a false ID, link analysis software can be used to search for associations to other accounts. The detection of a single individual using a false identification can lead to other accounts of suspected terrorists. If one individual receives an electronic funds transfer from another, link analysis could be used to discover the identity theft case and vice versa. Crimes of fraud, money laundering, and identification theft are usually not isolated crimes, but detecting these types of transactions requires more sophisticated technologies than link analysis or visualization, it requires advanced pattern recognition techniques and algorithms for autonomous profiling processes.

Access to multiple databases can also be used to combat identity theft. For example, an immigration database provides details on passports and permanent residency, travel activity, visa issuance, foreign visitors, entry, duration of stay, and so on. That single source of data can be enhanced with biometric information such as DNA prints, fingerprints or iris scans, and so on. Commercial demographics such as those discussed in Chapter 2, "Aggregation: How to Leverage the Web, Robots, and Commercial Demographics for Entity Validation," on data aggregation can be used to validate a Social Security number sequence, location of issue, created date, and so on, and other sources of information can be used to validate the identity of individuals, such as their last known addresses and vehicles associated with their names. The United States is implementing plans under the USA PATRIOT Act to use a biometric identifier scanning system at consular offices abroad and at U.S. ports of entry. This act also requires linking immigration databases with law enforcement agencies to enable more effective tracking of foreign visitors.

The next step to accessing multiple databases for validating someone's identity is the analysis of his behavior. This is especially critical in emerging digital industries such as financial services, credit card, wireless, banking, and the Internet, where an individual's transactions are his digital signature. Shared bank databases would enable banks to share information on customers for due diligence purposes only. However, banking secrecy and privacy issues need to be addressed before this happens. The USA PATRIOT Act introduces the concept of voluntary information sharing among financial institutions for anti-terrorist financing and anti-money laundering due diligence, and this is a start. Efforts are under way to pass laws facilitating customer information sharing among banks to crack down on identity fraud; in addition, countries worldwide are enacting new legislation to combat money laundering crimes.

Identity validation services such as those from ID Analytics and name recognition software such as that from Language Analysis Systems (LAS) can be used to perfect homeland security watch lists. Money laundering detection software, such as that from Searchspace, can also be used to examine and detect account deviations and behavioral inconsistencies in financial transactions. At the core of money laundering detection is the use of pattern-recognition technologies for monitoring abnormal account behavior, unusual transaction activity, and inconsistent monetary amounts.

A knowledge-based system such as that of ID Analytics can also be used for authentication of a person's identity. These types of authentication intelligence systems are being used to identify individuals by obtaining specific information that is general in nature and unique only to that person. Credit card companies are currently using several of these authentication systems and services, as well as data products to screen new applications. These same systems lend themselves to homeland security applications. All of these identity theft detection technologies do not dilute the need for banks, credit card companies, wireless providers, and government agencies such as DMV to standardize and scrutinize identification documentation. It is worth noting that identity theft complaints in the United States almost doubled last year, topping the FTC list of the most widespread forms of reported fraud.

In prior generations, identity theft was not the problem that it is today; people in the community knew each other. In our digital environment, individuals can go anywhere and buy anything, paying by credit or debit card. It is essential in today's world that we know that people are who they say they are. Airport and border personnel need to know that travelers and immigrants are who they say they are. To a large extent our whole financial system depends on people being who they say they are. False or stolen identities undermine our whole system of commerce as well as our national security. Because of the difficulty in developing the expertise for detecting these elaborate crimes, we will discuss specialized intelligence software and services that have been developed over the years for private industry, but which also can be used for homeland security purposes.

NATIONAL REPORT ON IDENTITY FRAUD

ID Analytics, Inc., a technology company providing businesses with solutions to detect and prevent identity theft and related fraud, conducted a lengthy and detailed study using application records from wireless providers, banks, and credit card companies, reporting its findings in the *National Report on Identity Fraud*. The year-long research project leading up to the report analyzed more than 200 million records, including valid and fraudulent consumer applications for credit, debit, and new accounts, together with the largest collection of cross industry-known frauds to date. A key finding of the report was that a surprising proportion of the identity fraud perpetrated against businesses is actually without a consumer victim because the fraudulent identity is fabricated. In fact, 88.4 percent of identity frauds discovered through the research were not originally reported as such by businesses due to the criminals' ability to obfuscate traces of the crime.

Undertaken in partnership with the Center for Information Policy Leadership, which develops global privacy concepts for the digital age, the report from ID Analytics is the largest and most comprehensive effort ever undertaken to analyze identity fraud. Based on tremendous interest from businesses to better understand the crime in an effort to prevent it, ID Analytics received extensive support from eight of the top ten card issuers, two of the top five wireless providers, and approximately 80 percent of U.S. retail banks.

This unprecedented collaboration of companies across multiple industries enabled ID Analytics to gain an accurate assessment of the size and scope of identity fraud, as well as understand the highly sophisticated and complex behaviors of the criminals who commit it. The report describes in detail the results obtained through analysis of this data, providing information never before available about how identity fraud occurs and why it is so difficult to detect. This type of report and findings can also assist homeland security organizations in detecting these types of crimes as they relate to sophisticated schemes for obtaining credit cards, opening bank accounts, and obtaining wireless phones by terrorists.

One of the key findings is that the most effective identity theft fraud prevention approaches are those that predict fraudulent behavior across industries by spotting applications not normally flagged as fraudulent. The report concludes that in order to curb the problem of identity theft, a more aggressive approach needs to be taken by financial institutions, focusing on stopping the fraud at the source, by the organizations and companies that extend credit. In other words, the best method for stopping identity theft is by detecting it during the application phase. Until now, there has been a lack of robust, empirical evidence detailing how identity theft is committed and how the ensuing fraud victimizes financial institutions. However, the *National Report on Identity Fraud* provides a statistically viable look into this costly epidemic that had previously been hidden from the industry. The results unveiled in the report are already playing a large role in the formulation of business solutions by the financial industry for preventing identity fraud before it starts. Other significant findings from the report include the following:

- The majority of fraudulent and suspicious accounts have no links to known fraud at the time of application. In fact, only 4 percent of identity frauds could be linked to another identity fraud at the time of application. As a result, current fraud detection methods that rely on links analysis to known fraud have limited value.
- While many cases of identity fraud are, in fact, the result of fabricated identities, the majority of applications contain actual, valid identity information. The research shows that 97 percent of all applications contain a valid Social Security number.
- Sophisticated identity frauds are extremely difficult to detect and prevent using current approaches. Because many of these frauds are associated with unreported identity theft and fabricated identities, they are often undetected and misclassified.
- Fraud rates vary greatly by the type of application, depending on whether it's a face-to-face transaction (such as in a store or bank) or a "faceless" transaction (such as online, by telephone, or via postal mail), in combination with whether it is instant credit granted at the point of initial purchase or non-instant credit where there is a waiting period (such as with a checking account). The highest rate of fraud detected was among instant credit transactions, at 6 percent, and also among faceless transactions, at 4.4 percent. By comparison, lenders had tagged instant credit fraud at .46 percent and faceless fraud at .23 percent.
- Participation and collaboration across multiple industries, including bank and retail credit card, wireless, retail banking, and online consumer finance, is vital to detecting and preventing fraud. No single corporation or industry has sufficient visibility to identify fraudulent patterns based on analysis of its applications alone. This finding is particularly important to homeland security because it points up the importance of data aggregation, integration, collaboration, and mining of multiple diverse databases in the detection of potential terrorists.

The main focus of the research was on studying identity fraud at the point of application and determining if there were ways to prevent fraudulent accounts from ever being opened. The research concentrated on the four U.S. industries that bear the vast majority of identity fraud losses: new wireless account setup and activation, major retailer and bank credit card applications, retail bank checking account openings, and instant loans for online and retail purchases. The research methodology was unique in several ways, including its examination of identity information across all applications rather than only approved credit or accounts that were ultimately tagged as fraud by the credit grantor. The research also looked at account performance information over time; each newly opened account was scrutinized for how it performed over the first six months of the account lifecycle—in other words, how many dollars were charged against the account, at what point in time, and whether or not payments were made. As a result, the findings were more comprehensive and more insightful than any identity fraud research findings to date.

The report also presents findings on current approaches to fraud detection, as well as insights into the best approach for stopping identity fraud before losses occur. A key finding from the research is that current fraud detection methods based on data matching and known fraud files are inadequate; only cross-industry collaboration can identify and predict fraudulent behavior patterns. The report also found that in most instances a genuine Social Security number was commonly used. A second strategy to evolve from the study was the recommendation for the proactive use of pattern recognition technologies to detect these types of entity crimes. A strategy for homeland security organizations also emerges from these findings: In order to combat identity theft by a future terrorist, a broad number of diverse data sources should be mined.

It was known at the start of the report that identity fraud was a problem, but what was not known was how the criminal patterns linked together. Also based on the research, it was discovered that identity fraud could be detected through the use of advanced pattern analysis technologies. The knowledge gained through this research, combined with new advanced technology, has led to the development of ID Score™ by ID Analytics that assesses the legitimacy of identity information provided by individuals at the point of application, before credit, debit, or new accounts are granted. Underlying the ID Score is a pattern recognition technology the company calls Graph Theoretic Anomaly Detection™ (GTAD™) that dynamically detects unusual behavior based on the identity data elements on an application, before the crime takes place. Today, the ID Score is being used by some of the nation's largest credit card, retail card, wireless, and online instant credit companies, daily helping to detect hundreds of frauds and saving many thousands of dollars in losses.

ID SCORE BY ID ANALYTICS

Established in 2002 by a team with deep experience in fraud prevention, the executive core of ID Analytics is made up of former HNC personnel, a firm that was the major credit card fraud detection provider prior to its merger with Fair Isaac. ID Analytics works with clients in the bank and retail credit card, wireless, retail banking, and online consumer finance industries to provide comprehensive analytical solutions for identity risk management, preventing identity fraud at the point of application and throughout the customer lifecycle, for the prevention of take-over identity thefts. From its start, ID Analytics engaged in a cross-industry consortium involving financial, wireless, and retailing companies with the objective of stopping identity fraud before it starts. While many of these companies already have multiple fraud detection systems in place, they are increasingly concerned that this type of fraud is becoming epidemic, and the only way to stop it is through large scale, multi-industry cooperation.

To study the problem of identity fraud, ID Analytics spent close to a year analyzing data from a variety of lenders from across different industries. The companies who contributed data to this study come from different market sectors, and the data they contributed forms the largest and most comprehensive effort ever undertaken to explore prior instances of application fraud in an effort to help reduce the occurrence of identity fraud for consumers and businesses alike. Participants from diverse industries joined with ID Analytics to create the first ever identity theft fraud consortium.

In collaboration with consortium members, consumer advocates, law enforcement and government agencies, ID Analytics reviewed more than 200 million records, including valid and fraudulent consumer applications for credit, debit, and new accounts, together with the largest collection of cross-industry known frauds to date. Working with this unique and unprecedented set of information, ID Analytics was able to gain insight into thousands of fraudulent behavioral patterns that were not identified with current fraud detection methods. These patterns, combined with new advanced machine learning techniques and a variety of other data sources, have enabled ID Analytics to build its proprietary ID Score.

Using the first-ever cross-industry, cross-company approach to the problem, ID Score is designed to identify fraud that is not detected by most fraud detection efforts. ID Score compares application information against hundreds of millions of encrypted accounts from multiple industries, in combination with known frauds and fraudulent behavior patterns. In real time, ID Score gives ID Analytics clients the information they need to evaluate the risk of identity fraud before approving credit for a particular applicant. ID Score assesses the legitimacy of identity information provided by an individual and is supported with reason codes that provide insight into why an applicant received a particular score. These reason codes help pinpoint which identity data might be suspect and how to most efficiently verify an application.

With this information-sharing model, ID Analytics' solution becomes more accurate with each company that joins the consortium. Also, its ability to detect fraudulent behavior patterns from a 360-degree view of the fraudster, rather than from his interactions with just one company or industry, provides good insight into fraud prevention. It's the absence of this panoramic view and pattern analysis technologies that has allowed identity crimes to flourish in recent years, especially as criminals become more sophisticated on how to stay one step ahead of detection methods.

Unlike other fraud detection products with high false-positive ratios that ultimately require tedious manual verification and lack the capability to identify new fraud patterns, this consortium-based, 360-degree view, cross-industry, multiple-company service enables the real-time delivery of a score at the point of application, with high detection rates. The key to this system is the use of cross-industry data. ID Score is being deployed by some of the nation's largest credit card, retail card, wireless, and online instant credit companies. Using a similar model, homeland security organizations may want to consider a similar type of consortium within multiple government agencies at the federal, state, and local levels, as well as partnerships with companies such as ID Analytics in its effort to detect and combat identity theft by terrorists.

ID FRAUD INTERCEPT BY FAIR ISAAC

Founded in 1956, Fair Isaac® helps thousands of companies in over 60 countries reduce fraud and credit losses. Most leading banks and credit card issuers rely on Fair Isaac's FICO® scores to evaluate credit risk of new and existing customers, as do insurers, retailers, telecommunications providers, healthcare organizations, and government agencies. Using its vast experience in assessing risk, Fair Isaac provides a new service to combat identity theft geared at consumers. Its ID Fraud Intercept is designed to detect potential identity theft early by monitoring hundreds of databases for changes to the consumer's personal address or phone number.

Fair Isaac believes that often this type of activity is the earliest indication and pattern of identity theft. The service also highlights signs of potential fraud that may appear in a customer's personal credit report and FICO score. ID Fraud Intercept is primarily a consumer service that monitors more than 400 public and commercial data sources every week to see if anyone has tried to establish a new address or phone number under someone else's name. The relevancy to homeland security organizations of this consumer service is in the data sources that it looks at in its attempt to detect this type of terrorist-related crime.

According to a recent report by the FTC, early detection is vital when detecting and preventing identity fraud. The FTC found that by discovering identity fraud within the first month, nine out of ten victims are able to prevent the opening of fraudulent new accounts in their names. However, when victims first discover identity fraud six months or longer after it begins, three out of five will experience substantial monetary losses. Unfortunately, victims often don't know how their personal information was stolen, and they don't know what they need to do to prevent significant losses. Recent data shows that as few as 15 percent of identity theft cases begin with a lost or stolen wallet, checkbook, or credit card, while only 5 percent of cases involve stolen mail. Other common ways criminals obtain personal information are through transactions by phone, mail, and the Internet or the misuse of information entrusted by a co-worker or family member.

With ID Fraud Intercept, Fair Isaac has combined its worldwide expertise in fraud detection technology with its industry-standard scoring solutions to directly assist consumers against this fastest-growing financial crime. The company's fraud detection solutions are already being used to protect more than 60 percent of all credit card transactions worldwide from fraud. Creditors use the FICO credit score to make billions of credit decisions each year: More than 40 of the nation's 50 largest financial institutions rely on the FICO score to help them determine an individual's credit risk.

Every week, ID Fraud Intercept scours more than 400 different sources of public and commercial data, looking for changes. Not only does Fair Isaac search for changes in credit bureaus, but it also looks at utilities, property deeds and assessments, bankruptcy filings, vehicle data, and other public sources. Although ID Fraud Intercept is geared as a service for consumers, the expertise, data sources, and technology could be used to assist homeland security organizations in monitoring and filtering visa applications, foreign visitors, and other individuals with questionable patterns of activity indicating the possible theft of identification.

THE FAIR AND ACCURATE CREDIT TRANSACTIONS ACT OF 2003

This new legislation will significantly combat the growing problem of identity theft. The various provisions of the Act include the following:

- Provide consumers with a free credit report every year.
- Give consumers the right to see their credit scores.
- Provide consumers with the ability to opt out of information sharing between affiliated companies for marketing purposes.
- Ensure that consumers are notified if merchants are going to report negative information to the credit bureaus about them.
- Allow consumers to place "fraud alerts" in their credit reports to prevent identity thieves from opening accounts in their names, including special provisions to protect active duty military personnel.
- Allow consumers to block information from being given to a credit bureau and from being reported by a credit bureau if such information results from identity theft.
- Restrict access to consumers' sensitive health information.
- Provide consumers with one-call-for-all protection by requiring credit bureaus to share consumer calls on identity theft, including requested fraud alert blocking.
- Require creditors to take certain precautions before extending credit to consumers who have placed fraud alerts in their files.
- Stop merchants from printing more than the last five digits of a payment card on an electronic receipt.

Aside from services for validating the identity of individuals, there is another genre of software that uses unique algorithms and linguistic patterns and rules for the recognition, perfection, and matching of names, such as those on suspected terrorist watch lists. This is especially important to intelligence and border control components of homeland security organizations; however, before discussing some of the premiere name recognition software systems, the following sidebar discusses a specialized intelligence construction platform.

MITOSYSTEMS

MitoSystems offers a unique approach to the construction of intelligence systems for homeland security organizations with its Mitopia platform. Mitopia is a fully integrated platform that focuses on intelligence problems by taking a bottom-up architectural approach rather than the traditional top-down approach, in which different software components are linked via enterprise-wide appiications or commercial off-the-shelf (COTS) software. Mitopia is an end-to-end system that may involve

(continued)

hundreds or thousands of computers, with every machine running the same software code base and with the configuration tools available to specify the desired local functionality. MitoSystems takes an ontology-based approach in the construction of the Mitopia unified architecture. Mitopia is a multithreaded, distributed architecture that fuses all applications, encapsulating all the data into a unified model and weaving the "threads" of disparate information into a composite whole for analytic and strategic intelligence use by private and public organizations.

Mitopia was designed to support the entire intelligence cycle, from heterogeneous data collection, fusion, storage, and retrieval to analysis, visualization, and dissemination. Mitopia supports multiple languages and multimedia formats and represents a complete, fully integrated, end-to-end intelligence workflow platform. The concept of an ontology, or data fusion formalization scheme, is central and pervasive throughout the system. For instance, both database storage and user interface are generated automatically through the ontology.

Mitopia data-flow architecture is transformed into any number of applications through a set of configuration components. One application differs from another primarily through the establishment of the system ontology, the definition of a set of scripts to ingest and fuse data streams, and building block components, which provide localized algorithms and functionality. The core infrastructural overhead of any typical application is completely handled by the Mitopia environment. One of its key aspects is the capability to fuse heterogeneous data from disparate sources to discover relationships and connections. It does this through unified system ontology. Mitopia is able to handle multimedia data feeds in multiple languages and formats and process them in real time. The same software runs on every machine in a system, with local functionality specified through a variety of configuration parameters.

Mitopia is a completely ontology-based system in which all data is fused to determine explicit and computational connections, relationships, and patterns. The storage of data is driven by the system ontology, so changes in the ontology are instantly reflected in the appropriate storage fields and data types to be ingested. Mitopia employs a real-time parsing engine called MitoMine, which is used to automatically identify and extract entities and ontological objects with all relevant links. MitoMine acts to fuse data to the ontology, and this capability integrates multimedia information such as video, audio, and imagery. Ingestion servers support user-specified alerts of "interest profiles" with automatic user notification.

Mitopia uses a complete client/server architecture at its core. Servers can be clustered logically but distributed geographically and scaled to any number of machines. A complete search infrastructure called MitoPlex acts as a federated search infrastructure between all servers and to all containers within a server, including multimedia. Search and querying is multilingual and language independent. Automated ontology-based hyperlinking of incoming data on a per-user basis can be set according to security clearance and user preferences.

(continued)

Incoming data is fused via the ontology, and the underlying architecture supports automated creation of arbitrary links. Visualization tools enable trends and anomalies to be uncovered via abstract vector spaces whose axes are user definable and can be used for querying or automated alerts and profiles. The system ontology is designed to enable automatic extraction of entities, events, actions, and the examination of these events for matches to known entity motives. Scenario modeling can be used as an analysis tool simply by introducing non-real data into the normal data stream.

A 3D visualization framework is in place to view data along multiple axes either derived from real data values or inferred via user-specified vector algorithms. Connections in data can be seen in three dimensions, with sounds attributed to data types. A complete, immersive 3D environment, including spatial data (maps), satellite images and flyovers, and building "walk-throughs" are provided and fully integrated with all abstract visualization tools. Video capture and streaming (multiple formats) are fully integrated and can be incorporated anywhere in the environment, including briefings and reports. A fully integrated GIS, topology, and mapping engine is provided and GIS-based query and data refinement are integrated with all other analytical techniques, including link analysis.

A multimedia report architecture is available with any number of customizable templates. Multimedia reports can be created through use of customizable templates, manual entry, and dragging and dropping collateral information and source documents to support analyses. Reports are available online in the system and can be published and distributed to select users on the system. Custom live reports can be created through the built-in visual data-flow programming language.

Reports and the data within them can be customized based on user privileges. Reports and all data at a client workstation can be collaboratively shared with others. All data in the system is permanently tagged with its source, and this information can be used to establish reliability. Support for tracking changes over time is inherent to the underlying model on which the system is built. Servers can be set up for any multimedia type; Mitopia can serve up images, videos, maps, text, and audio and stream them all to any client machine or integrate them in any analytical process. Video conferencing can be supported, as can plug-in encryption and biometric user authentication devices.

All data in the system can be shared. Users of the system are treated as specialized "feeds" and their input is shareable and can be queried or monitored in a homogeneous manner with all system data. Interest profile support provides automated push capability, as does the built-in mail server. User-definable workflows via visual dataflow language can be integrated into the process, enabling arbitrarily complex behaviors, including modification of distributed content. Once again, since users are feeds, their activity, interests, and the information they have requested can all be tracked and queried.

(continued)

The system supports and heavily uses the ability to define user-specific interest profiles or active agents that are automatically run on the user's behalf on all incoming information. These profiles can incorporate abstract processes defined via the visual programming language and include the capability to create new custom building blocks via compiled code. An API containing thousands of calls is provided to support the creation of such custom building blocks, which may incorporate any technology area or analytical techniques. The system supports both data and user-interface level sharing between arbitrary numbers of users on the system. A publish and subscribe collaboration model is built into the system data and architecture at the lowest levels. All system communication is handled via standard IP packets and thus will operate over any IP network.

MitoSystems believes this radical data-flow paradigm can be used to build massive, highly customized, distributed, multimedia applications for information acquisition, analysis, and management systems for strategic command and control purposes, including those for homeland security organizations.

NAME RECOGNITION

Name recognition technology has been gaining prominence since the 9/11 attacks, after disclosures that federal agencies failed to share information about two terrorists who had been on a law enforcement watch list. Months later, the former Immigration and Naturalization Service disclosed that it had issued visas to two of the hijackers. Many government agencies have started to implement name recognition software in systems ranging from taxation to child welfare and law enforcement and now homeland security in an effort to improve and perfect the matching of names in their systems.

Somewhat related to this process is name entity recognition (NER) software, programs used to extract references to people, organizations, geographical locations, and other entities automatically from documents in order to provide users with focused information on the major entities with respect to references in text sources. NER software is particularly useful when applied to large document collections because it is very efficient at identifying important aspects about individuals in text, enabling users to retrieve this information quickly, as well as to produce statistics on the contents of the whole document collection.

NER software is specialized information extraction tools and belongs in part to the genre of categorization software, text mining technologies, and natural language processing. As such, the tools will not provide perfect results, and some products will be more effective than others in locating the names being searched. Some of the most effective text analysis tools in this area have the capability to extract multilingual names of entities from documents, such as watch lists or other types of immigration or transportation databases, and as such may be of interest to homeland security organizations. These programs include the NER products discussed in the following sections.

AeroText (Lockheed Martin)

The AeroText™ product suite provides a fast, agile information extraction system for developing knowledge-based content analysis applications. Possible applications include automatic database generation, routing, browsing, summarizing, and searching. The AeroText Core Knowledge Base provides out-of-the-box capabilities to extract common entities such as persons, organizations, and place names and discovering relationships such as a person or an organization to a place. Languages supported include English, Spanish, Chinese, Japanese, and Arabic.

IdentiFinder (BBN/Verizon)

IdentiFinderTM extracts information from text or from speech to find people; places, companies, numbers, dates, amounts, or other categories defined by example. The software can be trained to scan text rapidly to locate these entities and apply contextual clues to locate names that would be impossible to specify in advance. The software can be set to look for aliases and specified entities regardless of formatting such as HTML, all capitals, mixed case, or lowercase. Languages supported include Arabic, English, and Chinese.

Intelligent Miner for Text (IBM)

This toolkit includes components for building advanced text mining and text search applications. The technology provided with this product has been merged into DB2, the Information Integrator for Content Linguistic analysis, and is provided for documents in 19 single-byte character set languages. Languages supported include U.S. English, U.K. English, Catalan, Danish, Dutch, German, Swiss German, Spanish, Finnish, French, Canadian French, Icelandic, Italian, Norwegian Bokmal, Norwegian Nynorsk, Portuguese, Russian, Thai, and Swedish. There is multi-byte language support for Hebrew, Arabic, Simplified Chinese, Traditional Chinese, Japanese, and Korean, but the Text Analysis Tools can be used only with English documents.

NetOwl (SRA)

SRA has been developing its line of NetOwl® text mining products since 1996. Beginning with research and development for the U.S. government in the early 1990s, SRA has gone on to develop several text mining products, including NetOwl TextMiner for automatically retrieving, analyzing, extracting, summarizing, and visualizing large amounts of unstructured data. NetOwl Extractor can be used for the extraction of names, where names are partially or completely unknown. Extractor can also pull links and events connecting people, organizations, and such items as weapons of mass destruction. NetOwl Extractor can handle several foreign languages, including Arabic, Chinese, Spanish, Japanese, German, French, and Russian. NetOwl InstaLink provides the homeland security analyst with the ability to maintain and update in real time crucial pieces of information that have been automatically extracted from very large quantities of text data as well as from already structured databases. InstaLink also enables collaboration capabilities for teams of analysts working on the same or related problems. These are the entity variables:

Types of entities extracted by NetOwl Extractor:

Address: DNS, e-mail, IP address, post office box, street, URL, ZIP Code, and so on.

Artifact: Drug, vehicle, weapon, and so on.

Numeric: Account, credit card, money, passport, percent, phone, SSN, and so on.

Organization: Company, education, facility, government, military organization, political publication, religious group, union, and so on.

Person: Civilian, military, and so on.

Place: Astronomical, city, continent, country, county, district, landform, province, region, roadway, water, and so on.

Time: Age, date, temporal, time of day, and so on.

Types of links and events extracted by NetOwl Extractor:

Event: Business, conflict, crime, family, financial, personnel change, political, transaction, vehicle, and so on.

Artifact Links: Maker, owner, and so on.

Organization Links: Founder, location owner, parent, stock market, and so on.

Person Links: Affiliation, associate, birthplace, grandparent, parent, sibling, spouse, other relative, and so on.

Thing Finder (Inxight)

Thing Finder™ Server is an Internet software tool for developers that enables them to implement extended search and browse functionality into their Web applications or pages. The server is a drop-in server-side product that supports JavaBeans, ActiveX, and ASP and JSP delivery mechanisms. The tool provides an automatic document and categorization analysis engine for indexing addresses, people, companies, URLs, and dates. Thing Finder supports the following languages: English, Chinese, Spanish, Japanese, French, and German.

Categories covered by Thing Finder:

Address: Address.

Internet Address: E-mail address, URL, and so on.

City: City name.

Company: Companies, corporations, retailers, and banks.

Country: Country name.

Currency: Currency and currency expressions.

Date: Date and date expressions.

Day: Day of the week.

Holiday: Holidays and special days.

Language: Noun referring to a language.

Measure: Measurement and measurement expressions.

Month: Month, including abbreviations.

Noun Group: Common noun phrase, that is, a phrase consisting of two or more related nouns.

Organization: Government, legal, or service agency, including non-profit associations and institutions.

Peoples: Name referring to a group of people based on country, ethnicity, or region.

Percent: Percents.

Person: Person's name.

Person Pos: Title that is also used to refer to a person.

Phone: Phone numbers.

Place Other: Geographical name that does not fit in other place categories.

Place Polit: Dependent and oversea territories of countries that are not generally included in the set of administrative divisions of a country.

Place Region: Geographical area that is larger than a city and typically captures significant geographical areas.

Product: Product name.

Prop Misc: Any proper noun without an unambiguous classification.

Publication: Name of a newspaper, magazine, journal, and so on.

SSN: Social Security number, including Canadian Social Insurance numbers and French INSEE numbers.

State: The major administrative divisions of countries.

Time: Time and time expressions.

Time Period: Measures of time expressions.

Year: Years, including abbreviations.

Government Use of Name Recognition Technologies

Name recognition software that has been used to help child welfare agencies locate delinquent parents and credit bureaus identify tardy payments can be adapted to help homeland security organizations perfect watch lists and track down potential terrorists. This type of linguistic-based name matching software can help homeland security organizations search databases for individuals on a watch list, such as the Terrorist Screening Center (TSC), to consolidate terrorist watch lists and provide 24/7 operational support for thousands of federal screeners across the country and around the world. The TSC will enable federal, state, and local officials to make better-informed decisions to protect the United States from terrorist attacks. For example, better access to information will make it easier for a consular officer posted in another country to determine whether to grant a visa, or an immigration official at a U.S. airport to decide whether a person is eligible to enter the United States.

The TSC builds on improvements to U.S. watch list capabilities that began in 2001, immediately following the 9/11 attacks, including, most recently, the president's creation of the TTIC. Name recognition software can improve search-matching capabilities for identification theft and screening of individuals, and some of these programs do not require databases to be reformatted into a specific model, prepared, or "scrubbed." Using this type of name recognition software, the TSC can consolidate watch list information into an unclassified terrorist screening database and make the database accessible to queries for federal, state, and local agencies for a variety of screening purposes.

The Internal Revenue Service and two federal intelligence agencies are using name recognition software because it is able to search and find matches despite extreme error and variation. The FBI is also using this type of software for its National Crime Information System, while the IRS is using it for its Name Search Project, for matching taxpayers with a tax identification number. The strength of this type of name recognition software is that it maintains all the translation tables and the patterns of common spelling. In addition, most of the high-end products are language independent, performing intelligent indexing, searching, and matching of names, addresses, and other specific identification. For homeland security organizations, the problem is compounded by the need to recognize variations in the spelling of foreign names from different cultural regions in the world, with variations in their structure and formats.

A large problem with personal names stems from the variations that take place when they are changed from their original script into Roman characters. Figure 6.1 illustrates several problems encountered when an Arabic name is transliterated

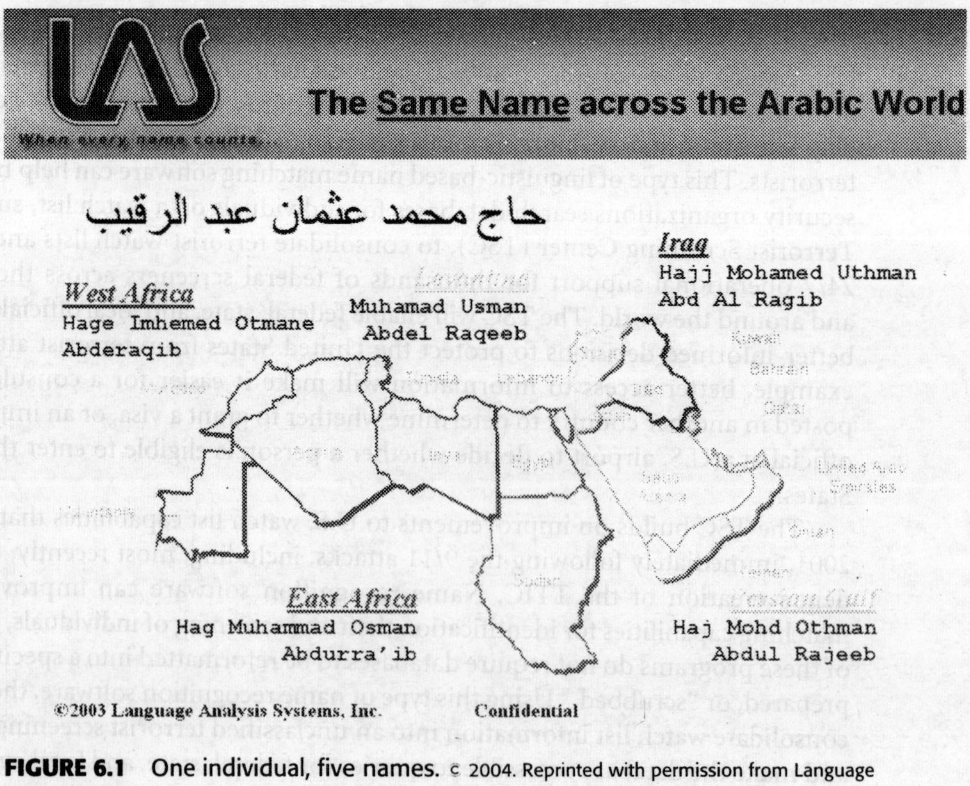

FIGURE 6.1 One individual, five names. © 2004. Reprinted with permission from Language Analysis Systems.

from its native script into the Roman character set. First, across the top, you see a man's name written in the Arabic script from right to left. However, different regions use a different method of transliterating the same name. These variations include four name parts, while some have six. There also are different versions of the same name; note that Mohammed, Imhemed, Muhammad, and Mohd are all valid spellings of Mohammed. Also, Haj or Hag is not a name but rather a title, meaning the person has made a pilgrimage to Mecca. Most computers would treat this title as the first name, an inaccurate assumption. Then there are whitespace parsing variations, such as Abdurra'ib and Abdul Rajeeb. Again, most computer programs would not recognize those names as equivalent, but specialized linguistic-based name recognition software such as that from LAS would.

Search Software America (SSA)

Search Software America (SSA) is another firm developing and marketing name recognition software that enhances an organization's ability to search, find, match, and group identity data within its computer systems and network databases. SSA specializes in software that adds intelligence and quality to critical name searching and matching applications such as counterintelligence, fraud detection, and now homeland security. Many aspects of intelligence and investigation operations rely on the perfection of data about the names, addresses, and other identification attributes of people and organizations. This identification data will be subject to the normal unavoidable variations and errors encountered in all data processing operations. In addition, in cases where the entity is committing fraud or identity theft, a perpetrator will attempt to defeat normal matching algorithms, and the identification data will often be subject to deliberate abnormal or extreme variations.

In systems that support intelligence and investigation work, databases of historical incidents and known perpetrators are maintained such that new incidents can be linked or matched against them, or new patterns discovered from within them. Such databases need to maintain indexes of the names or addresses of the perpetrators and organizations. In order to support such systems, it must be possible to reliably search or match large-scale databases using the names of people and watch lists as well as their prior and current addresses. SSA's software offers that type of matching, despite the unavoidable or deliberate variation and error in name, address, and other personal identification data.

The SSA software copes well with data of any quality and does not require the data to be cleaned or formatted. It also supports data from any country using any character set.

SSA's software is able to search for a name whether it is William, Bill, Billy, or Will, or Peter, Pete, Pietro, or Pierre for a wide range of purposes, including immigration matching and finding financial data. To automate the searching and matching process, the software mimics the way humans look for names, addresses, dates, identity numbers, and other data: It uses "tunable" matching algorithms to rank, score, or match entities.

The SSA Data Clustering Engine can be used to discover clusters of identities that may be of interest to investigators and to discover matches between external files, such as terrorist watch lists. The SSA Identity System (IDS) is an out-of-the-box search and matching system that performs online and batch searching, matching, and duplicate discovery of name and address data. The Text Name Identification (TNI) product is used to extract name, address, and other information from free text for indexing by products such as SSA-NAME3 or IDS, or for grouping and linking by the Data Clustering Engine. The process does not require the data to be cleaned or formatted and supports searches in 55 languages. The search server runs on IBM Corp. OS/390 mainframe, Microsoft Corp. Windows NT/2000, and UNIX platforms.

LANGUAGE ANALYSIS SYSTEMS (LAS)

Two computational linguists from Georgetown University founded Language Analysis Systems, Inc., almost 20 years ago. They began by working on an early project with the U.S. State Department. Since then LAS has been developing high-end name recognition software for various U.S. intelligence and border control agencies. Through this work, LAS has examined almost 1 billion names from more than 200 countries, classifying and creating statistics that are today being used in their multilingual recognition software. LAS has performed years of linguistic research on naming conventions around the world.

LAS is unique in its approach to name recognition, in that it first looks at a name to determine the name's name-type or culture of origin. Once that is determined, the name search system can bring a number of cultural/linguistic rules to bear on the name to get the most accurate match.

Through this approach, the software is also able to provide an in-depth understanding of names, their formats, gender associations, and likely countries of origin. This unique approach is necessary because foreign names do not always fit the three-part Western format of given name, middle name, and surname, as is typical of United States' citizens. There could also be different spellings of names identifying the same individual, which is especially relevant in the processing of terrorist watch lists, because homeland security requires managing information about people from all regions in the world and recognizing their names accurately.

To illustrate the problem of global diversity and the challenge of multilingual name recognition, note Figure 6.2. In the center, you see the person's name written in Chinese logograms. Note that there are multiple standard transliterations across regions of the world, resulting in extremely different versions of the name when it is converted to the Roman script.

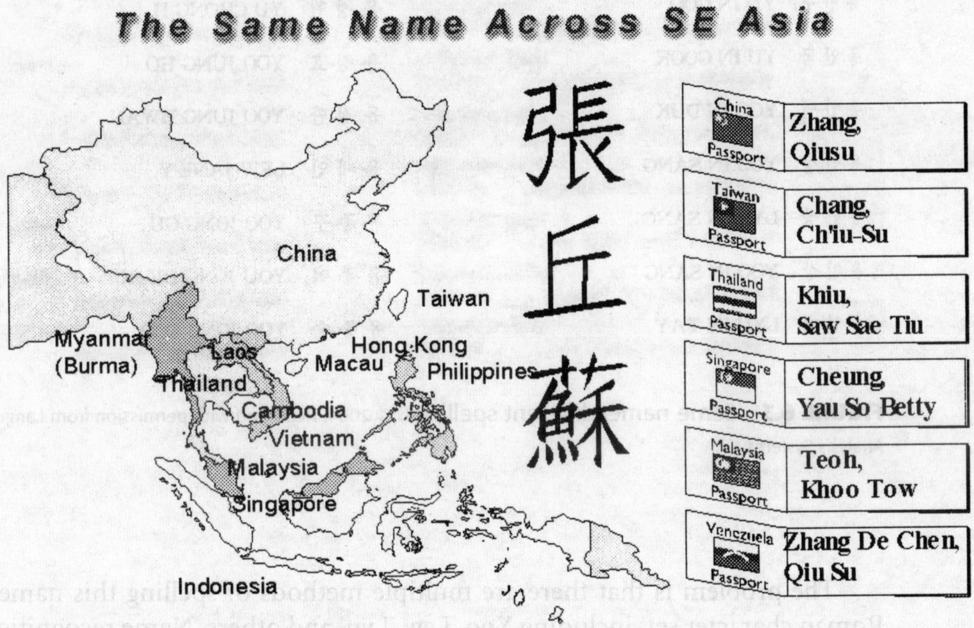

FIGURE 6.2 Same name in Asia, different names in the United States. © 2004. Reprinted with permission from Language Analysis Systems.

LAS has studied and encoded the various transliteration standards into its software so that it can detect that Zhang, Qiusu and Cheung, Yao So are most probably the same name, recognizing the variations stemming from cultural differences.

This bilingual directory illustrates the variations that commonly occur in the spelling of foreign names, such as that of Korean names. Note the symbols in Figure 6.3 for the names listed down the left side and the transliteration for the surname, Liu.

FIGURE 6.3 Same name, different spellings. © 2004. Reprinted with permission from Language Analysis Systems.

The problem is that there are multiple methods of spelling this name in the Roman character set, including Yoo, Lew, Lyu, and others. Name recognition software can detect these variations in the spellings of the same name. This type of software recognizes that a name is not just a string of characters. Rather, it focuses upon the cultural context, noting that a name has many properties such as title, nicknames, and so on that can be automatically understood by an intelligent processing engine. It also takes into consideration certain cultural and regional rules about names of individuals.

Character string-oriented mechanisms such as Soundex perform especially poorly in the searching of foreign names. For example, a match for Yoo will never be found when searching with Soundex for Lew. This is due to the fact that this type of string-based system favors Anglo sounds for names, performing poorly when applied to the recognition of transliterated names.

Here is an example of what happens: An individual enters the country and is recorded in various databases (see Figure 6.4). Problems can occur as this individual's name is input to each depository due to transliteration issues and/or human error. The results are that records and digital entities of the same name are created in a slightly different manner and can easily become invisible to subsequent searches.

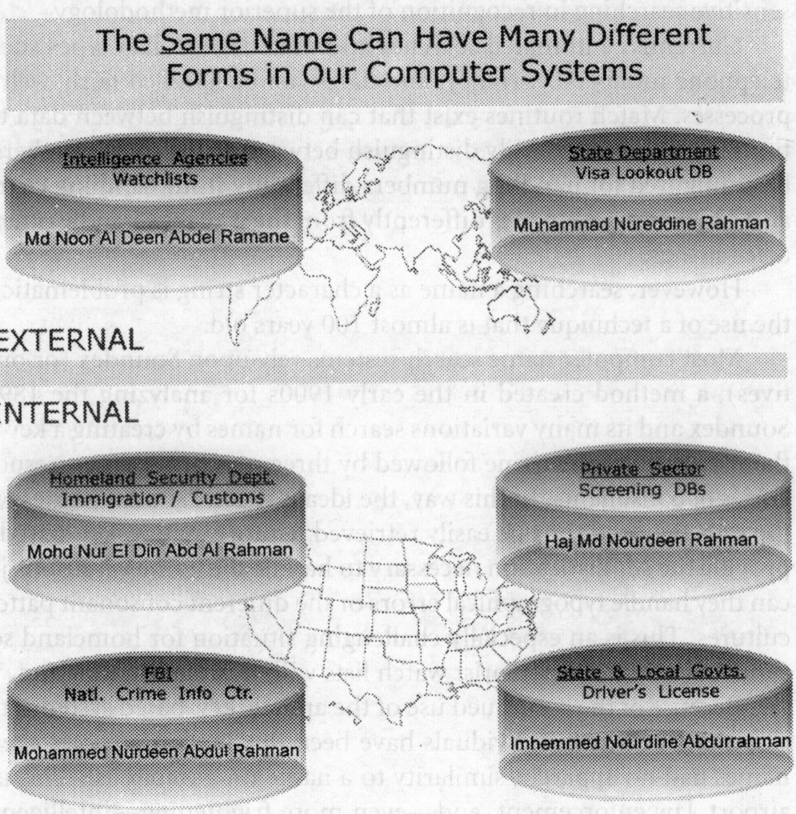

FIGURE 6.4 Same name, different records in multiple databases. © 2004. Reprinted with permission from Language Analysis Systems.

Subsequently, follow-up queries and searches for the name Mohammed Nurdine Abdurrahman are difficult to match across the various government, law enforcement, and commercial databases.

The input problem is almost impossible to fix. Even if the U.S. government were able to standardize how names are translated, there is no way to control how other governments translate names, and therefore an individual would still be able to obtain documents under different variations. Further, there is no way to control how the individual presents himself in most situations. However, a good way to improve these searches in order to reduce false positives is to use linguistic-based software for perfecting and matching names. In fact, as part of the Enhanced Border Security and Visa Reform Act of 2002, Congress mandated the use of linguistically sensitive searching in recognition of the superior methodology.

Currently, automated searches and matches for data types such as addresses, telephone numbers, currency, and dates can be handled fairly well via automated processes. Match routines exist that can distinguish between data types, and relational databases can easily distinguish between strings and numbers. Software can be configured for handling numbers differently from handling currency; and they also can process addresses differently from the way they handle other types of character strings.

However, searching a name as a character string is problematic, due in part to the use of a technique that is almost 100 years old.

Most computer name search systems rely upon Soundex (or one of its derivatives), a method created in the early 1900s for analyzing the 1890 census data. Soundex and its many variations search for names by creating a key that consists of the first letter of the name followed by three numbers that correspond to six categories of consonants. In this way, the idea is that all similar names will end up with the same key and thus be easily retrieved. Unfortunately, key-based systems fail to provide the sophistication necessary to handle the name variations just shown; nor can they handle typographical errors or the different consonant patterns from other cultures. This is an especially challenging situation for homeland security organizations dealing with terrorist watch lists with multicultural names.

Because of the continued use of the archaic key-based systems, there have been situations in which individuals have been detained at airports even though their names had no apparent similarity to a name on a watch list. This is because most airport, law enforcement, and—even more frightening—intelligence systems still use key-based algorithms, all of which are based on Soundex. Soundex is the most common algorithm bundled in today's popular databases such as Oracle and Microsoft SQL. There is at least one very applicable terrorist event that is partially attributable to having inadequate name matching in multiple systems, the case of Mir Aimal Kansi, who shot five people in front of the CIA.

The Pakistani immigrant Mir Aimal Kansi, responsible for the shootings outside CIA headquarters, passed through immigration checkpoints at John F.

Kennedy International Airport in New York with a passport and business visa listing his name as Mir Aimal Kasi. The discrepancy in Kansi's name hampered investigators in determining who he was and how he came to the United States. Kansi's case, of course, is not an isolated one, but is one of the most poignant examples of the frailty of current name tracking systems. Interestingly, Kasi and Kansi are both perfectly reasonable transliterations from the name in its normal orthographic form. Unfortunately, most of today's federal, state, and local law enforcement, immigration, and homeland security systems do not use the sophisticated name recognition technology that is necessary to make this determination. A key-based name search system could never have matched the name of Kasi to Kansi.

Studies have shown that Soundex fails to return from 25 to 60 percent of correct names. Soundex Plus tables are systems that have added nicknames to the basic Soundex matching method; it is better than Soundex, but it still is limited to the flawed premise of key-based character matching. In contrast, the LAS culture-based system is a departure from the key-based systems of the past. This culture-based system encodes cultural information from over 200 countries, treating a name not as a character string but instead as an object containing valuable data about the bearer.

The LAS system breaks the types of name variations into three levels. At the first level, the system considers the possible variation in the character string itself. At the second level, it automatically determines the culture of a name. At the third level, the software applies associated cultural rules for recognizing and processing the name. (By using culturally related nicknames and common variations of spellings, for example, LAS has found over 200 spelling variations of the name Mohammed.) Finally, the name recognition software also supports phonetic variations for names that sound alike but are not spelled alike.

LAS offers a complete line of products that parse, store, search, match, and generate names intelligently.

LAS also offers a Name Transliteration Server that enables organizations to search names in databases even though the query name and the database name(s) may be in different languages. The following is an example application using several LAS name recognition products, in this case it is the Name Reference Library™ (NRL), which was used to help track the 9/11 terrorists to their Florida connections (see Figure 6.5). After a perpetrator name is entered, the NRL automatically provides the following:

- Probable culture, using the NameClassifier™
- Probable gender, using the NameGender Toolkit
- Parsing information, using the Name Standardization Utilities
- Alternate valid spellings, using the NameVariation Server

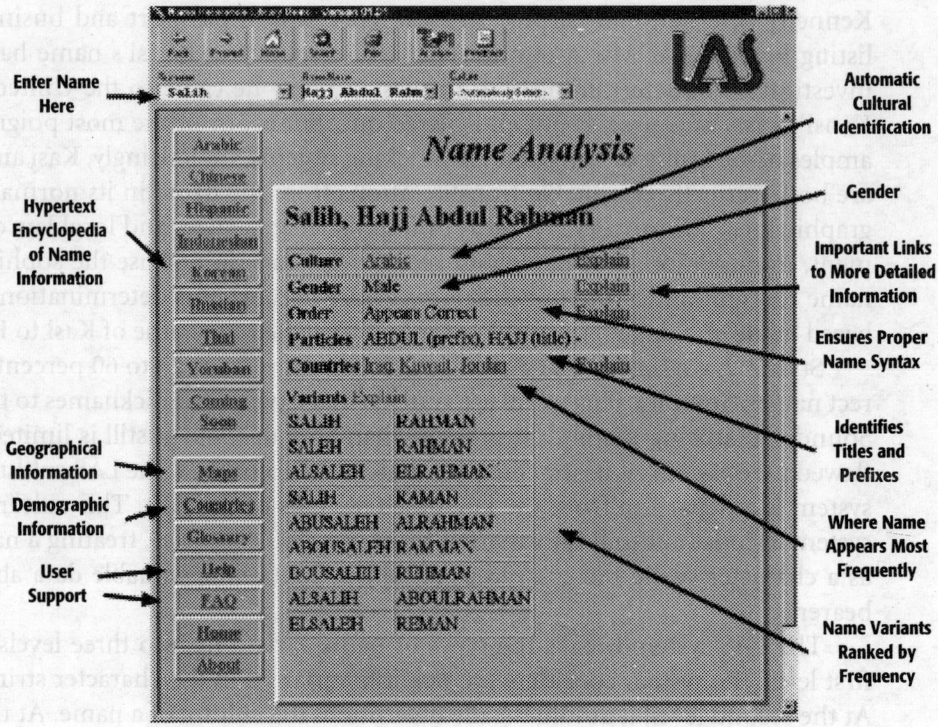

FIGURE 6.5 A Name Reference Library search. © 2004. Reprinted with permission from Language Analysis Systems.

The Name Reference Library is an interactive reference guide of culture-specific information about names, their use, their meanings, and their patterns of spelling variations. The NRL shows how names are used in key cultures and ethnic settings, showing gender associations for unfamiliar given names, and links names to specific geographic regions and locations where they are most commonly used. The NRL supports name recognition from the following cultures: Arabic, Hispanic, Chinese, Indonesian, Russian, Korean, Yoruban/Nigerian, and Thai. The NRL also provides an XML-based API, enabling its name-analysis functions to be integrated directly into many Web-enabled applications.

The following is an example of the *cultural scoring* of four individual names using NameClassifier on the names RYU IK HIE, CHAROEN, SAW SAE TIU; HAJJ MOHAMED UTHMAN ABD AL RAGIB; and MARIA LUZ RODRIGUEZ V. DE LUNA:

Name: RYU IK HIE

Count: 13

#1	**475**	**Korean**
#2	283	Japanese
#3	211	Anglo
#4	125	Arabic
#5	93	Farsi
#6	91	German
#7	57	French
#8	28	Pakistani
#9	26	Indian
#10	18	Hispanic
#11	18	Chinese
#12	10	Russian
#13	2	Thai

Name: CHAROEN, SAW SAE TIU

Count: 13

#1	**255**	**Thai**
#2	161	Pakistani
#3	148	Korean
#4	140	Indian
#5	136	Arabic
#6	100	Anglo
#7	98	Farsi
#8	77	French
#9	57	Hispanic
#10	57	Japanese
#11	51	Russian
#12	33	German
#13	25	Chinese

Name: HAJJ MOHAMED UTHMAN ABD AL RAGIB

Count: 13

#1	**1493**	**Arabic**
#2	919	Farsi
#3	676	Pakistani
#4	511	Anglo
#5	434	Indian
#6	188	Hispanic
#7	164	German
#8	140	Japanese
#9	123	Thai
#10	104	French
#11	104	Korean
#12	61	Russian
#13	52	Chinese

Name: MARIA LUZ RODRIGUEZ V. DE LUNA

Count: 13

#1	**1074**	**Hispanic**
#2	534	German
#3	395	Anglo
#4	393	Russian
#5	292	French
#6	241	Pakistani
#7	207	Indian
#8	202	Farsi
#9	176	Korean
#10	170	Arabic
#11	159	Thai
#12	147	Japanese
#13	121	Chinese

Next are examples of search and scoring of names using the NameHunter™ engine, which provides ranked results based on linguistic and cultural variation patterns. The user simply supplies NameHunter with a list of names and unique record IDs and the name-searching engine provides automated support for Level 1 and Level 2 variations in names. These include the following two processes:

Level One: Character Variation

Typos: Smith~Simth, Johnson~Jphnson

Noise: Thompson~Th9mp2on

Concatenations: Andrews~Andrewsjr

Truncation/Initials: Ivanov~Ivanovsky, Patrick~P

Level Two: Cultural Variation

Titles: Dr., Rev, Haj, Sri., Col., ...

Suffixes: -aldin, -oglu, -skii/-skaya, ...

Prefixes: Fitz, O', De La, Abdul, ...

Qualifiers: Jr., fils, neto, sobrinho, Ph.D., ...

Infixes: de, vde., ...

Nicknames: Johnny, Betty, Alyosha, Paco, ...

Cultural Variants: Imhemed/Mohamed/Mohd

When configured with the LAS NameClassifier, selection of the appropriate cultural- and linguistic-variation patterns by NameHunter can be fully automated, or this choice can be left for the end-user. The following is a sample of its search results on "Creighton, Bobby":

Name	Score
Creighton, Robert	0.970000
Creighton, Robert & Margie	0.970000
Creighton, B J	0.955000
McCreight, Robert E	0.690000
McCreight, Robert & Eileen	0.690000

The following are NameHunter matches on "Gomez de Gonzalez, Maria":

Name	Score ID
Gomez, Maria	1.000000
Gomez, Maria & Jose	1.000000
Gonzalez, Maria	0.965000
Gonzalez, Maria Isabel	0.965000
Gomez, M	0.955000
Gomez, M O	0.955000
Gonzales, Maria	0.931750
Gonzalez, M	0.920000
Gomez, Mario	0.900000

LAS Name Variation Demo

Name to process: Mena   Name-field: Surname   Culture: Arabic

Show Variants | Clear | About this demo | Back to LAS Demos

Name	Field	Rank	Percent
MENA	SN	1	76.44%
MEENA	SN	2	22.00%
MENNA	SN	3	0.32%
MENNAA	SN	4	0.24%
MENNAH	SN	5	0.21%
MEENE	SN	6	0.17%
MEENAA	SN	7	0.13%
BEN MENA	SN	8	0.09%
MNA	SN	9	0.04%
ELMENA	SN	10	0.04%
AL MENNAA	SN	11	0.04%
MNEH	SN	12	0.02%
MNE	SN	13	0.02%

FIGURE 6.6 A demonstration of LAS name variation match capability. © 2004. Reprinted with permission from Language Analysis Systems.

Another major problem is that languages written in non-Roman scripts may use multiple systems for converting names from native to Roman characters. For example, a common Chinese name may be written correctly as either Hsiao or Xiao, and the same Russian surname may occur as Ivanov or Ivanoff. Existing name search systems in use today do not always match each other; so one form of the name will not reliably retrieve the others. This is one of the biggest problems for homeland security organizations today.

Antiquated key-based name-matching systems provide only an engineering solution to a complex problem that is really a linguistics and culture-recognition problem. Names ultimately vary according to the culture they come from. For example, a common element of many Arabic names is the prefix Abdul, which means "servant of." Key-based systems do not know that matching on the Abduls in the database names is of little help in this type of search because doing so will result in a high number of mismatches or false positives.

New name recognition technology, such as that from LAS, addresses the problem of identifying the culture, components, and variations of names by combining computational linguistics and cultural knowledge with software engineering. In response to the terrorist attacks of 9/11, Congress passed the Enhanced Border Security and Visa Entry Reform Act of 2002. With the intent on strengthening the border protection for the United States, the bill mandates that all related agencies use linguistically sensitive technology to search and process names to maximize precision and minimize false positives. The Act recognizes that antiquated approaches such as Soundex and key-based algorithms are not adequate for the mission-critical application of national defense. LAS is currently the only commercially available product that is fully compliant with the Act.

MONEY LAUNDERING

Terrorist financing can be defined as the processing of property from any source to be used to finance terrorist activity that has been or will be committed. It is thought to use many of the same techniques as money laundering, and therefore many of the possible countermeasures are similar, using the same type of technological services. Terrorist financing differs from money laundering in that it may be more difficult to detect because it is directed mainly at future activity. It is possible that the only offense that has been committed when the financing takes place is conspiracy to commit a terrorist act.

Also, the amounts of money needed to finance terrorism are widely believed to be relatively small—the 9/11 attacks on the World Trade Center and the Pentagon were believed to have required less than $1 million—compared to either normal commercial transactions or typical volumes of money being laundered by, say, large drug trafficking operations, which might total several hundred billion dollars a year. If anything, the detection of money laundering for terrorist activity will be that much more difficult to discover.

The global nature of terrorist financing networks and the urgency of responding to terrorist threats requires the ability to use the most advanced pattern recognition technology, coupled with new levels of communication, cooperation, and collaboration between homeland security organizations and the private sector. The efficient and rapid dissemination of terrorist financing information requires the active participation of banks and the money laundering software and services they have come to rely on.

Already the Department of Treasury, the Financial Crimes Enforcement Network, and seven other federal regulatory bodies require that financial businesses implement systems to determine if a person opening an account is on any list of known or suspected terrorist organizations and maintain records of the information used to verify the person's identity. The banking sector is required by law to monitor and report suspicious transactions indicating the possibility of money laundering. This does not necessarily mean, however, that current bank procedures are fully adequate to meet the new challenges of anti-money laundering policy in the post-9/11 period.

Prior to the USA PATRIOT Act, a report had to be filed for transactions over US$10,000; now, transactions must also be reported at adjustable limits. Under the Act, a financial institution can be held liable—and punishable by both monetary fines and criminal indictment—if the institution is found to have handled illicit funds either knowingly or unknowingly. While it is virtually impossible to completely block the movement of illicit funds through a financial institution, banks find it necessary to implement more thorough monitoring programs in order to comply with this new regulatory stringency. In order to thoroughly monitor customer transactions, new account openings, and complex relationships between accounts for possible money laundering activity, large financial institutions have started to use technologies capable of handling high volumes of transactions and multiple relational categories.

Banks and other financial institutions will not only have to tighten procedural compliance, they may also have to reevaluate entire business lines. Banks have traditionally done a good business in providing international correspondent banking relationships for domestic customers wishing to move funds abroad, and for overseas customers wishing to establish accounts in the United States. The USA PATRIOT Act singles out correspondent banking in particular as a potential harbor for money laundering, and the Treasury Department is examining methods for ensuring positive identification of overseas account holders, barring relationships with shell banks, and other controls on correspondent banking.

The Act also affects various bank monetary services, such as check cashing, payment of government entitlements, and international money transfers, to individuals with no formal account relationship, or the *unbanked* sector. Because unbanked customers do not necessarily pass through a know-your-customer account opening procedure, banks may need to institute special monitoring procedures for unbanked service customers, particularly in regard to money transfers. These various considerations for banks will apply to other financial institutions as well with an even greater initial impact, because most of these institutions are starting from zero and must build their money laundering programs from scratch.

Anti-Money Laundering (AML) Technologies

Information technology systems capable of storing and analyzing massive amounts of data, coupled with developments in artificial intelligence, have led to advances in the fight against money laundering in recent years. Under the 1996 Bank Secrecy Act, banks have long had to report suspicious deposits and transfers above $10,000 to the Treasury Department. The events of 9/11 changed that; under the USA PATRIOT Act there is currently an aggressive enforcement of anti-money laundering laws, which widened the reporting requirements to securities brokers, insurers, car dealers, and travel agents. Using their own resources, they now must file suspicious-activity reports based on cross-checking of customer names against a Treasury list of criminal suspects.

Banks and businesses have little choice but to bulk up on software to help them comply with new legislation. It is estimated that U.S. financial institutions will spend $695 million on anti-money laundering software and hardware by 2005 and another $11 billion on staffing, training, legal issues, and reporting to the government. However, because of the complexity involved in detecting money laundering, many of these organizations are turning to software companies such as GIFTS Software, Mantas, NetEconomy, and Searchspace. Their systems use sophisticated algorithms, stochastic models, and artificial intelligence technologies to monitor and learn what bad behavior looks like, then to route accounts to human analysts to review before investigations are opened. Figure 6.7 shows how an account alert is created.

These money laundering software companies have evolved over the last 10 years through three distinct anti-money laundering (AML) phases. At the first AML phase they focused on threshold exception reporting at the financial product level,

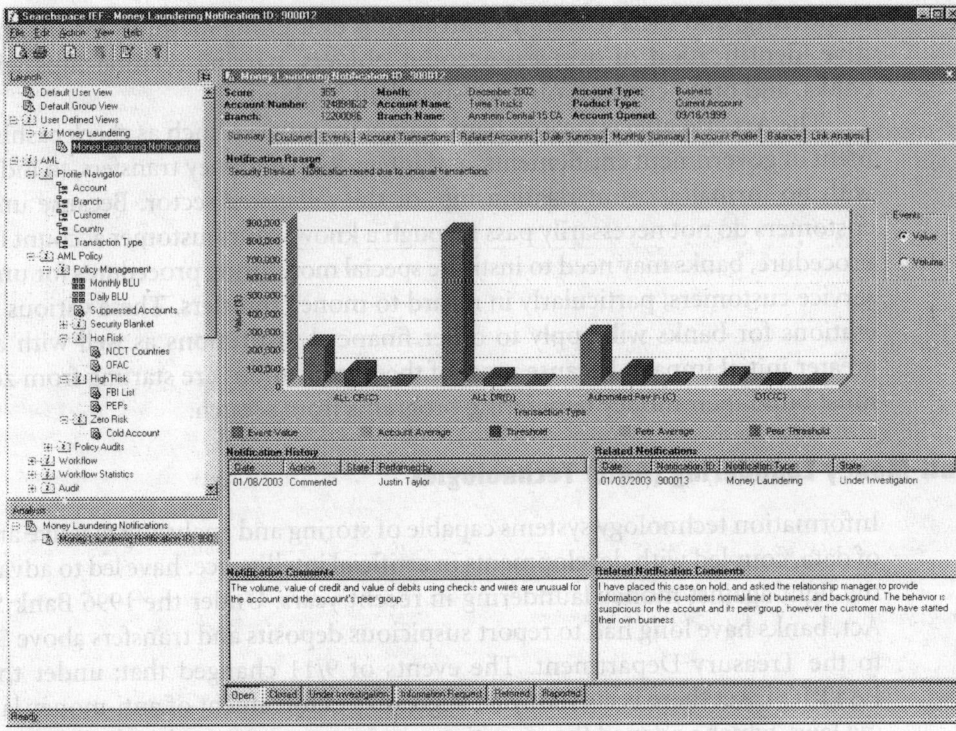

FIGURE 6.7 Notification generated by Searchspace due to unusual transaction.

so that, for example, if an individual withdrew more than $600 over a two-day period from an ATM, this activity would trigger an alert to a compliance analyst for review and possible investigation. Threshold-based systems relied on rules that tended to be static and that focused on specific products, such as checking accounts or credit cards. At the second AML phase, some of these money laundering detection software systems began to focus on the patterns of frauds, where, using neural networks, the programs begin to train and learn to detect criminal activity. However, with time this also becomes ineffective because new money laundering schemes are always evolving.

This brings us to the third AML phase of this evolution, where the software begins to monitor transactions at the individual level, creating profiles of customers. At this final phase, the more advanced money laundering systems are capable of profiling down to the amount of cash individuals normally draw from an ATM and what transactions they typically conduct with what merchants. At this level, patterns of criminal activity are discovered not by observing historical patterns, as was the case in the second phase of evolution. Instead, alerts are generated when deviations from the norm occur. At this phase, comparison of account behavior is also applied against peer industry groups in an effort to discover abnormal activities indicating money laundering schemes.

Prior to electronic payment channels, financial institutions relied on their tellers and bank officers to identify unusual behavior that signaled possible money laundering activity, but in the current digital environment with Internet banking, automated phone options, wireless transactions, and ubiquitous ATMs, this can no longer be the case. Today's environment requires the use of virtual machine learning agents, analogous to the human tellers or officers, that can provide the knowledge of each customer and the transactions associated with types of businesses. These virtual agents are found in the form of new anti-money laundering software and services.

FIGURE 6.8 Dynamic money laundering notification.

A new generation of AML technologies has emerged with the ability to monitor every single transaction, discovering all unusual behavior and looking for deviation from peer groups. These intelligent enterprise systems are able to learn and adapt, comprehending new money laundering schemes as they arise. They take an enterprise-wide approach, determining every transaction that is unusual, as opposed to looking for a specific pattern or behavior, which was the case with second generation AML systems. Money launderers often know the basic thresholds to avoid and are continuously developing new ways to evade them. Rather than pushing a large sum of money through an account in a single transaction, they may make multiple deposits that are less than the set threshold limit, using different accounts, and then later aggregate the funds into a single account. This is known as *smurfing* and can involve hundreds of small transactions.

The following sections discuss some of the more advanced AML systems in the market.

GIFTS Software

GIFTS's Enhanced Due Diligence (EDD) software enables banks to comply with new regulatory requirements such as the USA PATRIOT Act of 2001. The software is comprised of four modules: Transaction Patterning, the Treasury Office of Foreign Assets and Control (OFAC), the Bank Secrecy Act (BSA) Inquiry, and the Transaction Profiler.

The Transaction Patterning module enables the user to manually or systematically establish a transaction baseline for customer accounts. This enables the user to monitor and identify fluctuations that may be inconsistent with the customer's normal business practice. Any account activity that exceeds the allowed variance, as defined by the financial organization, is brought to the attention of the appropriate staff through a selection of an online report, offline report, or e-mail alert. The information contained in the database can be filtered or segregated by multiple customer account fields. Users can manually add customer account information to the database through a customer profile form.

Every transaction message that is sent to the OFAC module is filtered against the OFAC list. The results of this filtering are displayed, and transactions filtered and found clean are sent for regular processing and placed in the appropriate scrubbed folder. Transactions containing data that may be OFAC related are placed in the Possible Match queue so that an operator can review them to ensure compliance. Rules can be easily defined in the system by the end-user to reduce false positives.

Once a query is executed in the BSA Inquiry module, the user is presented with an online list of the results meeting the search criteria. The user can then drill down to the transaction details for each of the results displayed and can sort the information by any of the field columns. Results are viewed directly through a browser and easily printed or downloaded for presentation to the inquiring regulatory agency or internal audit department. The BSA Inquiry module can greatly reduce the amount of time and manual effort currently required to perform this type of research.

The Transaction Profiler module enables the user to perform both ad hoc inquiries and create standard/multiparty profiles (repetitive queries) that can be scheduled to run on a daily, weekly, monthly, or quarterly basis. Notification and hyperlink access to Profiler reports can also be established via an e-mail alert to the appropriate compliance staff. This staff may then click on the hyperlink to view the generated reports. Profiler reports are easily printed in hard copy form and can be downloaded to any Windows program for further analysis. The integrated AML software suite can be configured with other GIFTS financial products.

Mantas

The Mantas Behavior Detection Platform is a Web-enabled, end-to-end money laundering system that brings together data from existing legacy sources providing for enterprise-wide data monitoring and analysis. The platform can scale up or down to meet the needs of global financial organizations. Mantas behavior detection technology gives financial institutions the ability to automatically monitor and analyze customers, accounts, and transactions across the entire organization for a complete and accurate picture of behaviors of interest. As a result, the Mantas system enables financial organizations to detect suspect behavior early enough to mitigate risk, report and prioritize findings, and comply with changing regulations. Mantas relies upon specially designed *Link Analysis* and *Sequence Matching* algorithms designed to find hidden relationships and suspicious patterns.

Link analysis finds hidden links between accounts and then pieces this information into larger webs of interrelated accounts. At the simplest level, accounts may be linked in subtle ways, such as sharing a common beneficiary, or evidence that the parties involved do business with each other such as writing checks or wiring funds to each other. Once a group of linked accounts is found, the accounts' behavior can be examined as a group, which can unmask previously hidden suspicious patterns of behavior. This technology is particularly applicable when rings of perpetrators are involved, such as a terrorist cell.

The other technique that Mantas uses is that of sequence matching where a particular order of events, such as those transpiring over a period of time, contains some important clue that points to a hidden relationship or relationships. Because money launderers constantly adapt their behavior to get around the existing detection systems, their problem behavior grows ever more complex, spread out over time, and difficult to detect. As they vary their behaviors to defeat simpler and older detection methods, compliance officials at financial organizations must employ more and more sophisticated technology such as behavior detection technology and techniques such as link analysis and sequence matching in order to expose hidden relationships and uncover what otherwise would have remained covered tracks. Behavior detection technology untangles the webs of complex behavior that lie behind such problems as money laundering, and it enables organizations to uncover wrongdoing by finding suspicious patterns of behavior hidden within voluminous data. The key to behavior detection technology is its ability to identify suspicious events and related entities over time, separate them from normal everyday events, and then zero in on the perpetrators.

The Mantas Money Laundering Monitor analyzes all account and transaction activity from across the enterprise and across the globe via comprehensive surveillance of customers, accounts, and transactions, including wire transfers, demand account services, correspondent relationships, wireless and Internet banking, to reveal suspicious and previously unknown behaviors and provide alerts of suspected money laundering activities. The Mantas Money Laundering Detection System provides the capability to analyze factors across multiple dimensions; it generates reports to demonstrate observance of anti-money laundering rules and compliance with the Bank Secrecy Act and other regulations. It creates profiles of customers, accounts, products, and business activities across multiple dimensions that identify when behavior deviates from expectations. It issues alerts with supportive information to enhance the investigative processes, with audit trails to manage analyst investigations, and tracks the actions taken on a detected event or behavior.

The Mantas Money Laundering Detection System comes loaded with money laundering detection scenarios. These intelligent scenarios systematically and consistently monitor transactions and alert the user to behaviors of interest. These are some of the Mantas Money Laundering Monitor detection scenarios:

- High-risk geographies
- High-risk entities, including financial institutions, corporations, and individuals
- Hidden relationships
- Transfers between unrelated accounts
- Transfers between client or respondent banks and another institutions
- Patterns of recurring payor/payee in checks and monetary instruments

- Patterns of recurring payor/payee in electronic transfers and payment
- Changes in behavior, such as in number, frequency, dollar volumes, by geography, or by institution
- Rapid movement of funds; velocity of transactions
- Recurring or large wires, electronic transfers, or checks in round amounts
- Multiple checks or monetary instruments in the same amount or range
- Strings of monetary instruments with anomalies
- Currency transaction: possible Currency Transaction Record

NetEconomy

NetEconomy offers its Efficient Risk Analysis System Enhancement (ERASE) product to assist organizations in combating money laundering. ERASE can analyze data from disparate sources concurrently to provide a view on risk, and it can issue alerts in real time so that risk and compliance personnel can take immediate action. ERASE readily adapts to changing fraud or money laundering schemes without the need for retraining or reconfiguration. ERASE adapts even when the behavior of customers changes, such as when the financial organization introduces new products or services.

ERASE is a flexible and user friendly system that enables risk analysts and AML specialists to easily create new views as needed on high-risk activity within the bank. ERASE monitors account activity per client and per destination account. Profiles of these accounts, or electronic fingerprints, provide a powerful tool to detect unusual account activity and spot money laundering schemes. Once suspicious activity is detected, investigators can match fingerprints to follow trails of illegal activities. ERASE is built on a scalable architecture; it can run on standard Windows hardware and software platforms without losing its real-time and mission-critical performance characteristics.

Searchspace

One of the most sophisticated products on the market comes from Searchspace. Unlike most anti-money laundering software, which is based on models of past criminal activity or detection scenarios, Searchspace uses an ever-changing machine learning approach that gets wiser about crimes over time. Its clients include the Bank of New York; Wells Fargo, UBS, and the London Stock Exchange. In order to detect money laundering activity, financial institutions must have the capability to see all transactions throughout the organization as they occur in real time, including those through a teller or broker, over the Web, call sites, debit and credit cards, or ATMs. Third-generation anti-money laundering enterprise platform software such as Searchspace has the capability to pull all the disparate data sources together and enable adaptive profiling and analysis using advanced modeling algorithms.

Adaptive profiling is effective at discovering suspicious transactions by first comparing every transaction against its corresponding account history to determine if the behavior is unusual. It then compares the transaction against a relevant peer group, which is industry specific or customer type based, for a further analysis of risk. This process greatly reduces the number of false positives and provides a clearer understanding of actual risk. This type of adaptive anti-money laundering system monitors transaction volumes and amounts on individual accounts over dates and types. If a customer makes two deposits monthly for a set amount into an account over a two-year period and then suddenly makes a third deposit one month for a different amount, this could appear to be unusual, according to the account history. But when compared to the peer specific group, such a transaction may not appear suspicious. Conversely, the peer group analysis can also discover risks that the account history review would not. Accounts set up for the explicit purpose of laundering money can readily stand out based on their unusual behavior when profiled against their peer group.

For example, in one situation Searchspace discovered that a business account for a pizzeria was set up to launder money. The restaurant seemed to have consistently high sales throughout the year with no lulls or especially busy periods. A review of its account history would not reveal suspicious activity, because the deposits were consistent. However, by comparing the pizzeria's transactions against an industry peer group, the account suddenly appeared very suspicious because similar restaurants tended to experience a dip in sales after the Christmas holiday, and the profiled pizzeria did not. Similar types of industry-specific comparisons can draw out abnormal financial behavior indicating potential money laundering activity.

This approach automates the anti-money laundering operation by discovering unusual transactions considered to be risky. These are then communicated to the organization's compliance staff with an explanation as to why they are considered suspicious; this enables the compliance staff to take action as necessary. This explanation is accompanied by the associated data, providing an understanding as to the reason for the alert. The first generation of AML systems were only able to flag a transaction that triggered a dollar threshold amount or identified a known pattern. The second generation of AML system pattern detection technology, such as neural networks, are used to identify potential criminal behavior based on historical activity the system has been trained to detect. The third-generation type of software system, such as Searchspace, not only discovers unusual behavior, it also

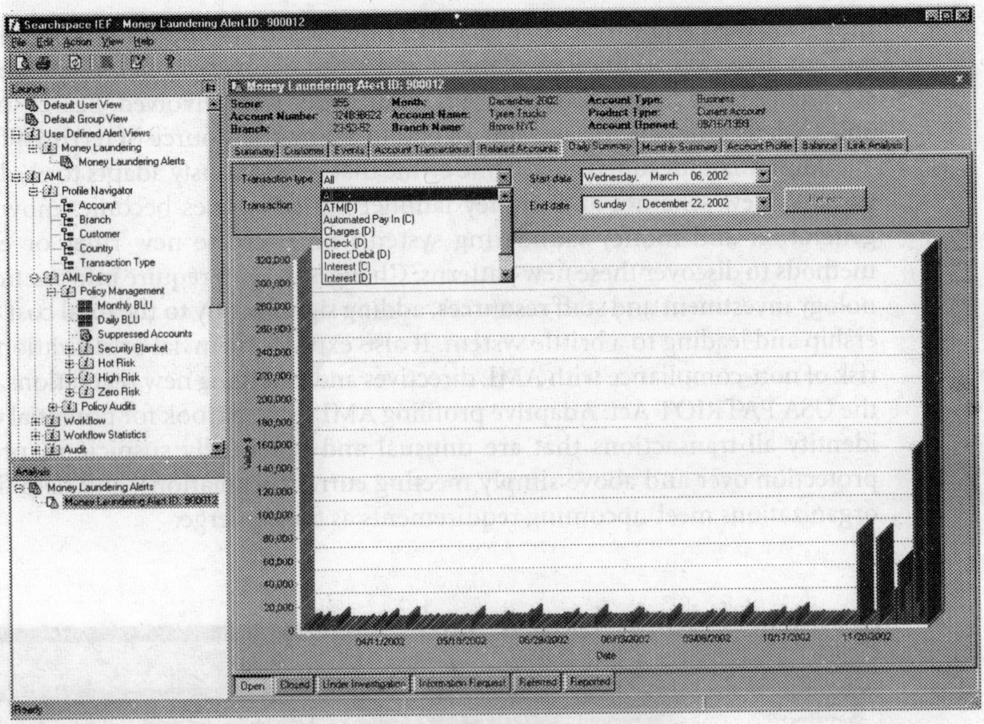

FIGURE 6.9 Searchspace monitoring date and type activity.

provides the supporting evidence as to why an alert was generated. The ability to understand risk associated with a transaction helps the compliance staff to prioritize analysis and focus on the highest risk transactions first.

The top priority for any AML program is the effective detection of money laundering activity to look for any form of unusual behavior as opposed to looking for specific known forms of money laundering. This enables financial organizations to find even highly sophisticated schemes designed to elude detection, such as a corporate account that was established to first launder funds and then move the money to an account in an African nation with a high level of terrorist activities. The money laundering operation was developed to evade AML techniques, but it was discovered by Searchspace through adaptive profiling. The corporate account was set up to receive deposits over a set of 11 different transaction types. The account holder posed as a food wholesaler and used a number of different electronic payment channels to remain relatively anonymous. The levels of deposit were not unusually high and would have eluded a rules-based system. It is also unlikely that pattern detection technology alone would have discovered the money laundering scheme because many different transaction types were involved. Searchspace was able to detect the scheme and put an end to a potential source of terrorist funding.

Money laundering is a dynamic crime that continuously adapts to elude detection. As new schemes and money laundering techniques become known, first-generation anti-money laundering systems must create new rules or establish methods to discover these new patterns. Changes in rules require information technology investment and staff resources, adding significantly to the total cost of ownership and leading to a brittle system. It also exposes financial organizations to the risk of non-compliance with AML directives and emerging new regulations, such as the USA PATRIOT Act. Adaptive profiling AML systems look for potential risk and identify all transactions that are unusual and potentially suspicious, providing protection over and above simply meeting current regulations, and help financial organizations meet upcoming requirements as they emerge.

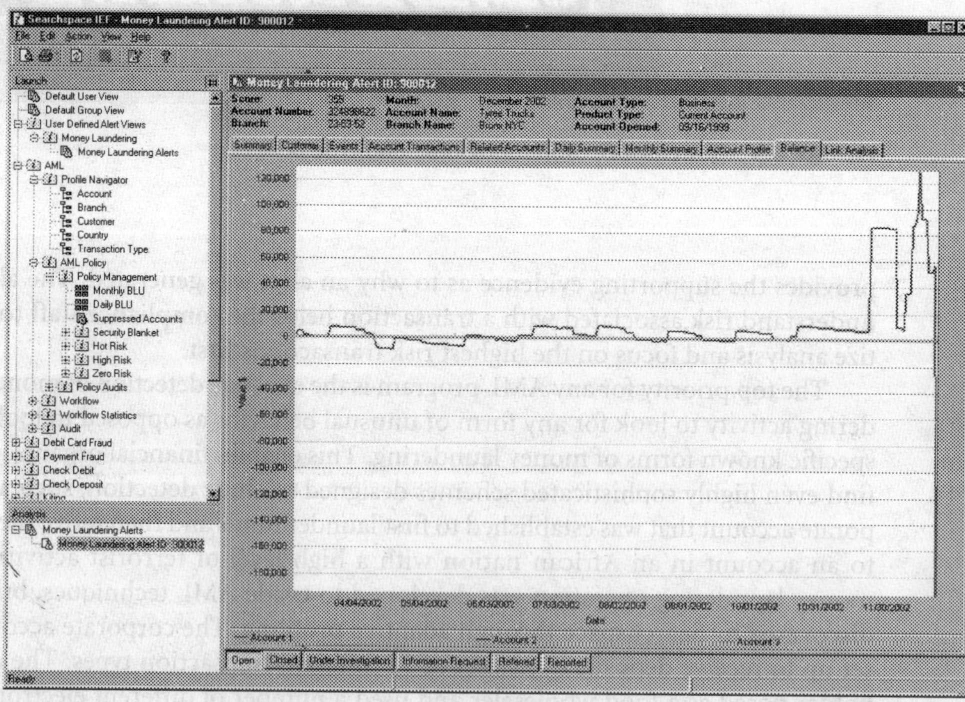

FIGURE 6.10 Searchspace money laundering alert.

The Searchspace system sits atop the transaction-processing system of a bank or brokerage firm and combs through many terabytes of information using specialized application components to address a broad range of critical risk and opportunity identification tasks. The software behaves like a teller in a smalltown bank who has enough time to watch every account, client, and employee. The software selects suspicious transactions and sends them to the desktop of the compliance officer or fraud analyst dealing with the particular type of crime, whether it's check fraud or money laundering. That person then decides whether to shelve the report or file it with Treasury's Financial Crimes Enforcement Network. At its core is technology that emulates human logic and reason on an immense scale to automate AML processes by monitoring huge volumes of data, automatically learning and continually updating what is normal for each business entity. This adaptive, contextual understanding is then used to decide if a transaction is unusual and determine whether it represents risk or opportunity. These decisions trigger an action for a compliance staff member to respond to this behavior at the right time.

Searchspace began developing software in 1995, and its first AML product went live in 1998. Its software includes the Intelligent Enterprise Framework (IEF)® and Sentinel® products that are designed to work with and integrate all existing data sources within an organization. It monitors all transactions to determine activity of interest that requires action. Sentinel products monitor, analyze, report, escalate, and drive action for specific money laundering functions. Searchspace technology uses a mix of approaches, ranging from AI-based methods such as genetic algorithms, fuzzy logic, pattern recognition, and supervised learning to statistical analysis, analytic methods, and rules-based techniques. The software seeks to provide an explanation for its money laundering alerts or for why some transactions are not judged relevant.

Searchspace stresses the importance of contextual computing; simple rules, it says, tend to generate too many alerts, which is costly to manage. Building in the capability to learn from data, however, should enable systems to apply individual context to decision-making, enabling more accurate and targeted notifications. Static rules are limited to detecting only a defined set of behaviors or patterns. Searchspace also points out that the ability to adapt means that the system is protected from costly upgrades and continuous retuning as and when patterns or methods of money laundering change. Its IEF is a parallel threaded *n* tier architecture and can scale according to the processing requirements. Some of the installed systems manage in excess of 40 million transactions per day. In its distributed form, the architecture has been benchmarked to 70 million transactions per day.

IEF is both modular and platform independent. The solution runs on all major hardware platforms, including IBM, Sun Microsystems, and Intel systems. Searchspace is a Global Strategic Alliance Partner with IBM, and the companies have

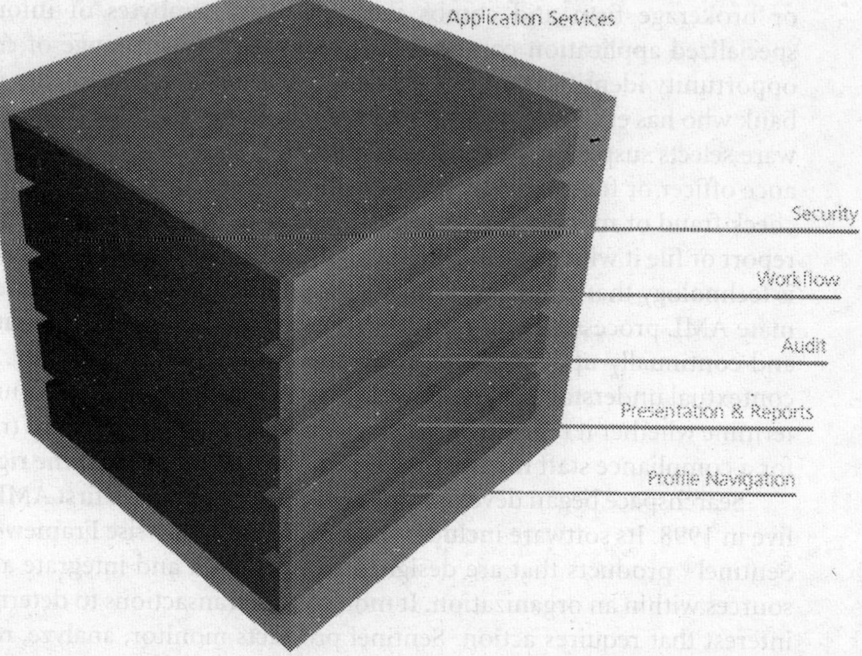

FIGURE 6.11 Searchspace application services. © 2004. Reprinted with permission from Searchspace.

jointly developed a standardized AML solution that typically is installed at customer sites and resides within their software infrastructure.

The Searchspace solution supports both a traditional Windows-based interface and a Web browser interface. For the end-user, the solution has the look and feel of an e-mail system. It identifies, in real time, transactions that require closer inspection by compliance and incorporates a workflow process for their reporting. Users are able to change system parameters on the fly, drill down to detailed information on a specific transaction or account, and compare results against a peer group with help from charts and graphics. All the data and any patterns discovered remain the property of the institution. On average, a Searchspace installation takes three to eight months. The standardized AML solution offered with IBM can be implemented in as little as three months. System configuration is performed as part of the deployment process. User training takes two days, but more can be provided if needed, in addition to the online help and hardcopy manuals. The AML product cost ranges from US$500,000 to US$5,000,000, depending on the scale of the solution chosen, hardware, and professional services and level of requirements.

Searchspace currently monitors hundreds of millions of transactions per day, and customers include Wells Fargo, the Bank of New York, UBS, UBS Financial Services (formerly UBS PaineWebber), Bank One, Lloyds, TSB, Fifth Third Bank, Barclays, and the Royal Bank of Scotland. The Searchspace IEF gathers data about all business entities such as customers, accounts, products, transactions, and branches. In IEF's modular architecture, this role is the responsibility of the Data Manager, which reconciles and cleanses transactional and reference data from sources across the organization. In IEF transaction data is used to generate adaptive profiles for every organizational entity. These automatically generated models describe the behavior of the entity in compact mathematical terms. Each model is automatically updated and refined based on each new action, such as a transaction. The profiles represent contextual knowledge of entity behavior. Adaptive profiles are maintained within the Operational Data Store, providing an optimized central knowledge repository.

Sentinel applications compare new actions with the activity that might be expected from an individual's behavioral context characterized by the adaptive profiles. In addition, specific patterns of behavior can be accurately detected. This automatic approach avoids overwhelming numbers of false notifications and enables the resources of the organization to be directed at high-quality and accurate money laundering notifications. Notifications and actions are fed automatically into IEF's active workflow component, driving responses and minimizing handling time. Each notification describes the exact reasons for the issue being raised. This complete transparency and automation of the administration process make the handling of alerts fast and cost effective.

The IEF enables each entity to be accurately profiled by creating an automatically maintained representation of its behavior. For each customer, information relating to accounts, products, transactions, and branches is compactly stored so that contextual decisions based on an individual's behavioral history can be made and updated. Entities and their relationships can be very complex in nature, and a single transaction can affect multiple profiles. Because they are modified by transactions as they occur, profiles are continually refined to match the up-to-date behavior of the individual. In order to optimize performance, IEF incorporates a data cache, based on standard RDBMS technology, known as the Operational Data Store.

The Searchspace Sentinels are the essential business process applications that continually prioritize actions based on specific business issues. Sentinels are analogous

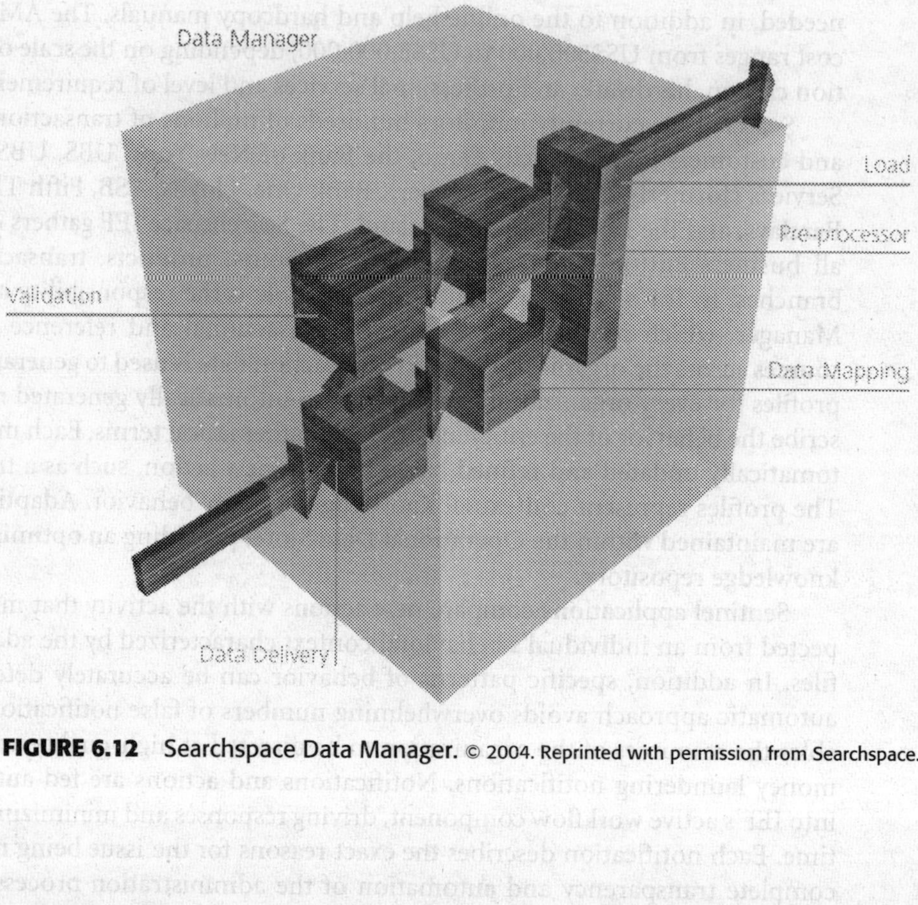

FIGURE 6.12 Searchspace Data Manager. © 2004. Reprinted with permission from Searchspace.

to electronic experts, automatically identifying specific situations such as potential money laundering or fraud, locating patterns of activity, and assessing unusual events, sequences of events, or associations, according to configurable business policies. Using the AML Sentinel as an example, unusual events based on an individual's activity are measured against mitigating factors such as account history and peer behavior to give a contextual assessment of an individual's behavior. Following the identification of unusual activity, which may be judged suspicious in the context of the individual, an automated assessment of all activity in the account is conducted. Any evidence suggesting risk or mitigation is scored and evaluated in the Dynamic Decision Matrix, an automated, multidimensional decision-making process.

Searchspace Case Study

A bank was required to ensure that effective AML compliance procedures and solutions were in place; the main concern for the bank was in the area of correspondent and international banking. The bank's existing rules-based solution produced a huge volume of alerts, which needed manual investigation. Genuine money laundering criminal transaction cases were at risk of being lost in the myriad of alerts. Additionally, the banks existing rules-based solution was limited by its ability to detect only known patterns of money laundering behavior.

The Searchspace AML Sentinel established adaptive profiles of account and bank activity across multiple lines of business. This enabled the bank to detect unusual flows of funds that failed to meet the expected patterns of behavior for individual customers, accounts, products, or services offered by the bank. For example, the Sentinel was able to detect the placement of multiple large amounts of cash into an account, followed by wire transfers and letter of credits when the

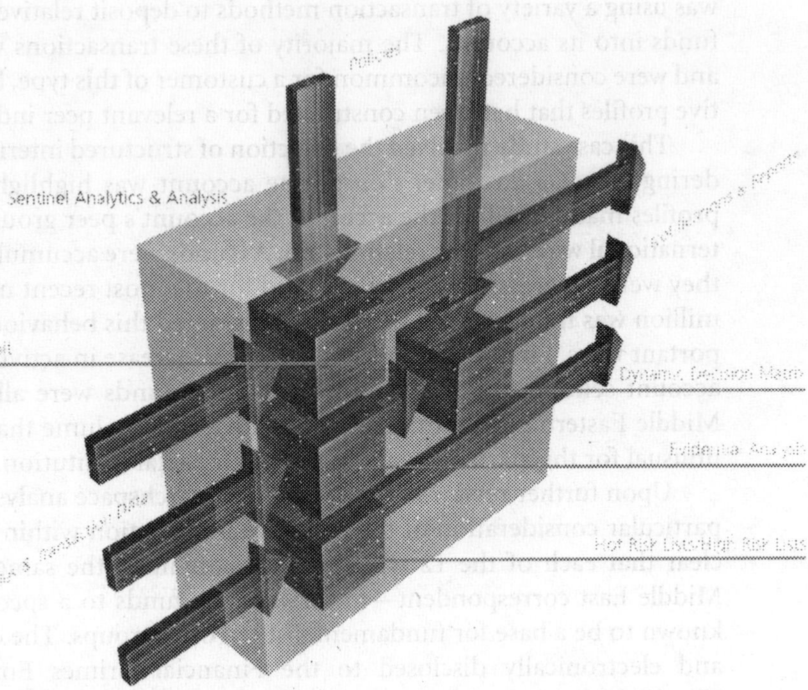

FIGURE 6.13 Sentinel analytics matrix. © 2004. Reprinted with permission from Searchspace.

account had previously been dormant. It was able to present this in a risk-ranked list for investigation.

Upon installation of the Searchspace system, the bank conducted a comparative study with its prior system. The relevancy of Searchspace produced alerts, as determined by a bank domain expert, was 80 percent, compared with a relevancy of only 20 percent for the rules-based solution. The biggest single improvement was in the sheer number of false alerts being generated. The rules-based system produced thousands of alerts per day, most of which were irrelevant. The Searchspace solution, using context-sensitive pattern recognition technology, was able to reduce the alert numbers by 98 percent, while still resulting in the improved alert relevancy outlined previously, not only enabling more effective detection of criminal behavior, but also enabling the bank to make significant operational savings.

Searchspace Case Study: Terrorist Financing Major U.S. Bank

A certain bank used Searchspace anti-money laundering Sentinel to meet USA PATRIOT Act obligations. A group of corporate bank accounts was set up by a customer who purported to be a food wholesaler. Sentinel identified that the customer was using a variety of transaction methods to deposit relatively small quantities of funds into its accounts. The majority of these transactions were not face-to-face and were considered uncommon for a customer of this type, based upon the adaptive profiles that had been constructed for a relevant peer industry-specific group.

This case study involved the detection of structured international money laundering where a customer's corporate account was highlighted by the adaptive profiles maintained for the account, the account's peer group, and the bank's international wire transfer relationship. As funds were accumulated in the accounts, they were progressively wired out, and for the most recent month, a total of $1.4 million was transferred. The system considered this behavior unusual in two important ways. First, this represented a large increase in activity for the customer's account sending the wires, and second, the funds were all directed through a Middle Eastern correspondent bank with a total volume that registered as being unusual for this particular international financial institution.

Upon further review of the alert at the Searchspace analyst workstation and in particular consideration of the narrative information within the wires, it became clear that each of the 12 wires present contained the same instructions to the Middle East correspondent—to forward the funds to a specific African republic known to be a base for fundamentalist terrorist groups. The case was investigated and electronically disclosed to the Financial Crimes Enforcement Network (FinCEN) division of the U.S. Treasury.

LEADMINER: NEW NIPS FOR ICE

To detect money laundering by terrorists, drug smugglers, and other criminals, the Homeland Security Department's Immigration and Customs Enforcement (ICE), an arm of the department's Border and Transportation Security Directorate, is using LeadMiner software from DataMining International. LeadMiner is an improved version of the Numerically Integrated Profiling System (NIPS) now used by ICE to track down financial crimes. ICE's predecessor agency, the Customs Service, began using NIPS in the early 1990s to investigate financial crimes. LeadMiner uses custom algorithms and artificial intelligence methods to analyze both structured and unstructured data to tease out relationships in the information. LeadMiner is a new generation of data mining software, which incorporates network and Web-based applications and new analytical algorithms.

ICE analysts use the software to crawl through multi-terabyte Oracle Corp. and SQL databases to detect patterns of financial activity by scanning files stowed in more than 25 databases. The data mining tool uses a trade discrepancy feature to automate comparisons of federal trade data with information from foreign governments' databases. Trade discrepancy analysis relies on the detection of unusual patterns of exports or imports to detect criminal activity. For example, shortly after the war, Iraq became one of the top five exporters of copper in the world, though it has no copper mines. That trade activity reflects widespread looting of copper from the Iraqi telephone and electricity systems.

International terrorist organizations also have used under-invoicing and over-invoicing of traded goods to shift revenue internationally—a practice that can be used either between companies or across subsidiaries of companies that operate in several countries. Such transfer pricing scams, which can be used to shift profits to jurisdictions with low taxes, have been outlawed by Congress and investigated by the IRS for decades. Most importantly for homeland security purposes, this invoicing scam can also be used for terrorist financing.

There are Visual Basic and Java versions of LeadMiner, and analysts can use either or both versions running under Microsoft Windows NT, Windows 2000, or Windows XP. The Java version is suitable for Internet applications; the Visual Basic version can be used for disconnected operations in secure facilities such as intranets.

AML Technology for Homeland Security

As this last case study demonstrates, this specialized type of intelligence system can be used to detect terrorist-related crimes, which in turn can assist homeland security efforts and organizations. Working in tandem, financial organizations can assist government agencies in combating terrorist financing. As seen, advanced money laundering software systems are highly adaptive, with the ability to learn the behavior of customers through a process known as adaptive profiling, such as that of the Sentinel software components from Searchspace to discover what is unusual and suspicious. With a full contextual understanding of each transaction and the associated customer behavior around it, these modern automated intelligence systems can guide human analysts and investigators through the entire AML process by issuing alerts and following up through resolution, including the reporting of suspected illicit activity to money laundering authorities as well as those involved in homeland security missions.

Money laundering patterns can be difficult to separate from legitimate behavior that is unusual, and adversely generating too many alerts could easily overwhelm an organization with false positives. In order to monitor and profile the common behavior of a customer, an AML system must have an understanding of the customer's normal number of transactions, products, and amounts at the account level. This is unlike first-generation money laundering systems that used rules or fixed thresholds for scenario detection or second-generation systems that relied on previously observed patterns of schemes to detect new ones.

The modern AML systems examine all dimensions of unusual behavior, building adaptive profiles that, in addition to comparing against predefined patterns, continually adjust according to both individual and peer or industry-specific group behavior to fully understand the norm for each account. It is through the core process of data mining that these modern AML systems are able to detect these crimes, which brings us to the last chapter of the book and the subject of pattern recognition for homeland security.

7 Mining: Pattern Recognition and Agent Technologies for Analyzing Text and Data Remotely

In This Chapter

- What Is Data Mining? Discovery and Exploitation
- Our Distributed Data World: Connecting the Dots
- Text Mining
- Data Mining
- The Future of Homeland Security: Hybrid Self-Evolving Systems

This is a pivotal and final section of the book. It deals with the core technology of what homeland security organizations must come to be proficient at—pattern recognition, which is prevalent in all the processes required for combating terrorism, whether it's the aggregation of disparate databases or the collaboration of information or experts, the categorization of unstructured content or the remote segmentation of distributed datasets. At the core of data aggregation, integration, collaboration, categorization, and intelligence is data mining in many different forms and formats.

Data mining is the engine of money laundering systems, identity theft detection services, and name recognition software. However, data mining for homeland security is especially challenging because events of interest occur very infrequently, in very large datasets that are often driven by non-intuitive variables and beyond the reach of experts and where events or profiles are ambiguous or unknown, or where they may change from what was initially modeled. As we will discuss in this chapter, it is the most challenging and innovative aspect of data analysis for homeland security and national defense, bringing to the forefront dynamic and innovative new approaches and algorithms with new developments in the area of cognitive science.

WHAT IS DATA MINING? DISCOVERY AND EXPLOITATION

Data mining is a two-fold process of discovery and exploitation. First of all, it is a process of using a group of algorithms to extract meaning from raw data. It is about using machine learning technologies for discrete classification, most commonly done in private industry to predict consumer behavior. In the context of homeland security, it may be used to anticipate possible attacks or intrusions or the profiling of potential perpetrators. Using statistic-based algorithms, this may involve continuous forms of regression, or it may involve the use of algorithms whose roots are based on artificial intelligence research for semantic processing and behavioral profiling. However, an essential part of data mining is that it must lead to some actionable outcome. Data mining leads to models that in the end lead to calibration for predicting behavior or events. The most common methodology of data mining is the creation of a model, using observed and captured historical data of behavior and then testing the model in predicting new unseen behavior. The value of data mining is in how accurate the model is in predicting that new behavior.

The data mining process of exploitation comes in the form of knowledge discovery, to identify and fill knowledge gaps and to discover the features and intervals of potential perpetrators, such as the signatures of identity theft or money laundering crimes. At its most basic form, data mining is about pattern recognition, but it may also be about entity extraction, such as providing human analysts a composite of what a potential perpetrator's features are, in the form of a profile based on the cross-analysis of multiple diverse databases. Data mining may be a simple report with a summary description to be disseminated within a homeland security organization, such as the statistics of intrusions into a computer network or the result of arrests at border crossings.

However, the most valuable form of data mining is predictive modeling and the influence it may have on a homeland security organization and its personnel.

For example, the U.S. Army performed a passenger-profiling project for segmenting JetBlue travelers into five groups: "short-trippers" (15 percent), "short

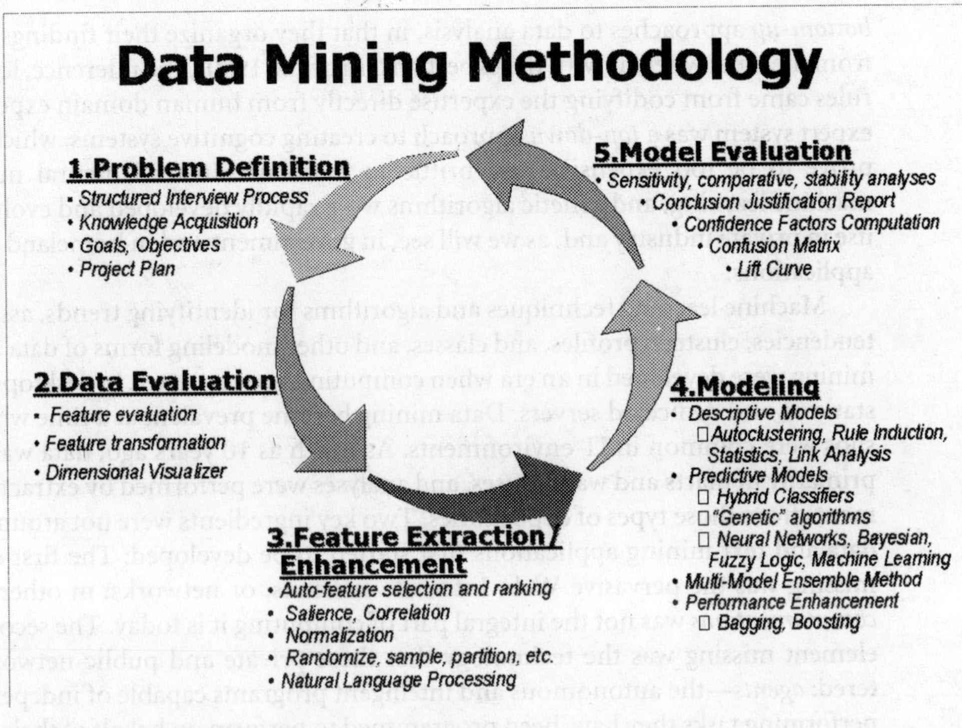

FIGURE 7.1 The data mining methodology.

notice/short stay" (25 percent), "high spenders" (17 percent), "stranded" or frequent one-way travelers (23 percent), and "non-descript" (20 percent). The profiles emerged from linking 2.2 million trip records with demographic data assembled by Acxiom; by using a hypothesis developed by studying the data, the project identified terrorists with 83 percent accuracy. This in its most raw form is what data mining is about.

OUR DISTRIBUTED DATA WORLD: CONNECTING THE DOTS

The roots of data mining are in artificial intelligence technologies. Beginning with the trainable knowledge-based expert systems from 20 years ago, data mining has evolved into two major strains: one set of technologies and algorithms dealing with structured databases, and one set that copes with free-form text. Both, however, are *bottom-up* approaches to data analysis, in that they organize their findings directly from the data, whereas with the expert system of the 1980s, the inference, logic, and rules came from codifying the expertise directly from human domain experts. The expert system was a *top-down* approach to creating cognitive systems, which would prove to be too expensive and brittle to maintain. Instead, neural networks, machine learning, and genetic algorithms were rapidly developed and evolved into use in private industry and, as we will see, in government and in homeland security applications.

Machine learning techniques and algorithms for identifying trends, associative tendencies, clusters, profiles, and classes, and other modeling forms of data and text mining were developed in an era when computing was restricted to desktops, workstations, and dedicated servers. Data mining became prevalent at a time when data silos were common in IT environments. As much as 10 years ago, data was stored primarily in marts and warehouses, and analyses were performed by extracting segments from those types of depositories. Two key ingredients were not around when data and text mining applications first started to be developed: The first element missing was the pervasive Web, Internet, intranets, or networks; in other words, *communications* was not the integral part of computing it is today. The second vital element missing was the technology that these private and public networks fostered: *agents*—the autonomous and intelligent programs capable of independently performing tasks they have been programmed to perform on behalf of their human creators over those pervasive networks.

In the current IT environment, however, data is inherently distributed and difficult, if not unlawful, to aggregate, especially in the case of homeland security where, for example, law prohibits the movement of state records, such as DMV files, outside their respective state borders. The issue of data security is paramount, and it imposes constraints on the architecture and process of data and text mining. Distributed data mining, however, mixes the use of modeling algorithms with agent technology, and this allows the merging of computation analysis and networked communication.

Distributed data mining accepts the fact that data may be inherently dispersed over multiple servers, in different locations, connected by networks, and housed in heterogeneous formats. The concept of distributed data mining is especially critical to homeland security because it allows data analysis applications to perform in remote environments. It also supports the scalability, security, and real-time response required to deal effectively with system or physical attacks. Distributed data mining enables private industry to support hosted customer relationship management (CBR) where the client keeps his data, and the service provider delivers data mining analyses over the Web or other networks, providing a return on investment

(ROI) as a utility. This same type of distributed design is ideal for homeland security organizations.

TEXT MINING

The Challenges of Unstructured Data Analysis: Extracting Knowledge

Homeland security organizations deal with an avalanche of unstructured data such as documents, government and private industry records, e-mails, chat, news feeds, and Web pages. However, the current retrieval techniques for indexing and searching this type of content, such as that of popular search engines like Google, are too ineffective and simplistic, resulting in hundred of "hits" based on their reliance on keywords. The problem with this type of text mining is that these search engines do not adequately take into account the context(s) in which these keywords are used within their original sources. The problem for a homeland security organization is that this type of engine will produce many search results that are irrelevant to the actual intelligence sought. This type of crude indexing results in lost time to the user and ineffective analyses by the organization and may even result in the detainment of an innocent person.

This type of "data noise" results also in wasted resources for a homeland security organization, requiring analysts to sort manually through too many unproductive hits without producing the desired information or intelligence. The full range of topics contained in documents may still not be adequately covered by the keywords used by homeland security personnel to express the content being searched. To assist homeland security organizations, text mining software can be used for searching large sources of unstructured content for the clustering of concepts. This type of software can be used to search, retrieve, and organize key topics, entities, events, views, and so on using natural language techniques so that a document becomes a sequence of linked concepts.

The challenges of text mining are many, such as that of synonymy, where many words can denote the same concept or meaning, or polysemy, where the same word can have different ambiguous meanings. Text mining software must cope with the generative uncertainty of languages, and it must also deal with scarcity, because in a typical document, half the words occur only once. Text mining software must organize its findings along the intended meaning of documents, via the interpretation of words. These programs must truly understand, much the way a human would. Most text mining software products can also deal with entity recognition, associating names with an individual, location, or event. They also are capable of coping with reference resolutions, recognizing and tracking entities throughout a source of text or across a multiple set of documents.

The Text Mining Technologies: Software That Understands

Text mining technologies differ from traditional information retrieval technologies in that they attempt to "understand" at some level the semantic context of the text being processed, as opposed to search engines that only search on keywords without taking context into account. The software products vary in how they summarize, organize, and cluster the meaning of unstructured content. Understanding the semantic context of what words and phrases are being used is very important for enhancing the value of these types of software for a homeland security organization. Many of these technologies use linguistic-based approaches to gain an understanding of the text. A number of them employ statistical or pattern matching-based methods, others rely on rules-based logic processing, and some exploit multiple styles. There is no definitive text mining methodology; the best search approach is driven by the application or need of the analysts from the homeland security organization.

As discussed in Chapter 5, "Categorization: The Techniques for the Clustering of Concepts from Unstructured Content," there are different linguistic-based techniques, which typically involve multiple types of activities. For example, word segmentation, also know as *tokenization*, identifies individual units of text, such as words, word particles, abbreviations, punctuation, and so forth. Some software goes through a stemming process that identifies the true base form of individual text tokens, such as bomb, bombing, bomber, and so on. In addition, sectional speech tagging identifies the part of speech—noun, verb, adjective, and such—of each word within the context of how it is being used and tags it accordingly. This all leads to the identification of proper nouns and noun and verb phrases that represent the entities, concepts, events, and their relationships that are contained within the text.

Statistical and pattern-matching techniques use mathematical models to identify entities and concepts. They can also be used to group similar documents into clusters, map them, and assemble them into autonomous or predefined topic categories. The algorithms used in these types of software vary and include Bayesian probability, neural networks, support vector machines, and k-nearest neighbors (a statistical clustering algorithm). Some, such as Recommind, use their own proprietary Probabilistic Latent Semantic Indexing (PLSI) algorithms. There also are more simplistic, rules-based systems that are very specific about the search criteria used to process documents. They rely heavily on subject matter experts to define taxonomies for them and usually work only with keywords, but they can incorporate decision trees and Boolean logic for greater accuracy. There is also rule-generating software using Learning by Constraint Relaxation (LCR) techniques, representing a soft computing approach, where words do not convey exact meanings but act as soft constraints over possible meanings.

Text Mining Processes: Categorization and Information Extraction

There is a wide variety of products that implement different techniques in an effort to extract the core concepts from unstructured content. However, they tend to fall into two main groupings: summarization (or categorization) and information extraction or ontology creation. In categorization, the software identifies the main topic and in some cases maps the text sources into subcategories with graphical display of the groupings. Categorization software identifies the entities and concepts in documents using statistical or artificial intelligence algorithms and organizing groups of text sources into a taxonomy of topic clusters.

Some of these categorization programs provide additional functions, such as routing their results via e-mail to users in an organization based on profiles they develop over time by scrutinizing the users' core interests or expertise. Other products concentrate on the creation of summaries, identifying the main topic or all the main topics in a group of text sources. They do this by excerpting and displaying a few sentences that best describe the core content. Summarization algorithms identify the sentence fragments or parts of text that best communicate the concise content of the source, whether it be a document, e-mail, news story, chat, or instant message.

The other main text mining process is information extraction, in which the software produces semantic element types from the unstructured text sources. This can include such intelligence as entities, concepts, events, facts, and relationships. One type of content that would be of interest to homeland security organizations is the extracted names of individuals, places, components, materials, and chemicals. In the previous chapter we discussed name entity recognition (NER) software, such as AeroText, IdentiFinder, NetOwl, and Thing Finder, which are specifically designed to extract this type of content.

Another product of these text mining tools is the extraction of key concepts from a vast array of text-based sources. This entity or concept extraction feature is a valuable function to a homeland security organization, which may be responsible for monitoring a large amount of data on a daily basis. This superior form of semantic sorting uses the power of machines to assist analysts in dealing with a voluminous amount of unstructured content. These types of text mining systems can also be programmed to discover relationships, such as affiliations of individuals with political or terrorist organizations. Some tools, such as Attensity, can extract these relationships from unstructured text and then parse it into a semistructured format, from which additional analyses via traditional data mining or visualization can be performed. This capability can be coupled with other software tools so that a flow of unstructured content can be converted into a structured format to create a stream of analyses for such applications as intelligence monitoring for homeland security purposes.

The need of homeland security personnel to discover relationships and associations rapidly and visually makes text mining tools very useful. At the most elementary level is the use of link analysis for displaying and discovering relationships among entities, such as in money laundering. This visualization feature can represent an aggregate of all the relationships found for entities across a collection of documents, e-mails, news stories, Web sites, instant messages, and so on. Visualization provides an additional level of understanding the relationships of text-based content such as star trees, time lines, and hierarchical and taxonomy structures.

What is most important about some of these text mining tools is their ability to produce a variety of structured outputs that can be linked to a variety of data mining tools for more sophisticated types of analyses, such as clustering or segmentation. Some analyses may involve event probability predictions or intelligence gathering and reporting. Simply organizing hundreds of unstructured sources of information into a graphical display is not enough when dealing with a continuous steam of data. Additional types of mining algorithms are required to compress and automate the task of detecting the needles in the moving haystacks.

The Text Mining Tools: From Unstructured to Structured

Although already covered in Chapter 4, "Collaboration: The Technologies for Communicating Content, Experts, and Analyses in Real Time," and Chapter 5, some of the premiere text mining tools will be reviewed in this section, due in part to how they can be incorporated in the overall context of analysis of structured and unstructured content for homeland security purposes. A single technology or paradigm will not be enough in ensuring a viable system of defense; multiple sources of data, services, and techniques will be required. The targets are not the same as they were on 9/11, and the intelligence systems for detecting and deterring them must also evolve and become sophisticated in the use of multiple technologies in a hybrid model.

Attensity

Attensity is capable of extracting event-specific information from unstructured text and then formatting in a way that it can be exported to other tools for subsequent analysis and visualization, such as clustering and link analysis. Attensity uses a linguistic approach to locate specific, known event information and then transform it into structured text or relational tables. Attensity uses a natural language processing engine coupled with a visualization component to generate a graphic parse tree of text content from sentences and paragraphs. Attensity servers are available designed with specific capabilities for government intelligence organizations. Attensity can be used for domain rule creation and dictionary management. The software supports document collection, conversion, filtering, metatag handling, event extraction, XML output, and event definition creation. Attensity can cope with misspelled words, shorthand, unknown terms, and so on and can pull data from multiple sources, including relational databases, intranets, e-mail, and the Web. Attensity works on Windows, Linux, and UNIX platforms and ODBC/JDBC-compliant databases and supports event notification.

Inxight

Inxight offers a suite of integrated tools to manage, extract, categorize, summarize, and analyze unstructured content from various data sources, and it can also be used to funnel structured information for subsequent data mining and visualization. Inxight software offers several components, including the Inxight Categorizer, which automates the classifying, analyzing, and administering of text. It automatically updates information when content is added, changed, or retrieved from multiple repositories, and it also updates the categorization scheme as new topics are identified or changes are made. The Inxight Categorizer Executive provides a graphical user interface for creating and maintaining taxonomy training datasets. The Summarizer extracts a summarized version of text sources.

The Thing Finder identifies a document's proper nouns, such as companies, products, places, and people, and then places them into appropriate categories; the user can chooses from 29 standard categories or create custom categories. The Concept Linker aids in searching a collection of documents for a keyword or phrase by generating a list of other words and phrases related to the keywords. The user then can conduct subsequent searches using those related words. The Similarity Finder finds subject and content similarities in multiple documents. Finally, the Inxight Star Tree Studio is a visualization tool for navigating through related text results and related information.

The Inxight text mining suite supports the use of machine learning algorithms for morphology, syntax, semantic, and contextual analysis in 12 languages. It can self-update categorization as more content is added, providing several levels of confidence thresholds for each category of the training dataset. The software supports over 70 common word processing file formats, including HTML, PDF, Word, e-mail, and Lotus Notes, and can connect to any database that supports XML-based queries, such as Oracle, Sybase, and Microsoft SQL Server. In the context of homeland security applications, this type of software suite with multiple modules makes a very flexible and robust tool for federal, state, and local organizations.

Recommind

Recommind's MindServer categorization software can automatically create taxonomies by clustering key concepts autonomously without training sample datasets. This is a unique text mining product, in that the software can learn autonomously how to categorize documents, files, news feeds, e-mails, and any other source of text. Concepts can be placed into multiple categories, and the software is flexible enough to work with structured, unstructured, or metadata sources. The MindServer software can be integrated with the company's Recommind Information Retrieval Solution so that users can browse and retrieve related information. The core of the self-categorization process is done by Recommind's proprietary PLSI algorithm. The software can handle multiple taxonomies on the same data and can import existing or custom-built taxonomies or automatically generate its own taxonomy from the text without the need of a data training set. The MindServer is flexible, allowing for manual intervention to modify taxonomies and make recommendations for new categories. Recommind manages multiple file repositories from diverse multiple locations, supporting over 300 file formats. The software is compatible with Java and C++-oriented software applications and runs on both UNIX and NT operating environments. Most of the Recommind engineers and developers are in the Germany office, which may make customization of the system for large organizations a concern.

Stratify

The Stratify Discovery System is another high-end text mining tool; it automatically adds structure to unstructured data and can be used in tandem with other data mining tools for more sophisticated, intelligent types of analyses. Users can retrieve information by querying the categorized data to gain knowledge from unstructured and structured data mining analyses. The Discovery System allows manual intervention to create custom taxonomies of topics relevant to a homeland security organization. The functions of this tool are extensive: The user can use existing taxonomies or create his own, and the software can generate metadata for each document and map it, allowing large groups of documents to be classified into multiple categories, as long as they meet the threshold for each grouping. Stratify supports over 200 formats, including HTML, plain text, Microsoft Office, and Adobe PDF.

It can classify in French, German, Italian, Spanish, and English. It also can pull documents from file servers, the Internet, intranet servers, Lotus Notes, and Microsoft Exchange through its optional crawlers. Lastly, it incorporates personalization features that learn users' interests automatically and provide them with matching documents, enabling collaborative workflow with topic-level security, making it an ideal tool for homeland security organizations.

DATA MINING

The Data Mining Processes: Prediction and Description

Data mining is an iterative process of knowledge discovery through automatic or manual methods. Data mining is most useful in an exploratory analysis scenario in which there are no predetermined notions about an outcome. For example, at the end of this chapter we will discuss how data mining can be used with certain scenarios, as determined by intelligence analysts, that could constitute indicators of possible hostile attacks. In the end, data mining is the search for new, valuable, and nontrivial information from large volumes of data. It always has been and will continue to be a joint effort of humans and machines, where the best possible results are achieved by balancing the knowledge and experience of human analysts and investigators who can describe or recognize problems and goals with the tremendously powerful search and number crunching capabilities of computers. In practice, there are usually two goals of data mining: prediction and description.

Prediction involves using variables or fields in a dataset to predict an unknown or future value of another variable. For example, a variable such as an out-of-sequence Social Security number coupled with a relatively new bank account might indicate a possible criminal transaction involving identity theft, yielding an IF/THEN rule such as the following, from a decision tree algorithm:

```
IF SSN is 456-87-9743
AND established date of account is @ 156 days
AND deposit = $6,034.00
THEN        ID THEFT              Y
            ID CONFIRMED          N
```

Very closely related but really quite different is the process of *description*, which focuses on discovering patterns describing the data that can be interpreted by humans. Therefore, data mining processes can be summarized as being *predictive* data mining, which produces the model of the system described by a given dataset, or *descriptive* data mining, which produces new, nontrivial information based on the available dataset.

The Data Mining Technologies: Rules, Ratios, and Code

There are several techniques and tools used to produce a model for predictive data mining that is expressed as a ratio, formula, or executable code and can be used to perform classification, prediction, estimation, or other similar tasks, such as the rule in the previous section. For example, a bank might use the rule described previously to generate an alert on a bank account, directing the transaction to a bank officer for review. A homeland security organization may require the implementation of hundreds or thousands of these type of rules or formulas of code for monitoring signs of attacks, either physical or virtual, for the protection of networks, borders, airports, ports, and cities.

On the descriptive side of data mining the goal is to gain an understanding by uncovering patterns and relationships in very large datasets. In the descriptive context, data mining can be used to discover the features, conditions, or characteristics that indicate possible alerts, threats, intrusions, attacks, or terrorist-related crimes. The relative importance of prediction or description for data mining applications can vary considerably, but both are achieved by using multiple techniques and tasks, such as the following:

Classification: Discovery of a predictive learning function that groups an item or a person into one of several predefined classes, such as a border crossing system that indicates pass versus inspect.

Clustering: A descriptive task in which categories or clusters are organized autonomously around a dataset, such as the clustering of IP addresses accessing a network indicating a potential system intrusion.

Summarization: A descriptive task for data reduction or for compacting a description of a dataset, such as the sequence of transactions for an account indicating potential money laundering activity.

Visualization: This involves three-dimensional views of data and decision tree or IF/THEN rules via geometric, icon-based, pixel-oriented, and hierarchical techniques.

Other data mining products include *dependency modeling* for finding a local model that describes significant dependencies between variables or between the values of a feature in a database or part of a dataset and *change and deviation detection* for discovering the most significant changes in dataset.

There are several types of artificial intelligence algorithms used for predictive and descriptive data mining. One of the most powerful is neural networks, which have been in use for over 20 years. Machine learning and genetic algorithms have also been used for creating data mining models both in private industry and in government. Law enforcement has used data mining to identify fraud and to associate crimes to criminals. As we learned in the previous chapter, this technology is also used for the detection of money laundering crimes. The intelligence community has used data mining techniques as part of activities relating to matters of national defense, which in the future will no doubt include homeland security tasks. The following sections briefly describe some of the most common algorithms of data mining.

Neural Networks

There are two main kinds of learning neural network algorithms: supervised and unsupervised. In *supervised* learning, the correct results (target values, desired outputs) are known and are given to the neural network during training so that it can adjust its weights to match its outputs to the target values. For example, if the attributes of prior intrusion detection have been captured, they can be used to train a neural network for the detection of future attacks. After training, the neural network can be tested by giving it only input values, not target values, and seeing how close it comes to outputting the correct target values. Very much like a child, a supervised neural network is trained by exposing it to examples until it recognizes the patterns it is designed to detect.

In unsupervised learning, the neural network is not provided with the correct results during training. Unsupervised networks usually perform some kind of data compression, such as dimensionality reduction or clustering. For example, a common architecture of this type of neural network is Self-Organizing Map (SOM), which has been used by criminal investigators to associate unsolved crimes with known *modus operandi* of perpetrators, clustering clues autonomously by the unsupervised process of SOM networks. In a previous book by the author, *Investigative Data Mining for Security and Criminal Detection*, several case studies are included in which SOM neural networks were used in burglary, rape, and murder investigations to cluster and associate crimes to criminals.

The distinction between supervised and unsupervised methods is that an unsupervised method can teach a summary of a probability distribution; it is commonly used to explore and cluster similar features of records stored in a database. In the supervised method, the most common application is the training of the network to classify or predict an output target based on a series of inputs. For example, based on a series of inputs such as the number of ATM transactions, the number of checking account deposits, the average amount of balances, the type of account, the number of wire transfers, and so on, a money laundering neural network-based system might be able to recognize and identify a potential money laundering scheme. There are many kinds of neural networks; the following is a collection of some of the most well-known architectures:

SUPERVISED, Feed Forward

Linear: Hebbian: Hebb (1949), Fausett (1994)

Perceptron: Rosenblatt (1958), Minsky and Papert (1969/1988), Fausett (1994)

Adaline: Widrow and Hoff (1960), Fausett (1994)

Higher Order: Bishop (1995)

Functional Link: Pao (1989)

Multi-Layer Perceptron (MLP): Bishop (1995), Reed and Marks (1999), Fausett (1994)

Backprop: Rumelhart, Hinton, and Williams (1986)

Cascade Correlation: Fahlman and Lebiere (1990), Fausett (1994)

Quickprop: Fahlman (1989)

RPROP: Riedmiller and Braun (1993)

RBF networks: Bishop (1995), Moody and Darken (1989), Orr (1996)

Orthogonal Least Squares (OLS): Chen, Cowan, and Grant (1991)

Cerebellar Model Articulation Controller (CMAC): Albus (1975), Brown and Harris (1994)

Learning Vector Quantization (LVQ): Kohonen (1988), Fausett (1994)

Probabilistic Neural Network (PNN): Specht (1990), Masters (1993), Hand (1982), Fausett (1994)

General Regression Neural Network (GNN): Specht (1991), Nadaraya (1964), Watson (1964)

SUPERVISED, Feed Back

Bidirectional Associative Memory (BAM): Kosko (1992), Fausett (1994)

Boltzman Machine: Ackley et al. (1985), Fausett (1994)

Backpropagation through time: Werbos (1990)

Elman: Elman (1990)

Finite Impulse Response (FIR): Wan (1990)

Jordan: Jordan (1986)

Real-time Recurrent Network: Williams and Zipser (1989)

Recurrent Backpropagation: Pineda (1989), Fausett (1994)

Time Delay NN (TDNN): Lang, Waibel, and Hinton (1990)

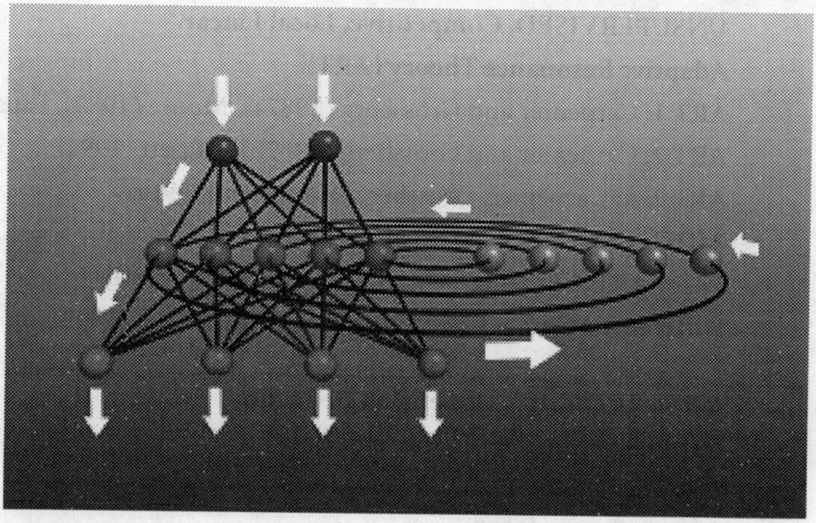

FIGURE 7.2 A neural network recycles the data as it trains to detect the desired phenomena.

SUPERVISED, Competitive

ARTMAP: Carpenter, Grossberg, and Reynolds (1991)

Fuzzy ARTMAP: Carpenter, Grossberg, Markuzon, Reynolds, and Rosen (1992), Kasuba (1993)

Gaussian ARTMAP: Williamson (1995)

Counterpropagation: Hecht-Nielsen (1987, 1988, 1990), Fausett (1994)

Neocognitron: Fukushima, Miyake, and Ito (1983), Fukushima (1988), Fausett (1994)

UNSUPERVISED, Competitive, Vector Quantization

Grossberg: Grossberg (1976)

Kohonen: Kohonen (1984)

Conscience: Desieno (1988)

Self-Organizing Map: Kohonen (1995), Fausett (1994)

GTM: Bishop, Svensén, and Williams (1997)

UNSUPERVISED, Competitive, Local Linear

Adaptive Resonance Theory (ART)

ART 1: Carpenter and Grossberg (1987a), Moore (1988), Fausett (1994)

ART 2: Carpenter and Grossberg (1987b), Fausett (1994)

ART 2-A: Carpenter, Grossberg and Rosen (1991a)

ART 3: Carpenter and Grossberg (1990)

Fuzzy ART: Carpenter, Grossberg and Rosen (1991b)

Differential Competitive Learning (DCL): Kosko (1992)

UNSUPERVISED, Dimension Reduction

Hebbian: Hebb (1949), Fausett (1994)

Oja: Oja (1989)

Sanger: Sanger (1989)

Differential Hebbian: Kosko (1992)

UNSUPERVISED, Autoassociation

Linear autoassociator: Anderson et al. (1977), Fausett (1994)

BSB: Brain State in a Box: Anderson et al. (1977), Fausett (1994)

Hopfield: Hopfield (1982), Fausett (1994)

Decision Trees

Decision trees and rules are methods for inductive learning developed mainly from the area of artificial intelligence. Decision tree and rule generators include the CART, the ID3, the C4.5, and the C5.0 algorithms. They are very powerful, fast, and accurate classifiers. They are supervised methods for learning algorithms and are used for constructing graphical decision trees, which are visual representations of important sub-segments in a data set, and conditional IF/THEN rules directly from very large datasets. Decision tree algorithms search for a solution within a search space in databases through a process akin to the game of 20 Questions: *What is the make of the vehicle? How many passengers are in the vehicle? Is the vehicle insured? What is the age of vehicle? How many border crossings during this week?* This machine-driven iterative process can involve hundreds of thousands of interrogations of the data, which only today's fast processors can perform, to instantly segment large databases to identify the most relevant features and attributes for detecting conditions for targeting a potential perpetrator, money laundering transaction, system intrusion, border crossing alert, and so on. What is most important for homeland security applications is that these types of data interrogations of databases can today be performed over networks on any dataset in the world through the use of agent technology.

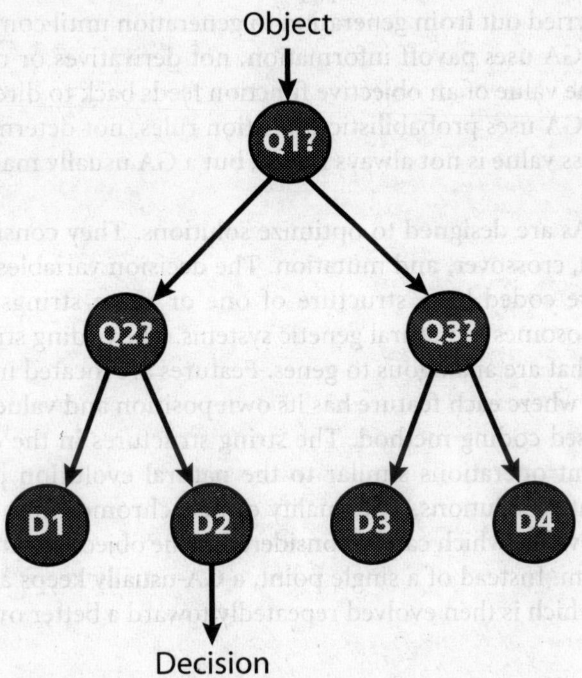

FIGURE 7.3 A decision tree performs thousands of tests in its classification routines.

Genetic Algorithms

Genetic Algorithms (GAs) are optimization search algorithms loosely based on the mechanics of natural selection. GAs were first proposed and designed by John Holland at the University of Michigan in 1975, based on the iterative process of "survival of the fittest." A genetic algorithm works with a population of individual strings (chromosomes), each representing a possible solution to a given problem. Each chromosome is assigned a fitness value according to the result of the fitness function. Highly fit chromosomes are given more opportunities to reproduce, and the offspring share features taken from their parents. GAs are different from other optimization and search procedures in three ways. A GA works with a coding of the parameter set, not the parameters themselves.

- A GA searches from a population of points, not a single point. The search is carried out from generation to generation until convergence.
- A GA uses payoff information, not derivatives or other auxiliary knowledge. The value of an objective function feeds back to direct a search.
- A GA uses probabilistic transition rules, not deterministic rules. The best fitness value is not always found, but a GA usually makes significant progress.

GAs are designed to optimize solutions. They consist of three operations: selection, crossover, and mutation. The decision variables of an optimization problem are coded by a structure of one or more strings, which are analogous to chromosomes in natural genetic systems. The coding strings are composed of features that are analogous to genes. Features are located in different positions in the string, where each feature has its own position and value, which complies with the proposed coding method. The string structures in the chromosomes go through different operations similar to the natural evolution process to produce better alternative solutions. The quality of new chromosomes is estimated based on the fitness value, which can be considered as the objective function for the optimization problem. Instead of a single point, a GA usually keeps a set of points as a population, which is then evolved repeatedly toward a better overall fitness value. In each

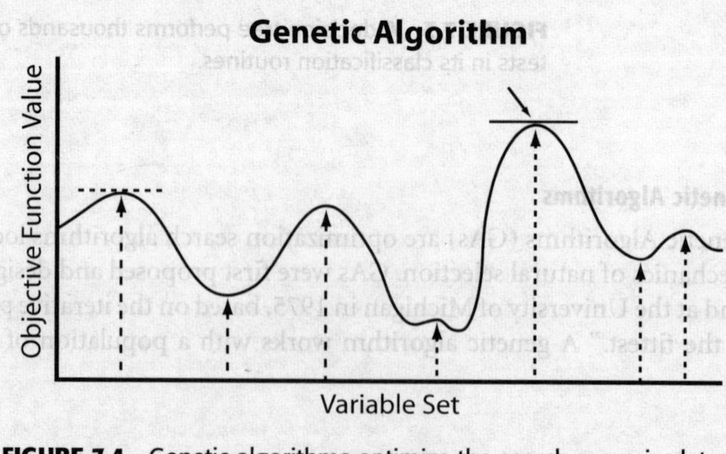

FIGURE 7.4 Genetic algorithms optimize the search space in data mining.

generation, the GA constructs a new population using genetic operators such as crossover and mutation. Members with higher fitness values are more likely to survive and participate in mating or crossover operations. Genetic algorithms are commonly used in tandem with neural networks in order to optimize the accuracy of their classification results.

There are other data mining algorithms (see *http://www.kdnuggets.com/*), including the following advanced modeling techniques:

Kernel Based Regressions

Kernel methods provide a powerful and unified framework for pattern discovery, motivating algorithms that can act on general types of data (such as strings, vectors, or text) to look for general types of relations (rankings, classifications, regressions, clusters). The application areas of this technique range from neural networks and pattern recognition to machine learning and data mining.

Radial Basis Functions

In many areas of mathematics, science, and engineering, it is sometimes necessary to estimate parameters, usually multidimensional, by approximation and interpolation. A radial basis function is a modern and powerful technique that works well in very general circumstances and is coming into widespread use as the limitations of other methods such as least squares, polynomial interpolation, or wavelet-based become apparent.

Support Vector Machines

Support Vector Machines (SVMs) are a new generation of learning systems based on recent advances in statistical learning theory. SVMs deliver state-of-the-art performance in real-world applications such as text categorization, hand-written character recognition, image classification, bioinformatics, and of course data mining.

Bayesian Inference

Inverse problems arise anywhere data is collected that is related to the unknown quantities by a mathematical model. Most data mining techniques such as decision trees or neural networks can predict an output when given a model and an input. Bayesian inference methods work when the problem is a bit more complex, such as when there is a need to:

- Estimate the input, given the model and the output
- Estimate the parameters of the model, given the input and the output
- Estimate both the input and the parameters of the model, given the output

Bayesian inference involves designing a system and collecting the data in a manner as to be able to solve optimally the aforementioned problems. Bayesian networks are ideal algorithms for homeland security applications because they can be used to model and make predictions in the presence of uncertainty and very little information. These types of algorithms are very important to homeland security applications, systems, and techniques because there are very few training examples for modeling such phenomena as terrorist behavior and attacks. A Bayesian network, as we shall see toward the end of this chapter, provides a highly plausible methodology for working with uncertainty, and yet they can be used to make some very reasonable decisions in support of homeland security organizations and applications.

Hybrid Models

Most data mining projects involve the use of multiple algorithms in combination, hence the creation and use of hybrid models. This is done in order to optimize both the speed and the accuracy of the modeling process. For example, later in this chapter a scenario will be presented in which a distributed data mining model is used combining a decision trees algorithm and Bayesian networks in an effort to optimize prediction and classification to the highest possible level.

Ensemble Estimation

Another data modeling technique involves taking different sections of a dataset used to create a model in order to test its accuracy. This involves random sampling, balancing, splitting, and rotating of the data in order to validate the accuracy of the models. There is also a *bootstrap* method in which the available data is resampled with a number of fake data records of the same size of the original dataset. These new training sets can then be used to define the bootstrap estimates of error rates.

The Data Mining Suites: Toolboxes of Algorithms

Because of the various data mining techniques that use hybrid models and ensemble estimation, high-end data mining software products have evolved into multi-algorithm suites. These data mining toolboxes not only incorporate text mining capabilities, but they also include multiple modeling algorithms for different types of analyses. For example, most of these data mining suites have multiple neural network architectures for estimation, classification, and clustering. Almost all pose some type of decision tree component for segmentation and classification. They also include a visualization component to enhance the value of the result of their analyses. The following is a description of the evolution of data mining tools and technologies, which have gone from standalone software to mining suites to database products that integrate data mining operations inside them and finally to agent-based programs capable of mining data anywhere, performing their analyses remotely over networks.

Megaputer

Megaputer Intelligence was founded in 1993 in Russia. The firm offers the PolyAnalyst™ data and text mining suite with an extremely large number of algorithms for knowledge discovery in large volumes of structured data and unstructured text. PolyAnalyst can perform analyses of structured and unstructured data, and it supports decision tree and link analyses, as well as visualization components, all well suited for homeland security and safety applications. PolyAnalyst provides the following machine learning algorithms for data exploration and analyses:

- Memory-based reasoning for multiple group classification
- Symbolic knowledge acquisition technology (SKAT)
- Decision forest for categorization of multiple classes
- Decision tree via information gain algorithms
- Discriminate via unsupervised classification
- Clustering for the localization of anomalies
- Multidimensional distribution analysis
- Taxonomy-based categorization
- Transactional data processing
- Stepwise linear regression
- Multiple neural networks
- Fuzzy logic classification
- Summary statistics
- Link analysis
- Text OLAP
- Link terms

PolyAnalyst supports the complete mining cycle, from data loading and cleansing to knowledge discovery to applying developed models for scoring data in external sources, visualization, and reporting operations. PolyAnalyst can load data from any major database, spreadsheet, statistical system, or collection of documents from popular formats. A broad selection of learning algorithms empowers the user of PolyAnalyst to predict values of continuous variables, explicitly model complex phenomena, determine the most influential independent variables, solve classification and clustering tasks, and find associations between events. PolyAnalyst provides the following machine learning algorithms for structured data:

- Classify (fuzzy logic classification)
- Cluster (isolating groups of similar cases)
- Decision tree (hierarchical rules classification)
- Decision forest (multiple class categorization)
- Find dependencies (multidimensional distribution analysis)
- Find laws (symbolic knowledge acquisition technology)
- Link analysis (visual multivariable correlation analysis)
- Market basket analysis (transactional data processing)
- Memory based reasoning (predicting through most similar cases)
- PolyNet predictor (neural network and GMDH)
- Stepwise linear regression
- Summary statistics

For free-form, unstructured text, PolyAnalyst provides the following:

- Link terms (term patterns and clusters visualization)
- Text analysis (linguistic and semantic analysis)
- Taxonomy-based classification
- Text categorization (automated taxonomy building)
- Text OLAP

As with most high-end data mining suites, PolyAnalyst was designed for both organizational users and data analysts. The interface shields the user from the complexities of data preparation and analysis. Users communicate with the system through a collection of standard dialogs and reports and flexible visualization functions equipped with drill-down capabilities. Reusable analytical scripts can be created and scheduled to execute on new batches of data at a given time. Industry-specific solutions are available from Megaputer, such as TotalRecall™, a module for automated analysis of large collections of incident reports, which can contain both structured data and text narratives.

The TextAnalyst component uses linguistic and neural network technologies to extract information from unstructured text and increase the speed and accuracy of search and retrieval activities. This allows users to quickly understand the information in a document repository. TextAnalyst can distill the meaning of unstructured

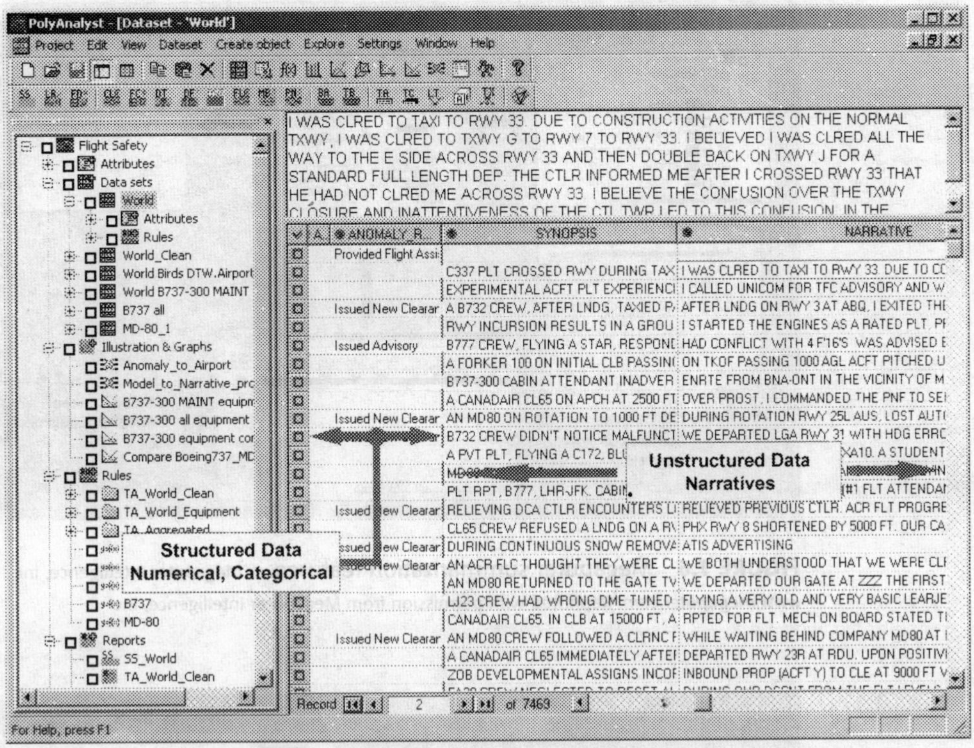

FIGURE 7.5 Megaputer text mining component interface. © Megaputer Intelligence, Inc., *www.megaputer.com*. Reprinted with permission from Megaputer Intelligence, Inc.

content by creating an accurate semantic network of the information, which can then be used for further analysis, using the other data mining algorithms.

The software also supports summarization of texts. The user can exclude or include specific words or phrases to guide the search for specific intelligence; hyperlinks are used to relate the semantic network concepts to the source documents and individual sentences. TextAnalyst supports the automatic creation of a hierarchical topic structure that represents the semantics of the analyzed text, with the more important subjects placed closer to the root of a tree structure, while weak relationships in the semantic network are also identified, enabling the user to interact with groups of documents and topics.

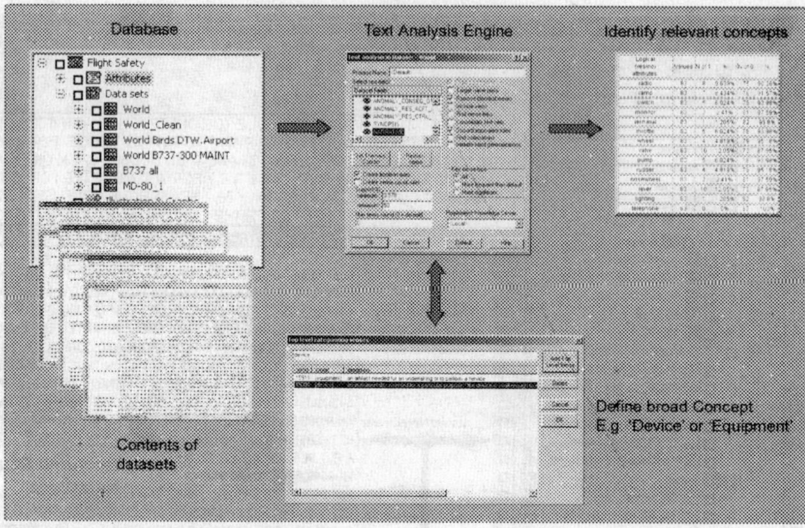

FIGURE 7.6 Megaputer summarization features. © Megaputer Intelligence, Inc., *www.megaputer.com*. Reprinted with permission from Megaputer Intelligence, Inc.

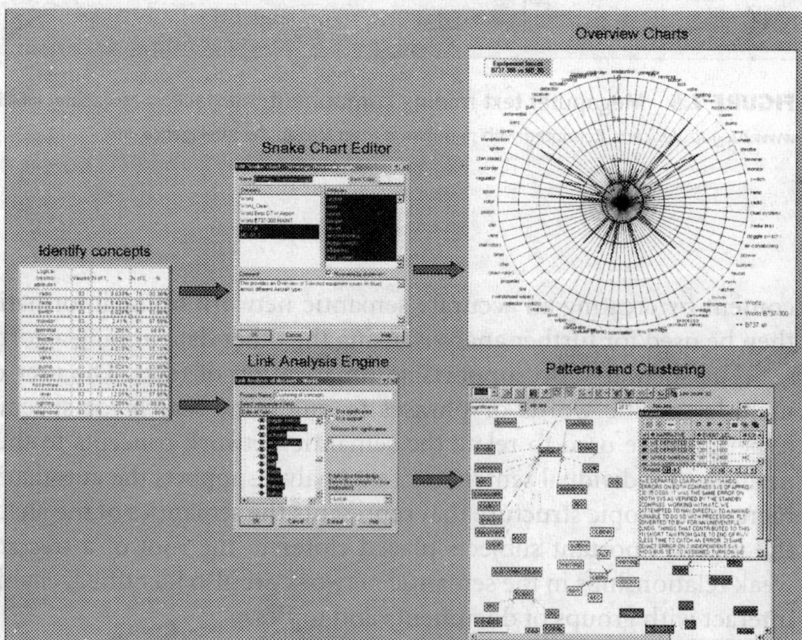

FIGURE 7.7 The clustering of concepts in Megaputer. © Megaputer Intelligence, Inc., *www.megaputer.com*. Reprinted with permission from Megaputer Intelligence, Inc.

MINING FLIGHT RECORDS: A MEGAPUTER CASE STUDY

This case study focuses on the use of the text mining technology from Megaputer in the analysis of flight records, and although the objective was safety, a similar type of analysis could be conducted for homeland security purposes. Megaputer completed a successful proof-of-concept project demonstrating the benefits of applying its PolyAnalyst data and text mining system to airline flight safety data analysis. The project was sponsored by the Federal Aviation Administration (FAA) Office of System Safety and carried out in cooperation with the Analytical Methods and Tools Working Group of the Global Aviation Information Network (GAIN). The purpose of the project was to develop new text mining methodologies for the analysis of flight safety data. PolyAnalyst was used for the analysis of data from the Aviation Safety Action Program (ASAP) Southwest Airlines database, with the ultimate goal of further enhancing long-term flight safety performance.

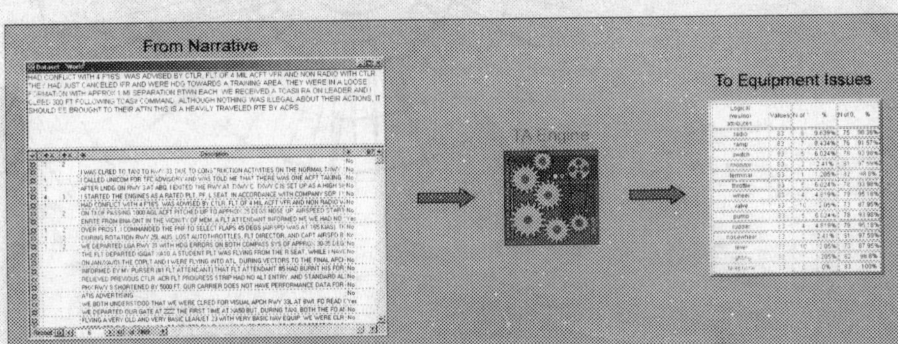

FIGURE 7.8 From flight narratives to key issues. © Megaputer Intelligence, Inc., *www.megaputer.com*. Reprinted with permission from Megaputer Intelligence, Inc.

PolyAnalyst was used to enable flight safety officers to quickly perform extraction of stable patterns of terms occurring in pilot narratives and present the results in visual formats. The Flight Operational Safety Office of Southwest Airlines used the visualization capabilities of PolyAnalyst to optimize the use of flight safety officers' time and help create easy-to-understand executive reports. In doing so they made the results of the analysis available to more decision makers in a timely manner.

PolyAnalyst demonstrated the efficiency of processing large volumes of mixed structured and unstructured data. The software automated the extraction of important patterns and clusters of terms from the text, reporting the results of the analysis

(continued)

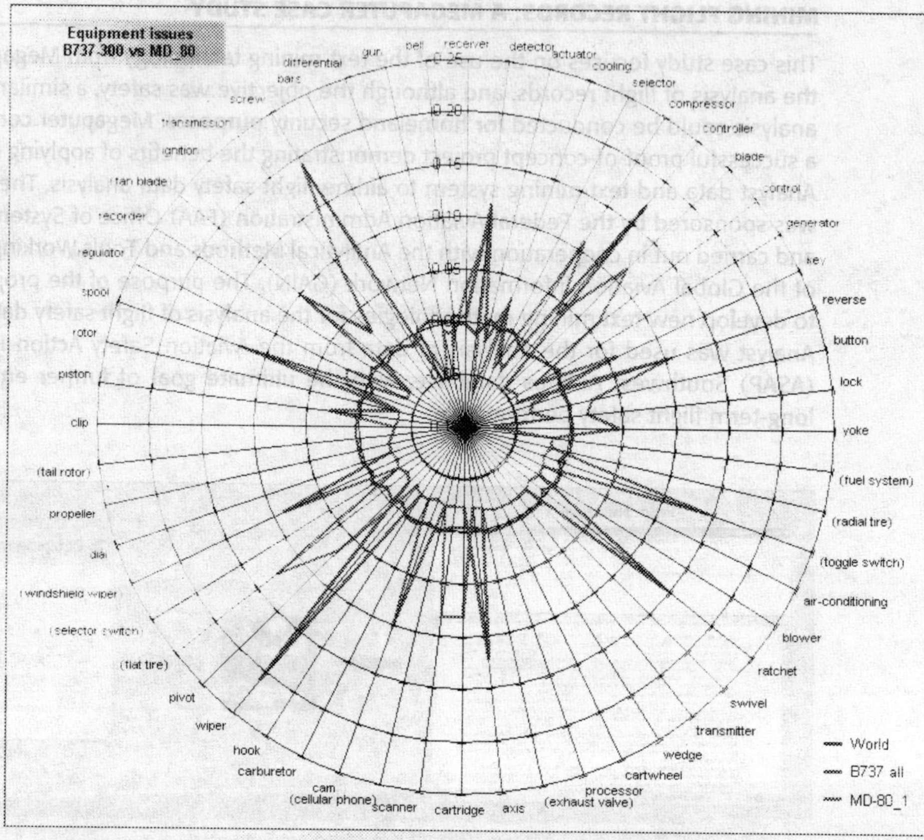

FIGURE 7.9 The mapping of unstructured content in Megaputer. © Megaputer Intelligence, Inc., *www.megaputer.com*. Reprinted with permission from Megaputer Intelligence, Inc.

as visual graphs. Users were able to perform intuitive drill down analyses to the original data records supporting their findings.

According to the FAA the project helped to demonstrate how much potential text mining has as a key safety data analysis technique. The agency's Assistant Administrator for System Safety, Christopher A. Hart, noted that exciting advances in text and data mining tools are enhancing the aviation community's ability to convert ever-growing volumes of data into valuable knowledge to further improve an already commendable safety record.

(continued)

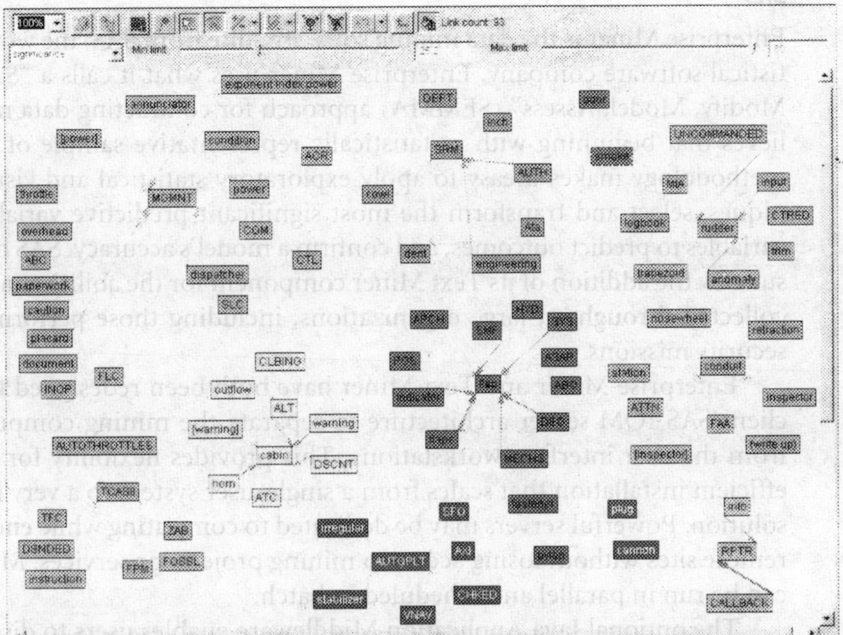

FIGURE 7.10 Link analysis map in Megaputer. © Megaputer Intelligence, Inc., *www.megaputer.com*. Reprinted with permission from Megaputer Intelligence, Inc.

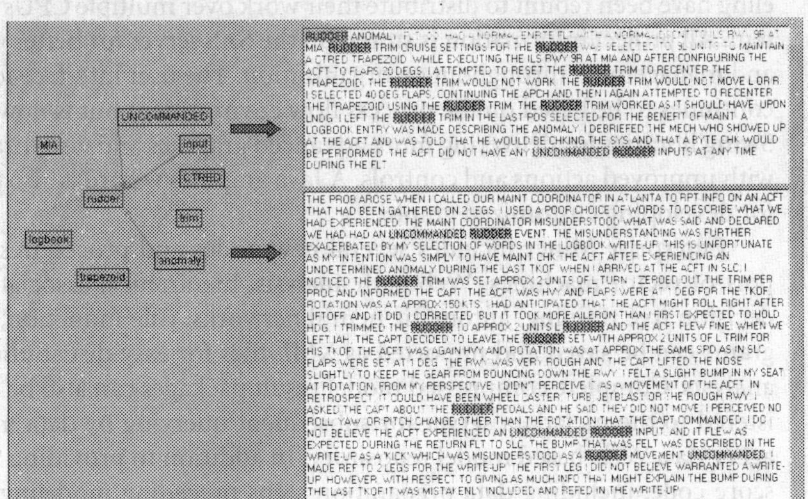

FIGURE 7.11 Megaputer is being used by the FAA to mine for trouble. © Megaputer Intelligence, Inc., *www.megaputer.com*. Reprinted with permission from Megaputer Intelligence, Inc.

SAS

Enterprise Miner is the data mining software suite from SAS, the world's largest statistical software company. Enterprise Miner uses what it calls a "Sample, Explore, Modify, Model, Assess" (SEMMA) approach for conducting data mining. SAS believes that beginning with a statistically representative sample of your data, this methodology makes it easy to apply exploratory statistical and visualization techniques, select and transform the most significant predictive variables, model the variables to predict outcomes, and confirm a model's accuracy. SAS has expanded its suite by the addition of its Text Miner component for the ability to analyze text data collected throughout large organizations, including those performing homeland security missions.

Enterprise Miner and Text Miner have both been redesigned for using a Java client/SAS IOM server architecture to separate the mining computational server from the user interface workstations. This provides flexibility for configuring an efficient installation that scales from a single-user system to a very large enterprise solution. Powerful servers may be dedicated to computing while end users move to remote sites without losing access to mining projects or services. Mining processes can be run in parallel and scheduled in batch.

The optional Java Application Middleware enables users to disconnect from a running diagram on the server or facilitate multiple users working with common SAS servers and a common SAS Metadata Server. Some process-intensive server tasks such as data sorting, summarization, variable-selection, and regression modeling have been rebuilt to distribute their work over multiple CPUs on the same system. All project information is stored on the SAS server for better wide-scale access and management throughout an organization. The user interface for both products continues to be based on the process flow environment but is now built using Java Swing libraries for delivering more advanced graphics and visualization techniques with improved actions and controls. A Java graphics wizard is also provided by SAS for developing customized graphs.

Enterprise Miner includes several new nodes and procedures, including support of vector machines, Web path analysis, hierarchical associations, interactive decision tree training, automatic neural networks, rule induction, and so on. Diagrams can be saved and imported as XML files for easy distribution to other data analysts. Complete compressed model result packages can also be created and registered to the metadata server for subsequent querying by data miners and managers via a Web-based model repository. In addition to providing SAS, C, and Java score code, including data preparation steps preceding modeling, model deployment through Predictive Model Markup Language (PMML) will be available. An experimental Java API is also included for building customized Java applications that embed Enterprise Miner processes in production systems.

The SAS Text Miner features include additional language support, interactive graphics for linking significant concepts and hierarchical clustering output, the ability to analyze multiple text fields, Web crawling, and additional parsing options. Text Miner is fully integrated with Enterprise Miner, hence the distributable algorithms in Enterprise Miner also can be used. SAS believes its SEMMA process can determine how to model new questions raised by previous results and thus return to the exploration phase for additional refinement of the data. Enterprise Miner incorporates decision trees and neural networks as well as regression components, memory based reasoning, bagging and boosting ensembles, two-stage models, clustering, time series, and association tools.

The complete scoring formula for all stages of model development can be automatically captured in the form of SAS, C, and Java languages for subsequent model deployment. A reporter tool provides output in HTML for distribution and viewing via a browser. SAS emphasizes that with the Enterprise Miner's graphical user interface and automated framework, users require little statistical expertise, with many corporations and most large government agencies already running the base SAS system, integration of Enterprise Miner facilitates the process of data mining and modeling. This is especially the case for those 22 agencies that have been incorporated into the Department of Homeland Security.

SPSS

Clementine® is the flagship data mining suite of SPSS. It is a totally icon-driven software system that supports a visual rapid modeling environment for data mining. The interactive stream approach to data mining is the key to Clementine's power. The system uses icons to represent steps in the data mining process. The user can mine data by building a *stream*—a visual map of the process. The data might be represented with a Sources icon, such as flat files or an ODBC connection. There are Record Operational icons for excluding, merging, sampling, and so forth of records in a database and Field Operation icons for filtering and designating data types.

There are also graphic icons for creating different types of visual reports and Modeling icons for placing neural networks and machine learning algorithms in the work palette for the construction of models and analyses. The user typically starts an analysis in Clementine by simply dragging a Source icon from the object palette onto the canvas to access a database. The user can start by exploring the data via a table or a graphic icon to display the data visually prior to bringing to the canvas various algorithm icons to construct models, the results of which are represented as gold nuggets.

The interactive, visual approach to data mining is the key to Clementine's ability to minimize time to solution. This visual approach makes it easy to see every step in the process clearly and enables the user to apply his domain expertise to quickly explore hunches or ideas by interacting with the data stream. Clementine visual data mining makes "train-of-thought" analysis possible, so the user can focus on solving problems rather than performing technical tasks such as writing code. Clementine's wide range of data visualization techniques also accelerates progress toward a solution by helping the user understand key relationships in the data and guiding the way to the best results.

Clementine comes with a wide range of analytical techniques, enabling the user to build and test numerous models to see immediately which model produces the best result or combine models by using the results of one model as input into another model. These "meta-models" consider the initial model's decisions and can improve results substantially. Cleo™, a new component of the Clementine family of data mining products, provides the ability to rapidly deploy predictive models online for real-time data scoring.

SPSS LexiQuest is the new text mining component of Clementine. It extracts textual information from target documents and categorizes them based on a taxonomy. When matching categories are found for the documents, the application allows the user to either apply metatags or simply forward the documents to an application repository. LexiQuest allows a user to visualize content relationships of terms found in a large database of documents. When interesting relationships are discovered, the system allows the user to view those associations via a link map. The taxonomy does not maintain ontological data other than synonyms.

As with other categorization software products, the initial grouping descriptions are obtained by the use of a training set of documents. These initial groups of documents serve to create a taxonomy of the relevant content for each category in a large body of text sources. From these, a series of terms is found and weights assigned based on the uniqueness of the term, with common words such as *terrorism* assigned a low weight because they are rather general and found in many documents assigned to many categories. A word such as *al-Qaeda* would receive higher weighting due to its specificity. The Categorize component is shipped with the Taxonomy Manager for the manual maintenance of the taxonomy, such as adding or removing terms and adjusting the weights of terms. The SPSS software currently supports English, French, and German.

The LexiQuest Mine component provides an approach for isolating, discovering, and processing content via linguistic and statistical techniques. The core content of documents can be viewed graphically, allowing easy identification of specific events in the flow of information. The software's core dictionary and grammars enhance the linguistic functions of the tool, while its dynamic clustering algorithms allow the user to interactively adapt the tool's graphics and output to his specific needs. LexiQuest can work with data from both internal sources and across the Internet, including HTML, XML, MS Office, PDF, plain text, and RTF. In the following case study, a demonstration is provided of how both text and data mining capabilities can be combined, in this case to detect potential hacker attacks.

MINING FOR SYSTEM INTRUSIONS: AN SPSS CASE STUDY

One of the concerns of homeland security organizations is the potential attack of computer systems: cyber-terrorism. In this case study, Clementine was used to demonstrate how an intrusion detection system could be constructed using the visual programming interface of the Clementine data mining suite. There was no programming or syntax required to perform this analysis.

First, a data mining stream is created to perform some preliminary data preparation on network IP address incident data. The raw data consists simply of a network IP address and an incident identification count. To make this raw data more useful to an analyst, Clementine was used to break the IP addresses into octets, with each octet then becoming a new variable, and then assigning each domain to a specified class and domain, which also become new variables. After performing this function on the raw data, the result is the table shown in Figure 7.12. Preparing the data in this format enables an analyst to glean more useful information based on the behavior within a certain class or domain.

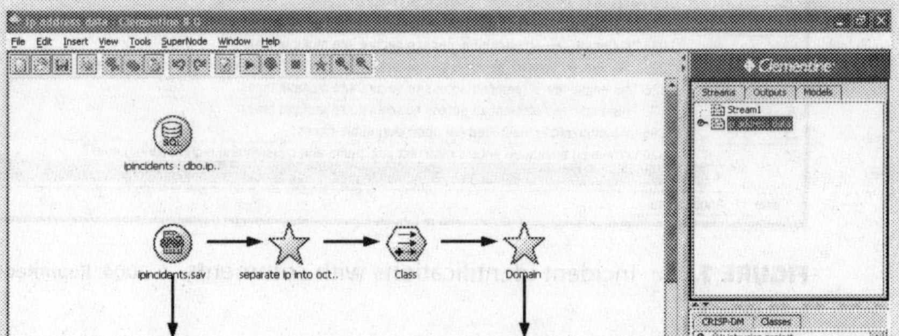

FIGURE 7.12 Raw data is processed via the graphical interface. © 2004. Reprinted with permission from SPSS, Inc.

(continued)

A typical challenge faced by almost every organization is in determining how to deal with unstructured text data. An example of one such data format is displayed in Figure 7.13. This dataset is comprised of security incident reports, labeled by an incident identification number and some incident comments describing the event. Typically, an analyst is required to comb through all of this data by hand and make some attempt at categorizing it into a structured format for analysis.

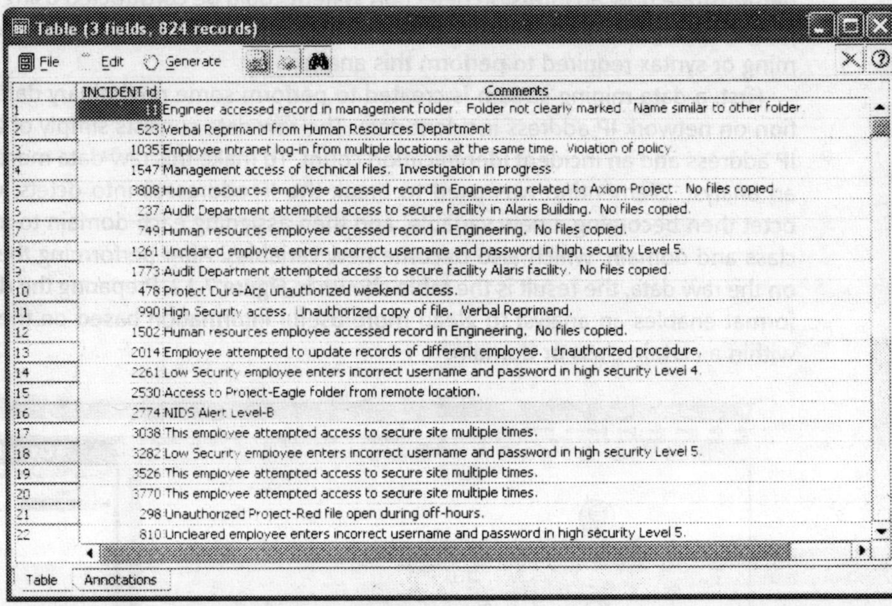

Table (3 fields, 824 records)

	INCIDENT id	Comments
1	11	Engineer accessed record in management folder. Folder not clearly marked. Name similar to other folder
2	523	Verbal Reprimand from Human Resources Department
3	1035	Employee intranet log-in from multiple locations at the same time. Violation of policy.
4	1547	Management access of technical files. Investigation in progress
5	3808	Human resources employee accessed record in Engineering related to Axiom Project. No files copied.
6	237	Audit Department attempted access to secure facility in Alaris Building. No files copied.
7	749	Human resources employee accessed record in Engineering. No files copied.
8	1261	Uncleared employee enters incorrect username and password in high security Level 5.
9	1773	Audit Department attempted access to secure facility Alaris facility. No files copied.
10	478	Project Dura-Ace unauthorized weekend access.
11	990	High Security access. Unauthorized copy of file. Verbal Reprimand.
12	1502	Human resources employee accessed record in Engineering. No files copied.
13	2014	Employee attempted to update records of different employee. Unauthorized procedure.
14	2261	Low Security employee enters incorrect username and password in high security Level 4.
15	2530	Access to Project-Eagle folder from remote location.
16	2774	NIDS Alert Level-B
17	3038	This employee attempted access to secure site multiple times.
18	3282	Low Security employee enters incorrect username and password in high security Level 5.
19	3526	This employee attempted access to secure site multiple times.
20	3770	This employee attempted access to secure site multiple times.
21	298	Unauthorized Project-Red file open during off-hours.
22	810	Uncleared employee enters incorrect username and password in high security Level 5.

FIGURE 7.13 Incident identifications with comments. © 2004. Reprinted with permission from SPSS, Inc.

In Figure 7.14, a data mining stream is created to perform text analysis of the unstructured data. The LexiQuest component within Clementine is used to perform concept extraction based on the linguistics of the narrative reports. This is done to pull from all the unstructured data as many concepts as exist and automatically present them in a structured format, which is by far superior to simply extracting on keyword searches.

The results of executing the functions of the text mining stream are seen in Figure 7.15, where multiple concepts from a single incident are displayed. For example, for incident identification number 11, three concepts were pulled from the statement: accessed record, folder, and management folder. This information is displayed and can be accessed in a format more conducive to close analysis.

(continued)

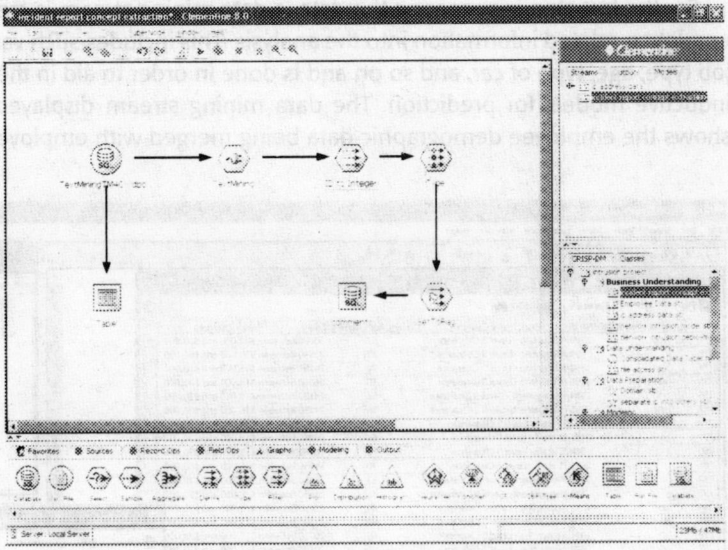

FIGURE 7.14 The text mining component is linked to the data stream. © 2004. Reprinted with permission from SPSS, Inc.

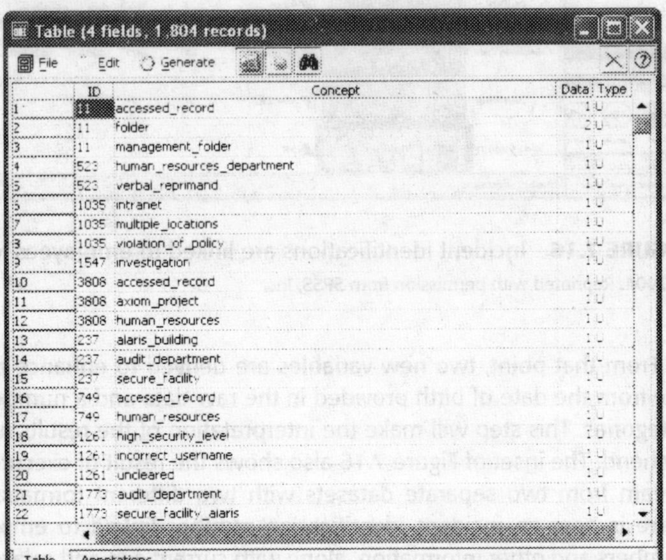
Table (4 fields, 1,804 records)

File Edit Generate

	ID	Concept	Data	Type
1	11	accessed_record	1	U
2	11	folder	2	U
3	11	management_folder	1	U
4	523	human_resources_department	1	U
5	523	verbal_reprimand	1	U
6	1035	intranet	1	U
7	1035	multiple_locations	1	U
8	1035	violation_of_policy	1	U
9	1547	investigation	1	U
10	3808	accessed_record	1	U
11	3808	axiom_project	1	U
12	3808	human_resources	1	U
13	237	alaris_building	1	U
14	237	audit_department	1	U
15	237	secure_facility	1	U
16	749	accessed_record	1	U
17	749	human_resources	1	U
18	1261	high_security_level	1	U
19	1261	incorrect_username	1	U
20	1261	uncleared	1	U
21	1773	audit_department	1	U
22	1773	secure_facility_alaris	1	U

Table Annotations

FIGURE 7.15 Incidents are clustered around concepts. © 2004. Reprinted with permission from SPSS, Inc.

(continued)

For the last step in preparing the data, a data mining stream is created that brings employee-related information into the analysis. This includes such variables as salary, job type, age, type of car, and so on and is done in order to aid in the construction of inductive models for prediction. The data mining stream displayed in Figure 7.16 shows the employee demographic data being merged with employee incidents.

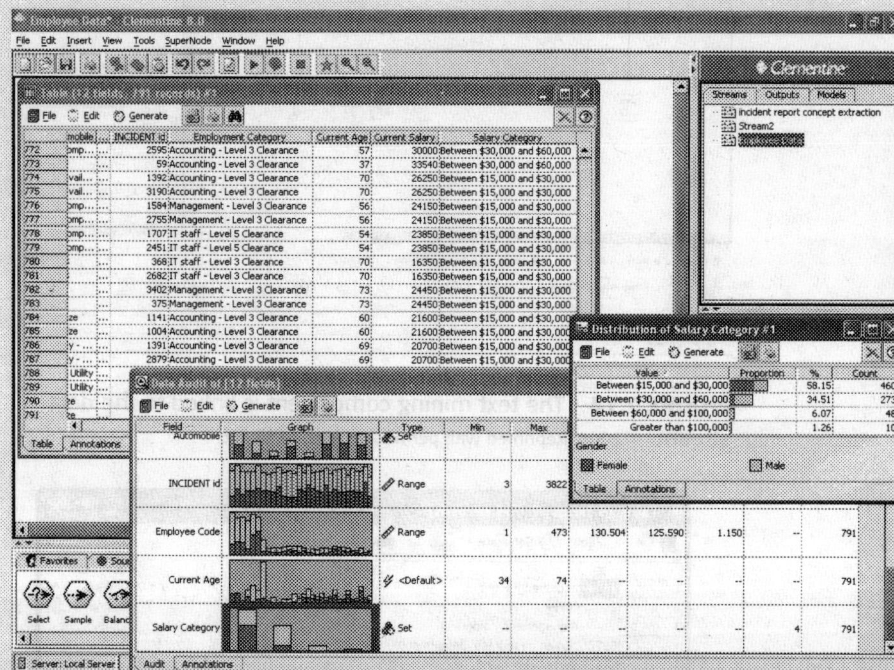

FIGURE 7.16 Incident identifications are linked to employees' demographics.

From that point, two new variables are derived to enhance analysis: the current age from the date of birth provided in the raw data and a number of different salary categories. This step will make the interpretation of the results much easier to comprehend. The inset of Figure 7.16 also shows the result of executing this data mining stream from two separate datasets with two different formats. With this merged, there is now an incident identification number linked to employee identification numbers and other information, along with current age and salary category, all within one table.

In Figure 7.17 the culmination of all the work up to this point is displayed graphically. In the top left part of the screen is the data stream of employee information

(continued)

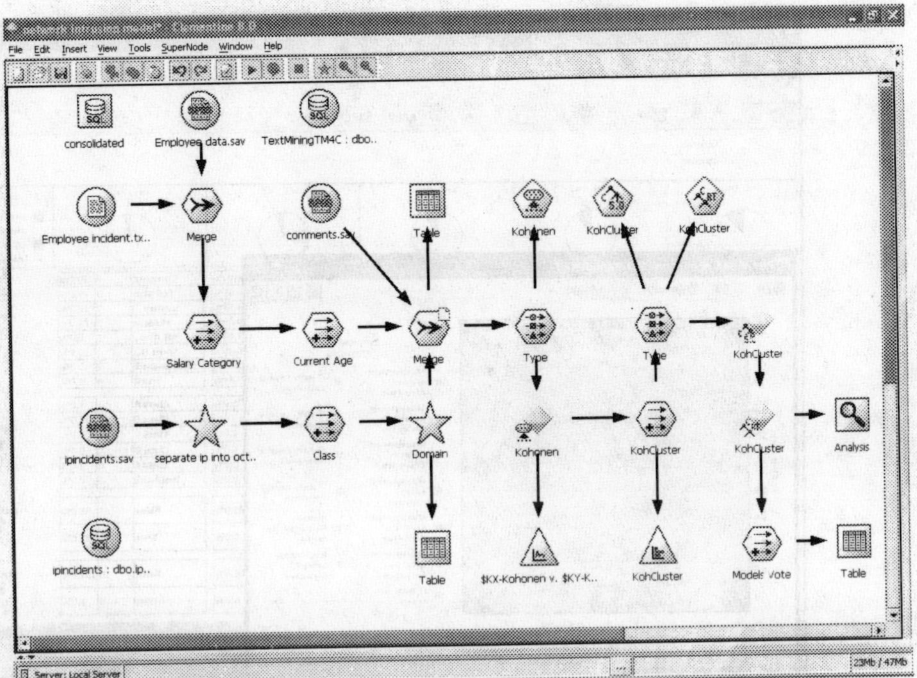

FIGURE 7.17 From data streams to mining by multiple algorithms. © 2004. Reprinted with permission from SPSS, Inc.

merged with incidents, and in the bottom left part of the screen is the network IP addresses stream. At the top center are the results of the text mining analysis saved to a file: comments.sav.

At this stage, what is important to note is that all these steps performed on raw data are now merged together to begin the data mining analysis, Figure 7.17 shows two data mining algorithms being applied to the data. The first gold nugget represents a Kohonen network algorithm, a neural network algorithm that performs clustering. The intent is to organize all of the data into groups that exhibit similar network behavior.

When the Kohonen clustering algorithm is executed against the data, output similar to that seen in Figure 7.18 is displayed. In looking at the output, note that along the top and along the bottom axis are large groups of incidents that contain large clusters that are somewhat populated. However, in looking along the center axis, note that there are some cases that did not make it into any of the other large clusters; these cases appear to be anomalous. From this point, those cases can be highlighted and extracted from the data stream in order to investigate them further.

(continued)

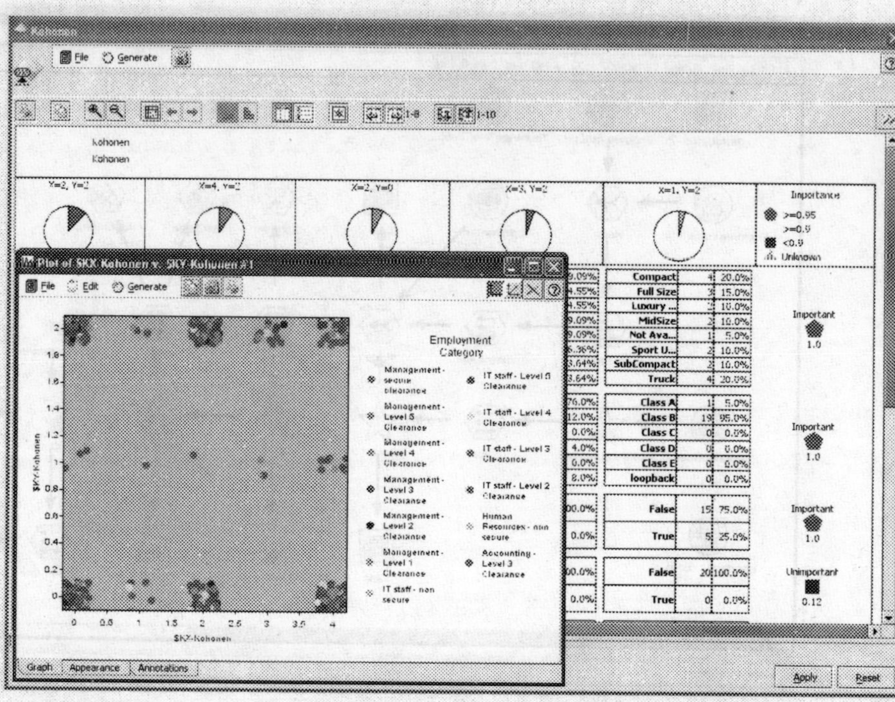

FIGURE 7.18 The clustering of incidents in the data. © 2004. Reprinted with permission from SPSS, Inc.

The second gold nugget represented in the data mining stream shown in Figure 7.17 is the C5.0 algorithm, an artificial intelligence program for segmenting and classifying data into IF/THEN rules via a decision tree process of induction. The idea here is to identify data points that are behaving slightly differently than the norm and extract descriptive rules that describe the conditional incident behavior of these anomalous transactions. This will allow the system and analysts to easily identify this type of unusual activity in the future. For purposes of the incident analysis, these anomalies can be labeled as those representing high risk. The C5.0 algorithm can be run against all the clustered data to begin to build a model that will predict high risk intrusion cases within new datasets. Figure 7.19 shows the output of what the C5.0 algorithm was able to create. Near the bottom of the screen, a certain number of descriptive rules were created for high risk cases. More importantly, these rules were generated from both structured and unstructured data sources, from which descriptive conditions are extracted for detecting future attacks.

(continued)

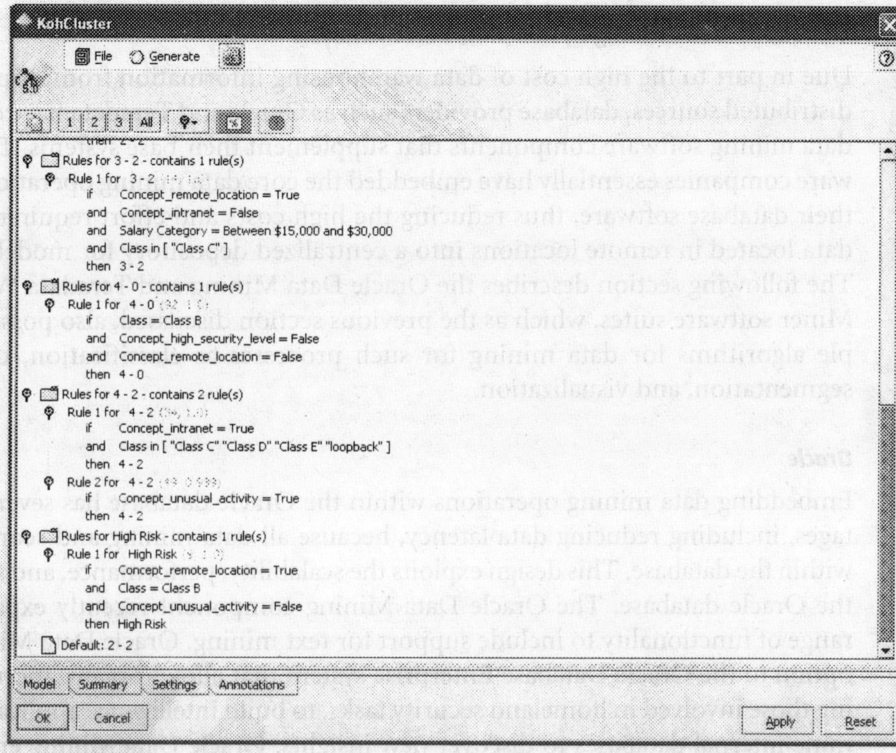

FIGURE 7.19 The extraction of incident rules. © 2004. Reprinted with permission from SPSS, Inc.

At this stage, a number of different operations can be performed within the Clementine data mining environment, such as testing and validating the accuracy of the model. In addition, more analyses can be performed to test different clustering and different predictive algorithms to try to increase the accuracy for detecting high risk incidents.

The final step in the modeling process is the deployment of its code to the organization. Clementine allows an analyst to encapsulate all of the work into an executable program that can then either be embedded into another application or run against new data for immediate scoring of high risk incidents. For example, the code can be shared with network security analysts whose responsibility is to prevent acts of cyber-terrorism and intrusion detection.

Embedded Data Mining

Embedded Data Mining Systems: In-Place Analysis

Due in part to the high cost of data warehousing information from disparate and distributed sources, database providers such as Oracle and Teradata have developed data mining software components that supplement their base systems. These software companies essentially have embedded the core data mining operations within their database software, thus reducing the high costs and effort required to move data located in remote locations into a centralized depository for model creation. The following section describes the Oracle Data Mining and Teradata Warehouse Miner software suites, which as the previous section discussed, also possess multiple algorithms for data mining for such processes as classification, clustering, segmentation, and visualization.

Oracle

Embedding data mining operations within the Oracle database has several advantages, including reducing data latency, because all data mining and scoring occur within the database. This design exploits the scalability, performance, and security of the Oracle database. The Oracle Data Mining component recently expanded the range of functionality to include support for text mining. Oracle Data Mining is an option to the Oracle Database Enterprise system that allows organizations, including those involved in homeland security tasks, to build intelligence applications that mine internal databases to discover new insights. Oracle Data Mining embeds the modeling functionality into the Oracle database for making classifications, predictions, and associations. All model building, scoring, and metadata management operations are initiated via a Java-based API and occur entirely within the relational database.

With embedded data mining design, all the data mining functionality is inside the database, so the data preparation, model building, and scoring activities remain internal. Because Oracle Data Mining performs all phases of analysis, modeling, and scoring within the database, each phase results in significant improvements in productivity, automation, and integration. By embedding these operations, significant productivity enhancements are achieved by eliminating the extraction of data from the database to special-purpose data mining tools and importing the data mining results back into the database. These improvements are notable in data preparation, which often can constitute as much as 80 percent of the data mining process.

With this embedded design, all the data preparation can be performed using standard SQL manipulation and data mining utilities within the database. Scoring to make predictions is greatly simplified as the data and the model are in the same location—inside the database. There is no need to move the data to the model or export the model as code (typically C, C++, or Java) and then move the model back to the data for scoring in the database. The benefits of *in-place mining* start with the first steps of a data mining project, including data preparation and the assembly of relevant data, the definition of a target field, and possibly the creation of new summary or calculated fields. The mining component accepts transactional and non-transactional, summarized, and single-record tables, as well as transactional tables; it automatically handles any conversion necessary.

The mining component supports *binning*, the process of collecting the values in a field into meaningful groups. This allows programmers to bin the data prior to building models for more problem-specific purposes. For example, for a money laundering problem, the number of transaction fields might be binned into the ranges 0–16, 17–21, 22–33, 34–50, and so forth. The Oracle Data Mining component provides programmatic access to two data mining algorithms embedded in the database through a Java-based API. They are Naïve Bayes for classifications and predictions and Association Rules for finding patterns of co-occurring events.

Teradata

Teradata also uses its Warehouse Miner component to provide data mining operations and algorithms inside its database. The technique is to generate Teradata SQL statements dynamically and execute them from a Windows client. In the case of algorithms, iterations may be required such that subsequent SQL statements are generated based on the results of previous SQL statements. Algorithms may also include traditional numerical processing using math library routines. Teradata Warehouse Miner breaks the algorithm into steps, and those that require data access are performed via SQL, while those requiring numerical processing may not be performed via SQL. Teradata Warehouse Miner does not move the detail data out of the database; only highly aggregated values are moved as needed.

The Teradata Warehouse Miner component includes a graphical user interface to its Statistical, Matrix, Algorithm, Graphing, and Scoring functions, as well as the Metadata and Teradata database. Although these components execute from a client, they all operate directly against a Teradata system and persist within a metadata model that resides inside the database. This metadata is persisted as a collection of one or more analyses contained within what Teradata calls a *data mining project*. This project acts as an index into the metadata, allowing analyses to be created, saved, removed, modified, and executed. All projects and analyses can be executed from within the graphical user interface or in batch mode, with or without the user interface.

The analysis user interfaces are divided into six separate components and are grouped according to functionality. Each component contains multiple controls, one for each algorithm. Each control uses smaller controls and dialog boxes to display all the parameters for the algorithm it represents. These parameters are represented internally as XML, which allows the control to load parameters onto the screen and save parameters to XML. The six components are as follows:

- Analytic Algorithms
- Descriptive Statistics
- Data Reorganization
- Data Transformations
- Matrix Functions
- Scoring and Evaluation

Each algorithm creates a report after it completes its analysis. The report is in XML and can display four different visualizations outputs: text, tables, data queries, and graphs. Once an algorithm is complete, the report is retrieved and displayed using a special report viewer object. The available graphs are

Descriptive Statistics: Histogram analysis, frequency analysis, scatter plot

Linear Regression: Scatter plot, bar chart for coefficients and t-statistics

Logistic Regression: Lift chart, bar chart for b-coefficients, t-statistics, p-values, and Wald statistics

Factor Analysis: Factor patterns, screen plot

Decision Trees: Tree browser, rule text

Cluster Analysis: Size and distances, similarity

The Teradata Warehouse Miner algorithms are packaged as separate executables that generate SQL, broken down into the following categories:

Descriptive Statistics: Univariate statistics, histograms, frequency, values analysis, overlap analysis, scatter plot

Transformations: OLAP, mathematical, statistical, trigonometric, bin coding, design coding, recoding, rescaling, derive (free-form SQL expressions), free-form SQL

Data Reorganization: Denonnalization, joining, sampling, partitioning

A second group of algorithms generate and execute SQL. They are usually iterative in nature or rely on previous results to further generate and execute additional SQL:

Matrix Functions: Create matrix, export matrix

Analytic Algorithms: Factor analysis, linear regression, logistic regression, cluster analysis, decision tree, affinity, and sequence analysis

Scoring and Evaluation: Factor analysis scoring and evaluation, linear regression scoring and evaluation, logistic regression scoring and evaluation, cluster scoring and evaluation, decision tree scoring and evaluation

All these functions enable in-place data mining directly against the Teradata database engine, enabling the model creation process in a massive relational database environment and providing a means of minimizing the steps to perform analytic operations. Traditional data mining techniques often require that the data be moved into proprietary or flat file structures; with in-place mining this is eliminated. For a homeland security organization this may be an issue because traditional data mining techniques require time to extract data from different locations, convert them into different data formats, and then import them into an application.

With an embedded data mining design, analytic operations can be performed on the data within the relational database itself, where the results can be managed in a single location and shared with the entire homeland security organization. This type of design uses the relational database management system (RDBMS) capability to handle a large number of multiple concurrent users and minimizes the number of steps to analyze and manage the data. However, using embedded data mining for a homeland security organization works only if all the data it requires resides in the same RDBMS, which is why the evolution of the technology moves to that of a distributed data mining architecture, which is agent based.

Distributed Data Mining

Agent Technology: Distributed Data Mining

Data mining, with its capability to predict human behavior within massive amounts of collected information, has been identified as one of the key technologies in the battle against terrorism. However, its application for homeland security and crimes often associated with terrorism is challenged by today's nature of data collection and operational IT environments, which are characterized by different database owners in distributed locations, with heterogeneous data schemas residing in diverse database platforms, coupled with strict security concerns prohibiting data exchange or movement of dynamic databases to a centralized data depository for analysis.

The distributed data mining approach can address these challenges and obstacles. In distributed data mining, the analytic processes of classification, clustering, segmentation, prediction, and so on and the machine learning algorithms used for these analyses are transported by software agents over networks to where the data resides. In this design, rather than moving the data to the algorithms, the algorithms go to where the data is stored, with only encrypted compressed pointers moving to a centralized mediator agent, which reassembles the pointer and the data processing findings from these multiple data sources into a cohesive data mining analysis.

At this juncture it is important that the concept of an *agent* be defined, especially in the context of how it relates to data mining and homeland security. An agent is an autonomous program designed to perform a function over a network or the Internet. Agents are often described as entities with attributes considered useful in a particular domain. This is the case with intelligent agents, entities that emulate mental processes or simulate rational behavior; personal assistant agents, which help users perform a task; mobile agents that are able to roam networking environments to fulfill their goals; information agents that filter and coherently organize unrelated and scattered data; and autonomous agents, which accomplish actions without supervision. For purposes of clarification, agents often possess the following traits or features:

They can react: They have the ability to selectively sense and act.

They are mobile: They can migrate in a self-directed way through networks.

They are autonomous: They can be goal driven, proactive self-starters.

They are intelligent: They have the capability to act on abstract task specifications.

They are adaptive: They possess the capability to learn and improve with experience.

They can collaborate: They can work with other agents to achieve a common goal.

They are persistent: They have temporal continuity and maintain an identity and state over long periods of time.

Because of these features, agents represent a key technology to homeland security organizations, with the most intelligent of these agents being capable of monitoring multiple diverse locations, communicating their findings and collaborating, analyzing conditions, issuing alerts at the first sign of a potential intrusion or attack, and profiling perpetrators or possible danger. For homeland security applications, the distributed data mining design is particularly important because in most situations the data these organizations rely on is in a different location, owned by different government agencies or departments, formatted in different schemas, stored in different types of relational databases, and, because of legislation or privacy laws, cannot be moved. Because of these factors, distributed data mining and agent technologies are especially unique solutions to homeland security organizations in today's IT environment. An excellent source of information exists for downloading from the Distributed Data Mining Bibliography maintained and managed by Kun Liu and Dr. Hillol Kargupta at *www.csee.umbc.edu/~hillol/DDMBIB/*.

In today's IT environment, two unique conditions exist, the first of which is that data is distributed in different and diverse databases. The second is that networks exist for linking all of these data sources, so agents can be used to mine them simultaneously. This type of distributed data analysis is a quantum leap from the first-generation type of mining analysis due to the ability to integrate a "real world" view of multiple data sources from diverse real-time databases. As changes occur in a dynamic environment in which conditions and transactions are continuously taking place, data mining can occur in real time. In this environment, data mining rules are created dynamically and can fire as conditions develop over a network of databases. In the past no direct correlation existed or was thought possible, but new knowledge discovery is possible via distributed data mining. This type of knowledge, distributed across a network of databases, organizes itself into a whole that is much greater that the sum of its parts.

Distributed Data Mining Techniques

Data mining as we have discussed deals with the capability to extract associations, clusters, and patterns from databases. The emergence of network-based distributed computing environments and the explosion of the Web during the 1990s have introduced an important new dimension to the data mining process: analyzing distributed, disparate, different data sources. As we have discussed, most of the current data mining software suites require the central aggregation of distributed data, usually in data marts or warehouses, which may not always be feasible for homeland security applications because of legislative restrictions, limited network bandwidth, security concerns, scalability problems, and the dynamic nature of today's modern databases.

Data mining in the Web, corporate or government intranets, sensor and wireless networks, especially as required by homeland security organizations, dictates the use of agent technology and pattern recognition technologies and a new paradigm for merging networks and data mining techniques. Distributed data mining supports the end-products of traditional data mining analyses: clustering, visualization, segmentation, classification, prediction, and modeling. However, it does this by analyzing data without moving it, at a lower cost, with improved efficiency and increased privacy and security for all concerned. When the datasets are large, scaling up the speed of data mining is crucial, which is why the embedded data mining process approach is an advancement, taking advantage of the parallel high-performance multiprocessor RBMS design. As we noted, this requires that all the data sources be centralized and be from a single database vendor, an unlikely scenario for homeland security organizations such as Terrorist Threat Integration Center (TTIC), which must integrate data from a vast array of sources.

The major reason why distributed data mining is the evolving method of accessing and analyzing multiple databases in different locations is security. New techniques in distributed data mining are being developed to encrypt and communicate the location of the data without actually moving the raw data from where it is stored. New methodologies hide sensitive data by using multiple types of random generating algorithms to preserve the privacy of the data being mined. These algorithms vary in the methods by which they encode the data, using various types of random "noise" designed to distort the original structure of the data. These distributed data mining techniques attempt to extract the patterns required for modeling without actually accessing or moving the raw data, in such a way that it cannot be reconstructed by others. Several distributed data mining methods are being developed for the analysis of structured content from sensor and wireless networks and other privacy-sensitive databases.

Exploratory studies have been done on privacy-preserving distributed data mining techniques in which multiple parts of databases are combined into a single consolidated cluster without accessing the features of the raw data. This is particularly relevant to homeland security organizations facing the dilemma in which different agencies and departments have some of the data elements of a common underlying population, possibly using different data features. Because of multiple constraints such as proprietary techniques, legal restrictions, and different data ownership, it is not feasible to pool all the data into a central location for clustering, link association, and modeling analyses.

There also have been recent developments in data reduction algorithms in which only small samples of entire databases are used to perform a distributed data mining model or rule-generation. Classical data mining algorithms require one or more computationally intensive pass over the entire database in order to perform their analyses, and this can be prohibitively slow. An effective method for dealing with this increasingly worsening scalability problem is to run special data mining algorithms on small samples of all the databases. For example, the FAST algorithm uses random sampling together with trimming of outlier transactions (out of range values).

Another program, the EA algorithm, repeatedly splits the data in halves to obtain its final data mining sample. Unlike FAST, the EA algorithm provides a guaranteed level of accuracy. Depending on the specific problem under consideration, either algorithm can be used to trade off speed and accuracy. The use of these types of data reduction algorithms is especially well suited for distributed data mining of streaming data systems, which is one of the challenges of homeland security organizations. The following section describes several distributed data mining systems, some of which, such as InferX, were originally developed for the military but represent ideal solutions for homeland security organizations in analyzing and collaborating findings from diverse immovable and extremely large databases.

Agnik

Agnik develops software in the area of mobile and distributed data mining. Its technology is based on years of research, developing data intelligence applications that can be used anywhere and anytime. Agnik specializes in customized applications in the areas of mining data streams, mobile data, distributed heterogeneous databases, and text data. Agnik's privacy-preserving data mining approach uses distributed analysis techniques. The emergence of network-centric IT environments has introduced many data-intensive applications in which the data, the computing resources, and the end users are distributed across different locations. The Internet, sensor and wireless networks, and other ubiquitous mobile appliances such as PDAs, palmtops, laptops, and cell phones are creating a need for a new breed of remote data mining for analysis of data at any time from anywhere. This is certainly the environment of homeland security organizations.

Agnik is creating a suite of ubiquitous data mining applications for these environments, geared toward the analysis of time-critical data streams, such as those required for homeland security purposes. Agnik is also developing distributed data mining applications that are designed to run in a network of desktop computers and high-end devices. The firm is currently developing applications in mining privacy-sensitive data without directly accessing it, which allows for detecting patterns without necessarily accessing the raw data directly. Agnik technology is being used for mining multi-organization databases for network-intrusion detection, regulatory data analysis, and counterterrorism.

Agnik is developing a Distributed Multi-organizational Collaborative Decision Support (MCDS) System for Emergency Preparedness for the Air Force. The project uses a kernel for a distributed, collaborative, multi-organizational decision support system for emergency preparedness, anti-terrorism, and homeland defense. The proposed research is based on a systematic approach that pays careful attention to both technical and human factors and offers a collection of solutions to manage, query, and mine distributed data sources efficiently. The project uses psychological, social, and organizational models. It provides graphical interfaces for creating domain ontology, distributed data mining techniques, interfaces for mobile devices developed using advanced techniques, and dynamic resource discovery for onsite emergency response teams.

The Air Force MCDS system provides a distributed approach to identifying and managing threats associated with physical and data assets that need to be protected. In Figure 7.20, a graphical user interface is displayed listing the assets under management.

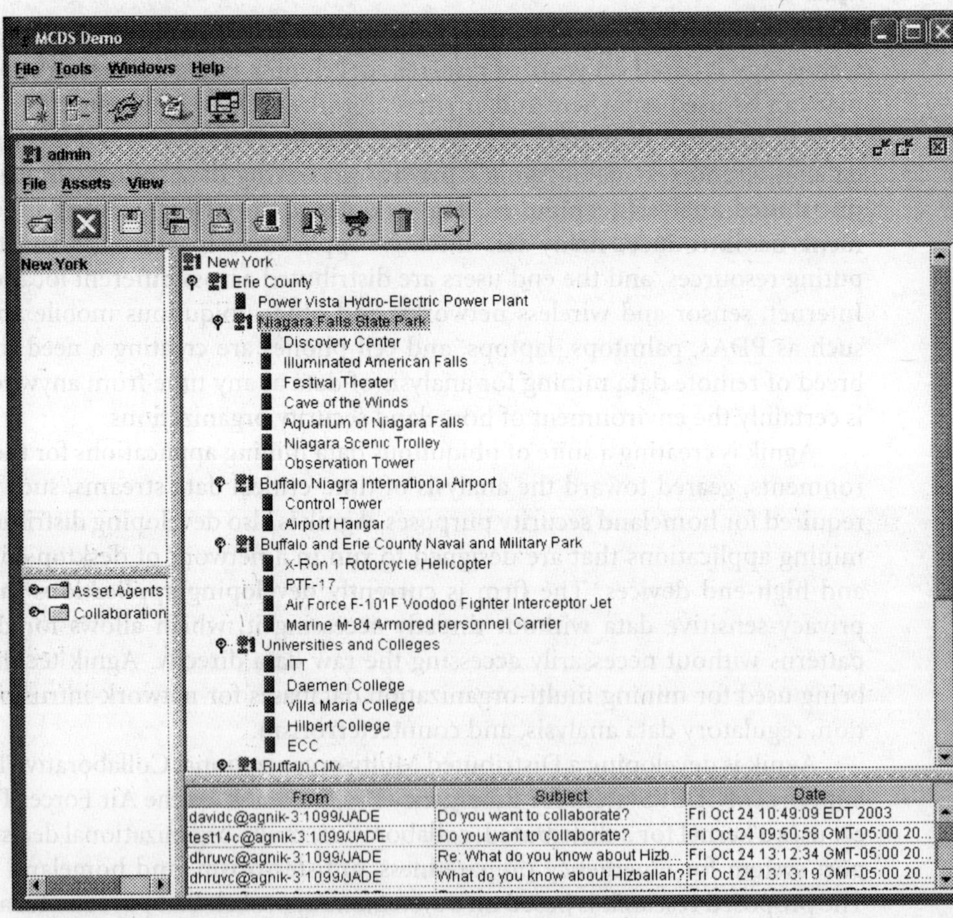

FIGURE 7.20 The asset tree management window.

The top half of the left frame lists the root nodes of the asset trees that the user has access to, and the bottom half lists different asset and collaboration agents that are currently logged into the same asset tree. Each node in the asset tree is managed by an intelligent agent and can be handled in a distributed fashion, depending on the location of the asset manager and the organization.

The top half of the right frame shows the asset tree structure. The bottom half of the right frame shows any important messages regarding any assets or any other messages that the user should know about. These messages are prioritized according to the user's preferences or depending on the output from the data mining modules. For example, detection of an outlier in the data stream mining module may create a message with high priority and show up on the top of the list, or a piece of human intelligence may also trigger such a collaborative alert.

Analyzing distributed data plays a critical role in the MCDS system. The purpose of the system's module is to link patterns from different data sources, such as data streams, relational data, and semistructured or unstructured data (text) detected by the corresponding local management and mining modules. For example, MCDS is designed to compare and associate multiple link structures from different sources, detected by an unstructured text analysis module and a stream-clustering module. Figure 7.21 shows a terrorist organization behavioral link analysis network generated after named entities are extracted by the system's Ontology Aware Information Extractor engine.

MCDS also has a Data Stream Management System (DSMS) designed to provide basic interface functions, such as how to design and load a query plan into the system. This operation includes parameters for specifying the data sources to access and where to send the data, and it can set an optional time period after which the query should be halted and eliminated from the user's system. Optional priority parameters are provided that will aid the DSMS in scheduling and allocating resources for the user. The interface of the DSMS continuous query plan designer can be seen in Figure 7.22, where the user can drag and drop the icons and the links for designing a continuous query over a data stream. These query plans will in turn be used for executing continuous queries over the data stream.

InferX

The agent-based technologies of InferX are designed specifically to perform distributed data mining over a dispersed network of databases, enabling the following new counterterrorism capabilities:

- Handling information fusion of diverse intelligence databases without moving or integrating the original data.

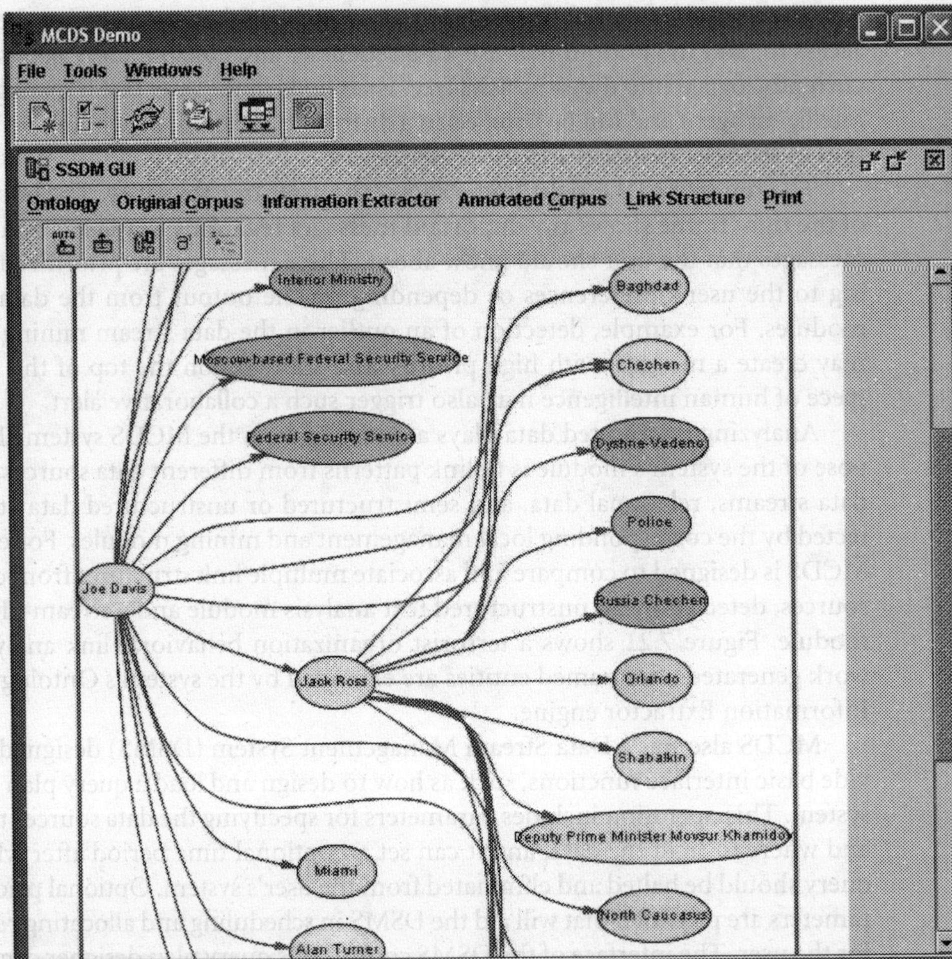

FIGURE 7.21 Link analysis network representing terrorist organizations' behavioral models.

- Identifying intricate patterns and relationships within information across distributed non-collaborative databases.
- Highlighting potential terrorist plans and possible attacks through early discovery of event patterns and causal actions or conditions.
- Providing distributed knowledge discovery to support collaborative decision-making over an entire network of dispersed intelligence data sources.

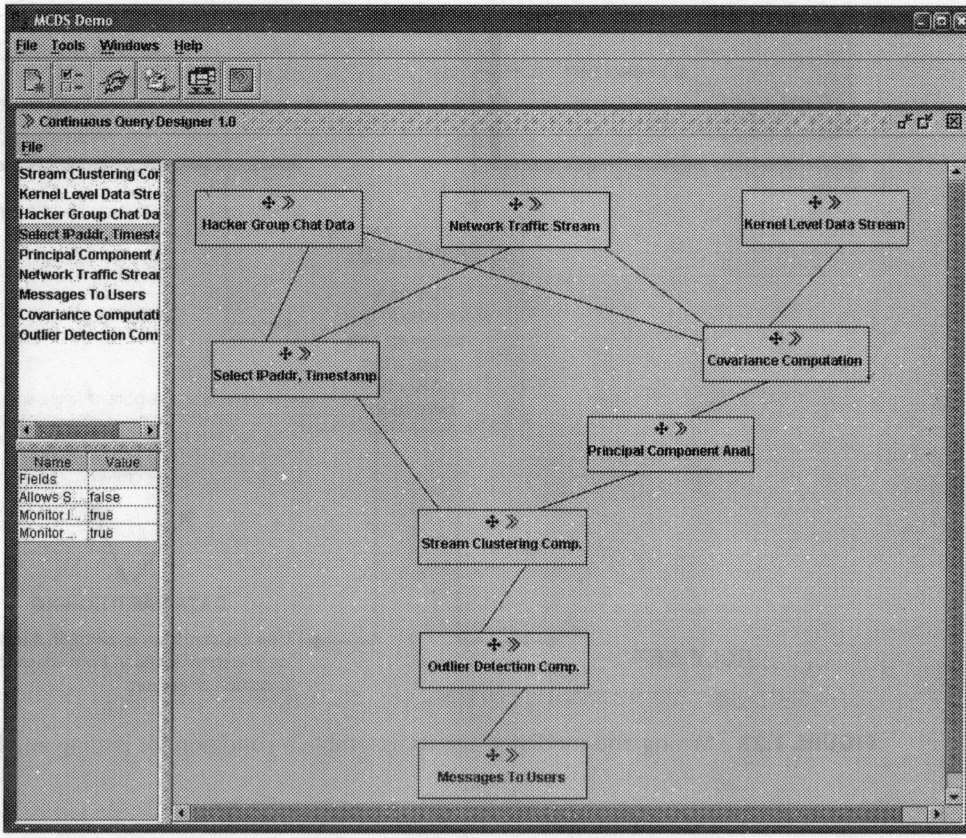

FIGURE 7.22 DSMS continuous query plan designer interface.

In the InferX design, machine learning agents are used to mine multiple databases remotely and simultaneously without moving any of the data. Only pointers to the results would be communicated, encrypted, and compressed to a centralized mediator agent. This type of remote data mining system incorporates the results of multiple distributed databases to detect potential terrorists, for instance at a point of entry border crossing in San Diego. For example, as shown in Figure 7.23, the InferX agents can remotely mine a database on homeland security border crossings records (DB1), a California DMV database (DB2), and so on—effectively utilizing a curtain of data sources much like a software sentry. Each agent computes the most optimal local condition using features available in each of the distributed databases.

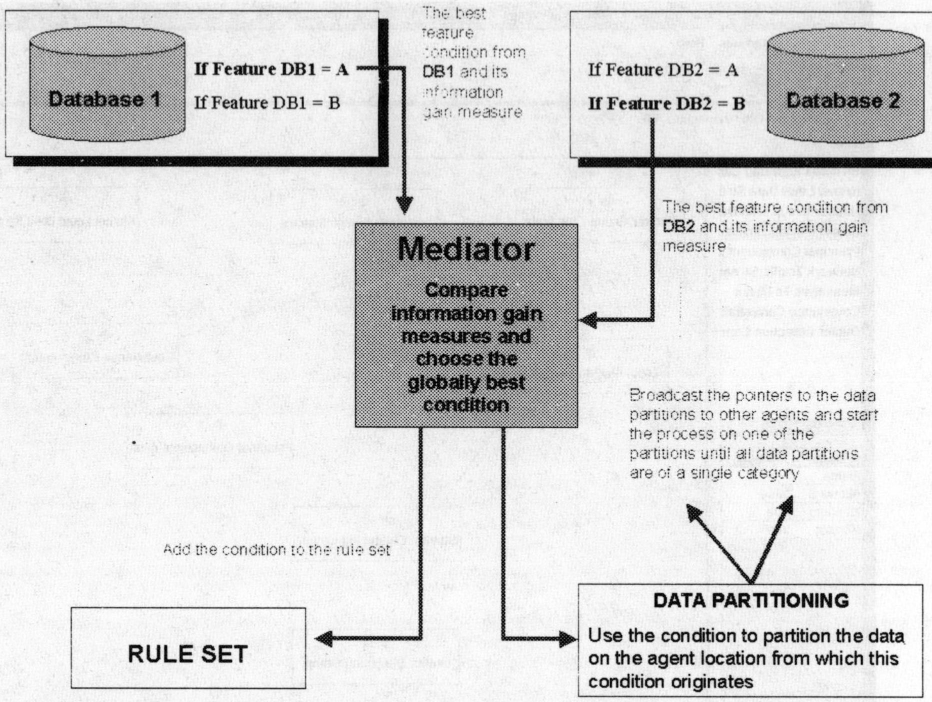

FIGURE 7.23 Mining and mediator agents assemble a condition for issuing an alert.

These conditions together with their *information gain measures* are sent to a centralized mediator agent that chooses the most globally optimal condition. This condition is input to a rule set structure or a group of conditions and is used to partition the data at the location from which it originated. The indices to the partitioned data are broadcast to other agents to partition the data accordingly. The system continues the same collaborative process of deriving the most globally optimal condition using the data from one of the partitions. It is a process by which a decision tree interrogates the distributed databases, segmenting them, and extracting from them the key data variables and values most significant in predicting the objective: identifying the conditional rule for targeting the objective, be that the profile of a smuggler or the location of a compromised cargo container. This repetitive process is executed until all partitions describe data belonging to a single category. Such a condition-generation process can assemble the rules for the eventual detection of potential terrorists, intrusions, or attacks.

While the InferX agent-based distributed data mining approach exhibits some resemblance to a mobile Multi Agent System (MAS), which is a loosely coupled network of software agents that interact to solve problems that are beyond the individual capacities or knowledge of each problem solver, the InferX design is radically different. An MAS mainly retrieves, filters, and globally coordinates information from sources that are spatially distributed. The InferX process goes beyond retrieval and filtering; its segmentation processes seek to discover conditions from which it generates a series of IF/THEN rules resulting from inductive generalization across distributed data locations. InferX does more than assemble data; it collaborates and analyzes it, and it does this without moving it. MAS systems are used mainly to support intelligent information retrieval, while the InferX design uses its agents to perform complex distributed inductive generalizations for information exploitation. The following is a sample of an InferX rule:

IF	Hamburg_Port_Security_State = Low
AND	Hamburg_Days_At_Port > 10
AND	Liverpool_Vessel_Type = Drive-off
AND	Liverpool_Delta_Weight : 800
THEN	Container Risk Classification is HIGH

MINING CARGO CONTAINERS DATA REMOTELY: AN INFERAGENT APPLICATION SCENARIO

To illustrate how an agent-based distributed data mining system would work, envision the problem facing a homeland security organization in monitoring the cargo containers it processes through its ports. The container traffic is a critical component of global trade, where it is estimated that about 90 percent of the international trade moves or is transported in cargo containers. In the United States, almost half of all incoming trade, by value, arrives by containers on board container ships, with almost 7 million cargo containers arriving and being offloaded at U.S. seaports each year. Following September 11, there was an urgent need for new techniques to screen containers with a high level of accuracy for protection against potential attacks. One of the core elements of the Container Security Initiative (CSI) is to use innovative intelligence and automated information to identify and target high-risk containers so that they can be screened before their arrival at U.S. ports.

A scenario has been developed to illustrate how the InferAgent system can be used for container security. Figure 7.24 illustrates a situation in which containers are

(continued)

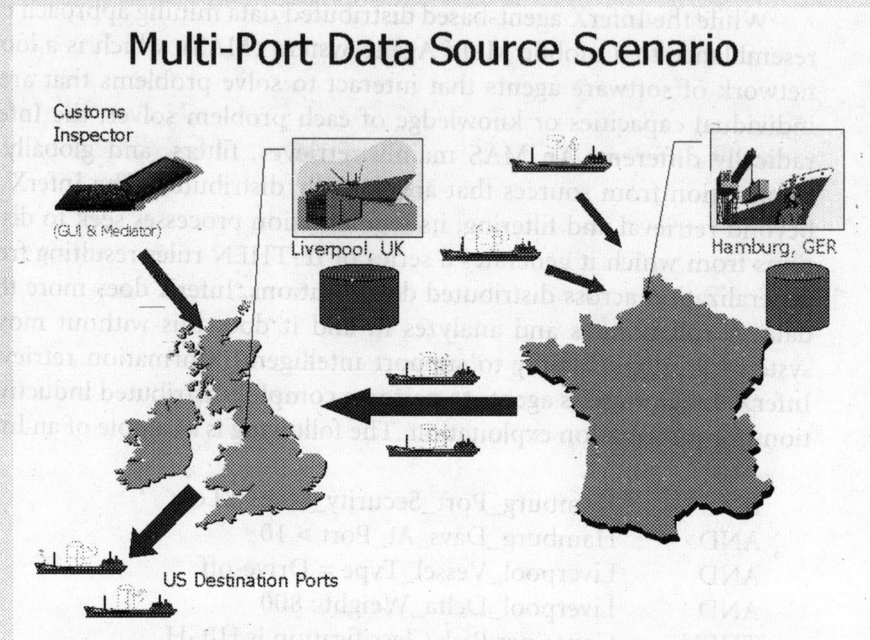

FIGURE 7.24 Multiport data source scenario.

shipped from Hamburg via Liverpool seaports to the United States. Each of the seaports maintains a database that contains information on container traffic and port daily activities and contains such information as vessel loading and unloading status, port security, and so forth.

Figure 7.25 shows some of the data fields in the Liverpool and Hamburg databases, which will be used by InferAgent for its analysis and detection of high risk alerts. A customs inspector at Liverpool, the en route port, analyzes the distributed databases using InferAgent and generates a security risk level report for the currently prescreened containers to be shipped to the United States. The report annotates containers as either low or high risk. The ones annotated high risk are subject to further elevated inspections by homeland security personnel.

To begin the process of distributed data mining, sections from both databases are used to extract and create a virtual database, which will be used to construct a model for detecting high risk containers. In Figure 7.26, InferAgent begins this process by extracting data fields from both databases.

The user can interact with the virtual database to select a group of data fields for the construction of the predictive models. InferAgent can access the databases in

(continued)

Demonstration Scenario Data Bases

Decision Port Data Base	Enroute Port Data Base
Liverpool_Country_of_Exporter	Hamburg_Exporter
Liverpool_Bill_of_Landing_Number	Hamburg_Bill_of_Landing_Number
Liverpool_Commercial_Destination	Hamburg_Commercial_Destination
Liverpool_Loading_Pier	Hamburg_Loading_Pier
Liverpool_Exporting_Carrier	Hamburg_Exporting_Carrier
Liverpool_Containerized	Hamburg_Containerized
Liverpool_Container_Gross_Weight	Hamburg_Container_Gross_Weight
Liverpool_Port_of_Origin	Hamburg_Port_of_Origin
Liverpool_Port_of_Destination	Hamburg_Port_of_Destination
Liverpool_Port_of_Transfer	Hamburg_Port_of_Transfer
Liverpool_Vessel_Type	Hamburg_Vessel_Type
Liverpool_Group_Size	Hamburg_Transfer_Unloading
Liverpool_Group_Size_Difference	Hamburg_Containers_In_Group
Liverpool_Transfer_Unloading	Hamburg_Container_Inspection_Level
Liverpool_Delta_Weight	Hamburg_Days_At_Port
Risk Classification	Hamburg_Number_Of_Vessels_At_Port
	Hamburg_Port_Security_State

FIGURE 7.25 Data components at two locations.

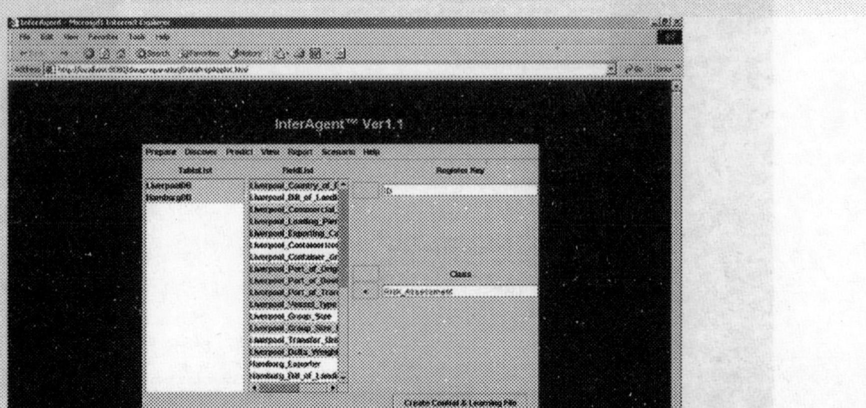

FIGURE 7.26 Fields from port of entry databases—one from Liverpool and one from Hamburg—are used to create a virtual database.

(continued)

Liverpool and in Hamburg simultaneously; InferAgent will look for the conditions identifying high risk containers and assemble them into a series of conditional IF/THEN rules. InferAgent will begin training itself using historical container traffic data, which results in confiscation of dangerous or tampered cargo. The model constructed by InferAgent will be used to monitor current and future flow of container traffic.

Once the distributed mining process is completed, the user can display the resulting rules or conditions for identifying high risk containers. Figure 7.27 illustrates one of these rules or conditions. This specific rule combines conditions found in the Liverpool and Hamburg databases, which under traditional data mining methods, such as those based solely on analytic algorithms without network communications, would have been impossible to discover. The agent components enable this type of system to perform global data analysis and discover conditions drawn from multiple databases located in different locations.

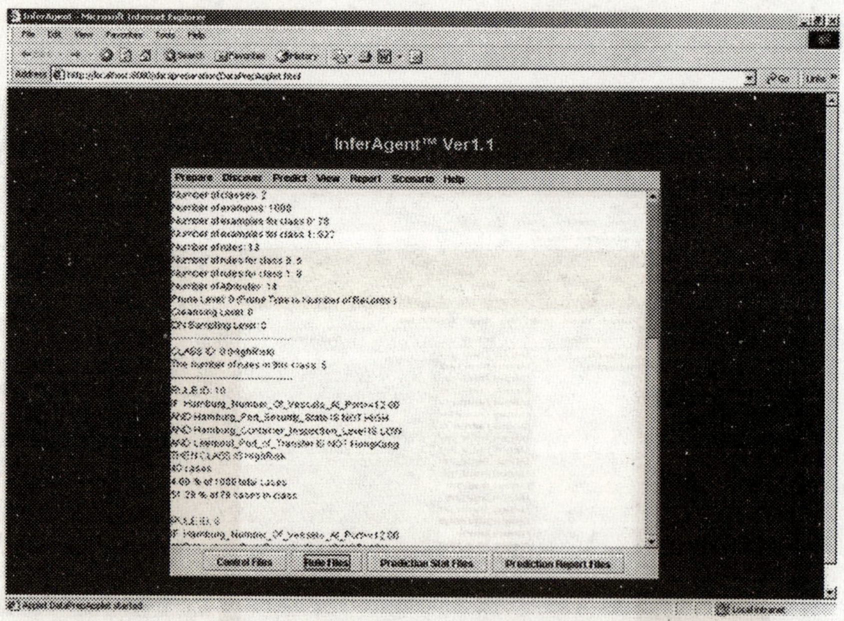

FIGURE 7.27 The resulting rules from the mining of both databases.

This type of rapid distributed data modeling design was created by InferX as a direct result of its contracts to develop image recognition systems for missile weapons for the Department of Defense. In dealing with large-scale sensory distributed database sensor systems as used by the Missile Defense Agency, InferX resorted to agent technology along with machine learning algorithms to deal with a real-time recognition problem for identifying potential targets from satellites. This was the adaptive modeling approach InferAgent took in analyzing multisensor information, which was deployed at the Vision Laboratory of Lockheed Martin Missiles and Fire Control. One of the major benefits of this design is that data ownership of multiple clients is maintained by these dispersed sources without the need to move any of the information. Instead, only the results and pointers to the data are transmitted encrypted.

This type of distributed analysis is accomplished via a synchronized collaboration of mining agents that analyze the information in remote databases where it is stored and a mediator agent component that assembles the communicated results simultaneously. Distributed data mining results in a set of conditional rules generated through a tree induction algorithm. The tree induction algorithm in an iterative interrogative process is used to determine the data feature that is most discriminatory. In other words, this data mining process focuses on discovering the single value or attribute that is the most significant in identifying high risk containers.

The next significant feature of each of the subsets of the data is then used to further split and narrow down the process of identification and classification of high risk containers. The resulting structure is called a decision tree, written as a collection of conditional rules, which in the distributed network framework of multiple databases is accomplished by communication between the mining agents and the mediator agent via the steps shown in Figure 7.28. In the end, a set of conditional rules is produced for identifying high risk containers.

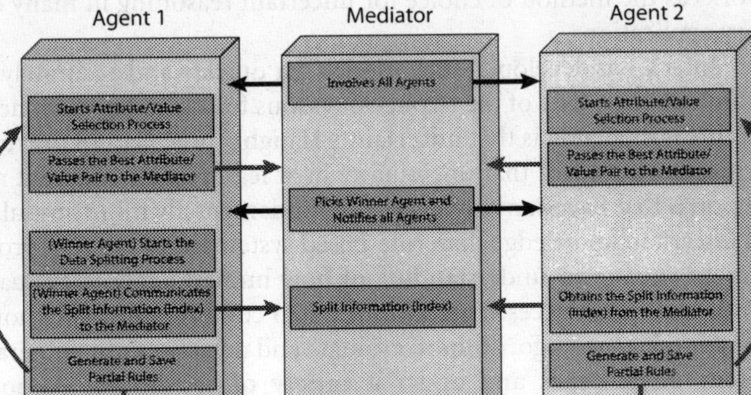

FIGURE 7.28 Agent-mediator communication mechanism (two-agent scenario).

InferX has developed a hybrid Bayesian Network Decision Tree algorithm to support the analysis of large databases, a fast and highly precise method for the detection of possible terrorist threats. One of the most daunting challenges for homeland security organizations is the modeling of uncertainty for the detection of potential terrorist activity. There is massive uncertainty encountered in attempting to construct such predictive models. It requires using probability estimates, because attempting to predict an attack cannot be obtained from the normal data mining methodology, which uses empirical frequency distributions. Terrorist attacks are events that are too uncommon or hypothetical.

For such modeling the probabilities must be derived using a combination of probabilistic modeling and analysis. A probability-based system should capture an expert's understanding of uncertain events. For example, an intelligence analyst is used to construct a probabilistic model, so that based on current event developments, news feeds, intelligence reports, and other information variables, the expert deduces a probable scenario: An attack is imminent. This expert generates probability weights that are used as inputs into the data mining system based on Bayesian network (to deal with uncertainty) and decision tree (to make quick decisions) algorithms to correlate these multiple complex factors and generate or suppress alerts about potential attacks.

These types of probability-based systems are most often used to incorporate uncertainty reasoning using Bayesian network algorithms. A Bayesian network is a graph-based framework combined with a rigorous probabilistic foundation used to model and reason in the presence of uncertainty. The capability of Bayesian inference to propagate consistently the impact of evidence on the probabilities of uncertain outcomes in the network has led to the rapid emergence of Bayesian networks as the method of choice for uncertain reasoning in many civilian and military applications.

InferX has developed such models for quickly and accurately detecting targets from satellites. One of the strongest reasons for using Bayesian networks in terrorist threat modeling is that uncertainty is highly prevalent in the real world, and it is critical to represent that uncertainty in at least a semi-coherent manner. Another reason is that Bayesian networks are a fundamentally more modular representation of uncertain knowledge than rule-based systems, and as such, provide an excellent way to encode an understanding of how human analysts evaluate developments from multiple sources. This hybrid design combines human knowledge with artificial intelligence algorithms to evaluate and detect certain vulnerabilities from different threat types and under a variety of conditions. Although this hybrid algorithm was developed to acquire targets for the military using sensor data, the technology could be migrated to detect multiple types of data for homeland security applications.

Working under contract with the military, InferX developed this hybrid algorithm, which incorporates features and functions from both Bayesian networks and decision tree algorithms for classification where the direct Bayesian inference is computationally intensive and prohibitively slow. Working with this hybrid approach, InferX has succeeded in using a decision tree to learn the patterns based on simulated data using forward sampling from the Bayesian network. Using this hybrid design, homeland security organizations could generate rules that are both strong and weak on the probability of attacks, using a combination of human knowledge from intelligence analysts and these machine learning algorithms. This hybrid design represents some of the most advanced techniques in distributed data mining for homeland security applications.

Infoglide

Infoglide Software's application suite, Bladeworks™, is a distributed data matching solution for risk assessment, decision automation, and non-obvious relationship discovery. Infoglide agent-based technology can also access multiple, disparate, remote databases, eliminating the need for data warehouses by creating virtual data warehouses. Infoglide has the capability to search data without having to combine databases, and this solves problems of data access and ownership between organizations as well as privacy, political, and legal issues. Infoglide uses patented *similarity search* technology to find relationships in data and can identify non-exact as well as exact matches. The software is highly configurable for real-time risk assessment of employee backgrounds, insurance and financial fraud, false aliases, identity theft, money laundering, underwriting losses, and homeland security risks. The firm recently announced a strategic alliance with American Management Systems (AMS) to provide its software to intelligence and law enforcement agencies in the global war on terrorism.

Infoglide software provides a matching technique it calls similarity searching to perform a special kind of entity match, even though the names of individuals might be misspelled. Infoglide searches not just names but other attributes, such as an address, a phone number, a place of birth, or a date of birth. The firm claims it is possible to find listings even though individuals have used aliases. Similarity searching never returns a null result-set as most exact matching search engines do when exact matches are not found. Instead, the similarity search returns a filtered list of values along with their respective rolled-up similarity scores. Rolled-up scores measure the closeness or similarity of the objects found relative to the search term, such as a name on a watch list. Infoglide has joined with Language Analysis Systems (LAS) to apply their name recognition technology.

A rolled-up score is one that combines similarity scores of children to produce a score for the parent. Scores "roll" all the way up the hierarchy until the whole document is scored. Scores range from 0 to 1, with 1 being an exact match. Attribute-level similarity scores are used to measure the similarity between a search term and the attribute instance being evaluated. Examples are the similarity of two database fields representing proper names, the relative similarity between two monetary values that might involve currency conversions, the geographical proximity of two ZIP Codes, or the geographical proximity of two telephone number area codes.

Infoglide's Fraud Investigator Enterprise has multiple features, functions, and attributes that enable the user to locate indicators of potential fraudulent activity, false aliases, and security threats. The software provides the following features:

Link Charting: Allows users to assemble suspicious claims records for further analysis. Every object brought onto the link chart is tied dynamically to the databases, allowing other searches to be performed.

Starting Point Analysis: Helps the user to search proactively for leads by surfacing the most common values and links.

Result Set Explorer: Allows the user to refine his original search. Provides the convenience of working with a relevant subset of the database rather than having to search the whole database again.

Batch Cross-Database Query: Allows the user to order searches that examine every search result in a result set to find matches across other databases.

Fraud Investigator Enterprise features four cross-database search methods:

Basic Search: Performed on data from one database.

SimLink Search: A method for quickly performing a predefined search for documents with the same or similar information as the anchor document.

Document Query: An advanced search in which the user can specify anchor values, change search weights within a group, change search measures, and specify the summary fields to be displayed in the result set.

Cross-Database Query: An advanced search in which the user can simultaneously search across several databases using the same query, even though the databases might be structurally different. Cross-database queries can compare data of the same data type, similar data types, or non-similar data types.

Infoglide's Similarity Search Engine (SSE) provides a library of data types and similarity scoring algorithms that are the result of years of applying similarity searching and scoring to real business problems in fraud detection and investigation. Infoglide software can also be extended to define new data types and scoring algorithms or change the algorithms for existing data types. The SSE can perform similarity scoring only after a domain expert has provided semantic and data type mapping to the set of data types for which similarity scoring algorithms are defined. For instance, a street address in a relational database may be a single string such as "123 Main Street." It may be valuable in similarity scoring to map this string data type to three built-in types: a numeric house number for which the similarity algorithm could determine if the house number is the same, next door, in the same block, or across the street from the search term street number; a primary street name, such as Main in the address 123 Main Street, for which similarity scoring might also identify Maine, Mane, and Man as closer than Elm; and a secondary street name such as Street, St, St., or "" (null, in this case).

The SSE uses *regular expressions* to split or join variables to facilitate optimal similarity matching and scoring. The SSE administrator has the capability to apply weightings to an individual similarity score so that its contribution to a rolled-up score is greater or less. The primary street name could be given more weight in the scoring process and thereby contribute a larger portion to the overall address similarity rolled-up score than the secondary name. Thus St. or null values would still result in a relatively high similarity score for the overall address if the secondary street name carried a lower weight.

Through the use of agent technology, SSE has the capability to create executable programs that will run on the platforms that host the databases; similarity searches on multiple databases can be performed simultaneously, thus maximizing performance. The agent technology provides remote filtering, which enables a result set from queries such as the "top 5 highest scoring results" or "results scoring over 90%" to be transported over a remote connection as opposed to all scored database records being returned for centralized filtering. When databases are horizontally striped, an agent may be deployed for each stripe, further increasing performance.

A major application of Infoglide Software's SSE is in identifying fraud in insurance claims, where both local and industry data sources have to be searched for indicators of abuse. Two very large property and casualty insurers use the SSE for detecting and investigating fraudulent claims. Major fraud rings have been uncovered, investigated, and successfully prosecuted using the SSE. Another existing application is with one of the most successful Web-based auction sites. The SSE is used to detect and deny access to individuals attempting fraudulent account registration. Through this name matching entity validation technology, Infoglide is providing fraud detection and alias identification solutions to the Transportation Security Administration (TSA) for homeland security purposes.

In summary, the Infoglide SSE excels in applications where data occurs in an unrefined state, where the search criteria of near misses should be included in results, and where data resides in several data sources, local or external. The technology also is applicable where a warehouse approach is too expensive or prohibited due to legislation and security. Infoglide Software's SSE offers programmatic interfaces to enable its search engine to be embedded in other organization applications. An API is available from Infoglide to provide connectivity either through the HTTP protocol or via sockets, where, search and configuration commands are passed as XML streams over the Internet connection. Using such APIs, a homeland security organization could use the name matching capabilities of Infoglide to monitor watch lists over disparate distributed databases, such as those of border points of entry or airline reservations.

The SSE uses agent technologies to maximize performance and scalability. With agent technology, an executable is transported to the platform hosting the database, usually a mirror of the operational database. This agent, along with configuration information, is used to do real-time mapping of the relational structures to Infoglide Software's data types. The agent also assists in similarity scoring for the single database and then passes the scored results as an XML stream to a master scoring engine that handles cross-database scoring and rolled-up scores. Because of the agent technology, access to multiple databases, money laundering, fraud and identity theft detection, and other types of homeland security applications, lookups can occur in parallel, thus maximizing performance.

Although both InferX and Infoglide use agents to perform their analyses remotely, they are quite different. InferX performs classification and rule generation of databases, while Infoglide does entity identification by performing name matching of multiple strings associated to individuals. Increasingly, however, these agent-based analysis systems will become important to homeland security organizations, enabling analysts to mine any database anywhere in the world, providing network-centric data and text mining capabilities. Next is a system that also uses agents to link and discover associations remotely over disparate databases: COPLINK®.

COPLINK

Connecting the dots in the future for homeland security organizations may come to mean linking the information already stored in multiple disparate databases in order for investigators and analysts to make the final correlations. One system which incorporates many of the technologies discussed so far in this book, that is data integration, categorization, visualization, name recognition and mining is that of COPLINK®, an intelligence system first prototyped by Dr. Hsinchun Chen at the University of Arizona's AI laboratory starting in the mid-nineties and commercialized by Knowledge Computing Corporation. As the name would suggest, the primary application of COPLINK has been in the area of law enforcement, but it also has possible value in the area of homeland security.

Since police departments have had to maintain extensive records management systems in order to roll out statistics on crimes for the federal government, a wealth of information exists in law enforcement databases. However, as with most information systems, the data exists in disparate and heterogeneous platforms and in multiple formats. This means that law enforcement officers have had to access several separate depositories, including records management and any number of homegrown databases such as gang, court citation, jail management, sex offender, and probation systems, via multiple queries requiring specialized key strokes or key assignments. This situation is very similar to the dilemma facing such organizations as the TTIC. COPLINK, however, can connect all these systems and allow access with a single query for discovering links and associations.

COPLINK searches through the separate databases of different agencies and identifies connections among suspects, vehicles, crimes, locations, and other data to provide investigative leads. Like InferX, COPLINK also uses artificial intelligence algorithms to learn patterns of association so that it can perform searches with intelligence. Intelligent systems such as COPLINK represent future homeland security designs that can provide large-scale analysis capabilities, including the identification of previously unknown relationships, using both text and data mining capabilities. COPLINK can take millions of pieces of seemingly random and often inconsequential information and find connections between things such as license plates, weapons, nicknames, speeding tickets, or tattoos.

The COPLINK interface, integration, and data mining features have evolved into a centralized operational system. Association detection algorithms within COPLINK allow investigators to detect people, places, and things with which a suspect has been associated. For example, one COPLINK feature allows investigators to track suspects by their previous addresses or people they have been associated with in order to come up with new locations and potential leads and additional information. Because COPLINK can point out relationships between objects, whether those objects are people, vehicles, organizations, locations, weapons, or crimes, it is an ideal system for counterintelligence applications. COPLINK can quickly determine if multiple people have ever had any object in common, such as a location, vehicle, phone number, IP address, address, organization, or contact. This makes it a highly effective intelligence tool in determining if there are physical or hidden associations. Vague physical descriptions and bits of information given by crime victims or witnesses—such as tattoos, car colors, and nicknames—take on new life when they can be plugged into the COPLINK system.

COPLINK does not house information from private or commercial databases such as credit reports. Depending on local conditions and regulations, public information can be used by the system, such as licenses and property tax records. In addition, COPLINK databases can contain information collected by police that isn't generally released to the public, such as gang-intelligence databases and officers' field notes. However, this information can be restricted to only specific users of the system. Because of privacy concerns on the public's part and inconsistent state and local regulations, law enforcement or homeland security agencies should carefully consider what information will be consolidated in a COPLINK system.

COPLINK works by sifting through a database of all sorts of police records, from traffic stops to murder investigations, to deliver a list of leads in just seconds. The same kind of process now takes hours or even days of a detective's time, if it is even possible. COPLINK automates the process of association, producing tables, link maps, and network-based displays of these relationships. In COPLINK all data is organized and displayed rapidly in a user-friendly, logical, and flexible format via a Web browser, so it can be learned and used by inexperienced computer users in less than a day. Queries can be made based on several categories, with the query results displayed in easy-to-sort summary tables showing key information in column format designed to find specific information fast. Summary tables contain hypertext links for each matched entry to underlying detail data and source documents. COPLINK is already in use in over one hundred jurisdictions around the country and has helped in many criminal investigations. For example, one case involved a victim who was found shot with his throat slashed and run over by the suspect's vehicle. The victim provided very little information: a man named "Shorty" who had "Caesar" tattooed on his arm. With only these clues, a Tucson detective (using COPLINK) found the potential suspect and printed out a mug shot. Shorty was arrested the same day.

The goal of COPLINK is to integrate law enforcement databases in a single consolidated data indexing server accessed by users through a Web-based interface to support intelligence and crime analysis. Since most crimes are committed by a relatively small percentage of the criminal population, there is a great likelihood that a given offender is already listed somewhere in a law enforcement information system. To solve crimes effectively, law enforcement personnel need access to a large and currently disparate set of data sources. At this time, if access exists at all, inconsistencies between systems makes them extremely difficult to use. COPLINK provides a consistent and intuitive Web-based interface that integrates different data sources. The multiplicity of data sources remains completely transparent, while law enforcement personnel learn a single, easy-to-use interface. COPLINK provides knowledge-based databases generated directly from multiple data sources that enable investigators to complete large-scale intelligence analysis, including the identification of previously unknown relationships.

Knowledge Computing Corporation

The COPLINK Solution Suite consists of four integrated software modules. COPLINK Connect™, a program that allows information sharing within and among various jurisdictions and government entities stored on widely differing systems and computer platforms. Users can query and view information gathered from different sources using a single easy-to-use interface. COPLINK Detect™ builds on COPLINK Connect so that users can perform sophisticated analysis of the shared data to discover hidden relationships and co-occurrences. COPLINK Mobile™ also builds on top of COPLINK Connect to provide query capability to an officer on the street through wireless access to a PDA device. The fourth component is COPLINK Administration™, which manages the tools necessary to perform routine security and maintenance on the COPLINK system. The system uses the techniques of concept space, text analysis, data mining, noun phrasing, and entity extraction, providing its output in formatted HTML tables and columns. COPLINK Active Agent™ is an add-on collaboration and notification module that can be set to watch for new data, meeting user-specified parameters and then automatically notifying the user when new data is migrated into COPLINK. At its core is agent technology, as with most of the other network-centric tools discussed in this book. Although first prototyped by Dr. Chen at the University of Arizona, Knowledge Computing Corporation developed and markets the commercial version of COPLINK.

COPLINK was designed to maintain a secure environment no matter the source of the data by protecting data transactions within a secure law enforcement communication network using data compression and 128-bit encryption. The system operates in a dedicated private network, a virtual private network (VPN), or an Intranet. Individual agencies have control over what data is integrated and updated. Knowledge assets are represented within law enforcement as a variety of disparate databases, each satisfying a particular need. Some examples of these disparate databases are Record Management Systems (RMS), gang databases, probation and parole databases, jail management databases, and dispatch systems, which can be integrated via the single COPLINK interface. Each of these knowledge assets provides information and data relevant to its classification, but the ability to search and analyze across multiple knowledge assets and discover associations and relationships makes COPLINK is an extremely effective weapon against crime and potentially homeland security. COPLINK is an effective, cost-effective way to link and analyze data within existing stovepipe systems and minimize training requirements.

The COPLINK crime analysis techniques include association rules, the process of discovering frequently occurring criminal elements in a database. This technique also includes intrusion detection to identify patterns of program execution and user activities as association rules. Another data mining technique is that of classification, the process of finding the common properties among different crime entities and classifying them into groups. Lastly, COPLINK is able to perform clustering, the process of grouping criminal items into classes of similar characteristics.

COPLINK is also able to conduct social network analysis; the system is able to establish a network that illustrates the roles of criminals, the flow of tangible and intangible goods and information, and the associations among those entities. COPLINK is able to perform sequential pattern mining to find frequently occurring sequences of items over a set of transactions that occurred at different times, such as to detect temporal patterns of a network attack. The system is able to perform string comparators for fraud and deception detection. Lastly, it is also able to perform entity extraction, identifying patterns of particular types from unstructured data such as text, image, or audio materials.

COPLINK incorporates name recognition algorithms superior to Soundex. As we found out in the previous chapter, this technology encodes a name with a format having a prefix letter followed by a three-digit number, but phonetic matching is particularly poor at finding matches. COPLINK uses a spelling string comparator that compares spelling variations between two strings instead of phonetic codes. See Figure 7.29 illustrating its formula.

Criminal association identification is performed via the shortest-path algorithms to find the strongest associations between two or more criminals in a network. Using a Social Network Analysis (SNA) process, the system can use block model analysis to detect subgroups and patterns of interactions between groups to identify leaders, gatekeepers, and outliers from a criminal or terrorist network. Simple association rule mining can be applied to discover criminal elements relationships, with common XML-based representation for criminal relationships being generated. Incremental data migration and association analysis of databases is supported via a graphical browser-based GUI interface for simple crime relationship analysis and case retrieval.

Privacy Software: Programmed Security

Because of privacy and security concerns, a homeland security organization may be required to employ proactive policies and new types of software for tracking how data is accessed by its personnel and systems. IBM is developing a technology that will give organizations a deeper understanding of their exposure to privacy problems and automate the process of defining which users are tapping a network's

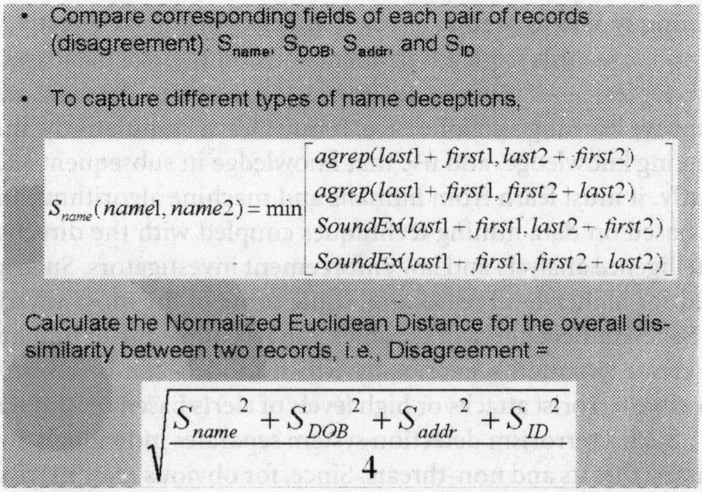

FIGURE 7.29 The COPLINK name recognition algorithm design.

assets and how they're using them. The software is at the forefront of an evolving trend in corporate and government in which privacy considerations are beginning to pervade many aspects of organizations' operations. Traditionally, privacy policies have centered on who can view what data. But software vendors, including Microsoft Corp., have begun using a data-centric model in which policies and procedures are built around a map of where data resides, which applications and processes use it, and where it goes.

This approach starts with the data, not the people, and to that end, this type of privacy software will help homeland security organizations develop a map of all their network assets, data paths, and employee use to locate privacy exposures. This type of privacy software is comprised of a batch of agents and a central server component, and its methods will be roughly analogous to those of a security vulnerability scanner. The software agents will crawl through a network, much like a Web spider does, touching each device and data path. The software reports to the mediator server, which will compose a map of the way data moves among servers, clients, and applications, as well as a picture of which employees use which data and in what way. The idea is to develop a process map depicting all interactions among people and data in a homeland security organization.

Mining Scenarios: Simulating Attacks

The amount of terrorist-related data is small, making it difficult to induce predictive patterns of such activity and profile the perpetrators. Development of a data mining system to predict terrorist attacks must make effective use of a wide variety of public records from government and commercial databases. Such a system must actively learn—it must be designed to request new data and analyses that optimally improve learning and inference. It must learn cumulatively, incrementally improve existing knowledge, and use that knowledge in subsequent learning and inference. Lastly, it must learn from humans and machine algorithms. Ideally the system will be based on data mining techniques coupled with the direction of knowledgeable intelligence analysts and law enforcement investigators. Such a system must be created for higher-level reasoning, using some of the most advanced algorithms such as Bayesian Belief networks, which can be coupled with human analysts in an effort to create situation scenarios by which models can be constructed for predicting possible terrorist attacks or high levels of alerts based on simulated model scenarios.

Such a terrorism detection system separates individuals and situations into two classes: threats and non-threats. Since, for obvious reasons, real threat class datasets are difficult to collect and often incomplete and noisy, the quality of detection models will have to be evaluated using artificial datasets. One solution to this challenge is to generate synthetic datasets using uncertainty models, which is framing datasets representative of plausible terrorist attacks. For example, relatively simple, fast-running, agent-based Bayesian network models can be used to capture the essential factors and behaviors of real-life scenarios, as those developed by human intelligence agents and analysts. Such a dataset can be developed by running the simulations thousands of times, varying the agent and scenario input parameters and the random seeds, the method by which the data is introduced to the model for prediction. More precise models of complex terrorism events can then be constructed by observing the behavior of these simulations over thousands of runs. Such data simulation applies a concept of data distillations, which are running simulations that distill the essence of a particular infrastructure scenario. These distillations are used to explore possible spaces using many runs. This large volume of data can then be further analyzed to discover additional knowledge and insights such as the conditions, intervals, and factors that are most important in anticipating possible attacks.

During the last two decades, much effort has been focused on the development of efficient probabilistic Bayesian network inference algorithms. These algorithms have for the most part been designed to compute the subsequent probability of a prediction efficiently. However, for decision-making purposes, these types of algorithms have computationally not been very feasible. They are complex, and the dense networks are slow. In other words, when using Bayesian networks, the simulation methods take a long time to converge to a reliable answer and are not suitable for real-time applications. Consequently, the computational time constraint is one of the most severe obstacles in incorporating Bayesian networks for predictive threat modeling. The dilemma is that while these types of algorithms are excellent in dealing with uncertainty, which makes them ideal for homeland security applications, they tend to be very slow.

An answer to such a modeling problem is the development of a hybrid Bayesian network that is accurate in dealing with uncertainty, along with a decision tree algorithm, which is fast, in modeling sparse data sets, such as that of potential terrorist attacks. To take advantage of the efficient process of the decision tree, it is used as a filter input to the Bayesian network. Such a decision-making mechanism combines the strength of the two data mining techniques to propose a hybrid approach that trades off the accuracy and computation speed. In such a system, homeland security intelligence personnel, specialists in their fields, would monitor news events and intelligence reports for the creation of intention-to-outcome analysis models, enabling early warning alerts based on antecedents with high-confidence indicator warnings. This type of event mining involves the use of very sparse data, commonly less than 100 events in sample set, with a very high level of possible combinations. In this hybrid system the analysts create new, realistic examples of rare events to automatically create inputs into the hybrid Bayesian network/decision tree algorithm for creating possible action plans. Where low-cost actions are used to provide the best outcomes, this antecedent intervention strategy is used to avert incipient outcome and induce desirable outcome.

Such a system would use classifiers that predict outcomes from antecedent behavior and would change the outcome if interfered with. This hybrid human and machine learning data mining system would use both deduction—"What is the probability that X will be next?"—and abduction, a reason backward model—"Given X, what is the chain of preceding events?" The system would be robust enough to handle missing data, a very common fact in the real world, especially that involving terrorism and its related crimes, such as money laundering. Such a system would be capable of handling multiple data types and subjective analyses from domain experts and homeland security personnel, as well as empirical data. It would be flexible enough to allow continuous improvement so that probabilities are updated with new human analysis and data as it becomes available.

THE FUTURE OF HOMELAND SECURITY: HYBRID SELF-EVOLVING SYSTEMS

Homeland security is a national strategy to develop and implement tasks for making the United States' sovereignty, domestic population, and infrastructure safe from terrorist threats or attacks. In the end this will require the implementation of multiple processes for using AI and the Web to combat terrorism by collaborating content, expertise, and analyses in real time, using warehousing and name recognition programs for entity validation, and using text and data mining technologies to mine databases remotely over networks. It will require the detection of crimes associated with terrorism such as ID theft and money laundering and the coordinated use of network-centric software to aggregate, integrate, collaborate, categorize, and analyze data. Effective learning and inference require large amounts of general and domain-specific knowledge, and because of this, experienced investigators and analysts need to guide the development of machine learning software for these homeland security processes.

A grid-based information infrastructure will prevail, linking data resources in support of virtualization, which hides the functions behind a generic interface that conceals the details of how data and functions are retrieved, organized, and implemented. In this grid, homeland security organizations will be able to assemble systems dynamically from distributed sources so that their personnel can call on remote resources for processing, storage, data, and software, regardless of their location or format. This homeland security grid can tailor the information and systems based on predetermined access profiles to make changes on demand with a need to access databases and software to retrieve data, audio, and video or experts and analyses. The necessary resources can be assembled from multiple sources as they are needed. In this grid-like environment, computing and information are virtualized so that any person or device can furnish data and software services to any other in a disparate collection of services over a secure network based on clearance levels.

Gradually, homeland security organizations will develop software that will enable the sharing of data, experts, analyses, and services, not by replacing legacy systems at participating sites but by linking them into a virtual organization of communities requiring similar technologies in a collaborative, controlled, secure, and managed manner. This will need to be accomplished by standardizing a variety of functions, such as authenticating the identity of users, authorizing requested data, activity, or analysis, defining and accessing the available databases and resources, and controlling the movement of all data. It will require tracking all interactions with privacy software. In such an environment, homeland security collaborators will need to agree on how services are described, how agencies and their personnel establish one another's identity, how access rules are described and verified, and how activities are conducted.

Data mining refers to the automatic extraction of underlying patterns or connections implicitly contained in huge corporate or government databases or data collections accumulated from structured and unstructured sources such as the Web or news feeds. Data mining for homeland security will no doubt evolve in many directions during the coming years, including these possible developments:

- Systems for integrating data streams from which analysts can set up profiles for assessing trends, anomalies, new events, and developments
- Systems that can analyze and summarize real-time data streams on the fly, correlate it, and notify decision makers when important conditions are detected them
- Systems that will scour for patterns, identifying correlations, rare or abnormal events, and subtle relationships, with the extracted results relayed to analysts for follow-up action
- Systems that collect, cluster, categorize, and summarize digital data streams for specific regions, highlighting details, conflicting facts, and unexpected developments
- Systems that understand the meaning of unstructured content and can automatically form semantic networks linking entities and events for analysts to review
- Systems that can learn more accurate predictive patterns from fewer data points, interpret very subtle indicators, and produce earlier warnings about emerging threats
- Systems to automatically detect and correlate names and pictured faces from audio and video sources

Finally, much of the knowledge homeland security organizations need focuses on patterns of events in time and space, often with large gaps introduced intentionally for the purpose of obscuring clandestine activities and perpetrator identities. Relevant data is drawn from many different sources, such as databases of sightings, Web pages, financial transactions, e-mail, server logs, intelligence reports, instant messages, phone calls, chat, travel records, and news feeds. Those sources contain many different types of items, such as numbers, text, photos, and audio and video feeds, and have varying degrees of reliability, overlap, and correlation. A major task of homeland security processes is to unify this mixed media into a cohesive view of profiles and scenarios. The available data represents only a fraction of what could be known; part of effective learning is reasoning about what additional data to request, and this will require the direction of experienced analysts in guiding and training the homeland security self-evolving software systems so that attacks like those of 9/11 do not occur again.

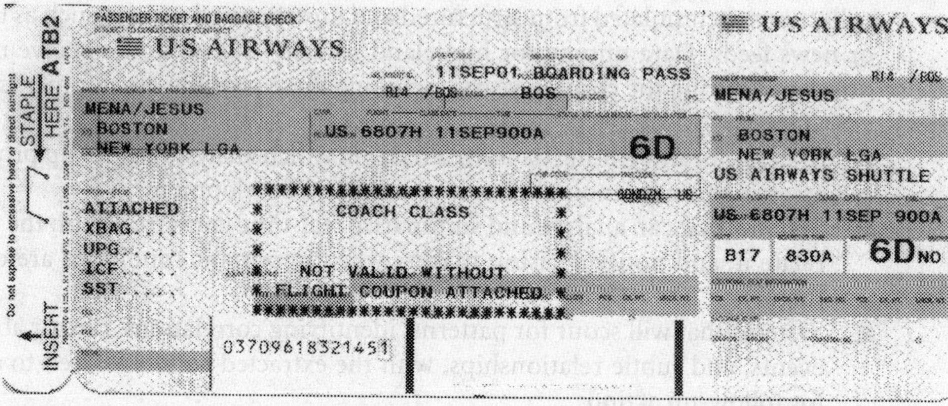

FIGURE 7.30 We all remember where we were on 9/11 at 9 A.M.: Seat 6D.

We face an enemy that never rests, one capable of obtaining weapons that come packaged in suitcases and envelopes, cargo and cars, and by desire and design, we are one of the most open countries in the world. We have 95,000 miles of shoreline to protect, 7,000 miles of borders shared with Canada and Mexico to safeguard, thousands of tons of cargo to inspect, and over a million people to process coming across our borders on a daily basis. It can seem an impossible task full of incredible obstacles, yet history teaches us that we can be undaunted by obstacles and choose instead to press on, using new and unique homeland security techniques and technologies.

Appendix About the CD-ROM

The accompanying CD-ROM includes demonstrations of several software products discussed in the book. Please visit the corresponding Web sites for exact system requirements, FAQs, updates, ordering information, licenses, and links to other tools and resources. The information contained on this CD-ROM is the property of the respective developers. It may not be distributed without their permission. Inquiries regarding the software contained on the CD-ROM should be directed to the developers of the products. In addition, please review the publisher's disclaimer at the beginning of the book. Please note that files not specifically mentioned below are support files and may not open on their own.

The CD-ROM also contains all of the figures from the book. These figures can be found in the Figures directory.

Overview of Entopia's Software Solutions

http://www.entopia.com
Entopia, Inc.
3200 Bridge Parkway
Redwood Shores, CA 94065

Double-click on the file `index.html` in the `Entopia` folder to launch Entopia's demonstration of their collaboration and categorization software.

Presentation of InferX Technology

http://www.inferx.com
InferX Corporation
1600 International Drive, Suite 110
McLean, VA 22102

Double-click on `InferX Demo` in the `InferX` folder to launch this presentation of the company's distributed data mining technology. Follow the prompts, and once the software is installed, click on the `supply~1.ppt` file (located in the folder you indicated during setup). Or, click on the `CSI.exe` icon to learn about InferAgent.

Information Builders and iWay Homeland Security Solutions

http://www.iwaysoftware.com/index.html
iWay Software
Two Penn Plaza
New York, NY 10121

To view a number of iWay's presentations and other documents, choose any of the files in the iWay folder. The file `ReadMe.doc` in the iWay folder contains more detailed descriptions. Adobe Acrobat is required to view some of the documents.

Demonstration of Data and Text Mining Software

http://www.megaputer.com
Megaputer Intelligence, Inc.
120 West 7th Street, Suite 310
Bloomington, IN 47404

Evaluations of the software discussed in this presentation are available at the company's Web site. To begin the demonstration, double-click on `PolyAnalyst FLASH demo` in the `FLASH` subdirectory of the `Megaputer` folder. A case study is also available in the `Megaputer` folder; to access it please double-click `crime_pattern_case.pdf`. More information is available in the documents `PolyAnalyst for Homeland Security.doc` and `Text Mining with PolyAnalyst_with pix.doc`.

MetaBase Modeler Workspace Introduction

http://www.metamatrix.com
MetaMatrix
680 Fifth Avenue
10th Floor
New York, NY 10019

This demonstration introduces the user interface, various models, virtual documents, and other features of the data integration program MetaBase Modeler. Double-click on `workspace_viewlet_swf` in the `Metamatrix` directory to begin; more information is available in the document `MetaMatrix.doc`.

Demonstration of Search Software Technology

http://www.searchsoftware.com
Search Software America
1445 East Putnam Ave.
Old Greenwich, CT 06870

To begin this demonstration of Search Software America's name recognition technology, please double-click on `index.html` in the `Export` folder, in the `SearchSoftwareAmerica` folder.

Presentation of Searchspace Solutions

http://www.searchspace.com
Searchspace
60 Broad Street
New York, NY 10004

Double-click on the Flash file `fraud.exe` in the `SearchSpace` folder to view the presentation about their money-laundering prevention systems. Two informational .pdf documents are also available within the `CD_Searchspace.zip` zipped directory.

Index

FIREWALL MEDIA

(An imprint of Laxmi Publications Pvt. Ltd.)

Computer Books *for School, BCA, MCA, IGNOU, DOEACC and Engineering Students and Professionals*

ISBN	TITLE	AUTHOR	PRICE	PAGES
	.NET			
8170087155	**Building Business Intelligence Applications with .Net**	Robert Ericsson	Rs. 295.00	404
8170083567	**Learning VB.Net Through Applications**	Clayton Crooks	Rs. 295.00	450
8170082463	**Magic of C# with .Net Frame Work**	Shibi Panikkar, Kumar Sanjeev	Rs. 495.00	950
8170082471	**Magic of ASP.Net with C#**	Shibi Panikkar, Kumar Sanjeev	Rs. 395.00	750
	A TO Z SERIES			
8170083214	**Access 2002 from A to Z**	Julie Kelly, Stephen L. Nelson	Rs. 75.00	208
8170083222	**Excel 2002 from A to Z**	Stephen L. Nelson	Rs. 75.00	208
8170083230	**Front Page 2002 from A to Z**	Heather Williamson	Rs. 85.00	208
8170083249	**Outlook 2002 from A to Z**	Stephen L. Nelson	Rs. 75.00	208
8170083257	**Page Maker 7 from A to Z**	Marc Campbell	Rs. 75.00	202
8170083265	**Power Point 2002 from A to Z**	Stephen L. Nelson	Rs. 75.00	208
8170083273	**Windows XP from A to Z**	Pat Coleman	Rs. 95.00	256
8170083281	**Word 2002 from A to Z**	Stephen L. Nelson	Rs. 75.00	208
817008329X	**XML from A to Z**	Heather Williamson	Rs. 75.00	208
8170083303	**Dreamweaver 4 from A to Z**	Heather Williamson	Rs. 85.00	215
	BEGINNERS & GENERAL INTEREST			
817008248X	**Shortcuts to Success in Computing**	Dheeraj Mehrotra	Rs. 55.00	110
8170083311	**Pictorial Computer Dictionary**	Dheeraj Mehrotra	Rs. 45.00	156
8170083486	**Pocket Net Browser**	Dheeraj Mehrotra	Rs. 95.00	302
8170084261	**1000 IT Quizzes**	Dheeraj Mehrotra	Rs. 75.00	120
	CALL CENTERS			
8170082196	**Call Centers Made Easy**	Stephen Medcroft	Rs. 195.00	320
	CISCO			
8170087481	**Enabling IP Routing with Cisco Routers**	R. Das, K. Chakrabarty	Rs. 295.00	486
817008749X	**Designing Networks with Cisco**	H. Pasricha, D. Jagu	Rs. 195.00	316

Please write for a free color Firewall Media Catalog for details on the above books.

ISBN	TITLE	AUTHOR	PRICE	PAGES
8170087503	**Cisco IP Routing Protocols: Troubleshooting Techniques**	V. Anand, K. Chakrabarty	Rs. 295.00	409

DATABASES

ISBN	TITLE	AUTHOR	PRICE	PAGES
8170087147	**DBMS-Complete Practical Approach**	Sharad Maheshwari, Ruchin Jain	Rs. 230.00	530
8170082404	**Learn to Program Visual Basic-Examples**	John Smiley	Rs. 295.00	500
8170082412	**Learn to Program Visual Basic-Databases**	John Smiley	Rs. 325.00	670
8170082420	**Learn to Program Visual Basic-Objects**	John Smiley	Rs. 325.00	700
817008475X	**IT Resources-Access 2002 VBA Programming Access**	Michele Amelot	Rs. 195.00	424
8170084512	**The Power of Oracle 9i**	Rajiv Parida, Vinod Sharma	Rs. 475.00	1100

DOEACC 'O' LEVEL

ISBN	TITLE	AUTHOR	PRICE	PAGES
8170088089	**DOEACC 'O' Level Model Test Papers**	Ramesh Bangia	Rs. 175.00	296
8170085640	**Programming and Problem Solving Through "C" Language**	Harsha Priya, R. Ranjeet	Rs. 95.00	306
8170084474	**IT Tools and Applications**	Ramesh Bangia	Rs. 145.00	392
8170085594	**Business Systems**	Ramesh Bangia	Rs. 175.00	452
8170085454	**Internet & Web Design**	Ramesh Bangia	Rs. 120.00	321

ELECTRONIC COMMERCE

ISBN	TITLE	AUTHOR	PRICE	PAGES
8170085497	**Electronic Commerce**	Pete Loshin, John Vacca	Rs. 295.00	472
817008119X	**E-Commerce**	Mamta Bhusry	Rs. 95.00	215
8170083524	**Marketing in The Cyber Age**	Kurt Rohner	Rs. 295.00	250

HARDWARE/EMBEDDED SYSTEMS

ISBN	TITLE	AUTHOR	PRICE	PAGES
8170087473	**Essentials Electronics for PC Technicians**	John W. Farber	Rs. 295.00	**546**
8170086264	**Grid Computing: A Practical Guide to Technology and Applications**	Ahmar Abbas	Rs. 295.00	408
8170088186	**CD Cracking Uncovered Protection Against Unsanctioned CD Copy**	Kris Kaspersky	Rs. 295.00	422
8170083435	**Practical Linux Programming: Device Drivers, Embedded Systems**	Ashfaq A. Khan	Rs. 295.00	420

Please write for a free color Firewall Media Catalog for details on the above books.

ISBN	TITLE	AUTHOR	PRICE	PAGES
8170083575	**TCP/IP Application Layer Protocols for Embedded Systems**	M. Tim Jones	Rs. 295.00	350
	INTERNET			
8170083206	**The Internet Hand Book for Writers, Students & Teachers**	Mary McGuire, Linda Stillborne	Rs. 195.00	288
8170084776	**Way in-Internet Getting Started**	Elizabeth Bramire	Rs. 95.00	165
	KEEPING AHEAD SERIES			
8170084652	**Keeping Ahead Exchange 2002 Server**	Philippe Levesque	Rs. 145.00	285
8170084660	**Keeping Ahead Windows 2000 Professional**	Jose Dardoigne	Rs. 175.00	388
8170084679	**Keeping Ahead Windows 2000 Server**	Philippe Mathon	Rs. 175.00	360
8170084687	**Keeping Ahead Linux Administration Kernel Version 2.0 to 2.2**	Bruno Guerin	Rs. 125.00	240
8170084695	**Keeping Ahead Using Linux Kernel Version 2.0 to 2.2**	Bruno Guerin	Rs. 125.00	258
8170084709	**Keeping Ahead Java 2**	Benjamin Aumaille	Rs. 145.00	284
8170084717	**Keeping Ahead SQL Server 7**	Joelle Mosset	Rs. 145.00	329
8170084725	**Keeping Ahead Java Script and VB Script**	Benjamin Aumaille	Rs. 145.00	313
8170084733	**Keeping Ahead C++ Programming Language**	Bruno Dubois	Rs. 125.00	234
8170084741	**Keeping Ahead TCP/IP in the NT Environment**	Bruno Ferec	Rs. 125.00	230
	MCSE			
817008489X	**MCSE-Administering SQL Server 7.0**	Jerome Gabillaud	Rs. 295.00	580
8170084903	**MCSE-Networking Essentials**	Jose Dordoigne	Rs. 245.00	453
8170084911	**MCSE-Windows 2000 Professional**	Jose Dordoigne	Rs. 325.00	665
817008492X	**MCSE-Windows 2000 Server**	Philippe Mathon	Rs. 345.00	712
	MULTIMEDIA AND ANIMATION			
8170088208	**3 DS Max 6 Animation with Character Studio 4 and Plug-Ins**	Boris Kulagin, Dmitry Morozov	Rs. 175.00	216
8170088216	**Adobe Audition: Soundtracks for Digital Video**	Roman Petelin, Yury Petelin	Rs. 195.00	278

ISBN	TITLE	AUTHOR	PRICE	PAGES
8170086205	**Building A Digital Human**	Karl Brilliant	Rs. 295.00	380
8170086213	**Making Digital Videos**	Ben Long	Rs. 295.00	284
8170087171	**Illustrating with Macromedia Flash TM MX 2004**	Robert Firbaugh	Rs. 245.00	366
8170082439	**Multimedia Basics-Technology (Vol. I)**	Andreas Holzinger	Rs. 195.00	285
8170082447	**Multimedia Basics-Learning (Vol. II)**	Andreas Holzinger	Rs. 195.00	300
8170082455	**Multimedia Basics-Design (Vol. III)**	Andreas Holzinger	Rs. 195.00	280
8170083532	**Maya Feature Creature Creations**	Todd Palamar	Rs. 295.00	450
8170083540	**Sound Forge Power**	Scott R. Garrigus	Rs. 195.00	250
8170086116	**Multimedia and Web Technology**	Ramesh Bangia	Rs. 295.00	706

NETWORKING

ISBN	TITLE	AUTHOR	PRICE	PAGES
817008721X	**Networking Essentials**	Jose Dordoigne	Rs. 195.00	453
8170087023	**Computer Networks**	Ajit Kumar Singh	Rs. 95.00	181
817008203X	**Telecom & Networking Glossary**	Robert Mastin	Rs. 300.00	250
8170082048	**Data Networking Made Easy**	Karen Patten	Rs. 360.00	350
8170082056	**Digital Convergence**	Andy Covell	Rs. 300.00	250

OFFICE AUTOMATION

ISBN	TITLE	AUTHOR	PRICE	PAGES
8170088003	**Desk Top Publishing**	Dinesh Maidasani	Rs. 125.00	210
8170087805	**Learning Computer Programming, MS Office and Internet & Web Tech.**	Dinesh Maidasani	Rs. 95.00	318
8170087686	**MS Word 2000 Thumb-Rules and Details**	Snigdha Banerjee	Rs. 175.00	390

ON YOUR SIDE SERIES

ISBN	TITLE	AUTHOR	PRICE	PAGES
8170084830	**On your side-Powerpoint 2002**	Andrew Blackburn	Rs. 145.00	282
8170084849	**On your side-Excel 2002**	Adrienne Tommy	Rs. 125.00	275
8170084857	**On your side-Word 2002**	Adrienne Tommy	Rs. 125.00	289
8170084865	**On your side-Access 2002**	Adrienne Tommy	Rs. 125.00	303
8170084873	**On your side-Frontpage 2002**	Andrew Blackburn	Rs. 95.00	220
8170084881	**On your side-Windows XP**	Adrienne Tommy	Rs. 125.00	310

OPERATING SYSTEMS

ISBN	TITLE	AUTHOR	PRICE	PAGES
8170087236	**Linux-A Practical Approach**	B. Mohamed Ibrahim	Rs. 95.00	187
8170083427	**The MS-Windows XP Professional Handbook**	Louis Columbus	Rs. 295.00	330
8170084784	**Way in-Windows XP Home Edition**	Andrew Blackburn	Rs. 95.00	183

Please write for a free color Firewall Media Catalog for details on the above books.

ISBN	TITLE	AUTHOR	PRICE	PAGES
8170086221	**Cyber Rookies—Operating System Fundamentals**	D. Irtegov	Rs. 295.00	498

PROGRAMMING

ISBN	TITLE	AUTHOR	PRICE	PAGES
8170087791	**The Art of Programming Through Flowcharts & Algorithms**	Anil Bikas Chaudhuri	Rs. 95.00	160
8170086248	**Preventative Programming Techniques**	Brian Hawkins	Rs. 295.00	322
8170083443	**Learning Computer Programming : It's not about Languages**	Mary Farrell	Rs. 295.00	375
8170086256	**Object-Oriented Programming From Problem Solving to Java**	Jose M. Garrido	Rs. 295.00	360
8170088038	**Assembly Language Programming for Intel Processors Family**	Vasile Lungu	Rs. 295.00	577
8170088178	**The Assembly Programming Master Book**	Vlad Pirogov	Rs. 395.00	726

PROGRAMMING - C#, C, C++

ISBN	TITLE	AUTHOR	PRICE	PAGES
8170083702	**The Power of C#**	Rajiv Parida	Rs. 295.00	592
8170085632	**Mastering Graphics Programming in 'C'**	Sudhir Dawra	Rs. 145.00	286
8170087074	**Mastering C Programs**	J.B. Dixit	Rs. 195.00	434
8170081262	**Programming in C**	J.B. Dixit	Rs. 245.00	505
8170087619	**Unix and C Programming**	Ashok Arora, Shefali Bansal	Rs. 295.00	606
8170086140	**Data Structure for 'C' Programming, 2nd Edition**	Ajay Kumar	Rs. 145.00	290
8170081270	**Programming in C++**	J.B. Dixit	Rs. 260.00	601
8170088194	**Hackish C++ Pranks & Tricks**	Michael Flenov	Rs. 245.00	326
8170082889	**Basics of C++ Programming**	Nishant Kundalia	Rs. 95.00	168
8170083648	**Mastering C++ Programs**	J.B. Dixit	Rs. 295.00	614
817008623X	**Cyber Rookies—C++ Programming Fundamentals**	Chuck Easttom	Rs. 295.00	41[illegible]

SECURITY

ISBN	TITLE	AUTHOR	PRICE	PAGES
8170083419	**Computer Forensics : Computer Crime Scene Investigation**	John Vacca	Rs. 445.00	600
8170083494	**Firewall Architecture for the Enterprise**	Norbert Pohlmann, Tim Crothers	Rs. 295.00	480
8170086272	**Net Spies**	Andrew Gauntlett	Rs. 195.00	210

Please write for a free color Firewall Media Catalog for details on the above books.

ISBN	TITLE	AUTHOR	PRICE	PAGES
	SOFTWARE ENGINEERING AND TECHNOLOGY			
817008718X	**Human Aspects of Software Engineering**	James E. Tomayko, Orit Hazzar	Rs. 195.00	338
8170087899	**Management Information Systems**	Avdhesh Gupta, Anurag Malik	Rs. 175.00	362
8170087953	**Human Computer Interaction**	Rajendra Ranjan Kumar	Rs. 95.00	210
8170088097	**System Analysis and Design**	Preeti Gupta	Rs. 125.00	192
817008802X	**Autocad 2005 for Engineers**	Ionel Simion	Rs. 175.00	271
8170088054	**Digital Signal Processing Fundamentals**	Ashfaq A. Khan	Rs. 295.00	391
817008363X	**Practical Project Management**	Ivan Bayross	Rs. 195.00	342
	STRAIGHT TO THE POINT SERIES			
8170084601	**STTP : Word 2002**	Corinne Hervo	Rs. 45.00	154
817008461X	**STTP : Excel 2002**	Corinne Hervo	Rs. 45.00	153
8170084628	**STTP : Dreamweaver 4**	Corinne Hervo	Rs. 45.00	135
8170084636	**STTP : Flash 5**	Corinne Hervo	Rs. 45.00	126
8170084644	**STTP : Photoshop 6**	Corinne Hervo	Rs. 45.00	152
8170084482	**STTP : MS Office 2000**	Ramesh Bangia	Rs. 95.00	300
8170086108	**STTP : MS Office 2003**	Ramesh Bangia	Rs. 145.00	288
8170087651	**STTP : MS Word 2003**	Ramesh Bangia	Rs. 60.00	150
8170088011	**STTP : Photoshop CS**	Firewall Media	Rs. 60.00	150
8170088143	**STTP : MS Excel 2003**	Firewall Media	Rs. 60.00	150
8170088151	**STTP : Coreldraw 12**	Firewall Media	Rs. 60.00	150
	STUDIO FACTORY			
8170084792	**Studio Factory-Photoshop 6**	Christophe Aubry	Rs. 175.00	364
8170084806	**Studio Factory-Flash 5**	Sami Ben Yahiya	Rs. 145.00	314
8170084814	**Studio Factory-Dreamweaver Ultradev 4**	Philippe Chatellier	Rs. 95.00	240
8170084822	**Studio Factory-Dreamweaver 4**	Christophe Aubry	Rs. 175.00	373
8170087627	**Studio Factory-Flash MX**	Arnaud Blanche	Rs. 145.00	337
8170087643	**Studio Factory-Dreamweaver MX**	Christophe Aubry	Rs. 195.00	407
817008766X	**Studio Factory-Photoshop 7**	Cyril Guerin	Rs. 175.00	390
	WEB TECHNOLOGY			
8170087163	**Web Design with Macromedia Studio MX 2004**	Eric Hunley	Rs. 295.00	558

ISBN	TITLE	AUTHOR	PRICE	PAGES
8170083400	**Professional Web Design (Techniques and Templates)**	Clint Eccher	Rs. 295.00	425
8170088046	**HTML, XHTML, CSS and XML**	Teodoru Gugoiu	Rs. 195.00	355
8170083583	**FrontPage 2000 for Visual Learners**	Chris Charuhas	Rs. 95.00	200
8170083591	**HTML & Java Script for Visual Learners**	Chris Charuhas	Rs. 95.00	200
8170083605	**The Visual Learner's Guide to Managing Web Projects**	Chris Charuhas	Rs. 95.00	130
8170083613	**Dreamweaver 4 for Visual Learners**	Chris Charuhas	Rs. 95.00	200
8170084768	**IT Resource-Implementing XML: Managing and Formatting Data**	Johhny Brochard	Rs. 125.00	279
8170085470	**Design Your Web World**	Sunil Jalota	Rs. 45.00	103

ORDER FORM

LAXMI PUBLICATIONS (P) LTD.

7/19, Ansari Road, Daryaganj, New Delhi-110002
Phones : 23262368, 23262370 ; *Faxes* : 011-2325 25 72, 2326 22 79
Email : colaxmi@hotmail.com
Website : www.laxmipublications.com

Please send me the following books by V.P.P. I have sent Rs. .... by M.O./Draft on Date ....

☐ ____________________

☐ ____________________

☐ ____________________

☐ ____________________

☐ ____________________

☐ ____________________

☐ ____________________

(Please use separate sheet if you need more books)

Fill in this coupon in BLOCK letters only.

Name ____________________

Address ____________________

____

P.O. ____________ Distt. ____________

State ____________ Pin Code ☐☐☐☐☐☐

Phone ____________ Email ____________

Please do not refuse to accept the V.P.P. Honour it and write to us if there is any complaint. We shall set right your complaint, if any.

Our books are available at all leading bookshops.

Please mention Name of Books, clearly.

It is necessary to send Rs. 50.00 per book as an advance. Without advance order will not be sent.

Terms and Conditions for the supply of Books by V.P. Parcels to Students

1. Mention your name, address and nearest post office, with Pin Code No., in capital block letters for quick compliance of your order.
2. You can also send complete payment in advance by Money Order.
3. V.P. Parcels are detained by the Postal Authorities for only 5 days. Hence the same should be honoured on receiving intimation to avoid legal action against the defaulter.
4. Half Postage free.
5. All disputes will be settled in Delhi Courts only.
6. V.P. Parcels are not accepted for stations served by A.P.O. 56 and A.P.O. 99. While ordering for our Books from these stations, please ascertain and send the amount in full, in advance, on receipt of which, the books will be sent by registered post.
7. (*i*) V.P.P. Orders should be accompanied with advance of Rs. 50.00 per book. Without advance, ordered book(s) will not be sent.

   (*ii*) While sending advance by money order, please write your requirements on the last part of money order (space for communication). On its reverse side write your complete name and address.

   (*iii*) **Please note that the upper part of the money order form here you have written your address, remains with post office. So it is necessary to write your address again on last part of the M.O. form.**
8. Order placed will not be cancelled.
9. For books which are not supplied to you due to their being out of stock, please write again after 30 days with 25% advance.
10. Requests for our Books from students who did not honour their previous order will not be considered unless they send us full advance payment plus the postage charges for the returned parcel.
11. Prices are subject to change without notice.

Please write your letters to :

LAXMI PUBLICATIONS (P) LTD.

7/19, Ansari Road, Daryaganj, New Delhi-110002

Phones : 23262368, 23262370 ; *Faxes* : 011-2325 25 72, 2326 22 79

Email : colaxmi@hotmail.com

Website : www.laxmipublications.com

